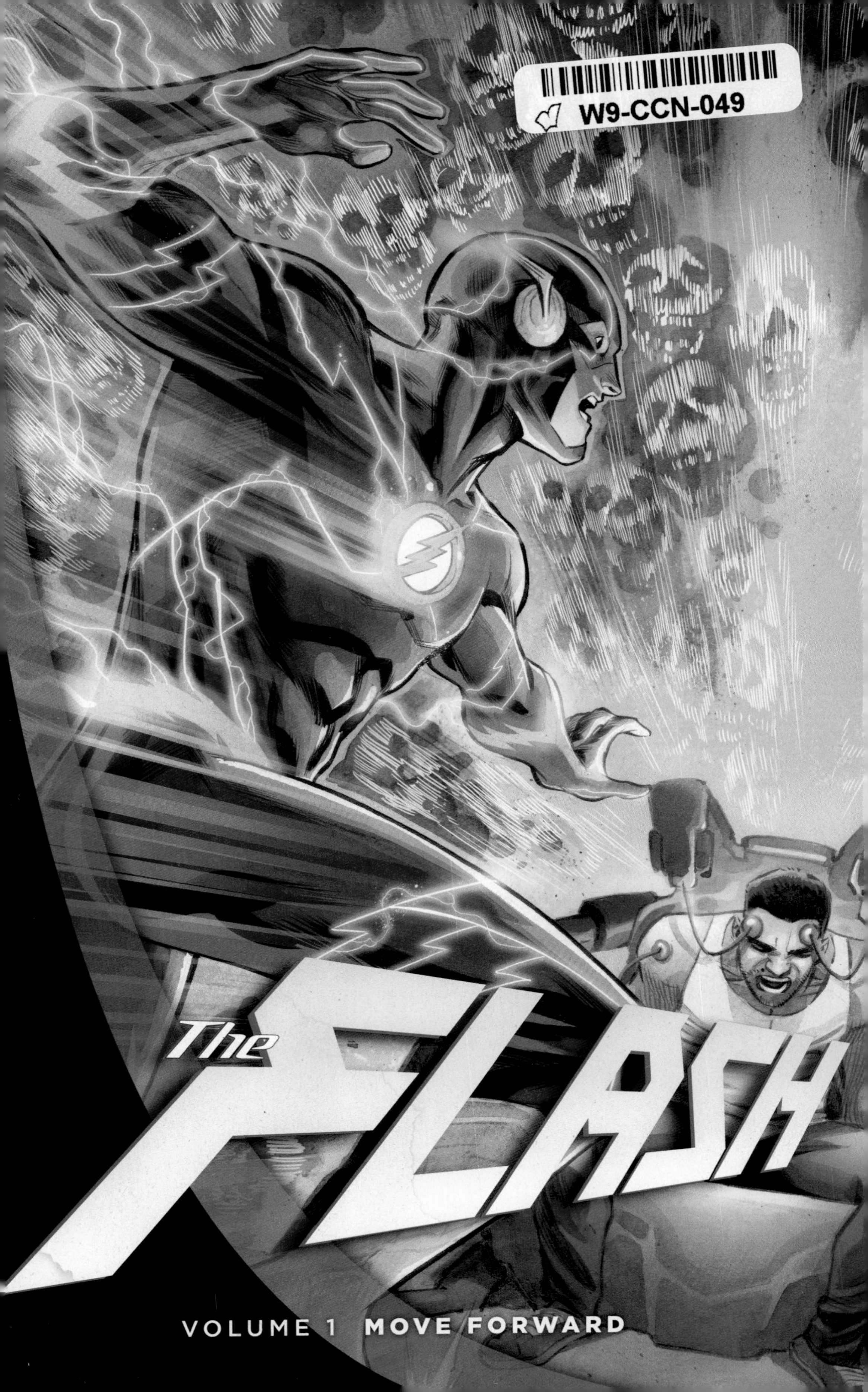
The FLASH
VOLUME 1 MOVE FORWARD

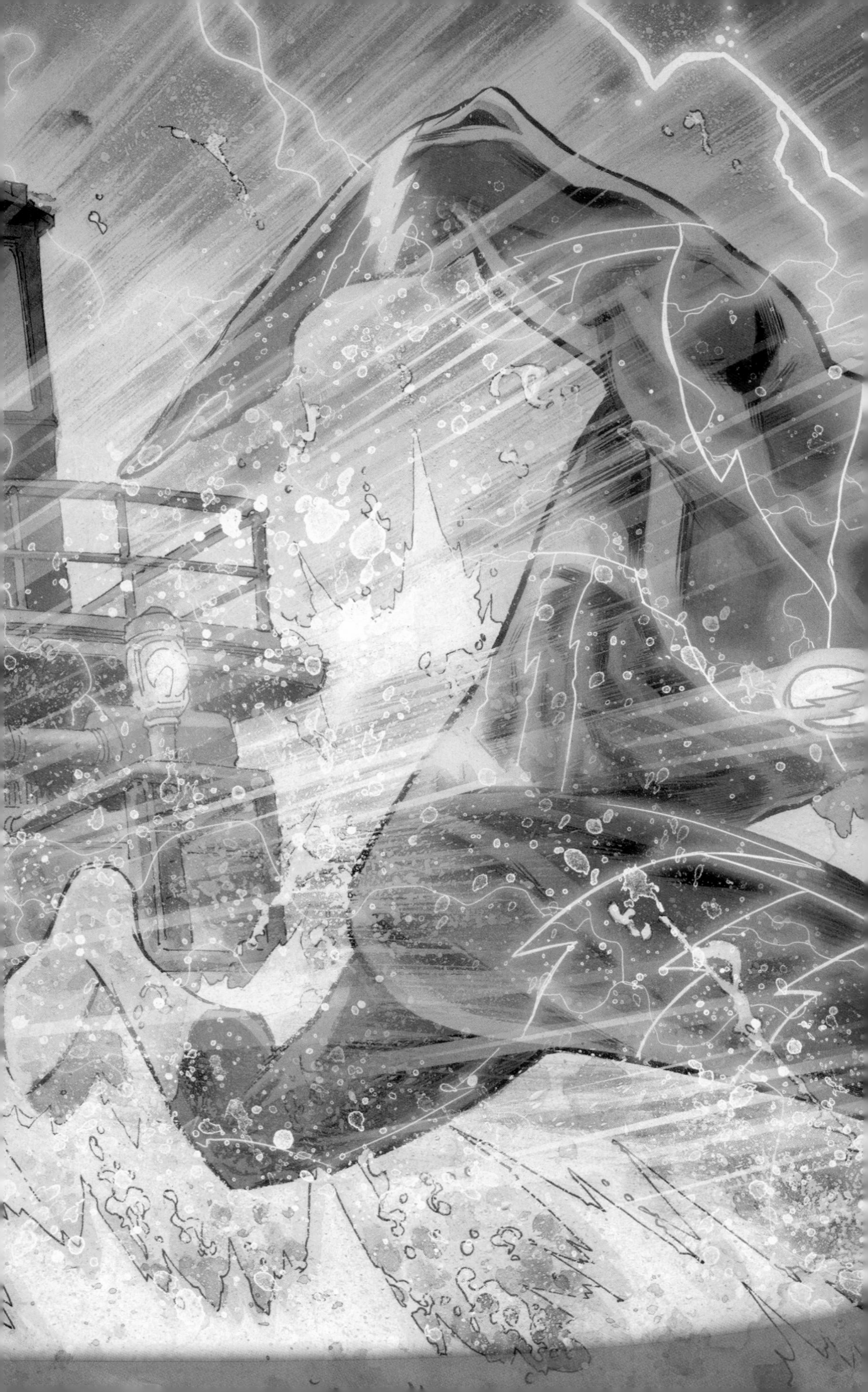

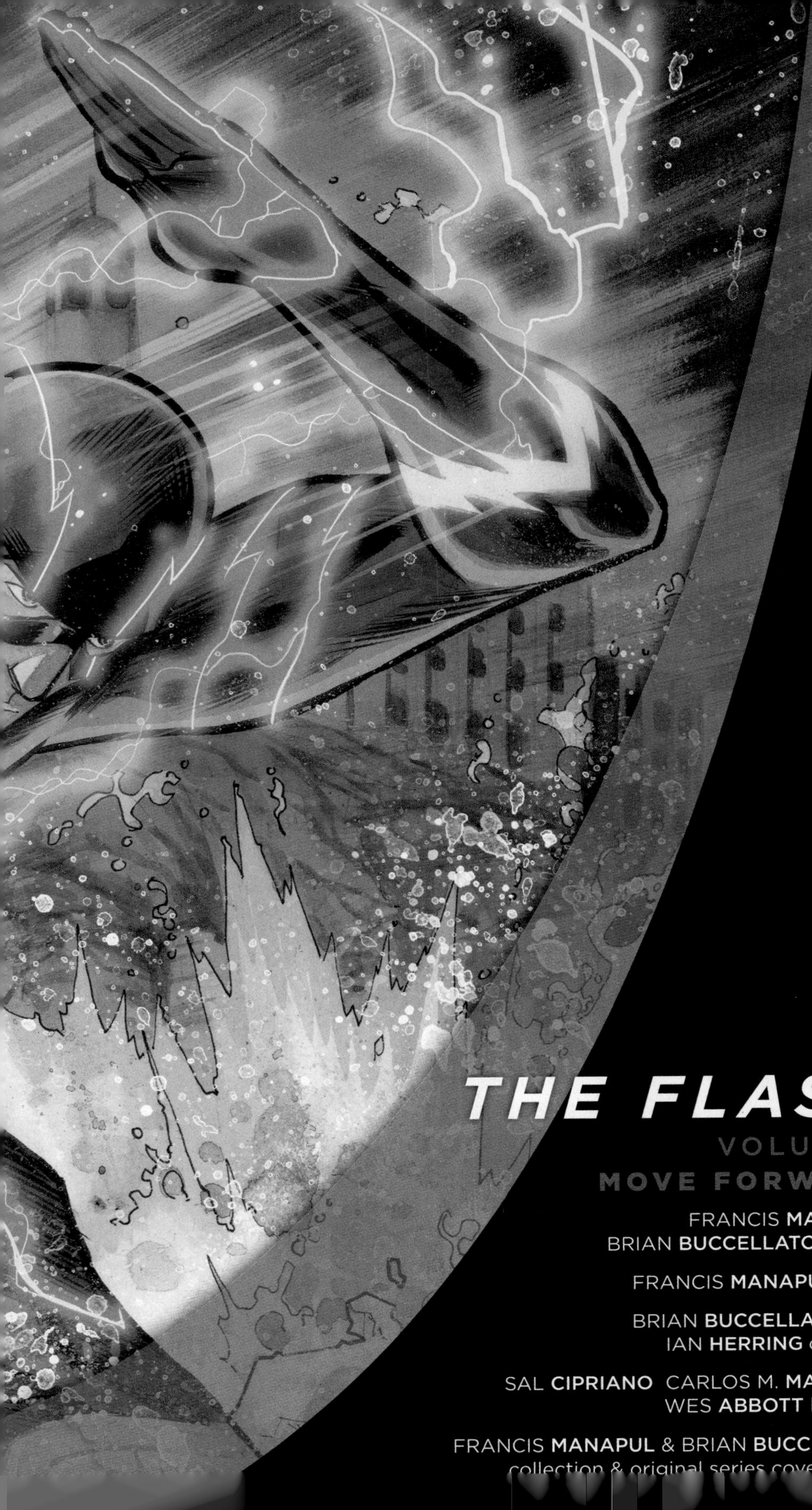

THE FLASH

VOLUME 1

MOVE FORWARD

FRANCIS **MANAPUL**
BRIAN **BUCCELLATO** writers

FRANCIS **MANAPUL** artist

BRIAN **BUCCELLATO** with
IAN **HERRING** colorists

SAL **CIPRIANO** CARLOS M. **MANGUAL**
WES **ABBOTT** letterers

FRANCIS **MANAPUL** & BRIAN **BUCCELLATO**
collection & original series cover artists

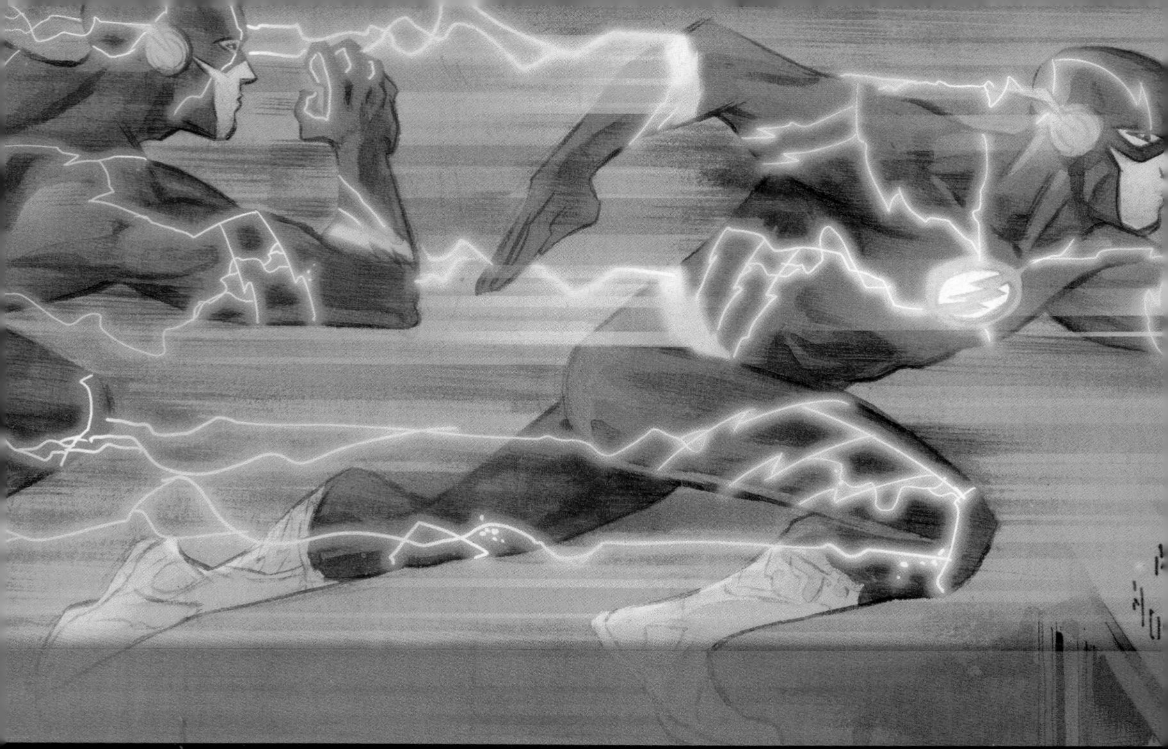

BRIAN CUNNINGHAM Editor – Original Series DARREN SHAN Assistant Editor – Original Series
PETER HAMBOUSSI Editor ROBBIN BROSTERMAN Design Director – Books
ROBBIE BIEDERMAN Publication Design

BOB HARRAS Senior VP – Editor-in-Chief, DC Comics

DIANE NELSON President DAN DIDIO and JIM LEE Co-Publishers
GEOFF JOHNS Chief Creative Officer
AMIT DESAI Senior VP – Marketing and Franchise Management
AMY GENKINS Senior VP – Business and Legal Affairs NAIRI GARDINER Senior VP – Finance
JEFF BOISON VP – Publishing Planning MARK CHIARELLO VP – Art Direction and Design
JOHN CUNNINGHAM VP – Marketing TERRI CUNNINGHAM VP – Editorial Administration LARRY GANEM VP – Talent Relations and Servi
ALISON GILL Senior VP – Manufacturing and Operations HANK KANALZ Senior VP – Vertigo & Integrated Publishing
JAY KOGAN VP – Business and Legal Affairs, Publishing JACK MAHAN VP – Business Affairs, Talent
NICK NAPOLITANO VP – Manufacturing Administration SUE POHJA VP – Book Sales FRED RUIZ VP – Manufacturing Operations
COURTNEY SIMMONS Senior VP – Publicity BOB WAYNE Senior VP – Sales

THE FLASH VOLUME 1: MOVE FORWARD

DC Comics, 4000 Warner Blvd., Burbank, CA 91522
A Warner Bros. Entertainment Company.
Printed by Solisco Printers, Scott, QC, Canada. 8/12/15. Fifth Printing.

HC ISBN: 978-1-4012-3554-3
SC ISBN: 978-1-4012-3554-3

Library of Congress Cataloging-in-Publication Data

Manapul, Francis.
The Flash volume 1 : move forward / Francis Manapul, Brian Buccellato.
p. cm.
"Originally published in single magazine form in The Flash 1-8."
ISBN 978-1-4012-3554-3
1. Graphic novels. I. Buccellato, Brian. II. Title. III. Title: Move forward.
PN6728.F53M36 2012
741.5'973—dc23
2012023703

PEFC
PEFC/26-31-02

PEFC Certified

This product is from sustainably managed forests, recycled and controlled sources

www.pefc.org

This Label only applies to the text section

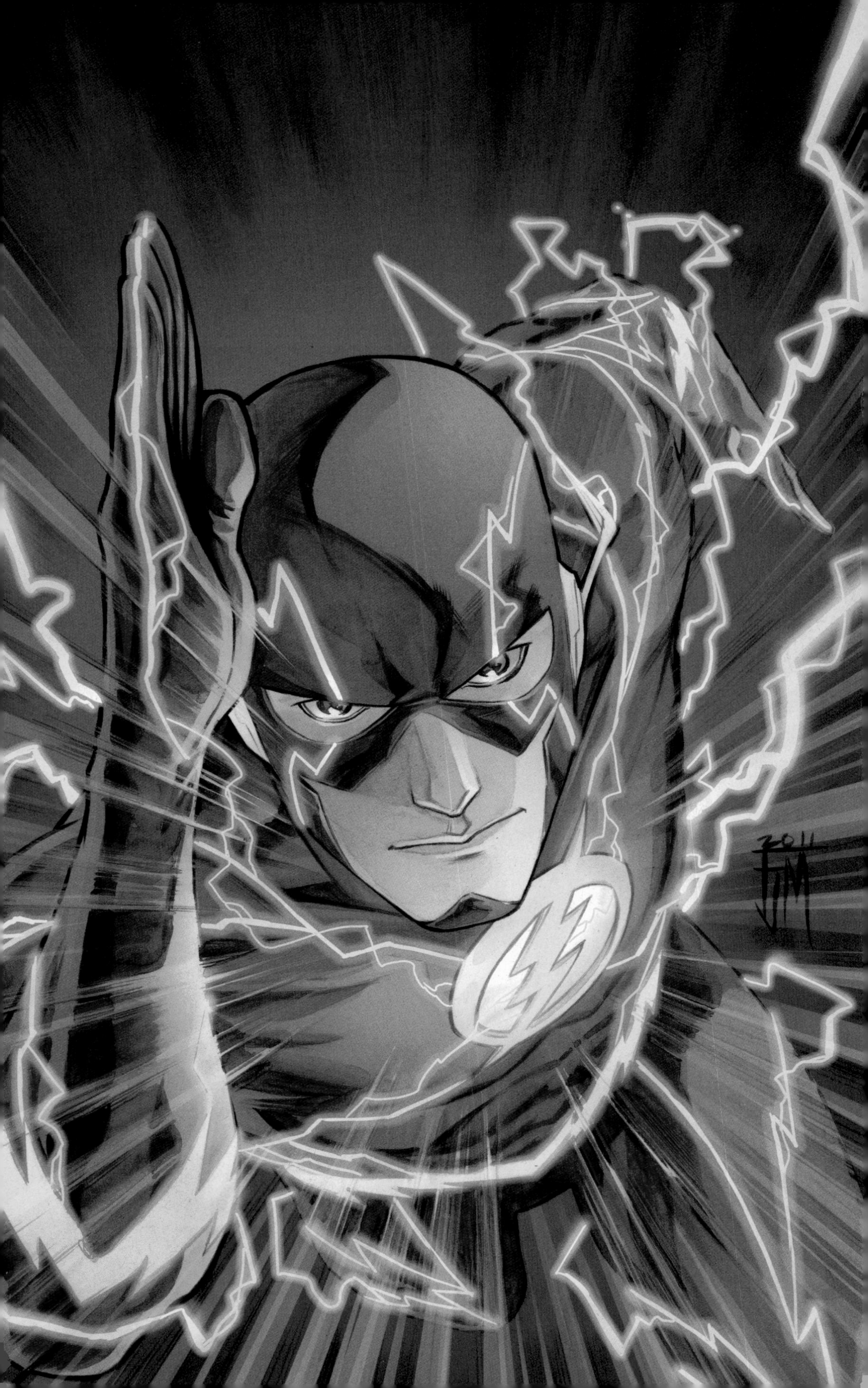

THE FLASH #1

variant cover by IVAN REIS , TIM TOWNSEND & ROD REIS

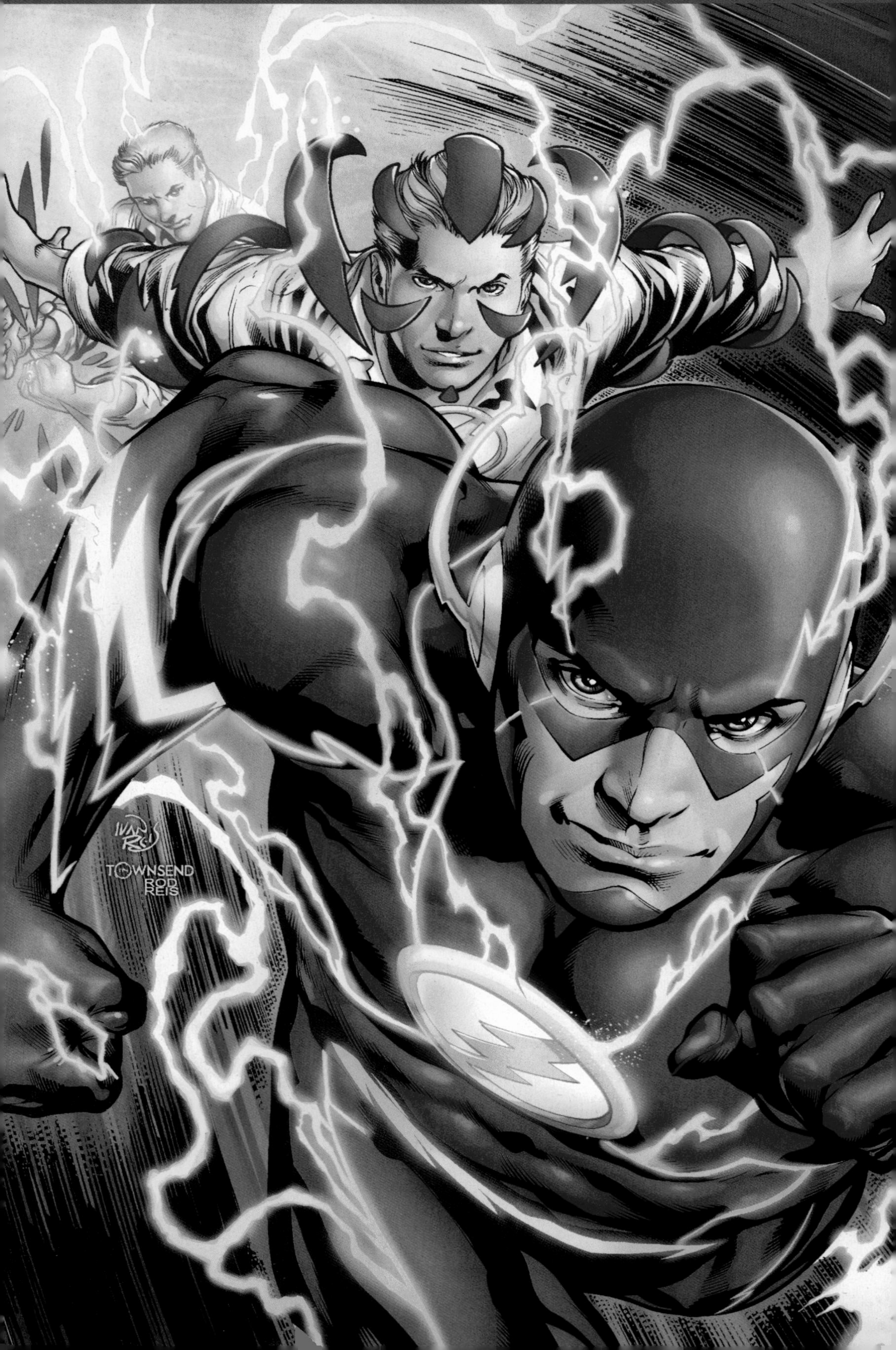
TOWNSEND
ROD
REIS

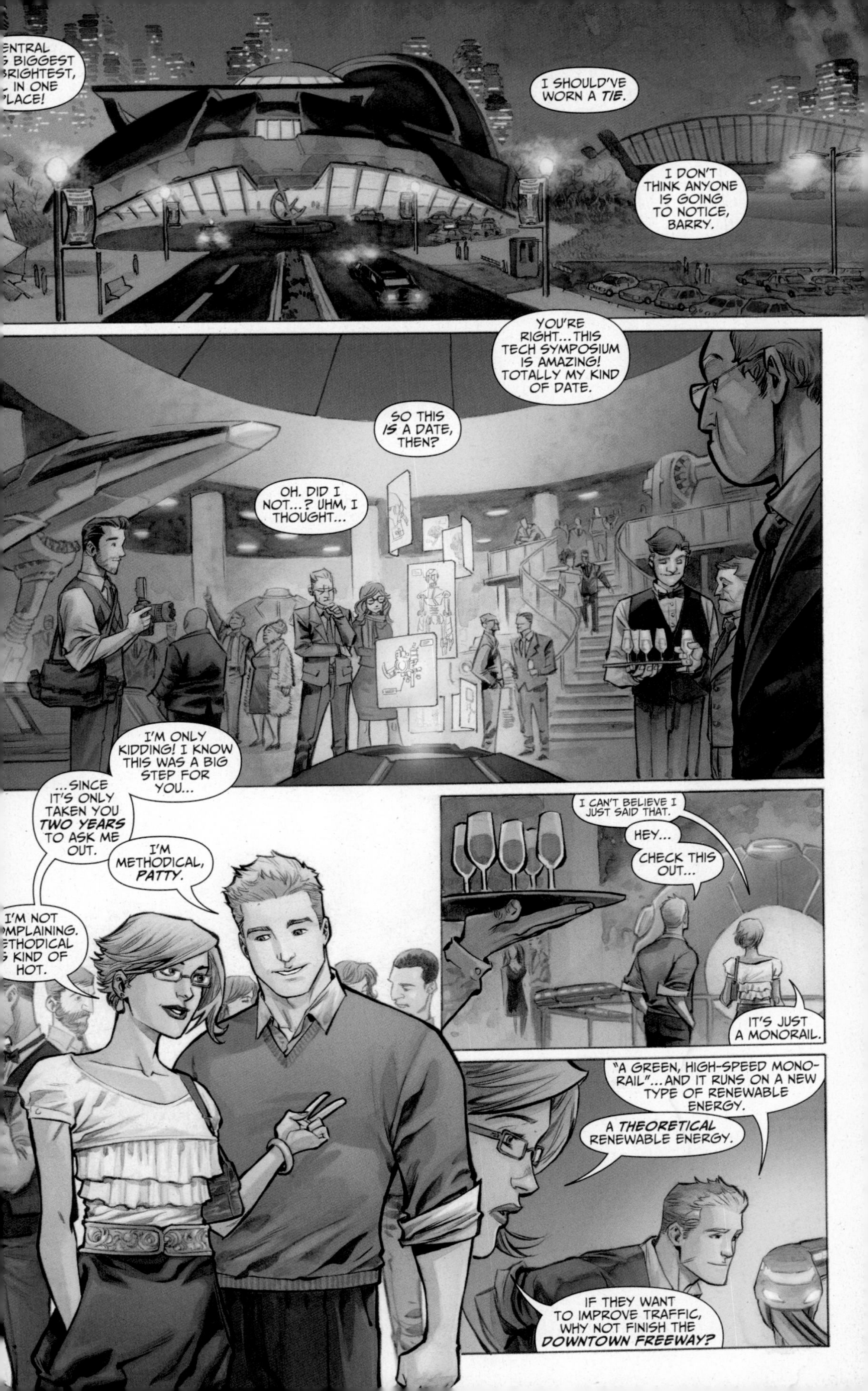

ENTRAL
G BIGGEST
BRIGHTEST,
IN ONE
PLACE!
I SHOULD'VE WORN A TIE.
I DON'T THINK ANYONE IS GOING TO NOTICE, BARRY.
YOU'RE RIGHT... THIS TECH SYMPOSIUM IS AMAZING! TOTALLY MY KIND OF DATE.
SO THIS IS A DATE, THEN?
OH. DID I NOT...? UHM, I THOUGHT...
I'M ONLY KIDDING! I KNOW THIS WAS A BIG STEP FOR YOU...
...SINCE IT'S ONLY TAKEN YOU TWO YEARS TO ASK ME OUT.
I'M METHODICAL, PATTY.
I'M NOT
MPLAINING.
ETHODICAL
S KIND OF
HOT.
I CAN'T BELIEVE I JUST SAID THAT.
HEY...
CHECK THIS OUT...
IT'S JUST A MONORAIL.
"A GREEN, HIGH-SPEED MONORAIL"... AND IT RUNS ON A NEW TYPE OF RENEWABLE ENERGY.
A THEORETICAL RENEWABLE ENERGY.
IF THEY WANT TO IMPROVE TRAFFIC, WHY NOT FINISH THE DOWNTOWN FREEWAY?

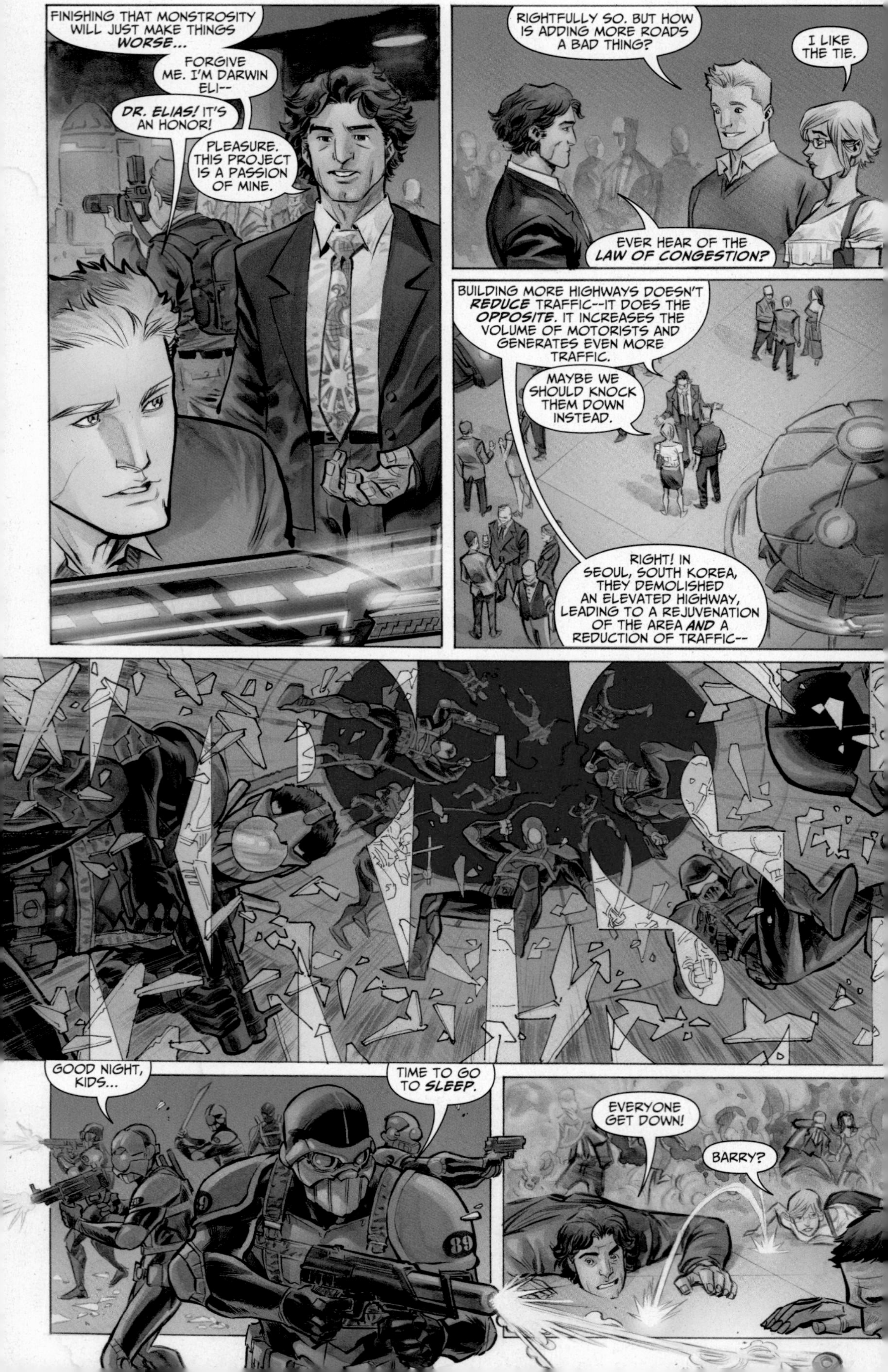
FINISHING THAT MONSTROSITY WILL JUST MAKE THINGS WORSE...
FORGIVE ME. I'M DARWIN ELI--
DR. ELIAS! IT'S AN HONOR!
PLEASURE. THIS PROJECT IS A PASSION OF MINE.
RIGHTFULLY SO. BUT HOW IS ADDING MORE ROADS A BAD THING?
I LIKE THE TIE.
EVER HEAR OF THE LAW OF CONGESTION?
BUILDING MORE HIGHWAYS DOESN'T REDUCE TRAFFIC--IT DOES THE OPPOSITE. IT INCREASES THE VOLUME OF MOTORISTS AND GENERATES EVEN MORE TRAFFIC.
MAYBE WE SHOULD KNOCK THEM DOWN INSTEAD.
RIGHT! IN SEOUL, SOUTH KOREA, THEY DEMOLISHED AN ELEVATED HIGHWAY, LEADING TO A REJUVENATION OF THE AREA AND A REDUCTION OF TRAFFIC--
GOOD NIGHT, KIDS...
TIME TO GO TO SLEEP.
EVERYONE GET DOWN!
BARRY?

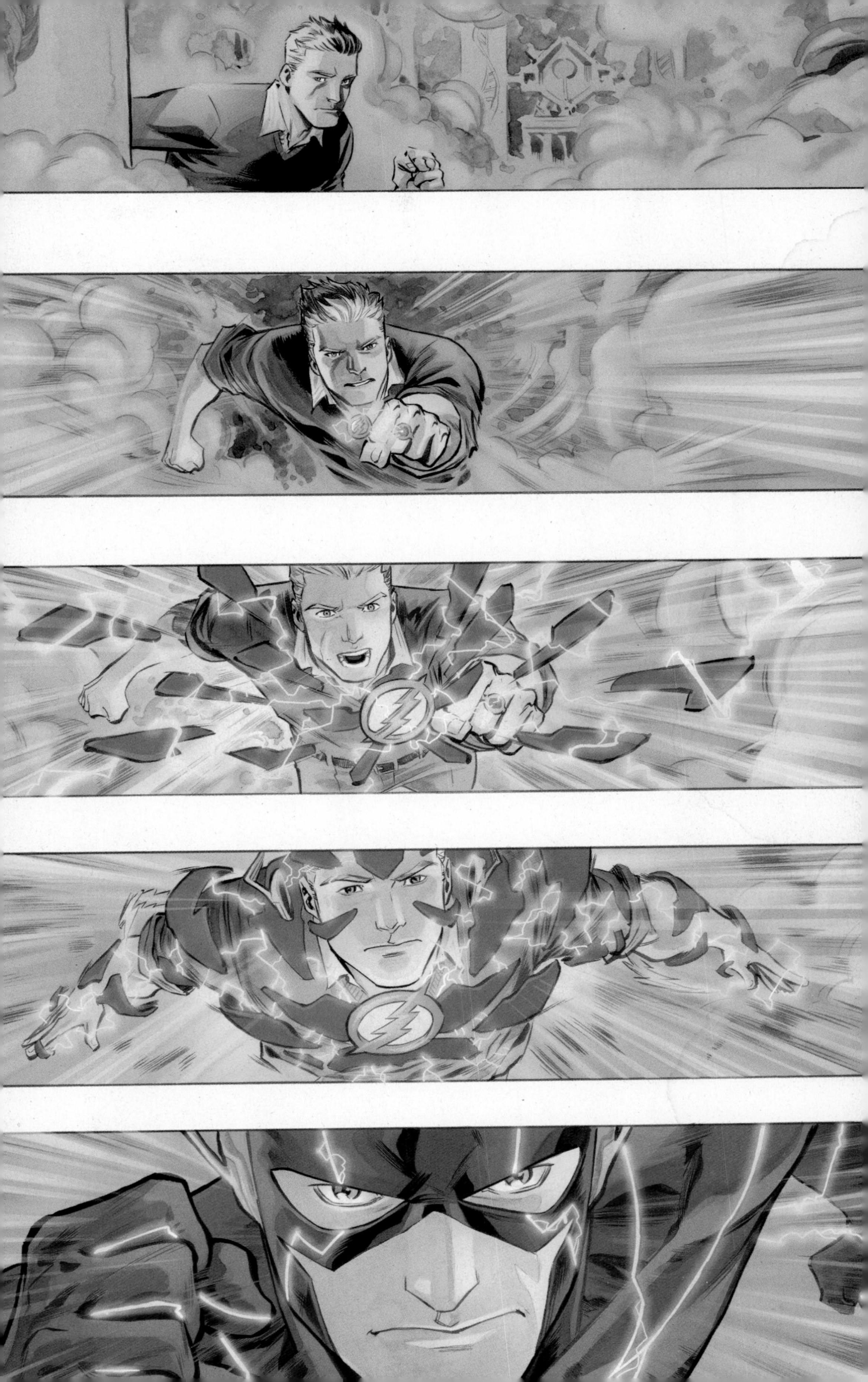

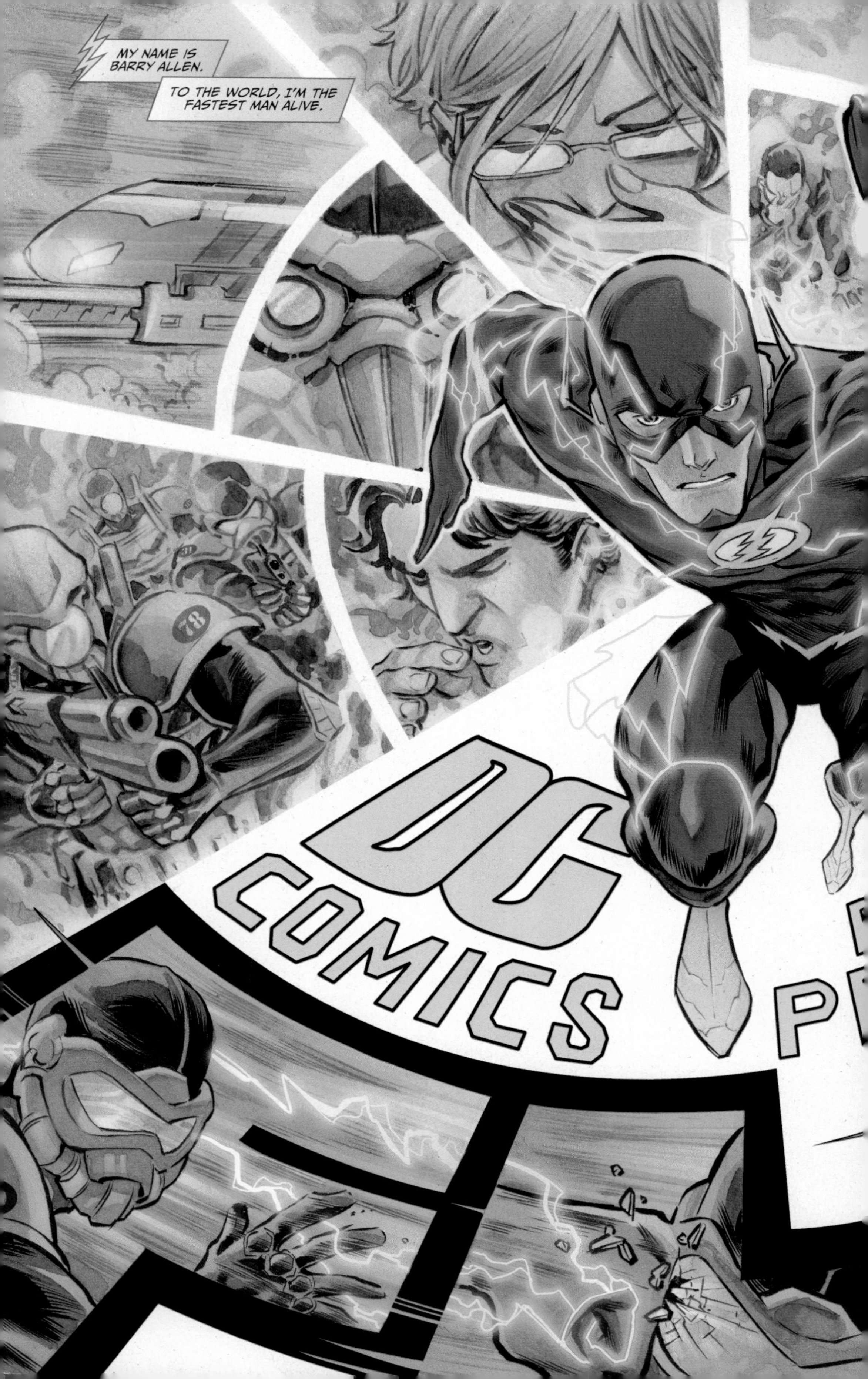
MY NAME IS BARRY ALLEN.
TO THE WORLD, I'M THE FASTEST MAN ALIVE.
DC COMICS

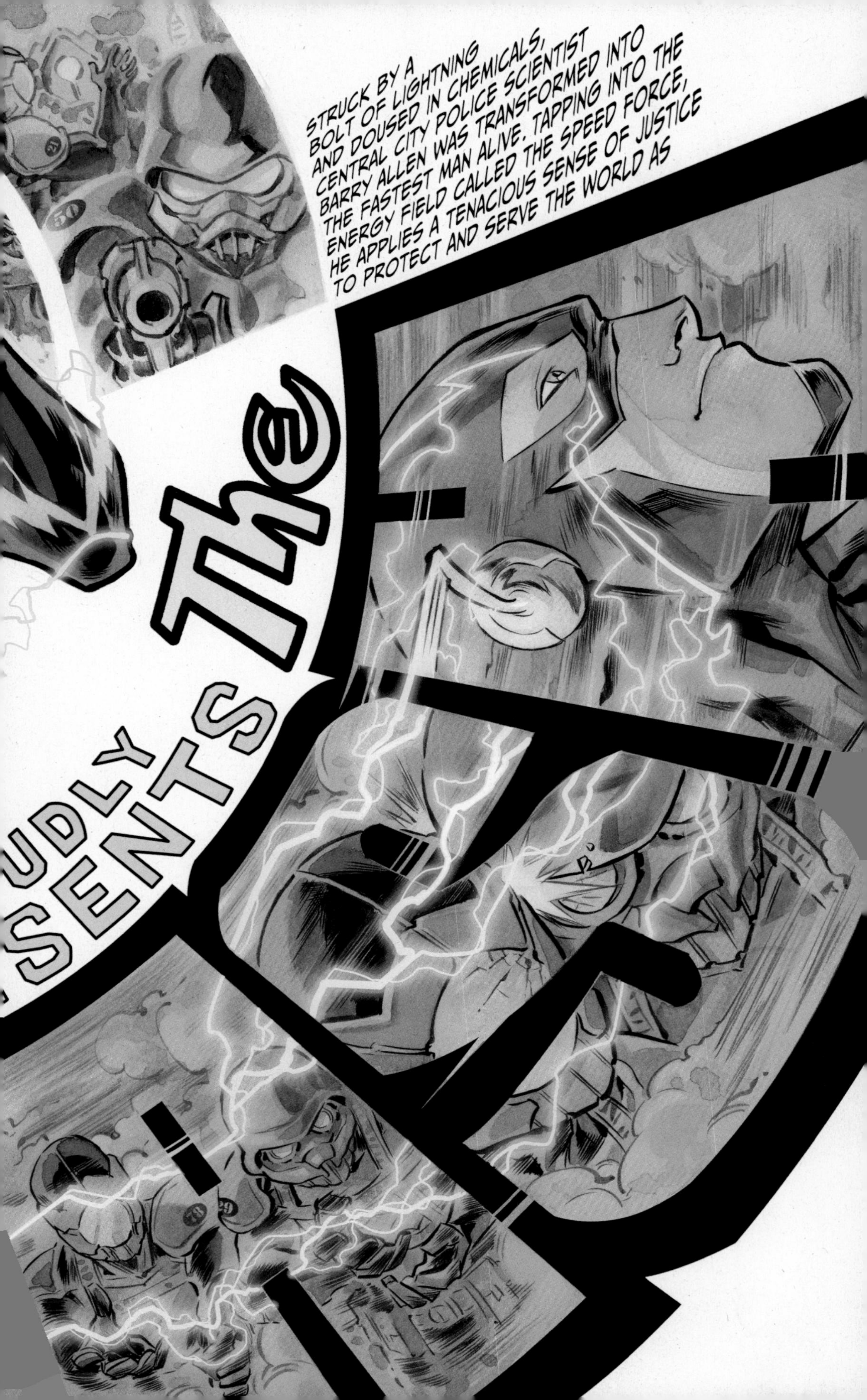
STRUCK BY A BOLT OF LIGHTNING AND DOUSED IN CHEMICALS, CENTRAL CITY POLICE SCIENTIST BARRY ALLEN WAS TRANSFORMED INTO THE FASTEST MAN ALIVE. TAPPING INTO THE ENERGY FIELD CALLED THE SPEED FORCE, HE APPLIES A TENACIOUS SENSE OF JUSTICE TO PROTECT AND SERVE THE WORLD AS
UDLY
SENTS
The

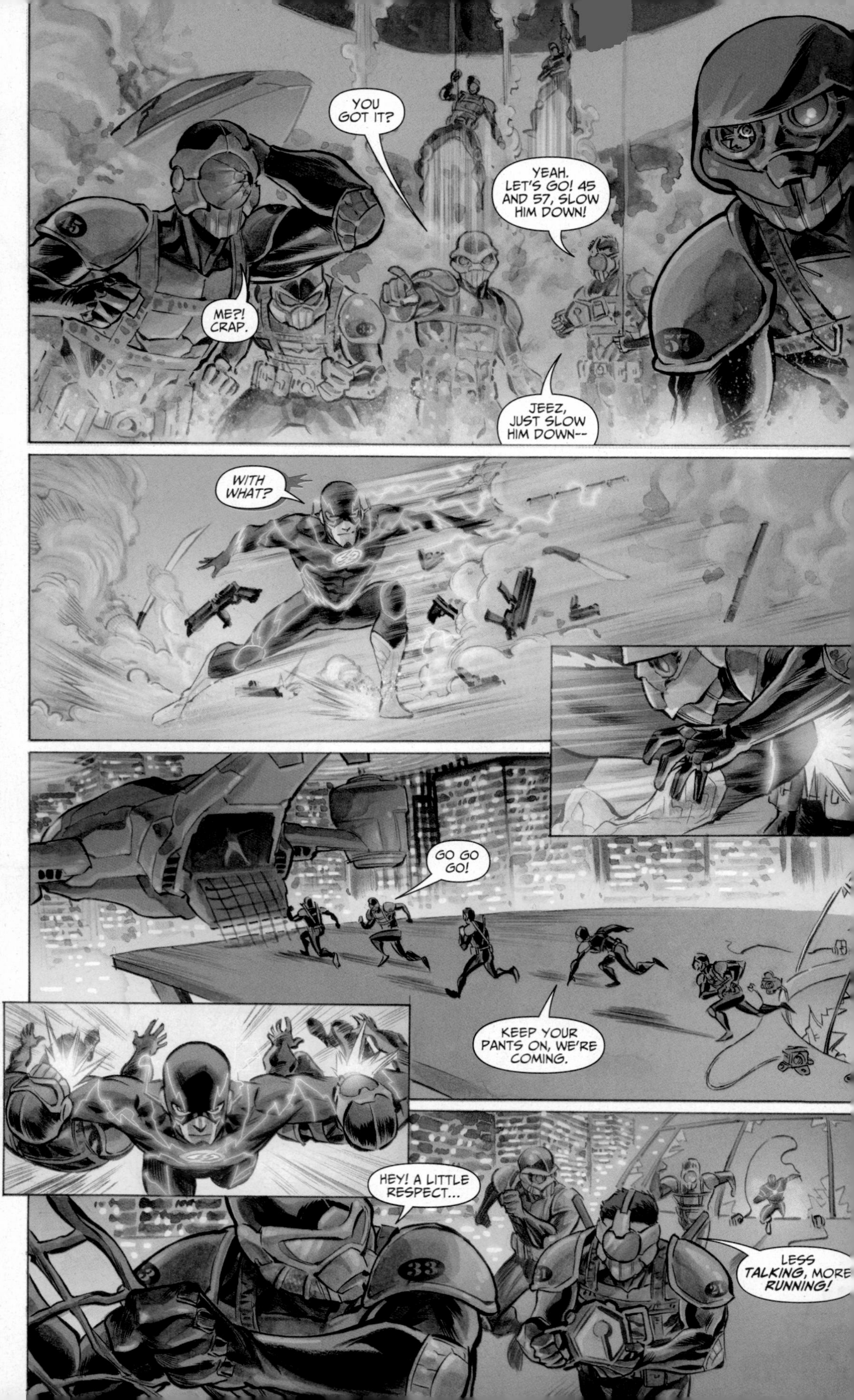

YOU GOT IT?
YEAH. LET'S GO! 45 AND 57, SLOW HIM DOWN!
ME?! CRAP.
JEEZ, JUST SLOW HIM DOWN--
WITH WHAT?
GO GO GO!
KEEP YOUR PANTS ON, WE'RE COMING.
HEY! A LITTLE RESPECT...
LESS TALKING, MORE RUNNING!

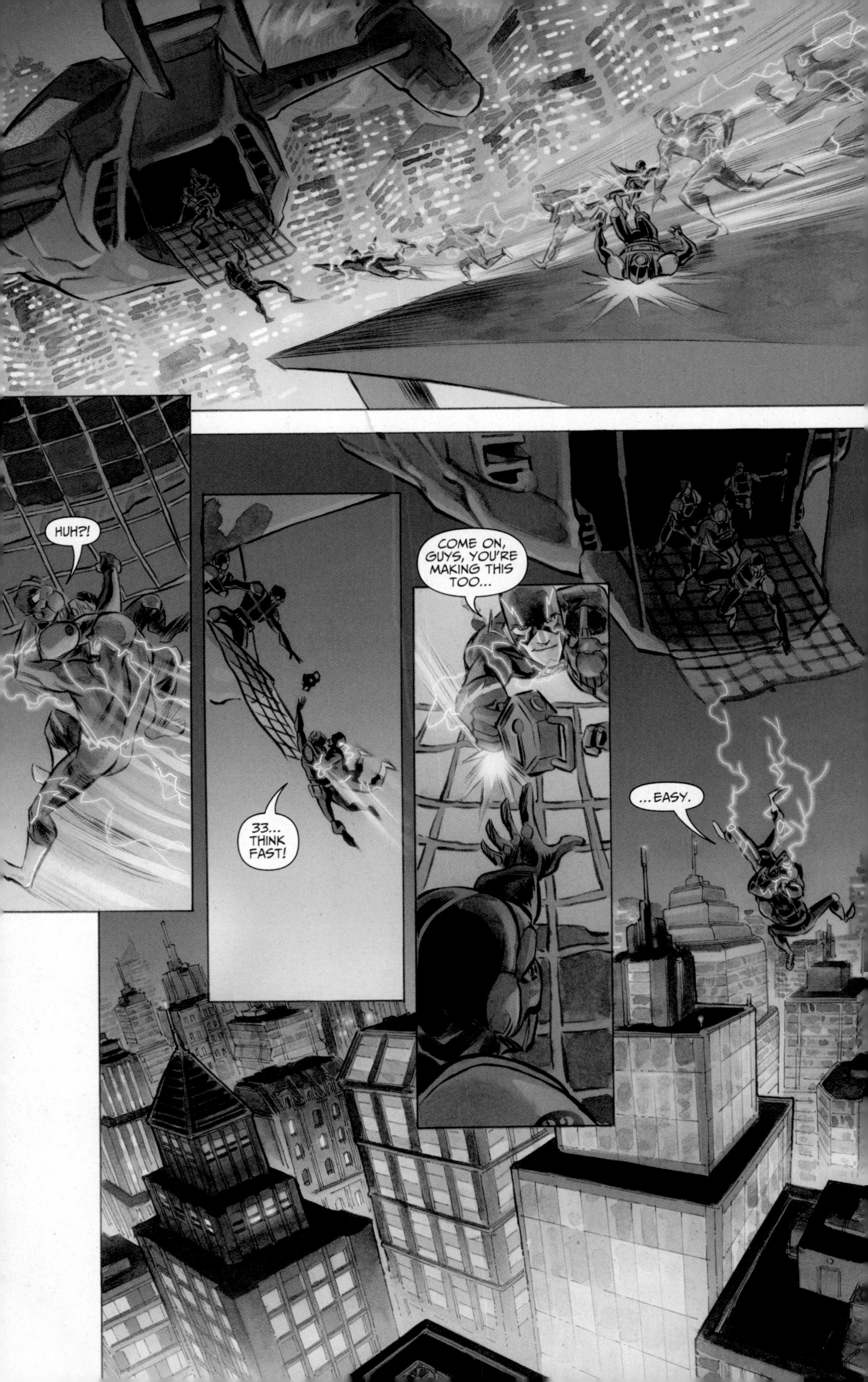
HUH?!
33... THINK FAST!
COME ON, GUYS, YOU'RE MAKING THIS TOO...
...EASY.

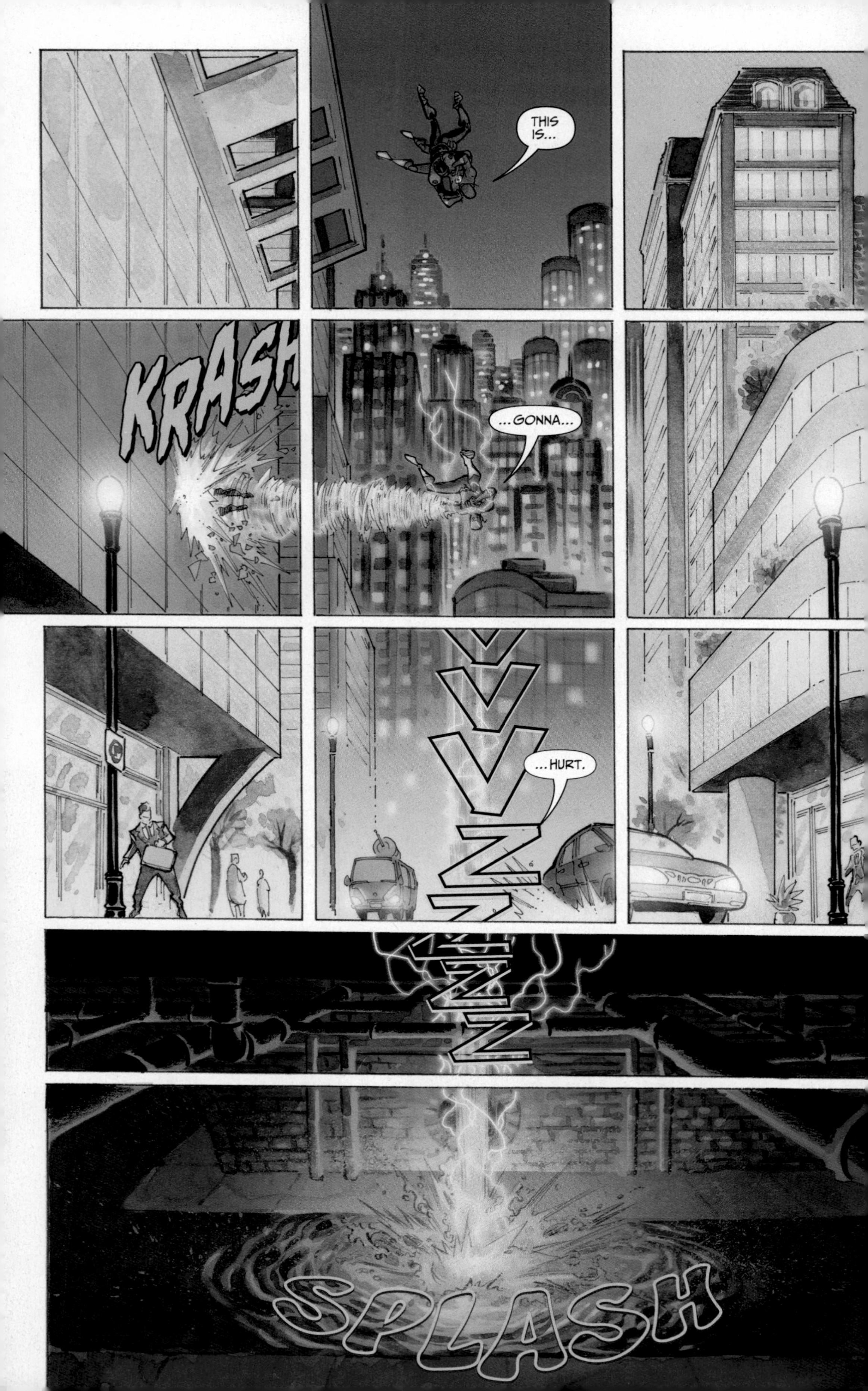
THIS IS...
KRASH
...GONNA...
...HURT.
SPLASH

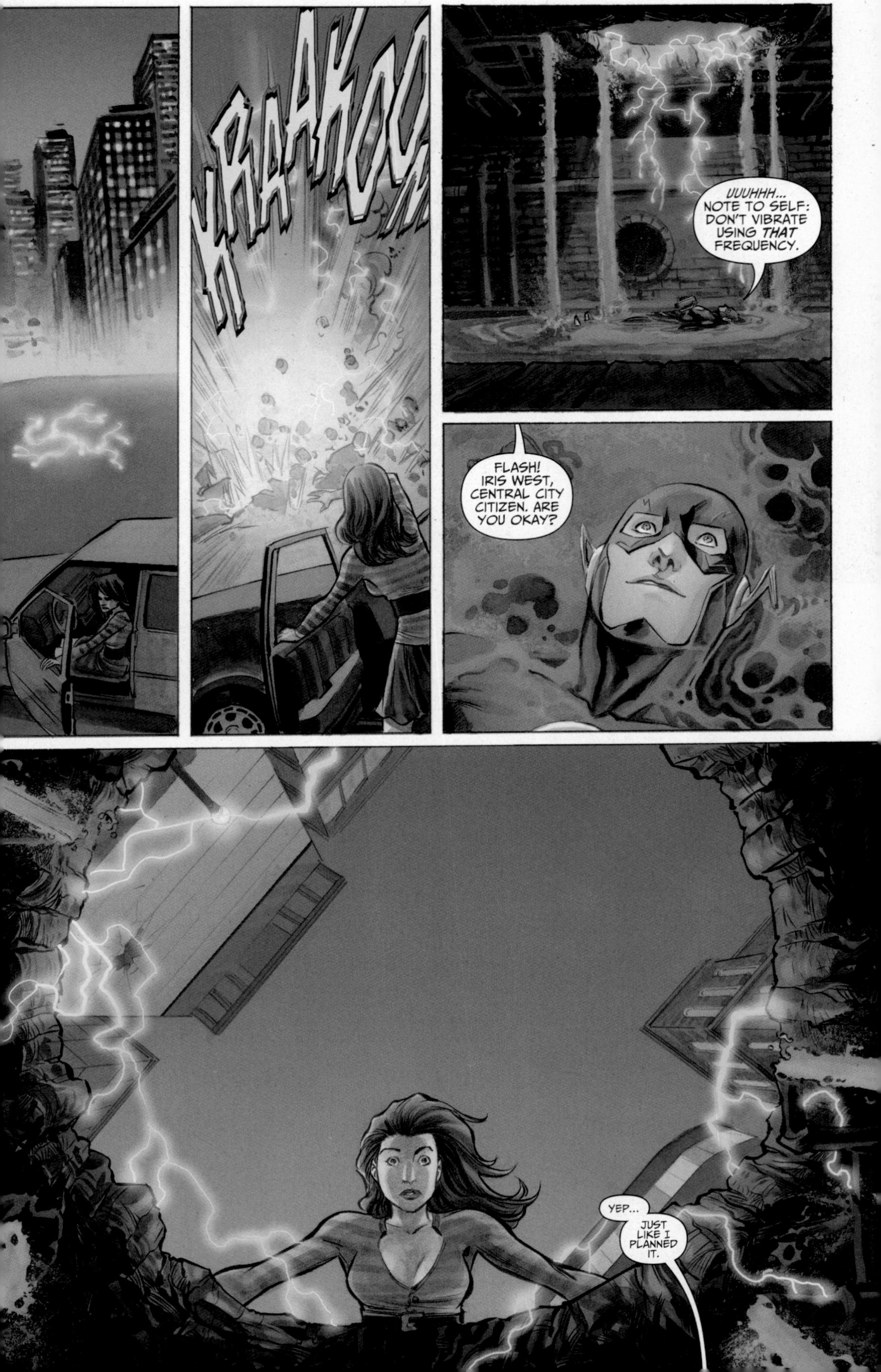
KRAKOOM
UUUHHH... NOTE TO SELF: DON'T VIBRATE USING THAT FREQUENCY.
FLASH! IRIS WEST, CENTRAL CITY CITIZEN. ARE YOU OKAY?
YEP...
JUST LIKE I PLANNED IT.

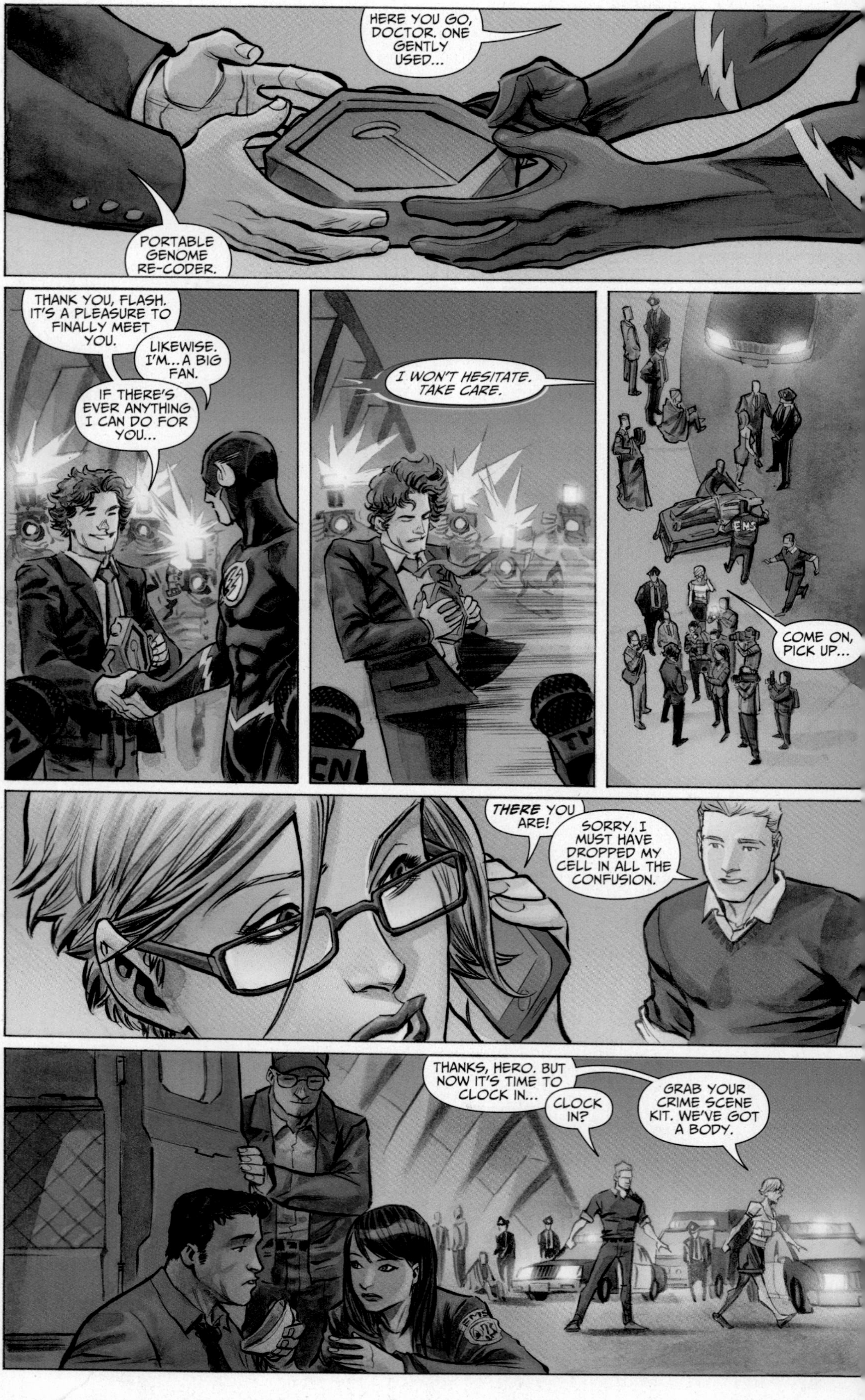
HERE YOU GO, DOCTOR. ONE GENTLY USED...
PORTABLE GENOME RE-CODER.
THANK YOU, FLASH. IT'S A PLEASURE TO FINALLY MEET YOU.
LIKEWISE. I'M...A BIG FAN.
IF THERE'S EVER ANYTHING I CAN DO FOR YOU...
I WON'T HESITATE. TAKE CARE.
EMS
COME ON, PICK UP...
THERE YOU ARE!
SORRY, I MUST HAVE DROPPED MY CELL IN ALL THE CONFUSION.
THANKS, HERO. BUT NOW IT'S TIME TO CLOCK IN...
CLOCK IN?
GRAB YOUR CRIME SCENE KIT. WE'VE GOT A BODY.

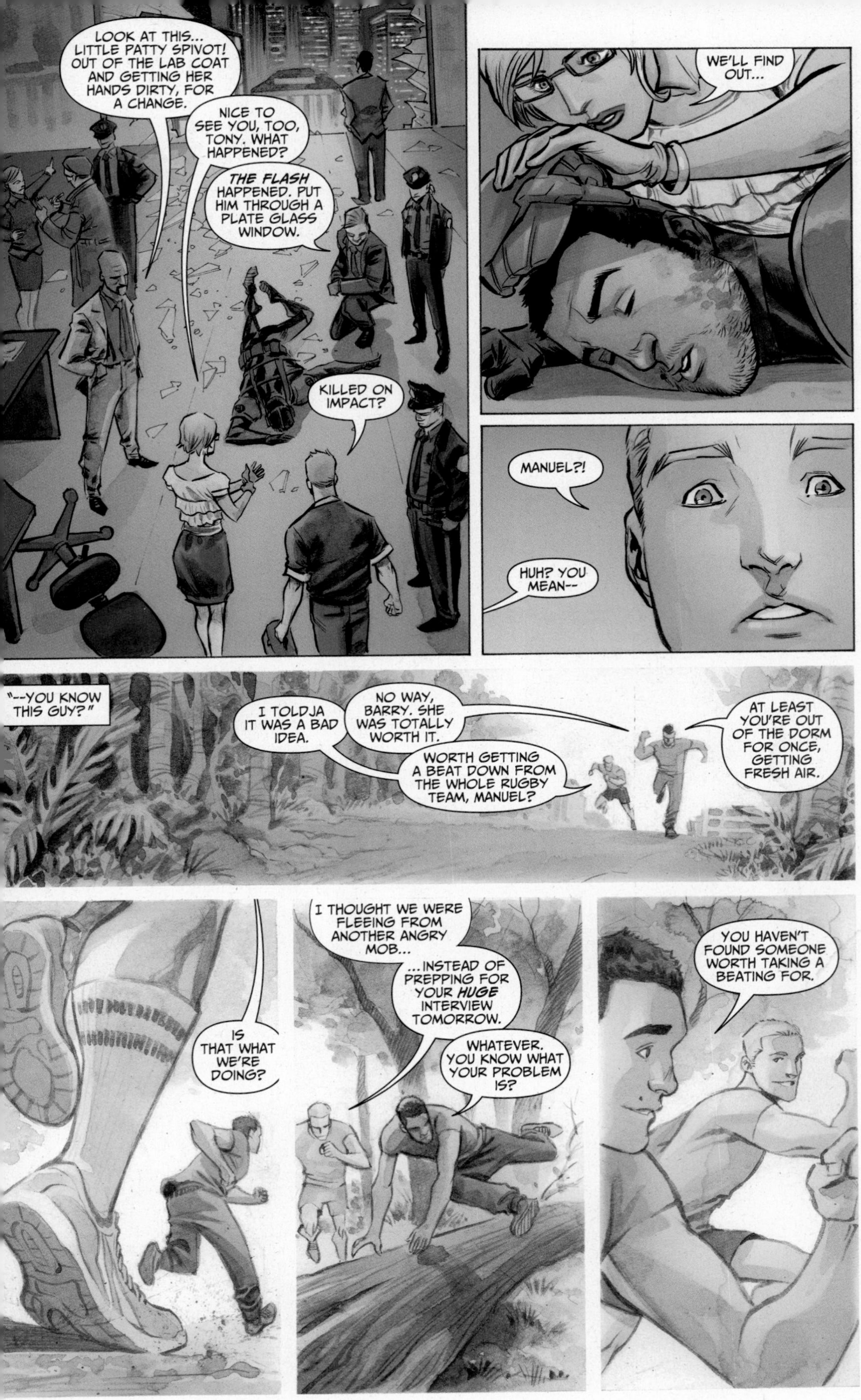
LOOK AT THIS... LITTLE PATTY SPIVOT! OUT OF THE LAB COAT AND GETTING HER HANDS DIRTY, FOR A CHANGE.
NICE TO SEE YOU, TOO, TONY. WHAT HAPPENED?
THE FLASH HAPPENED. PUT HIM THROUGH A PLATE GLASS WINDOW.
KILLED ON IMPACT?
WE'LL FIND OUT...
MANUEL?!
HUH? YOU MEAN--
"--YOU KNOW THIS GUY?"
I TOLDJA IT WAS A BAD IDEA.
NO WAY, BARRY. SHE WAS TOTALLY WORTH IT.
WORTH GETTING A BEAT DOWN FROM THE WHOLE RUGBY TEAM, MANUEL?
AT LEAST YOU'RE OUT OF THE DORM FOR ONCE, GETTING FRESH AIR.
IS THAT WHAT WE'RE DOING?
I THOUGHT WE WERE FLEEING FROM ANOTHER ANGRY MOB...
...INSTEAD OF PREPPING FOR YOUR HUGE INTERVIEW TOMORROW.
WHATEVER. YOU KNOW WHAT YOUR PROBLEM IS?
YOU HAVEN'T FOUND SOMEONE WORTH TAKING A BEATING FOR.

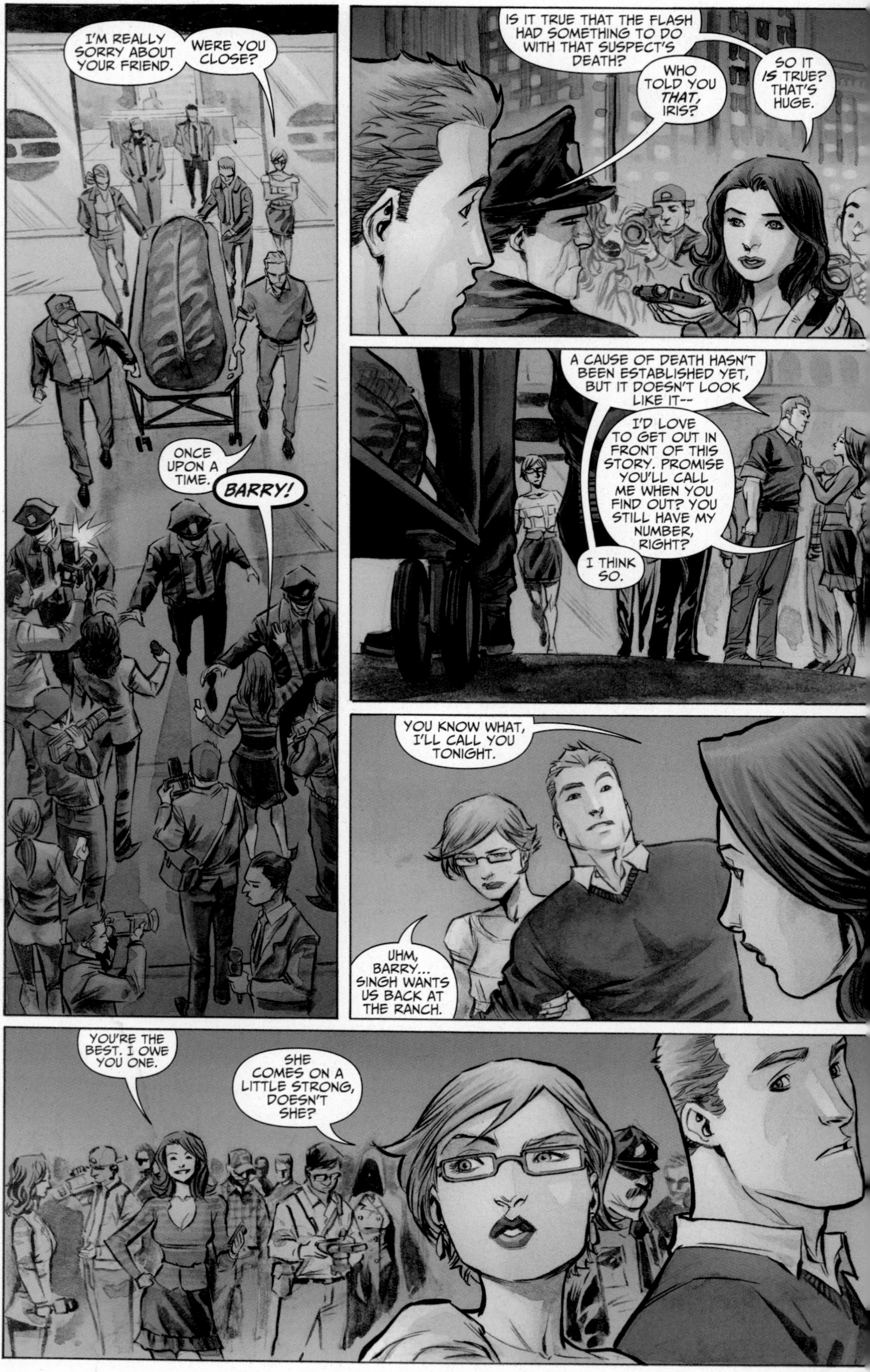

I'M REALLY SORRY ABOUT YOUR FRIEND.
WERE YOU CLOSE?
ONCE UPON A TIME.
BARRY!
IS IT TRUE THAT THE FLASH HAD SOMETHING TO DO WITH THAT SUSPECT'S DEATH?
WHO TOLD YOU THAT, IRIS?
SO IT IS TRUE? THAT'S HUGE.
A CAUSE OF DEATH HASN'T BEEN ESTABLISHED YET, BUT IT DOESN'T LOOK LIKE IT--
I'D LOVE TO GET OUT IN FRONT OF THIS STORY. PROMISE YOU'LL CALL ME WHEN YOU FIND OUT? YOU STILL HAVE MY NUMBER, RIGHT?
I THINK SO.
YOU KNOW WHAT, I'LL CALL YOU TONIGHT.
UHM, BARRY... SINGH WANTS US BACK AT THE RANCH.
YOU'RE THE BEST. I OWE YOU ONE.
SHE COMES ON A LITTLE STRONG, DOESN'T SHE?

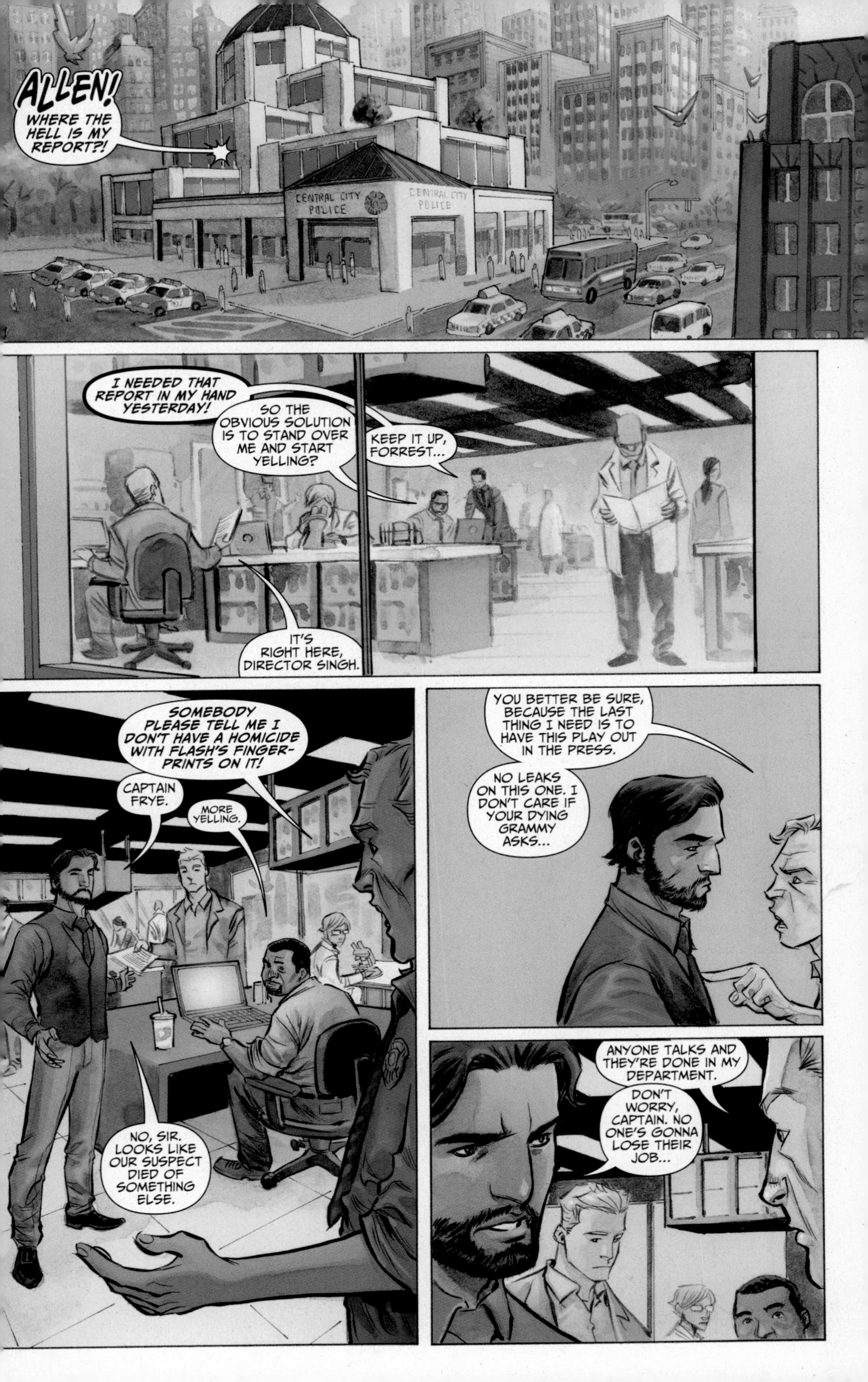
ALLEN!
WHERE THE HELL IS MY REPORT?!
CENTRAL CITY POLICE
CENTRAL CITY POLICE
I NEEDED THAT REPORT IN MY HAND YESTERDAY!
SO THE OBVIOUS SOLUTION IS TO STAND OVER ME AND START YELLING?
KEEP IT UP, FORREST...
IT'S RIGHT HERE, DIRECTOR SINGH.
SOMEBODY PLEASE TELL ME I DON'T HAVE A HOMICIDE WITH FLASH'S FINGER-PRINTS ON IT!
CAPTAIN FRYE.
MORE YELLING.
NO, SIR. LOOKS LIKE OUR SUSPECT DIED OF SOMETHING ELSE.
YOU BETTER BE SURE, BECAUSE THE LAST THING I NEED IS TO HAVE THIS PLAY OUT IN THE PRESS.
NO LEAKS ON THIS ONE. I DON'T CARE IF YOUR DYING GRAMMY ASKS...
ANYONE TALKS AND THEY'RE DONE IN MY DEPARTMENT.
DON'T WORRY, CAPTAIN. NO ONE'S GONNA LOSE THEIR JOB...

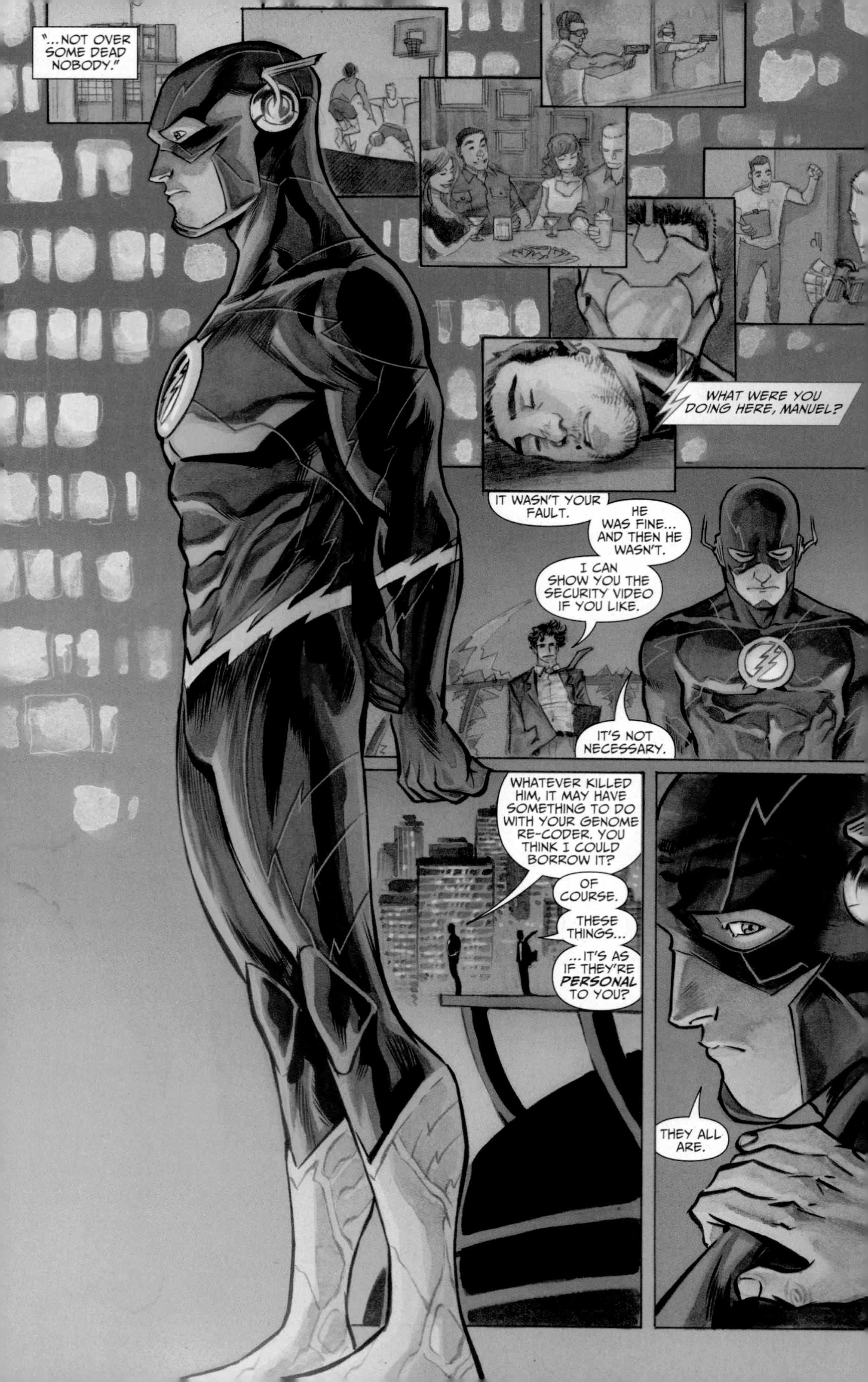
"...NOT OVER SOME DEAD NOBODY."
WHAT WERE YOU DOING HERE, MANUEL?
IT WASN'T YOUR FAULT.
HE WAS FINE... AND THEN HE WASN'T.
I CAN SHOW YOU THE SECURITY VIDEO IF YOU LIKE.
IT'S NOT NECESSARY.
WHATEVER KILLED HIM, IT MAY HAVE SOMETHING TO DO WITH YOUR GENOME RE-CODER. YOU THINK I COULD BORROW IT?
OF COURSE.
THESE THINGS...
...IT'S AS IF THEY'RE PERSONAL TO YOU?
THEY ALL ARE.

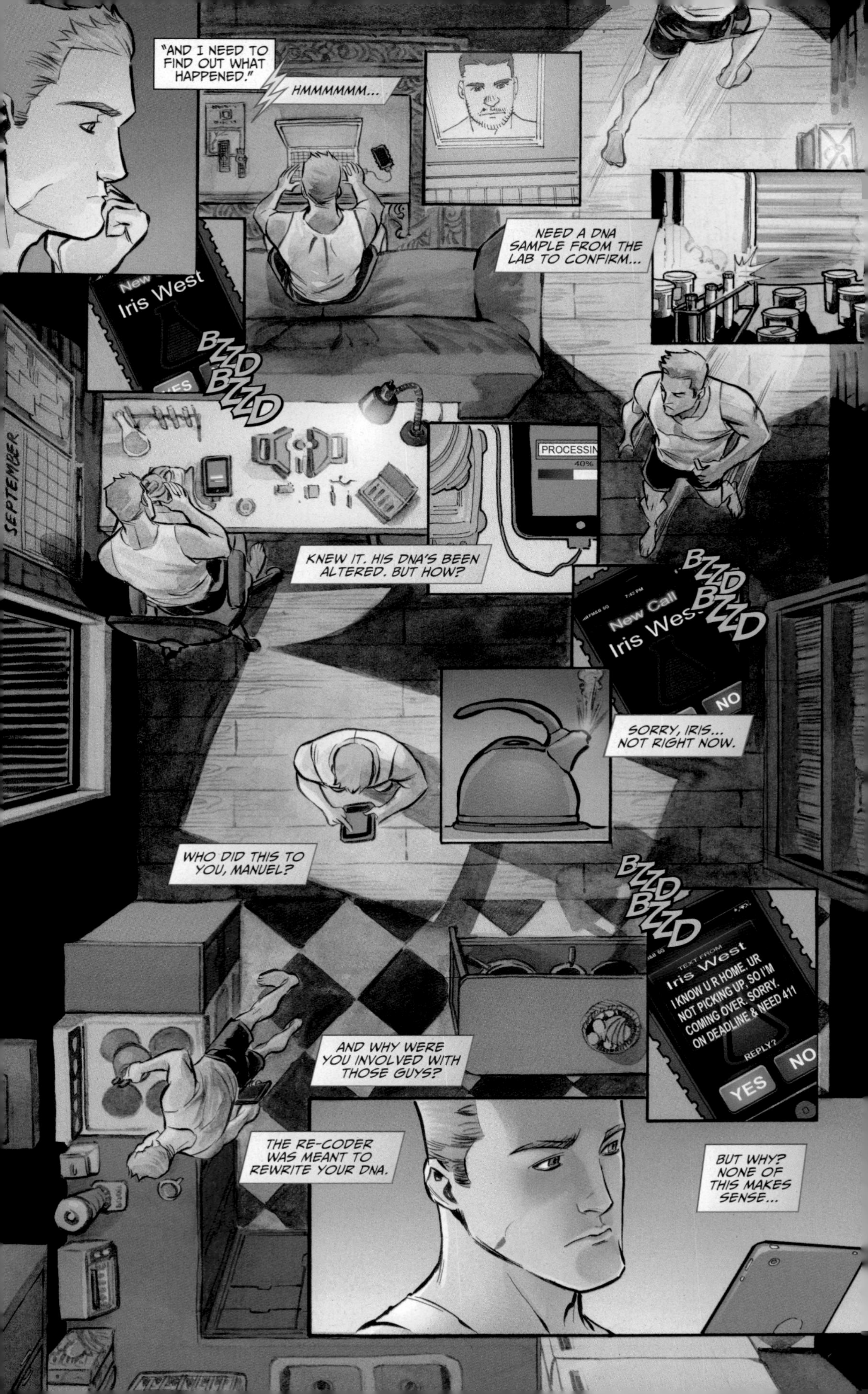
"AND I NEED TO FIND OUT WHAT HAPPENED."
HMMMMMM...
New
Iris West
YES
BZZD BZZD
NEED A DNA SAMPLE FROM THE LAB TO CONFIRM...
SEPTEMBER
PROCESSING
40%
KNEW IT. HIS DNA'S BEEN ALTERED. BUT HOW?
New Call
Iris West
BZZD BZZD
NO
SORRY, IRIS... NOT RIGHT NOW.
WHO DID THIS TO YOU, MANUEL?
BZZD BZZD
TEXT FROM
Iris West
I KNOW U R HOME. UR NOT PICKING UP, SO I'M COMING OVER. SORRY. ON DEADLINE & NEED 411
REPLY?
YES
NO
AND WHY WERE YOU INVOLVED WITH THOSE GUYS?
THE RE-CODER WAS MEANT TO REWRITE YOUR DNA.
BUT WHY? NONE OF THIS MAKES SENSE...

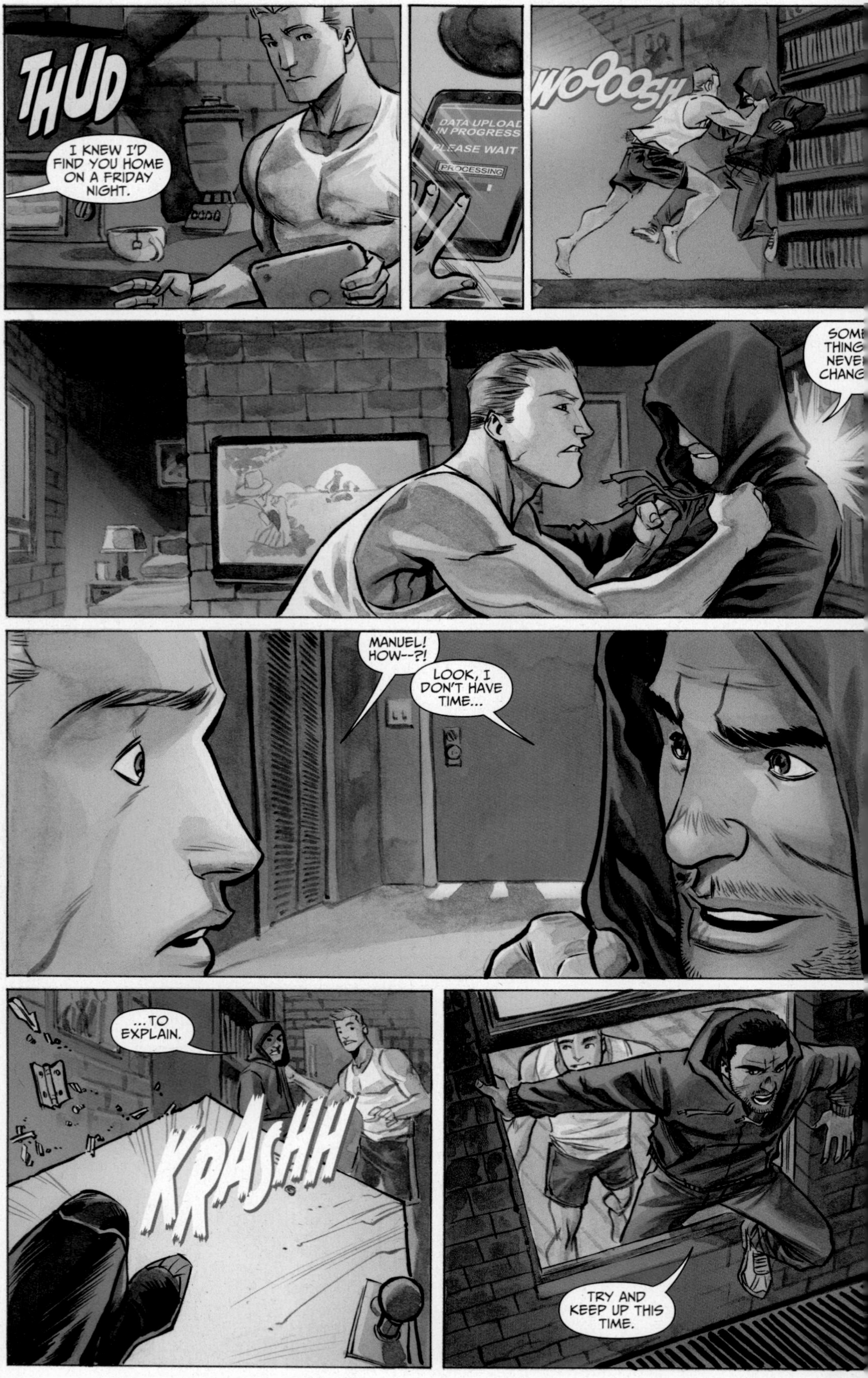
THUD
I KNEW I'D FIND YOU HOME ON A FRIDAY NIGHT.
DATA UPLOAD IN PROGRESS
PLEASE WAIT
PROCESSING
WOOOOOSH
SOME THING NEVE CHANG
MANUEL! HOW--?!
LOOK, I DON'T HAVE TIME...
...TO EXPLAIN.
KRASHH
TRY AND KEEP UP THIS TIME.

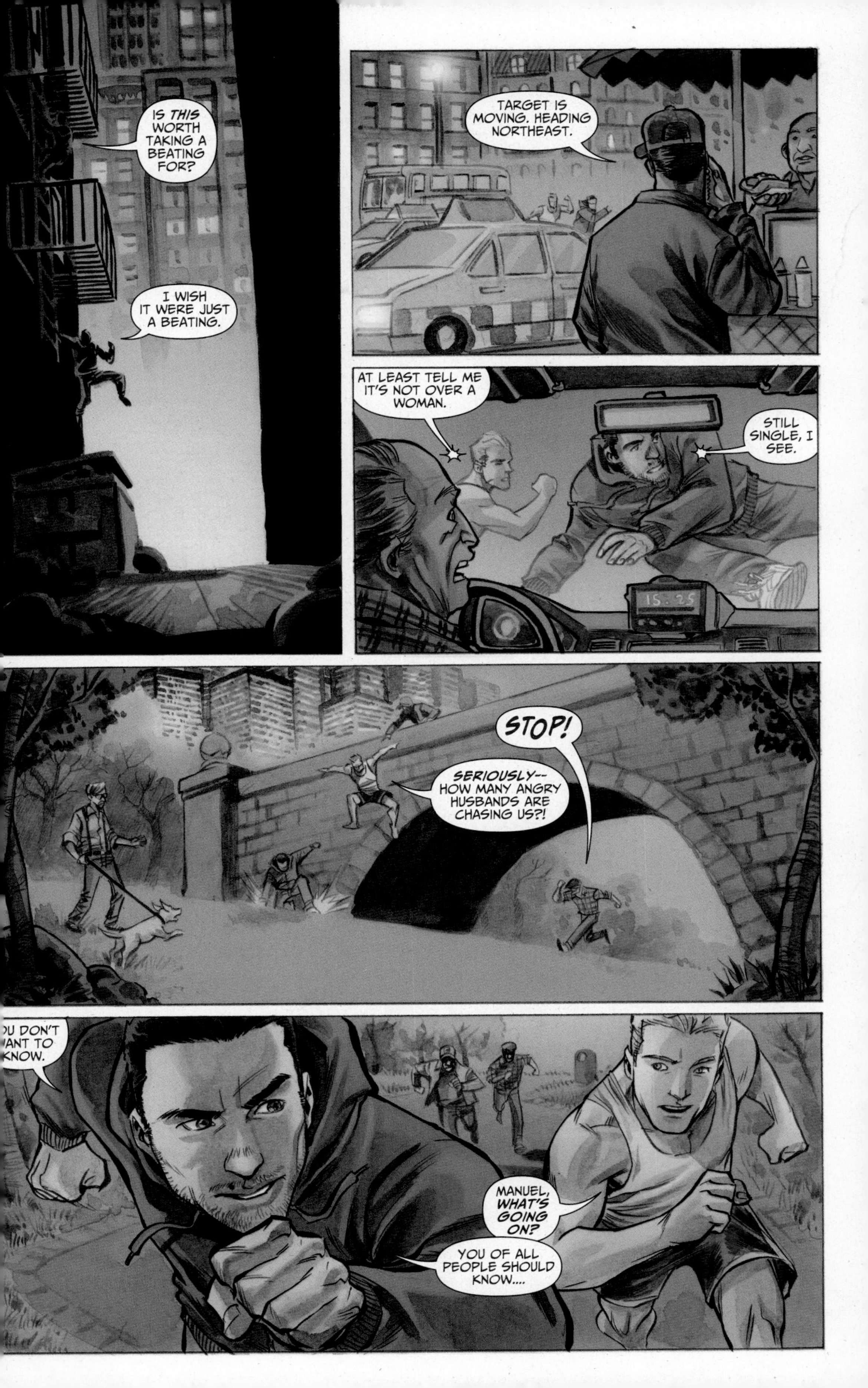
IS THIS WORTH TAKING A BEATING FOR?
I WISH IT WERE JUST A BEATING.
TARGET IS MOVING. HEADING NORTHEAST.
AT LEAST TELL ME IT'S NOT OVER A WOMAN.
STILL SINGLE, I SEE.
15:25
STOP!
SERIOUSLY-- HOW MANY ANGRY HUSBANDS ARE CHASING US?!
OU DON'T ANT TO NOW.
MANUEL, WHAT'S GOING ON?
YOU OF ALL PEOPLE SHOULD KNOW....

...WE'RE ALWAYS RUNNING FROM SOMETHING.

HE'S HALF RIGHT.

MY MOM ONCE TOLD ME THAT "LIFE IS LOCOMOTION..."

"IF YOU'RE NOT MOVING, YOU'RE NOT LIVING.

"BUT THERE COMES A TIME WHEN YOU'VE GOT TO STOP RUNNING AWAY FROM THINGS...

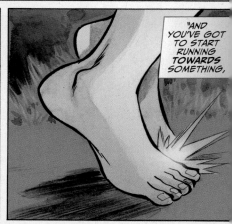

"AND YOU'VE GOT TO START RUNNING TOWARDS SOMETHING,

"YOU'VE GOT TO FORGE AHEAD.

BARRY?!

"KEEP MOVING."

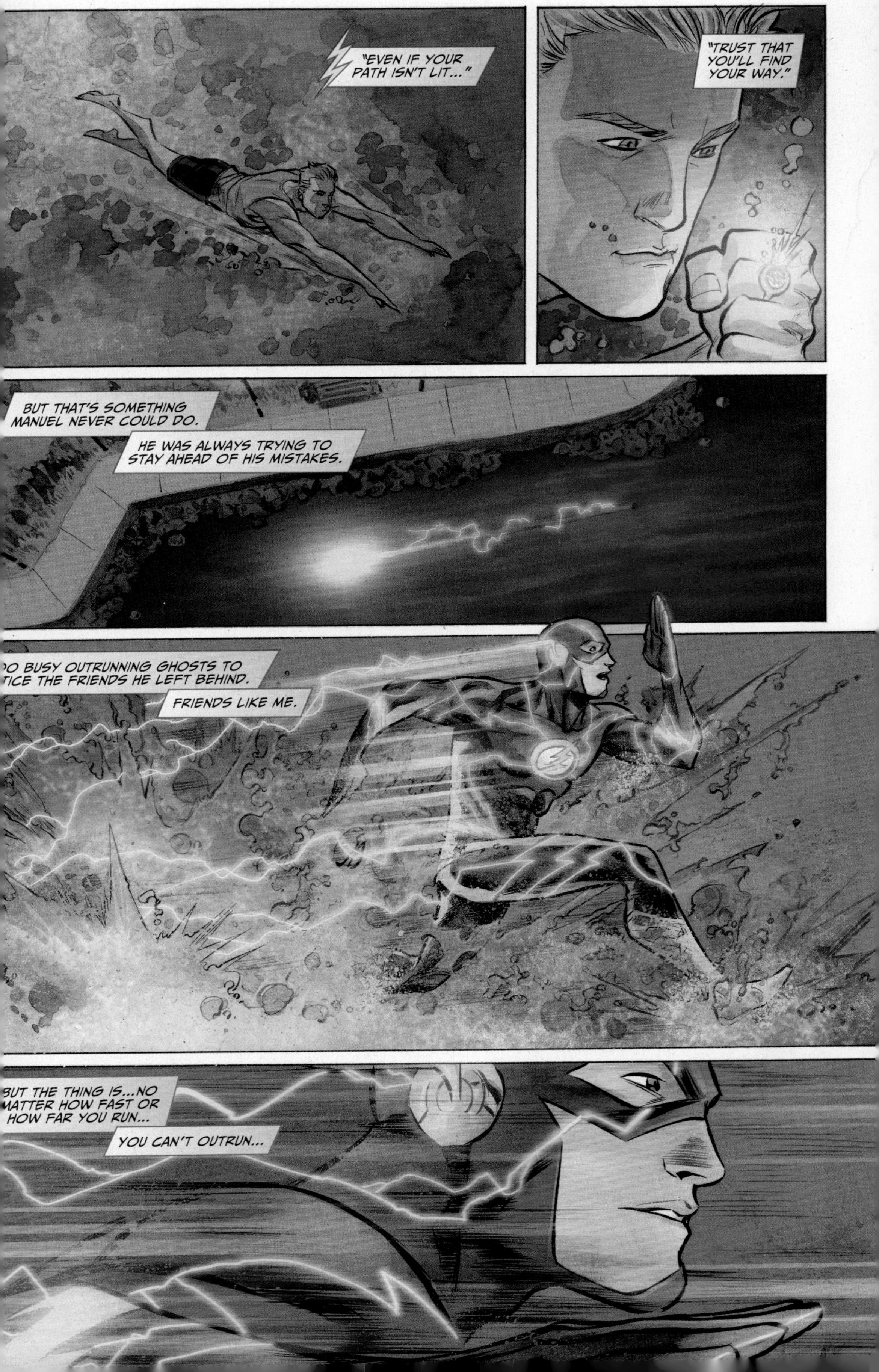
"EVEN IF YOUR PATH ISN'T LIT..."
"TRUST THAT YOU'LL FIND YOUR WAY."
BUT THAT'S SOMETHING MANUEL NEVER COULD DO.
HE WAS ALWAYS TRYING TO STAY AHEAD OF HIS MISTAKES.
O BUSY OUTRUNNING GHOSTS TO TICE THE FRIENDS HE LEFT BEHIND.
FRIENDS LIKE ME.
BUT THE THING IS...NO MATTER HOW FAST OR HOW FAR YOU RUN...
YOU CAN'T OUTRUN...

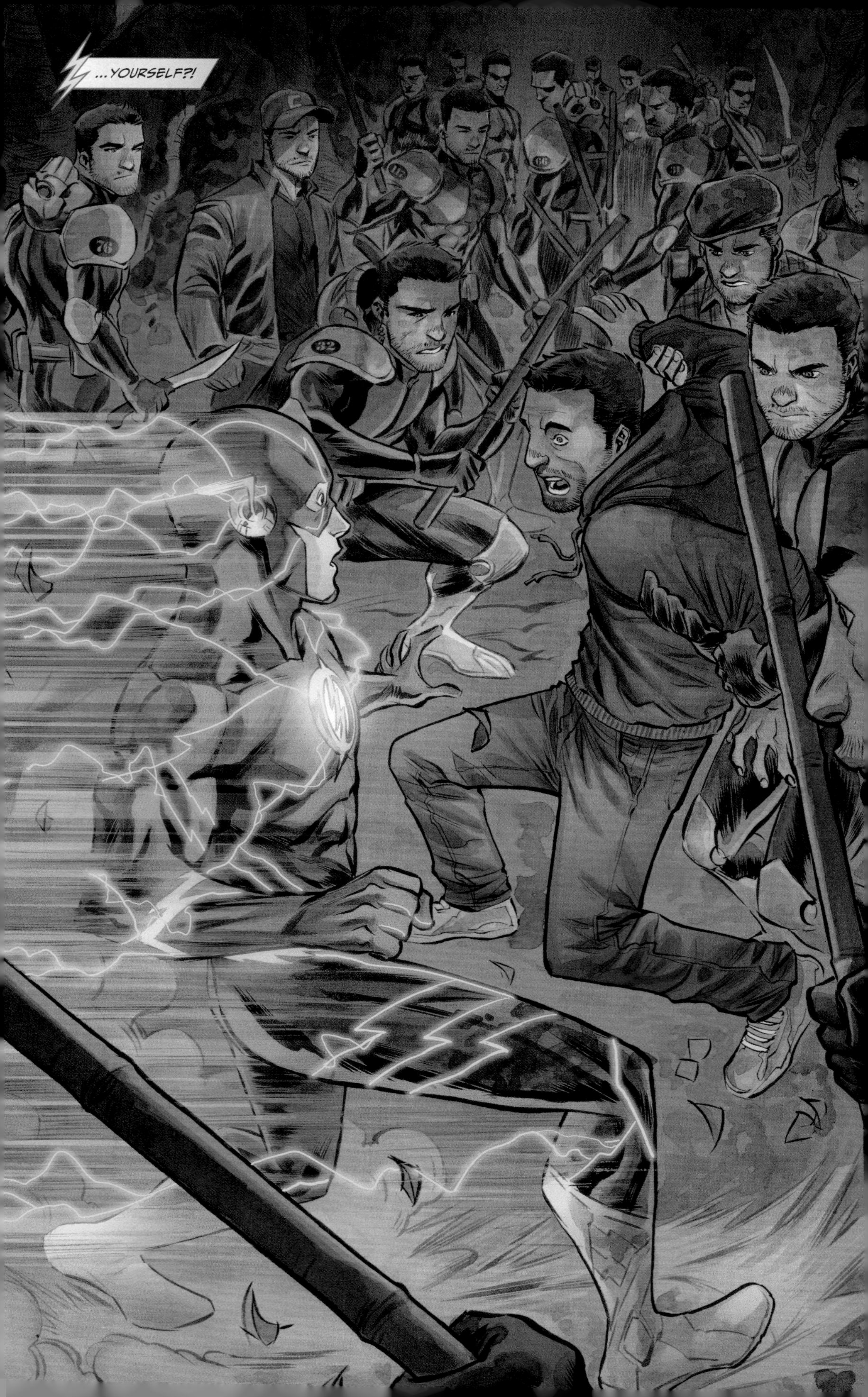
...YOURSELF?!

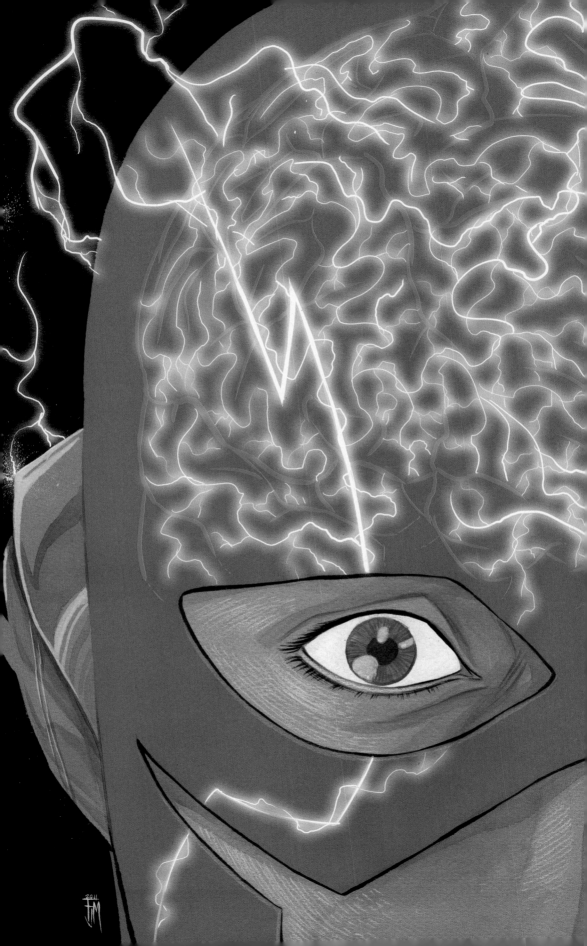

THE FLASH #2

variant cover by GREG CAPULLO & FCO

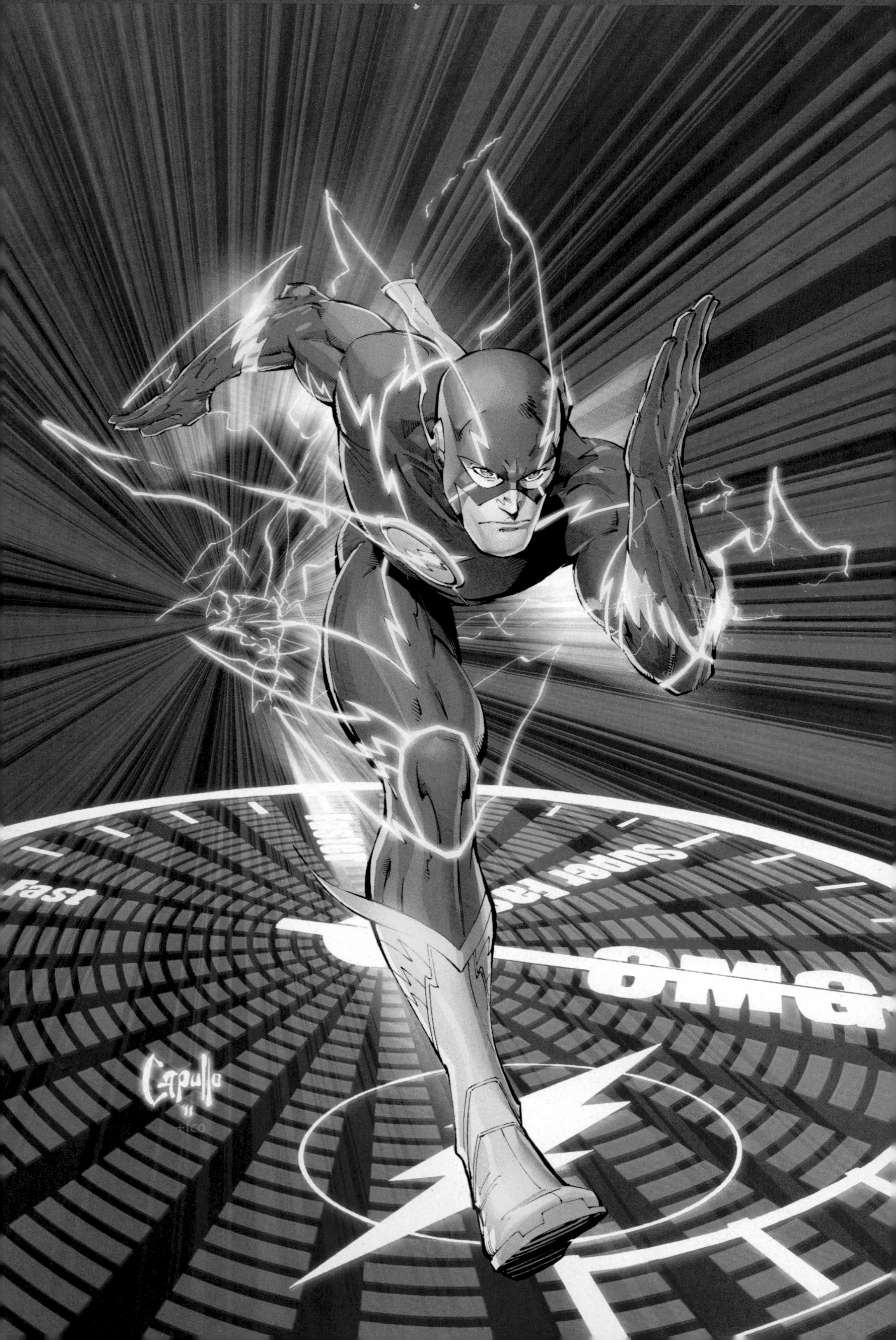
Fast
Capullo

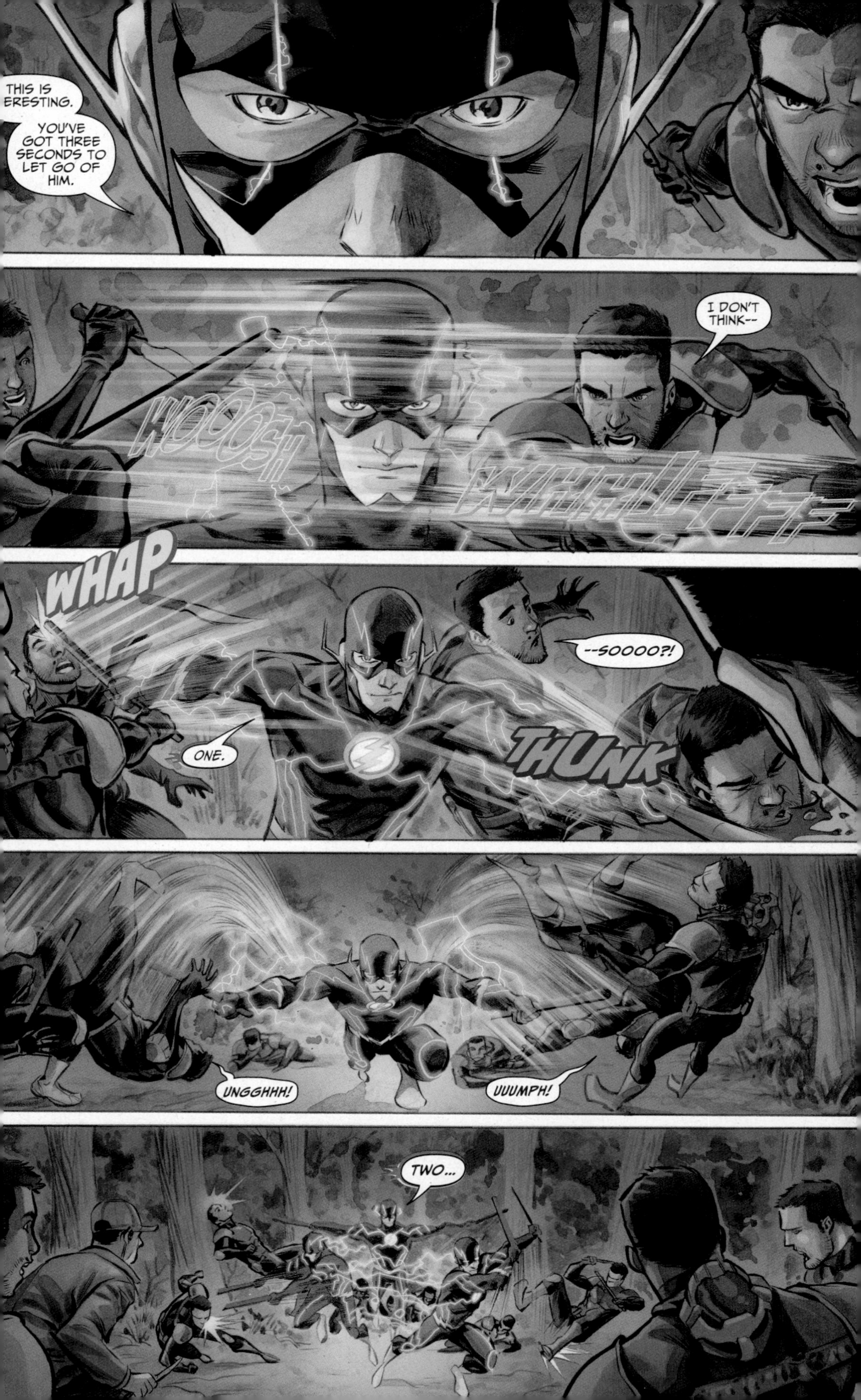
THIS IS
ERESTING.
YOU'VE GOT THREE SECONDS TO LET GO OF HIM.
I DON'T THINK--
WOOOSH
--SOOOO?!
WHAP
ONE.
THUNK
UNGGHHH!
UUUMPH!
TWO...

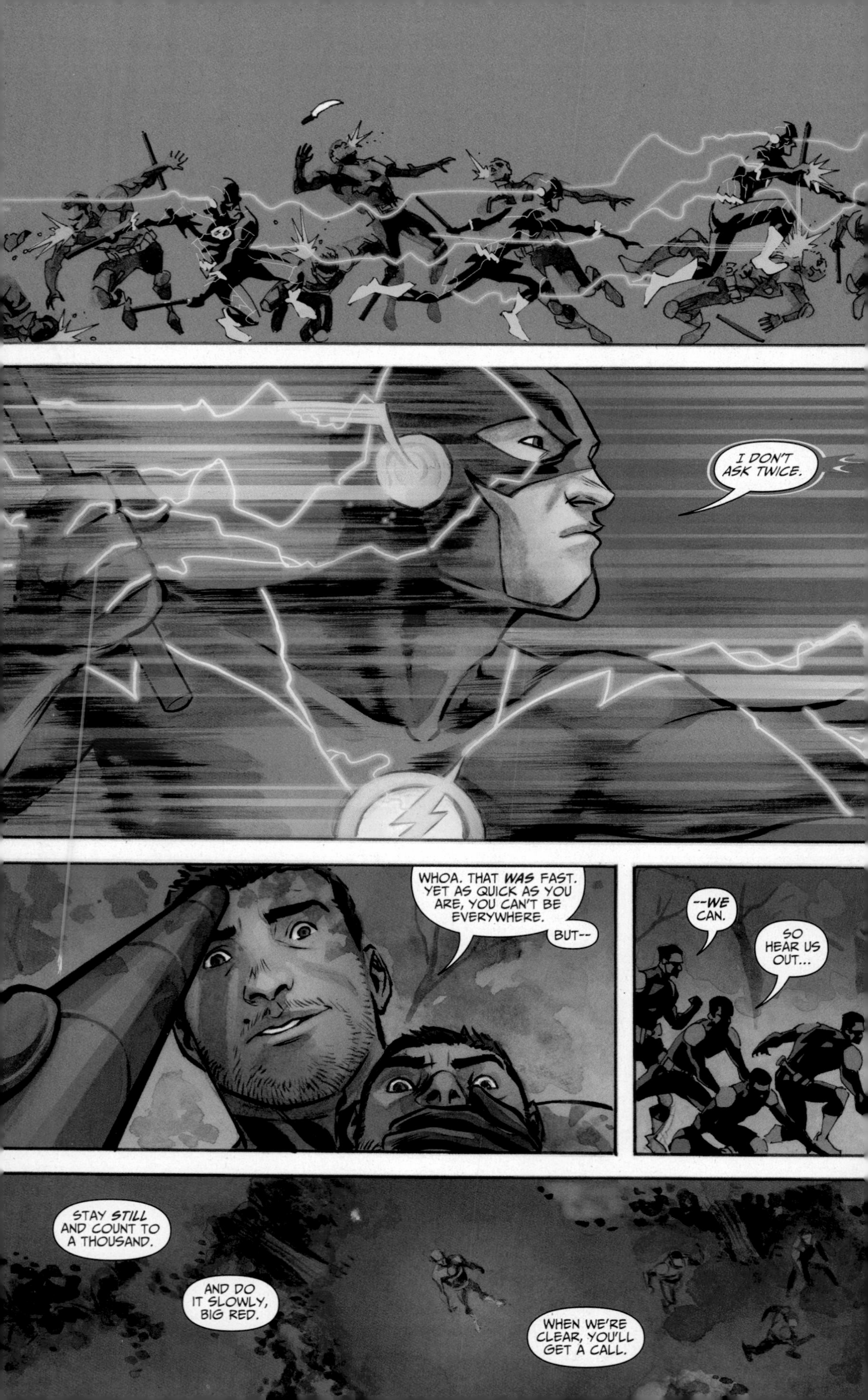
I DON'T ASK TWICE.
WHOA. THAT WAS FAST. YET AS QUICK AS YOU ARE, YOU CAN'T BE EVERYWHERE.
BUT--
--WE CAN.
SO HEAR US OUT...
STAY STILL AND COUNT TO A THOUSAND.
AND DO IT SLOWLY, BIG RED.
WHEN WE'RE CLEAR, YOU'LL GET A CALL.

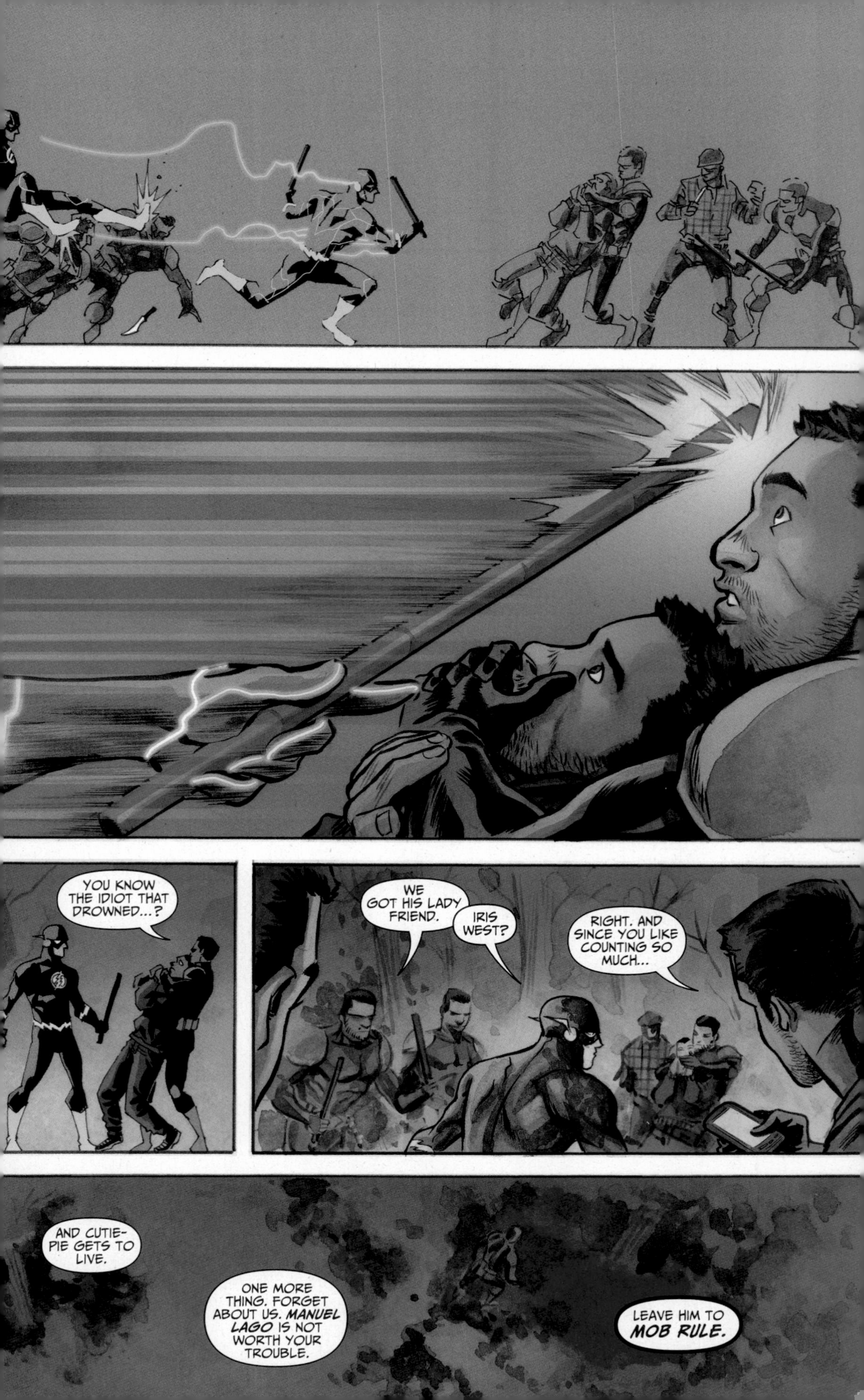
YOU KNOW THE IDIOT THAT DROWNED...?
WE GOT HIS LADY FRIEND.
IRIS WEST?
RIGHT. AND SINCE YOU LIKE COUNTING SO MUCH...
AND CUTIE-PIE GETS TO LIVE.
ONE MORE THING. FORGET ABOUT US. MANUEL LAGO IS NOT WORTH YOUR TROUBLE.
LEAVE HIM TO MOB RULE.

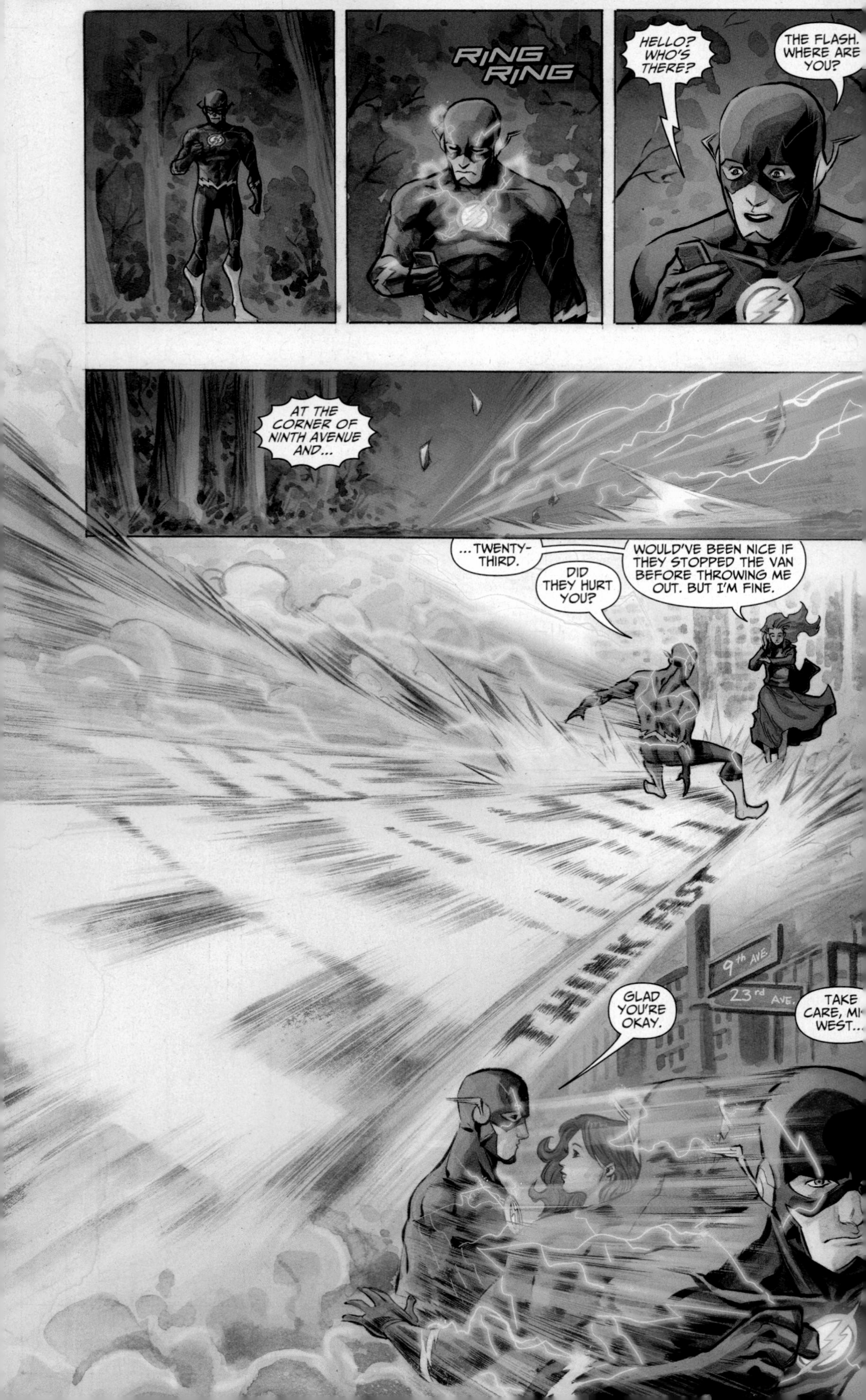
RING RING
HELLO? WHO'S THERE?
THE FLASH. WHERE ARE YOU?
AT THE CORNER OF NINTH AVENUE AND...
...TWENTY-THIRD.
DID THEY HURT YOU?
WOULD'VE BEEN NICE IF THEY STOPPED THE VAN BEFORE THROWING ME OUT. BUT I'M FINE.
THINK FAST
9th AVE.
23rd AVE.
GLAD YOU'RE OKAY.
TAKE CARE, MI WEST...

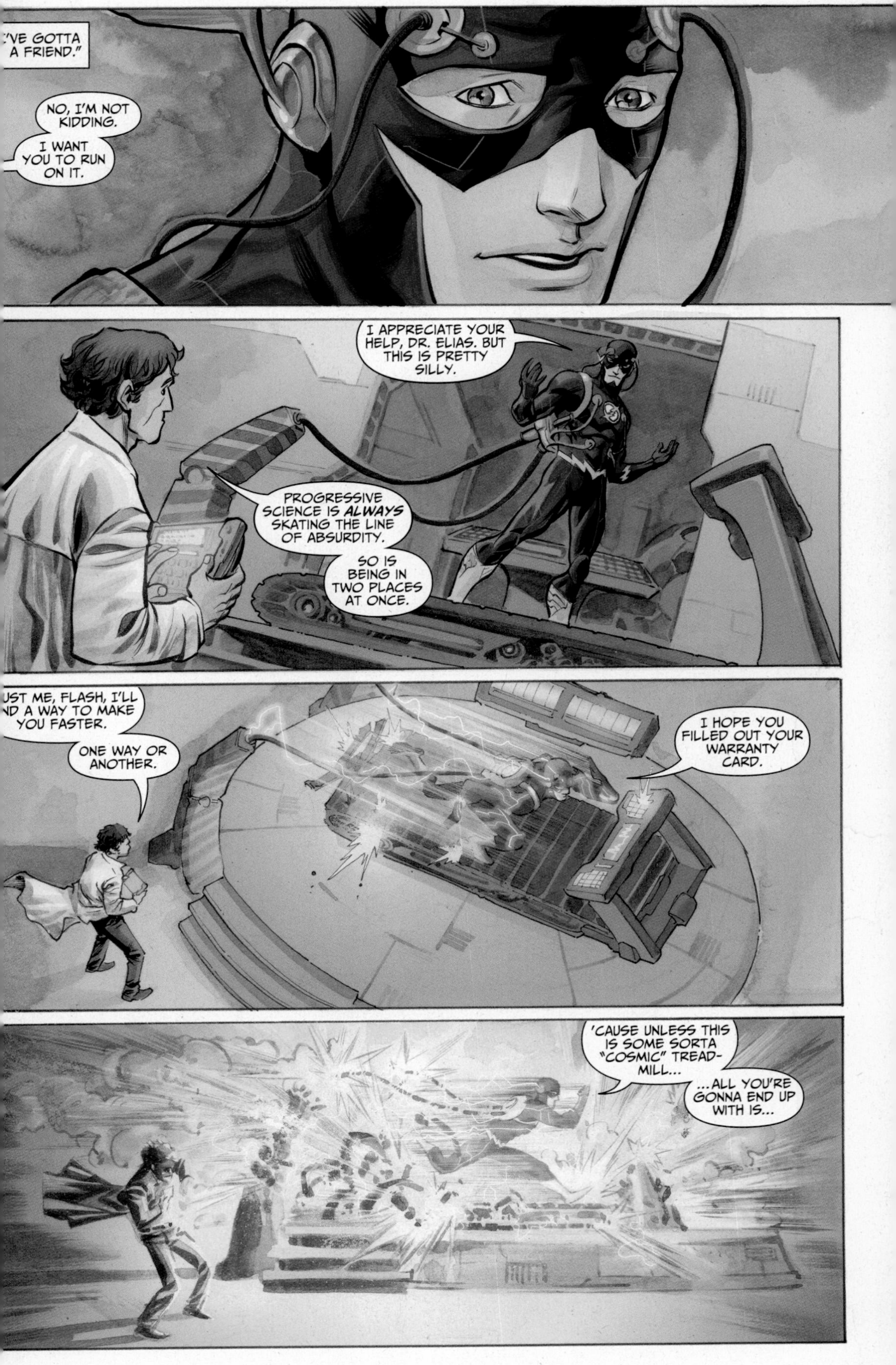

'VE GOTTA
A FRIEND."
NO, I'M NOT KIDDING.
I WANT YOU TO RUN ON IT.
I APPRECIATE YOUR HELP, DR. ELIAS. BUT THIS IS PRETTY SILLY.
PROGRESSIVE SCIENCE IS **ALWAYS** SKATING THE LINE OF ABSURDITY.
SO IS BEING IN TWO PLACES AT ONCE.
UST ME, FLASH, I'LL
ND A WAY TO MAKE YOU FASTER.
ONE WAY OR ANOTHER.
I HOPE YOU FILLED OUT YOUR WARRANTY CARD.
'CAUSE UNLESS THIS IS SOME SORTA "COSMIC" TREAD-MILL...
...ALL YOU'RE GONNA END UP WITH IS...

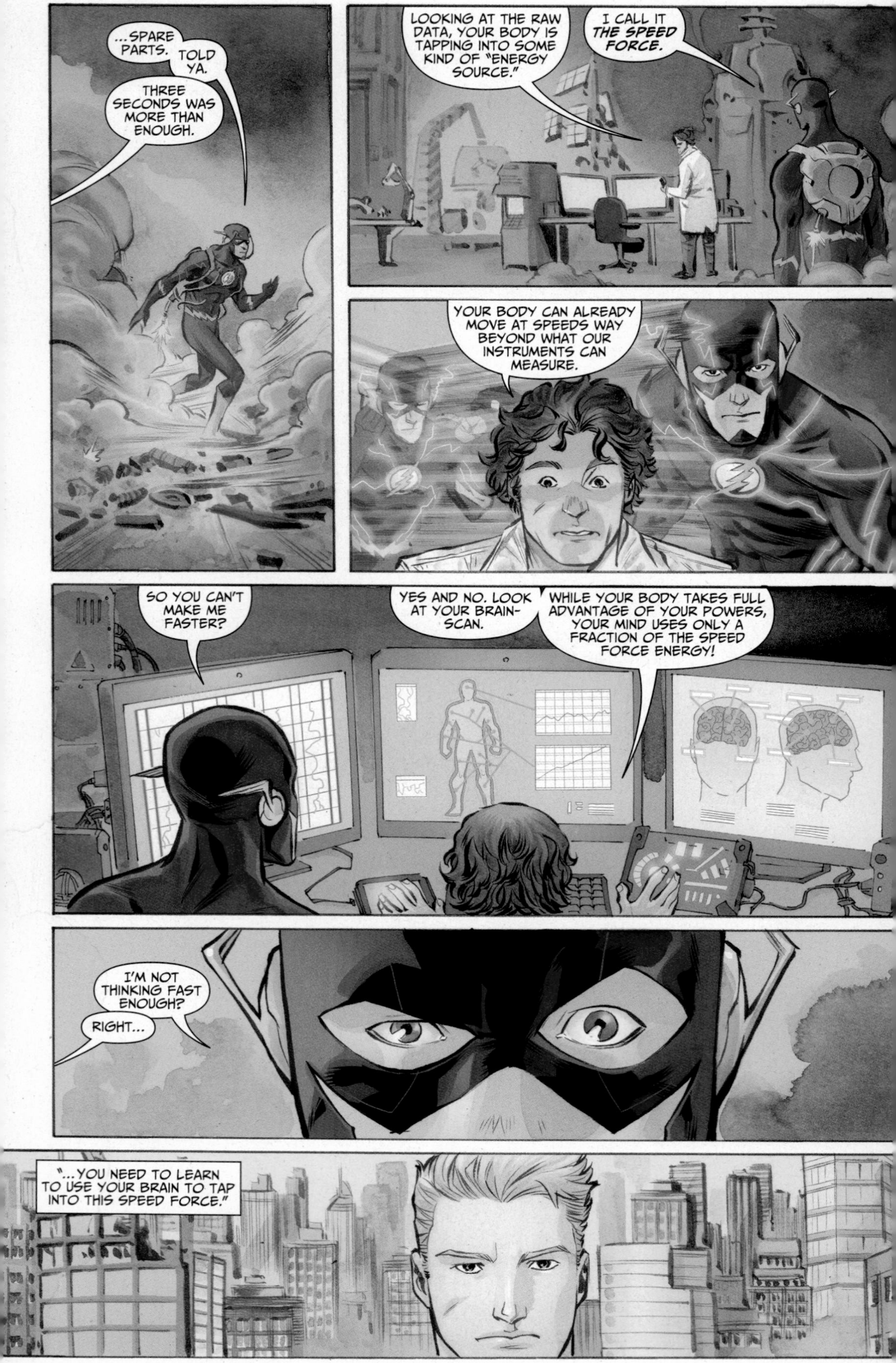
...SPARE PARTS.
TOLD YA.
THREE SECONDS WAS MORE THAN ENOUGH.
LOOKING AT THE RAW DATA, YOUR BODY IS TAPPING INTO SOME KIND OF "ENERGY SOURCE."
I CALL IT THE SPEED FORCE.
YOUR BODY CAN ALREADY MOVE AT SPEEDS WAY BEYOND WHAT OUR INSTRUMENTS CAN MEASURE.
SO YOU CAN'T MAKE ME FASTER?
YES AND NO. LOOK AT YOUR BRAIN-SCAN.
WHILE YOUR BODY TAKES FULL ADVANTAGE OF YOUR POWERS, YOUR MIND USES ONLY A FRACTION OF THE SPEED FORCE ENERGY!
I'M NOT THINKING FAST ENOUGH?
RIGHT...
"...YOU NEED TO LEARN TO USE YOUR BRAIN TO TAP INTO THIS SPEED FORCE."

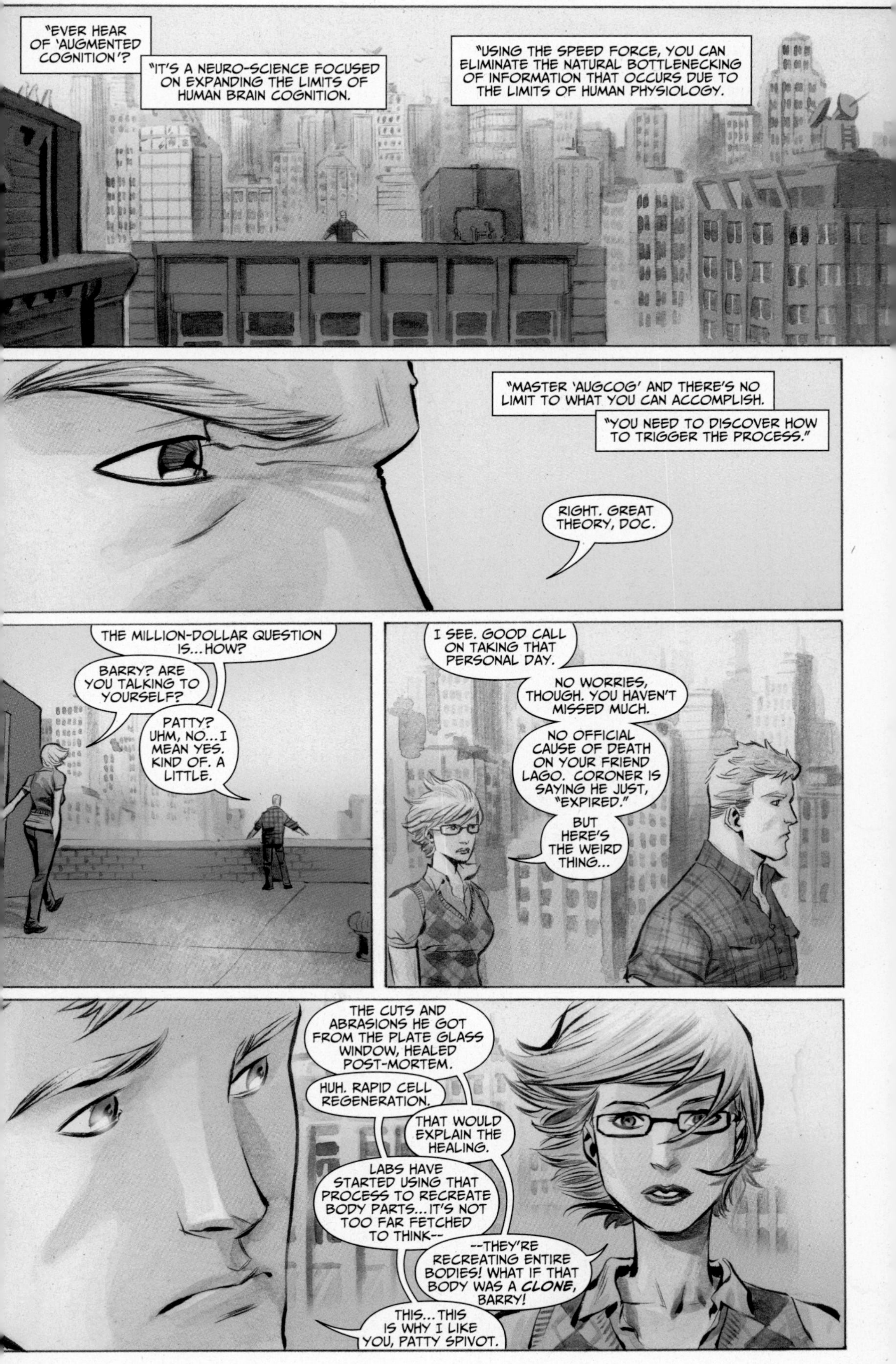

"EVER HEAR OF 'AUGMENTED COGNITION'?
"IT'S A NEURO-SCIENCE FOCUSED ON EXPANDING THE LIMITS OF HUMAN BRAIN COGNITION.
"USING THE SPEED FORCE, YOU CAN ELIMINATE THE NATURAL BOTTLENECKING OF INFORMATION THAT OCCURS DUE TO THE LIMITS OF HUMAN PHYSIOLOGY.
"MASTER 'AUGCOG' AND THERE'S NO LIMIT TO WHAT YOU CAN ACCOMPLISH.
"YOU NEED TO DISCOVER HOW TO TRIGGER THE PROCESS."
RIGHT. GREAT THEORY, DOC.
THE MILLION-DOLLAR QUESTION IS...HOW?
BARRY? ARE YOU TALKING TO YOURSELF?
PATTY? UHM, NO...I MEAN YES. KIND OF. A LITTLE.
I SEE. GOOD CALL ON TAKING THAT PERSONAL DAY.
NO WORRIES, THOUGH. YOU HAVEN'T MISSED MUCH.
NO OFFICIAL CAUSE OF DEATH ON YOUR FRIEND LAGO. CORONER IS SAYING HE JUST, "EXPIRED."
BUT HERE'S THE WEIRD THING...
THE CUTS AND ABRASIONS HE GOT FROM THE PLATE GLASS WINDOW, HEALED POST-MORTEM.
HUH. RAPID CELL REGENERATION.
THAT WOULD EXPLAIN THE HEALING.
LABS HAVE STARTED USING THAT PROCESS TO RECREATE BODY PARTS...IT'S NOT TOO FAR FETCHED TO THINK--
--THEY'RE RECREATING ENTIRE BODIES! WHAT IF THAT BODY WAS A *CLONE*, BARRY!
THIS...THIS IS WHY I LIKE YOU, PATTY SPIVOT.

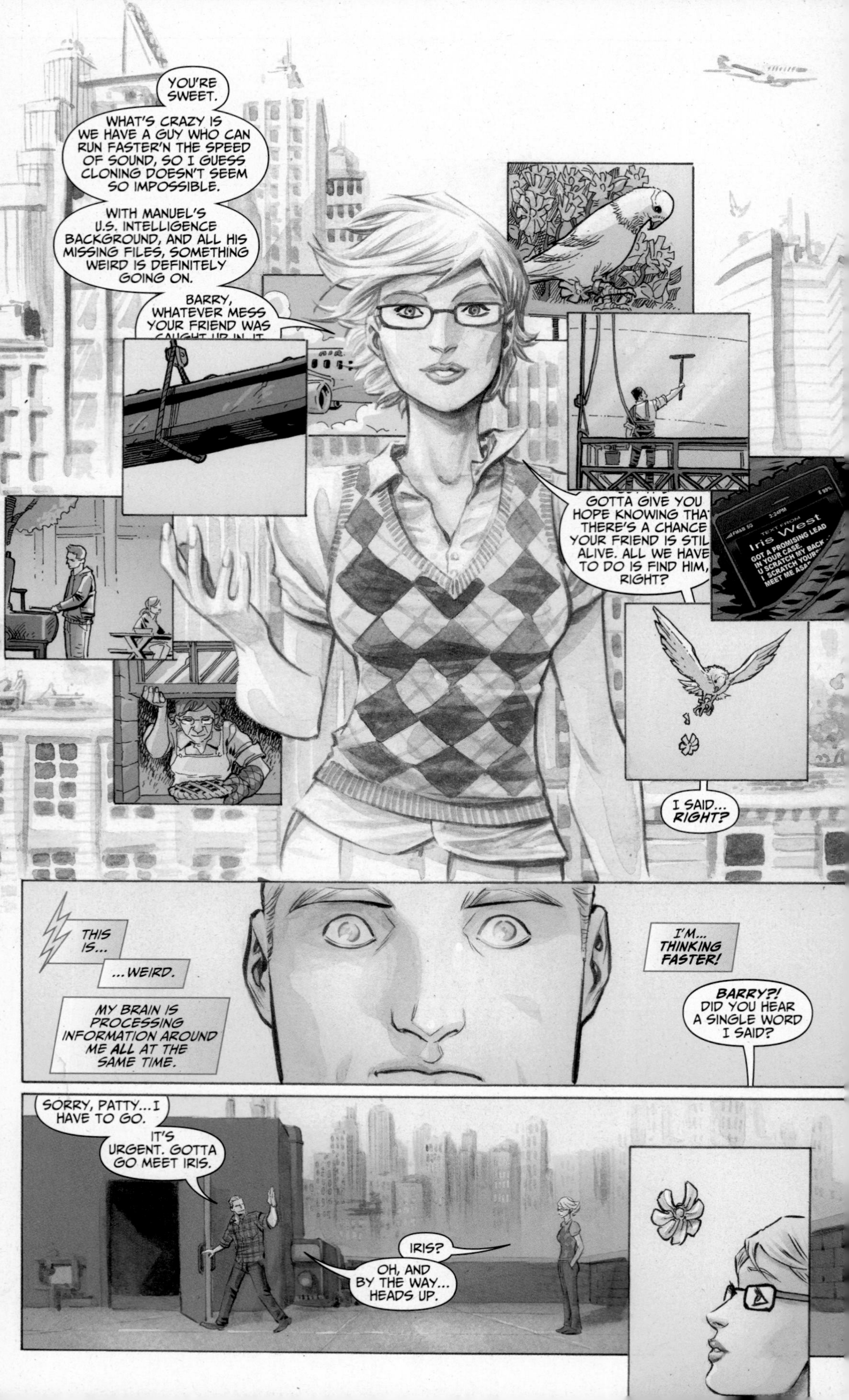
YOU'RE SWEET.
WHAT'S CRAZY IS WE HAVE A GUY WHO CAN RUN FASTER'N THE SPEED OF SOUND, SO I GUESS CLONING DOESN'T SEEM SO IMPOSSIBLE.
WITH MANUEL'S U.S. INTELLIGENCE BACKGROUND, AND ALL HIS MISSING FILES, SOMETHING WEIRD IS DEFINITELY GOING ON.
BARRY, WHATEVER MESS YOUR FRIEND WAS
GOTTA GIVE YOU HOPE KNOWING THA THERE'S A CHANCE YOUR FRIEND IS STIL ALIVE. ALL WE HAVE TO DO IS FIND HIM, RIGHT?
TEXT FROM
Iris West
GOT A PROMISING LEAD
I SAID... RIGHT?
THIS IS...
...WEIRD.
MY BRAIN IS PROCESSING INFORMATION AROUND ME ALL AT THE SAME TIME.
I'M... THINKING FASTER!
BARRY?! DID YOU HEAR A SINGLE WORD I SAID?
SORRY, PATTY...I HAVE TO GO.
IT'S URGENT. GOTTA GO MEET IRIS.
IRIS?
OH, AND BY THE WAY... HEADS UP.

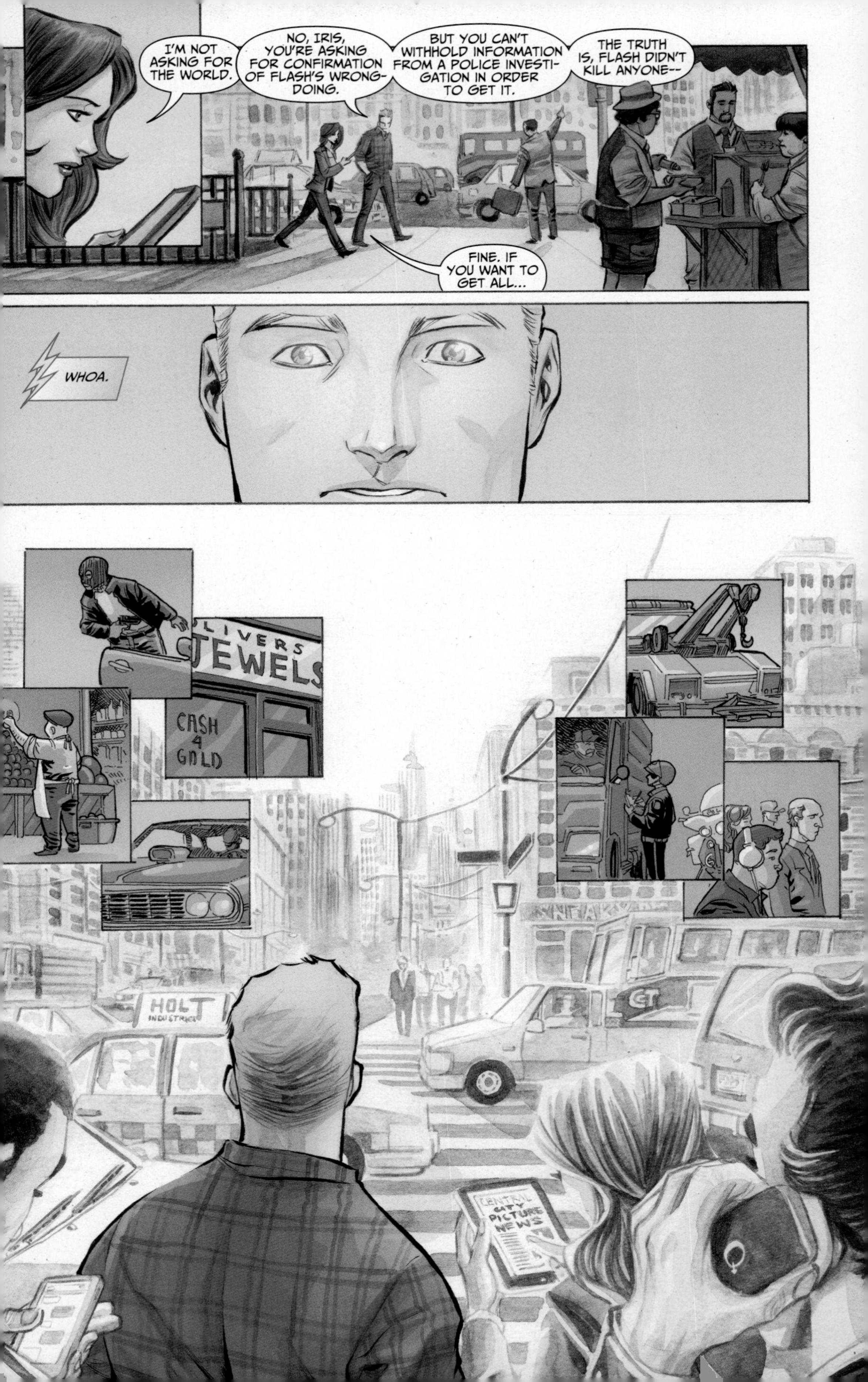
I'M NOT ASKING FOR THE WORLD.
NO, IRIS, YOU'RE ASKING FOR CONFIRMATION OF FLASH'S WRONG-DOING.
BUT YOU CAN'T WITHHOLD INFORMATION FROM A POLICE INVESTI-GATION IN ORDER TO GET IT.
THE TRUTH IS, FLASH DIDN'T KILL ANYONE--
FINE. IF YOU WANT TO GET ALL...
WHOA.
OLIVERS JEWELS
CASH 4 GOLD
HOLT INDUSTRIES
CENTRAL CITY PICTURE NEWS

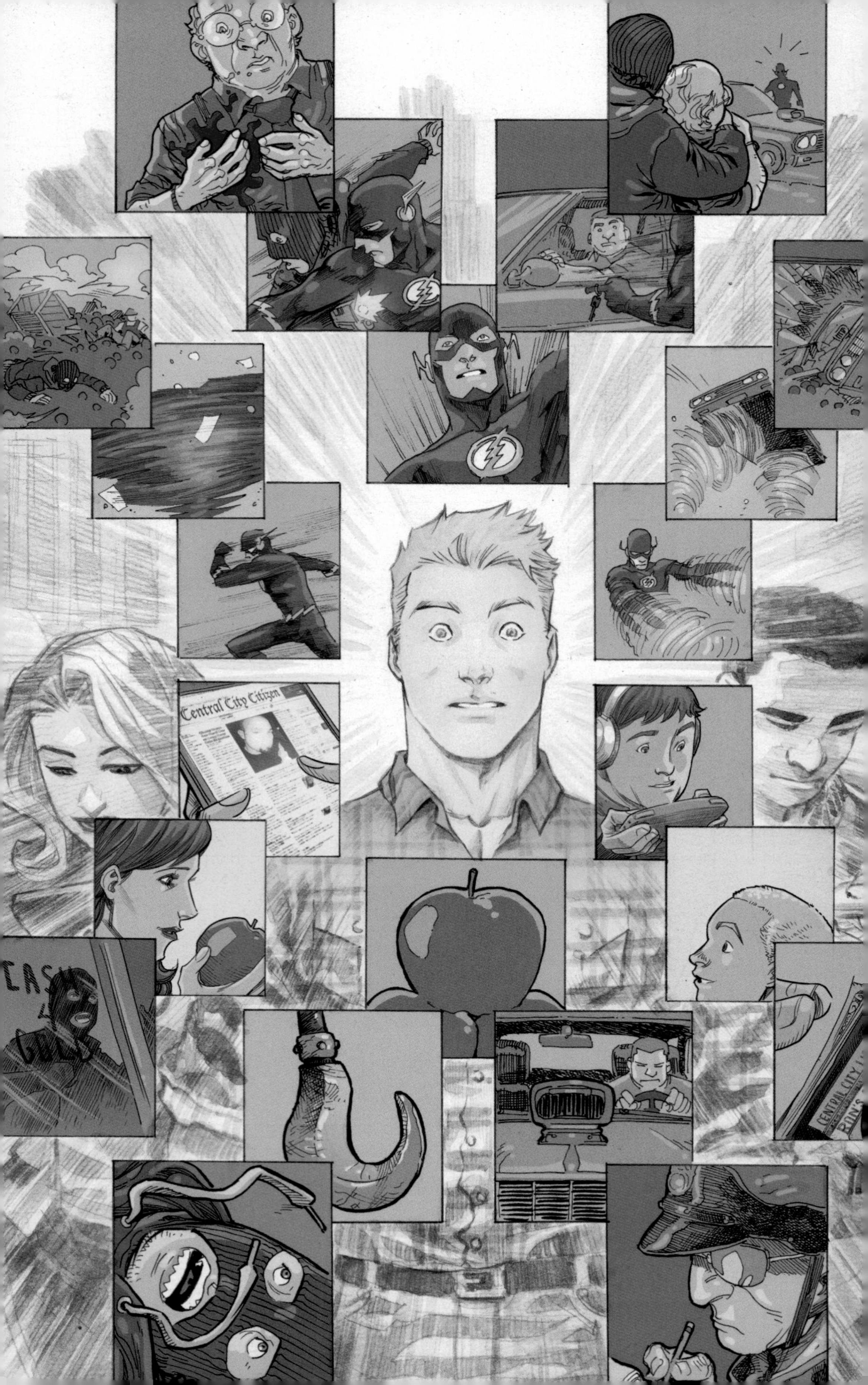
Central City Citizen

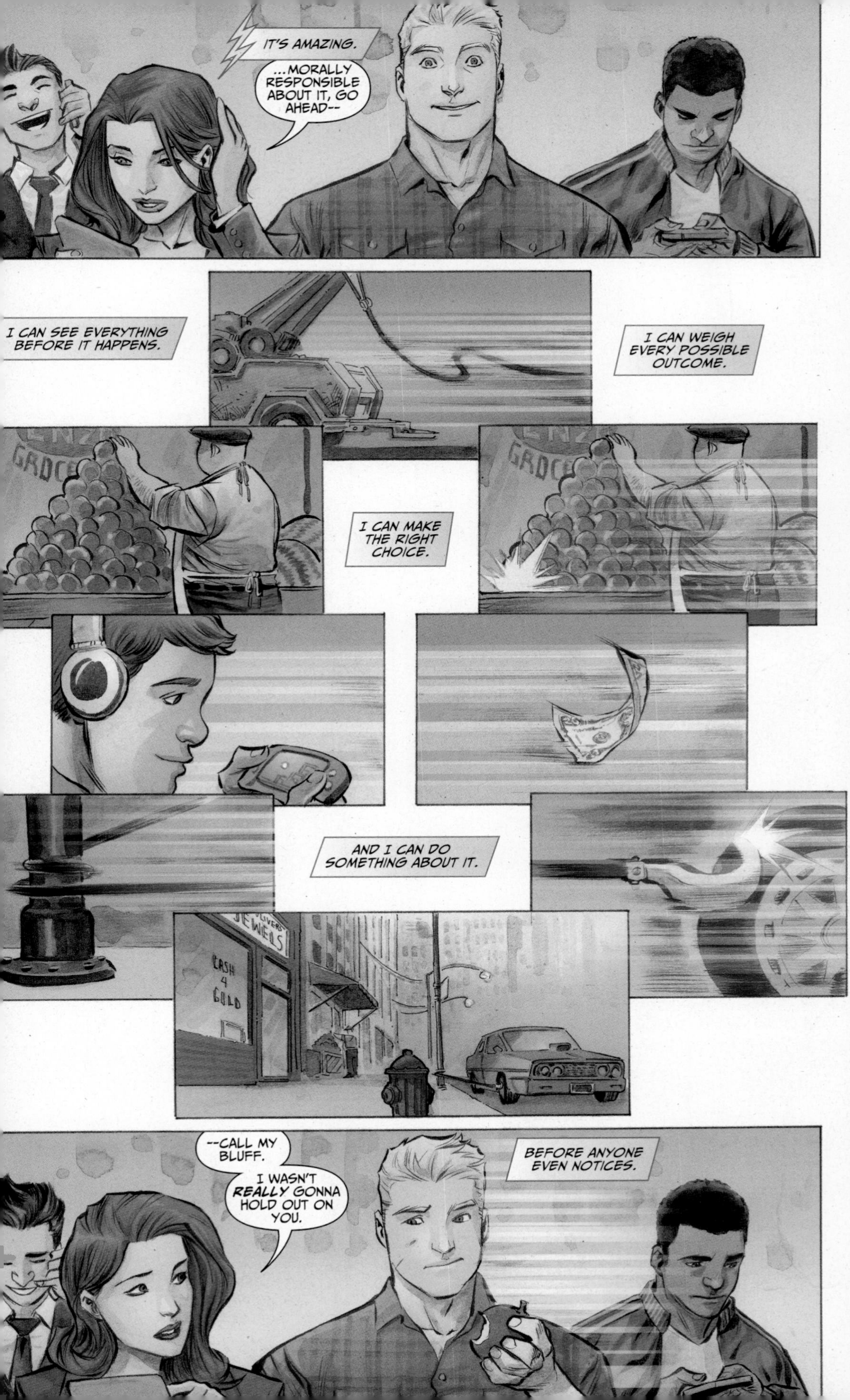
IT'S AMAZING.
...MORALLY RESPONSIBLE ABOUT IT, GO AHEAD--
I CAN SEE EVERYTHING BEFORE IT HAPPENS.
I CAN WEIGH EVERY POSSIBLE OUTCOME.
GROCE
I CAN MAKE THE RIGHT CHOICE.
AND I CAN DO SOMETHING ABOUT IT.
JEWELS
CASH 4 GOLD
--CALL MY BLUFF.
I WASN'T REALLY GONNA HOLD OUT ON YOU.
BEFORE ANYONE EVEN NOTICES.

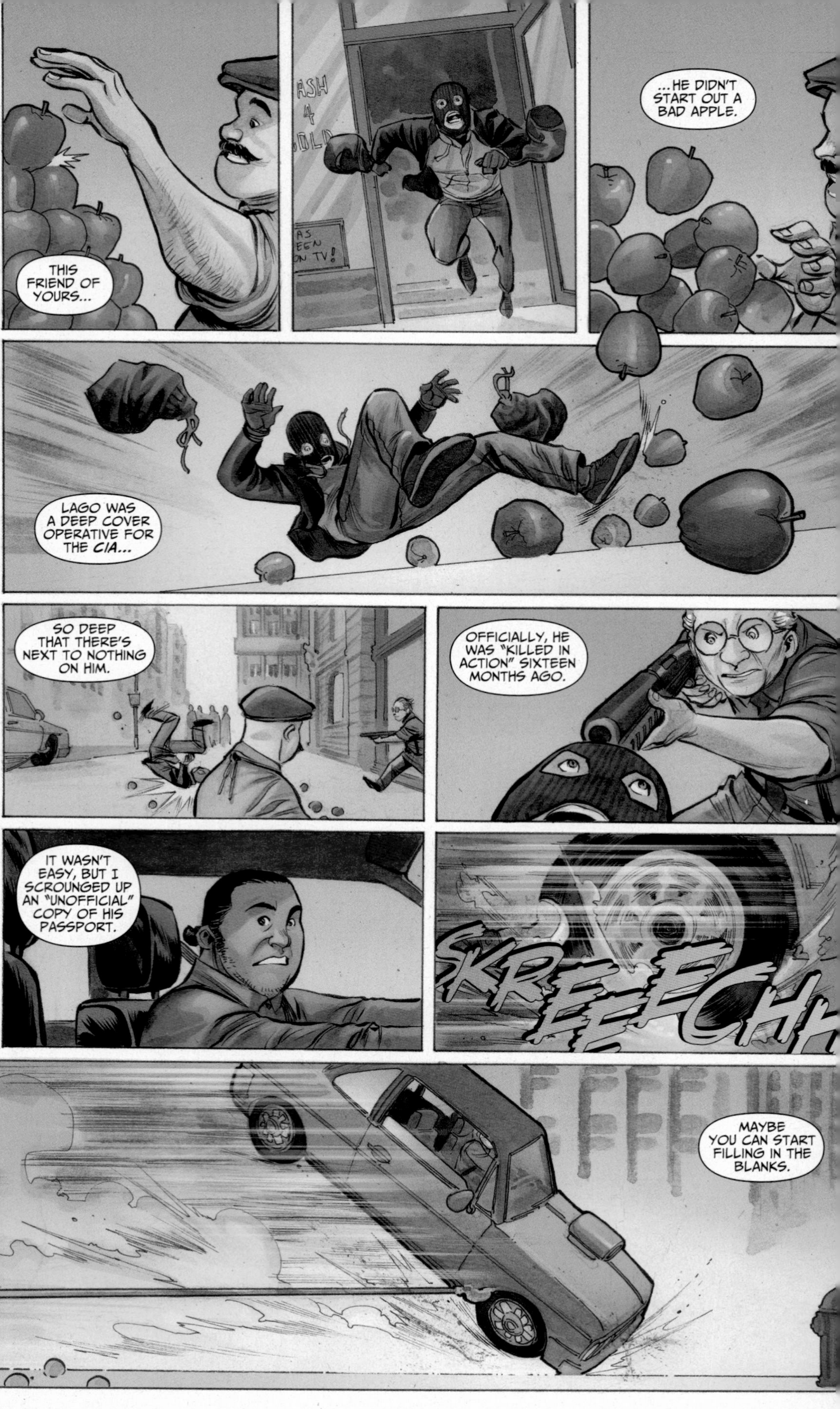
THIS FRIEND OF YOURS...
ASH 4 GOLD
AS SEEN ON TV!
...HE DIDN'T START OUT A BAD APPLE.
LAGO WAS A DEEP COVER OPERATIVE FOR THE CIA...
SO DEEP THAT THERE'S NEXT TO NOTHING ON HIM.
OFFICIALLY, HE WAS "KILLED IN ACTION" SIXTEEN MONTHS AGO.
IT WASN'T EASY, BUT I SCROUNGED UP AN "UNOFFICIAL" COPY OF HIS PASSPORT.
SKREEEECH
MAYBE YOU CAN START FILLING IN THE BLANKS.

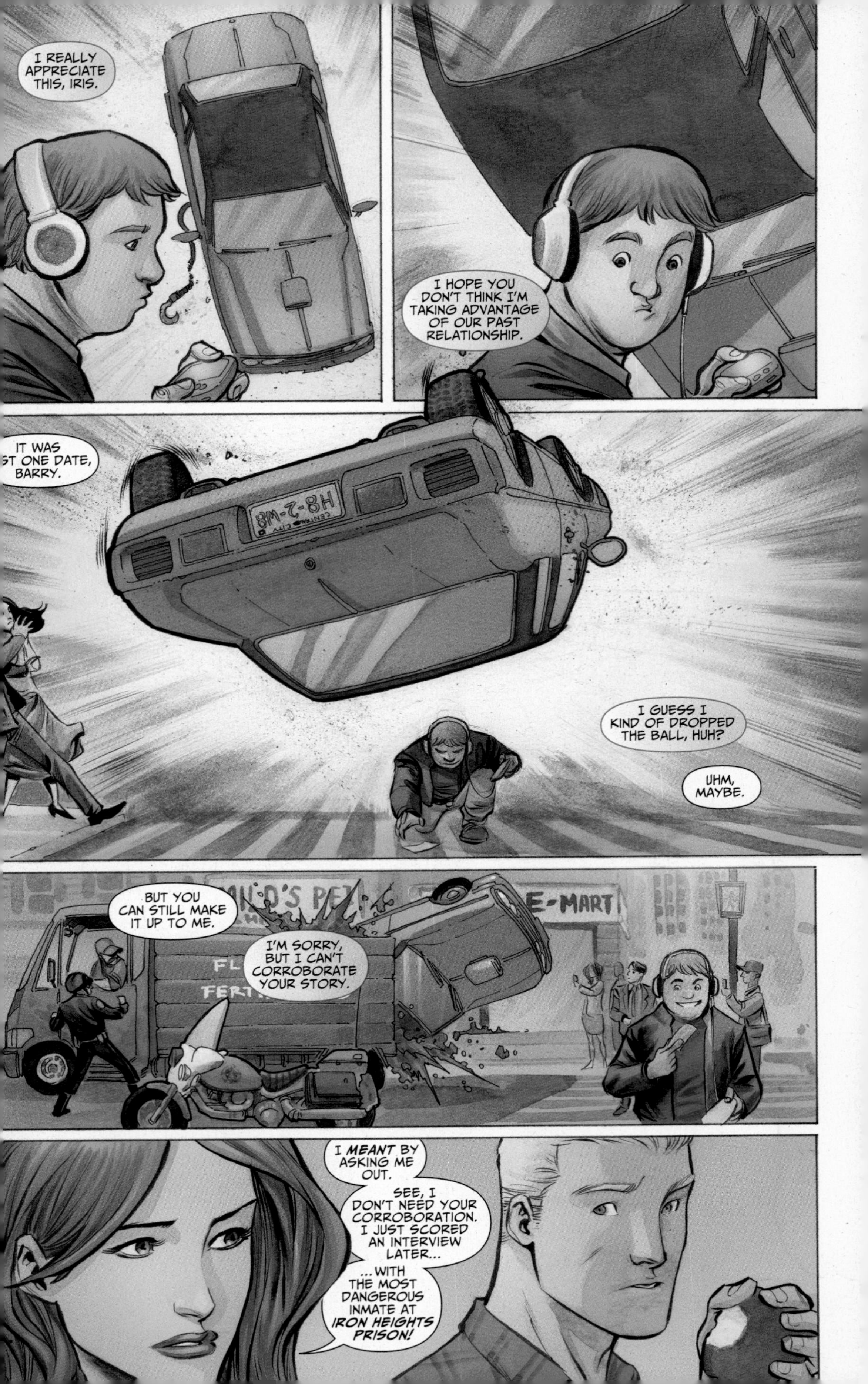
I REALLY APPRECIATE THIS, IRIS.
I HOPE YOU DON'T THINK I'M TAKING ADVANTAGE OF OUR PAST RELATIONSHIP.
IT WAS ST ONE DATE, BARRY.
I GUESS I KIND OF DROPPED THE BALL, HUH?
UHM, MAYBE.
BUT YOU CAN STILL MAKE IT UP TO ME.
I'M SORRY, BUT I CAN'T CORROBORATE YOUR STORY.
I *MEANT* BY ASKING ME OUT.
SEE, I DON'T NEED YOUR CORROBORATION. I JUST SCORED AN INTERVIEW LATER...
...WITH THE MOST DANGEROUS INMATE AT *IRON HEIGHTS PRISON!*

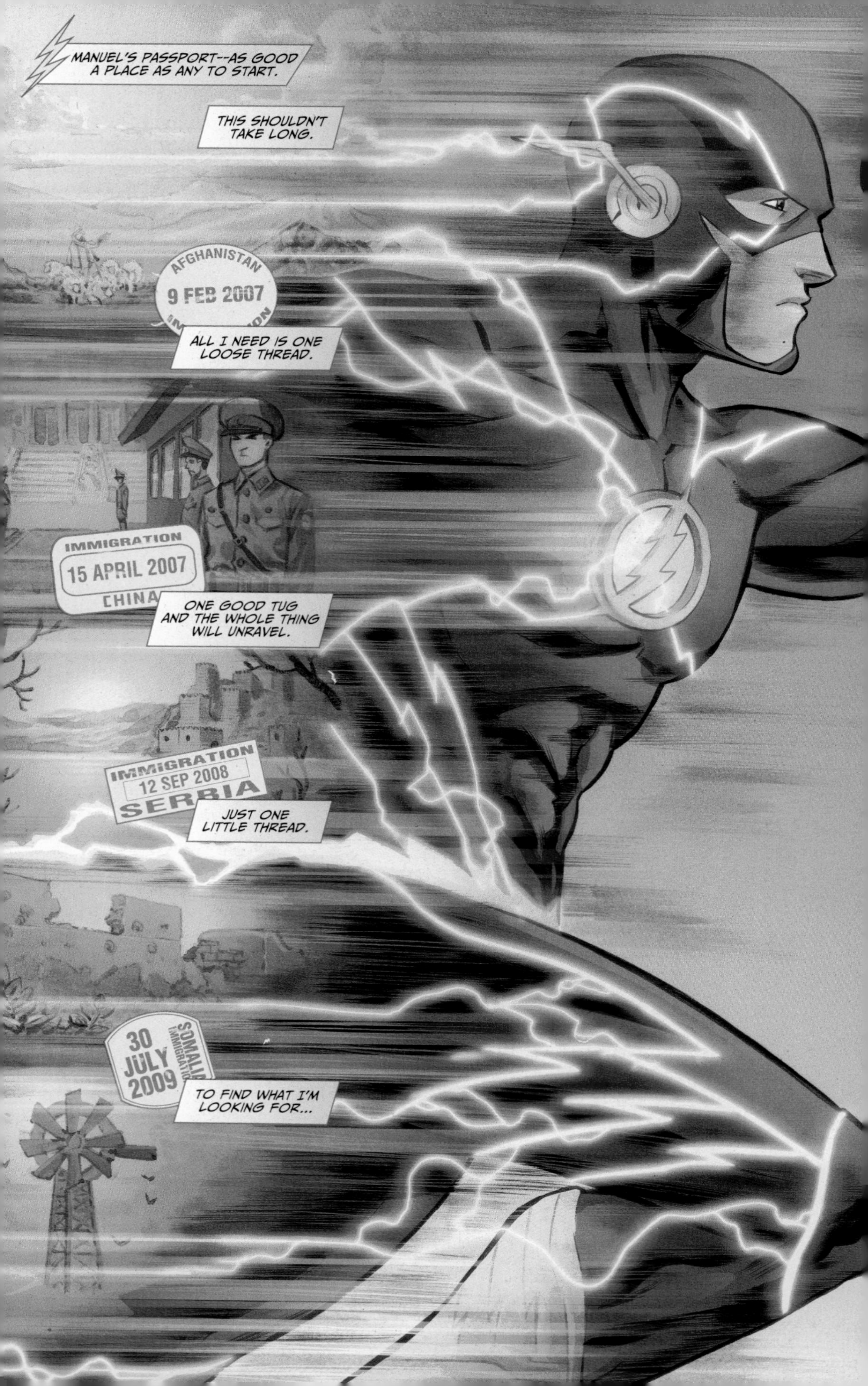
MANUEL'S PASSPORT--AS GOOD A PLACE AS ANY TO START.
THIS SHOULDN'T TAKE LONG.
AFGHANISTAN
9 FEB 2007
ALL I NEED IS ONE LOOSE THREAD.
IMMIGRATION
15 APRIL 2007
CHINA
ONE GOOD TUG AND THE WHOLE THING WILL UNRAVEL.
IMMIGRATION
12 SEP 2008
SERBIA
JUST ONE LITTLE THREAD.
30 JULY 2009
TO FIND WHAT I'M LOOKING FOR...

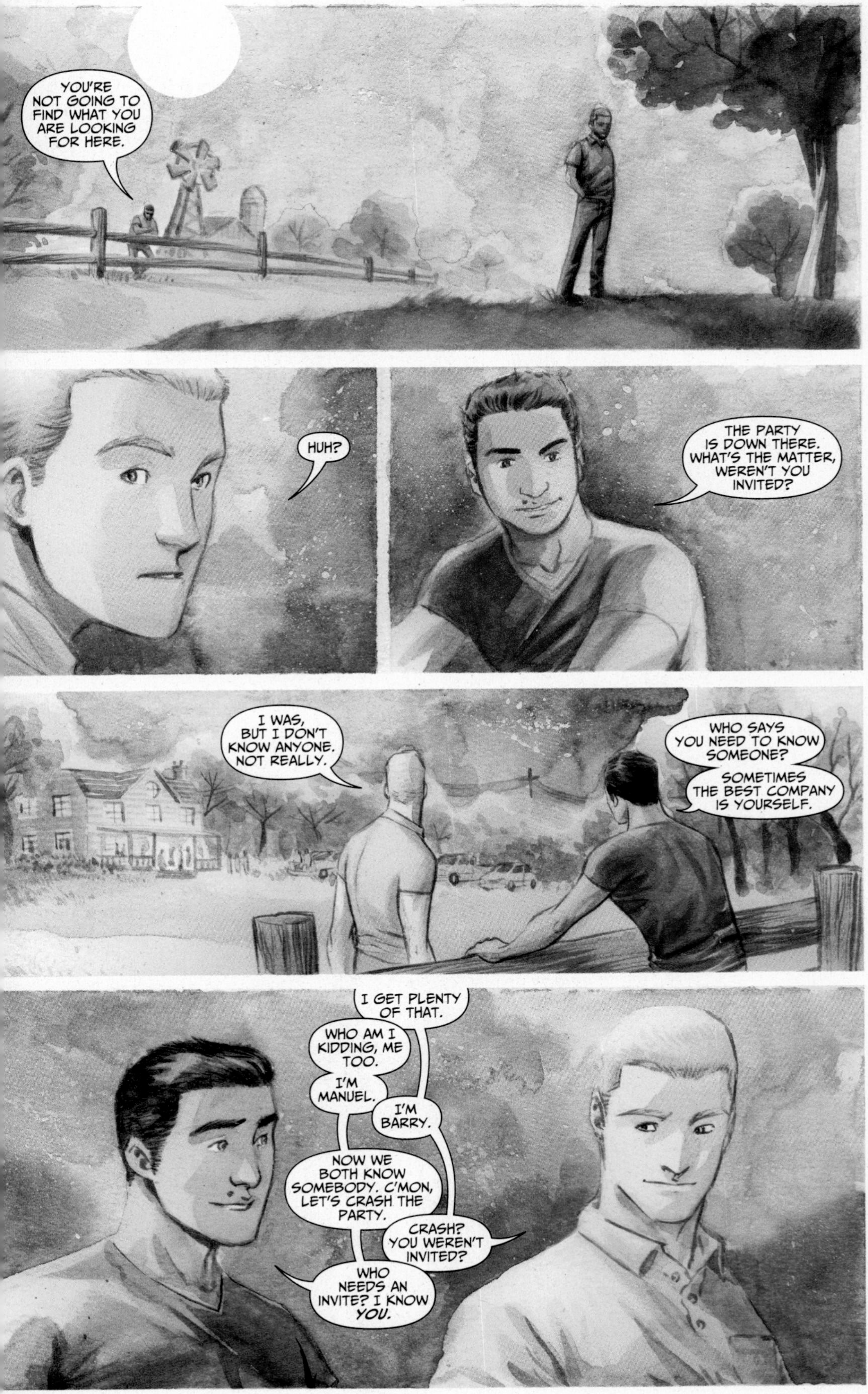
YOU'RE NOT GOING TO FIND WHAT YOU ARE LOOKING FOR HERE.
HUH?
THE PARTY IS DOWN THERE. WHAT'S THE MATTER, WEREN'T YOU INVITED?
I WAS, BUT I DON'T KNOW ANYONE. NOT REALLY.
WHO SAYS YOU NEED TO KNOW SOMEONE?
SOMETIMES THE BEST COMPANY IS YOURSELF.
I GET PLENTY OF THAT.
WHO AM I KIDDING, ME TOO.
I'M MANUEL.
I'M BARRY.
NOW WE BOTH KNOW SOMEBODY. C'MON, LET'S CRASH THE PARTY.
CRASH? YOU WEREN'T INVITED?
WHO NEEDS AN INVITE? I KNOW *YOU.*

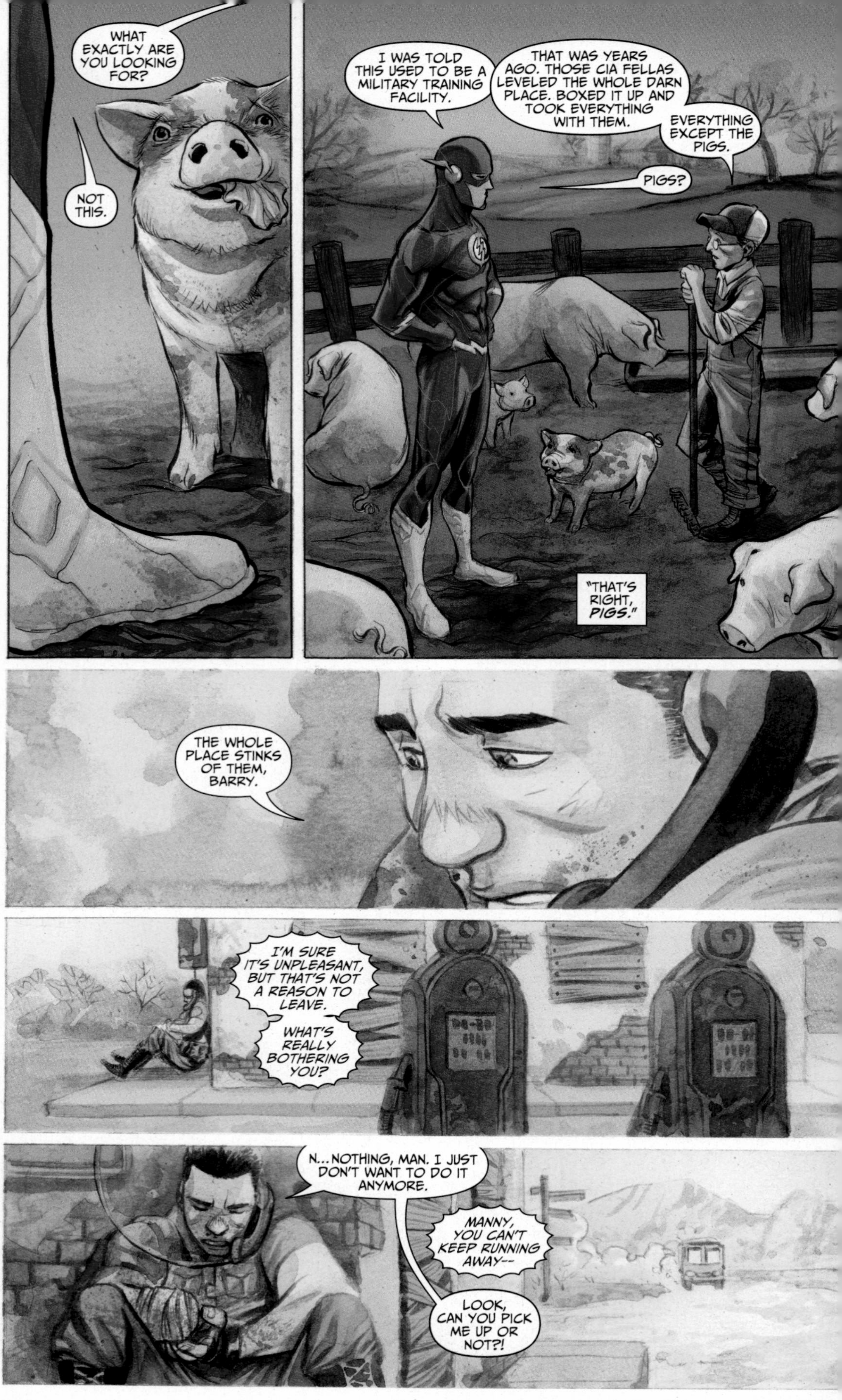
WHAT EXACTLY ARE YOU LOOKING FOR?
NOT THIS.
I WAS TOLD THIS USED TO BE A MILITARY TRAINING FACILITY.
THAT WAS YEARS AGO. THOSE CIA FELLAS LEVELED THE WHOLE DARN PLACE. BOXED IT UP AND TOOK EVERYTHING WITH THEM.
EVERYTHING EXCEPT THE PIGS.
PIGS?
"THAT'S RIGHT, *PIGS.*"
THE WHOLE PLACE STINKS OF THEM, BARRY.
I'M SURE IT'S UNPLEASANT, BUT THAT'S NOT A REASON TO LEAVE.
WHAT'S REALLY BOTHERING YOU?
N...NOTHING, MAN. I JUST DON'T WANT TO DO IT ANYMORE.
MANNY, YOU CAN'T KEEP RUNNING AWAY--
LOOK, CAN YOU PICK ME UP OR NOT?!

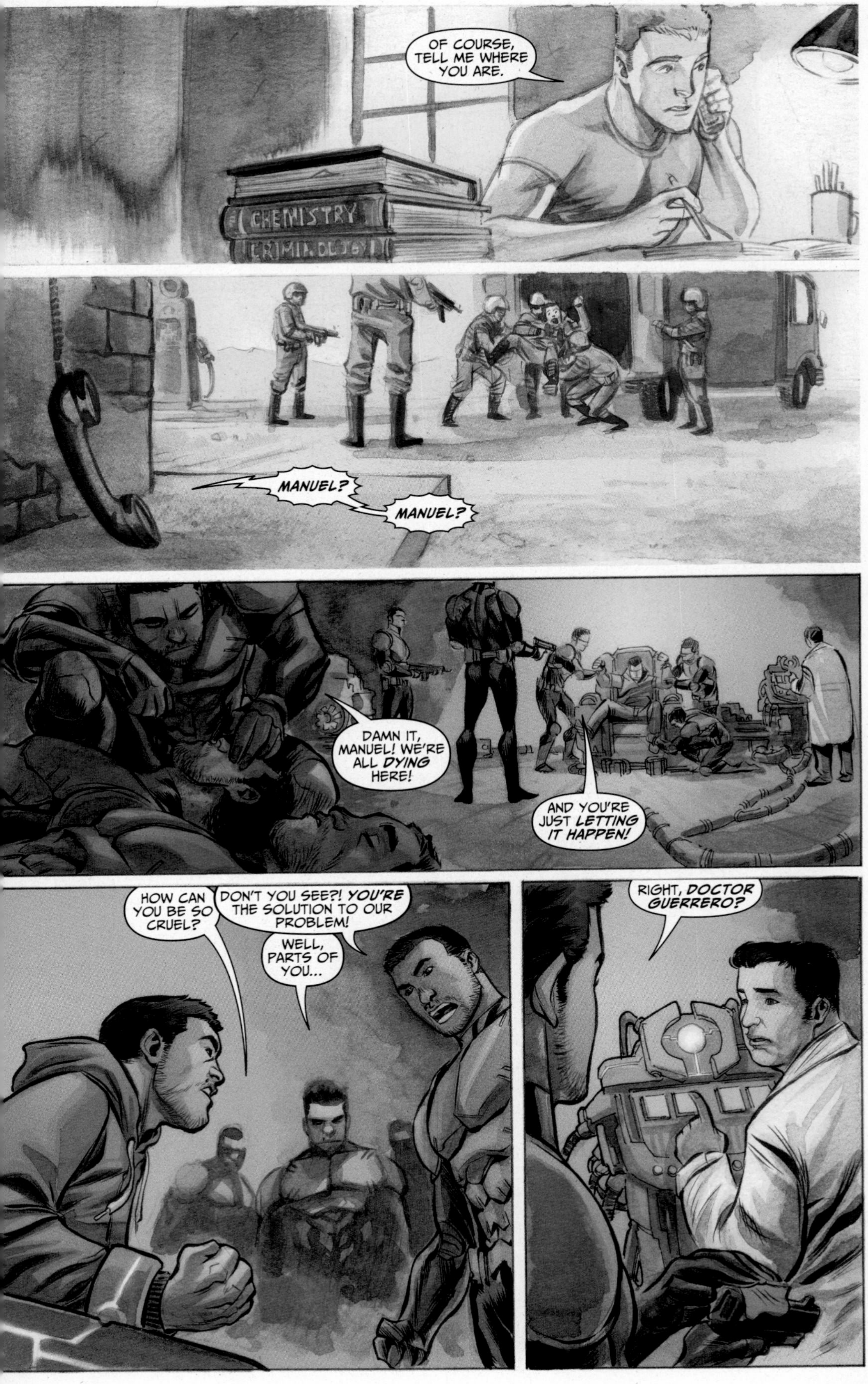
OF COURSE, TELL ME WHERE YOU ARE.
CHEMISTRY
MANUEL?
MANUEL?
DAMN IT, MANUEL! WE'RE ALL DYING HERE!
AND YOU'RE JUST LETTING IT HAPPEN!
HOW CAN YOU BE SO CRUEL?
DON'T YOU SEE?! YOU'RE THE SOLUTION TO OUR PROBLEM!
WELL, PARTS OF YOU...
RIGHT, DOCTOR GUERRERO?

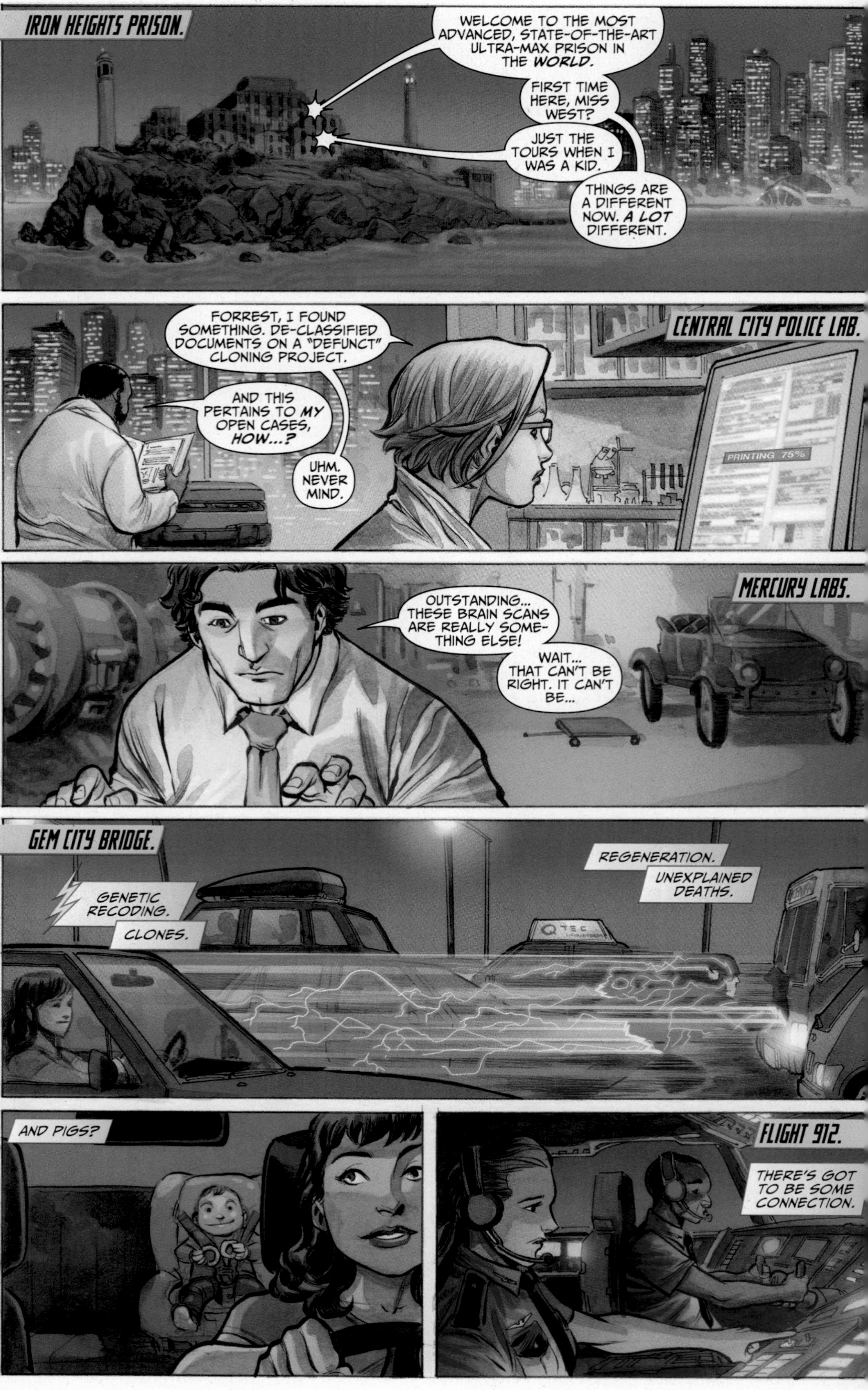
IRON HEIGHTS PRISON.
WELCOME TO THE MOST ADVANCED, STATE-OF-THE-ART ULTRA-MAX PRISON IN THE WORLD.
FIRST TIME HERE, MISS WEST?
JUST THE TOURS WHEN I WAS A KID.
THINGS ARE A DIFFERENT NOW. A LOT DIFFERENT.
CENTRAL CITY POLICE LAB.
FORREST, I FOUND SOMETHING. DE-CLASSIFIED DOCUMENTS ON A "DEFUNCT" CLONING PROJECT.
AND THIS PERTAINS TO MY OPEN CASES, HOW...?
UHM. NEVER MIND.
PRINTING 75%
MERCURY LABS.
OUTSTANDING... THESE BRAIN SCANS ARE REALLY SOME-THING ELSE!
WAIT... THAT CAN'T BE RIGHT. IT CAN'T BE...
GEM CITY BRIDGE.
GENETIC RECODING.
CLONES.
REGENERATION.
UNEXPLAINED DEATHS.
AND PIGS?
FLIGHT 912.
THERE'S GOT TO BE SOME CONNECTION.

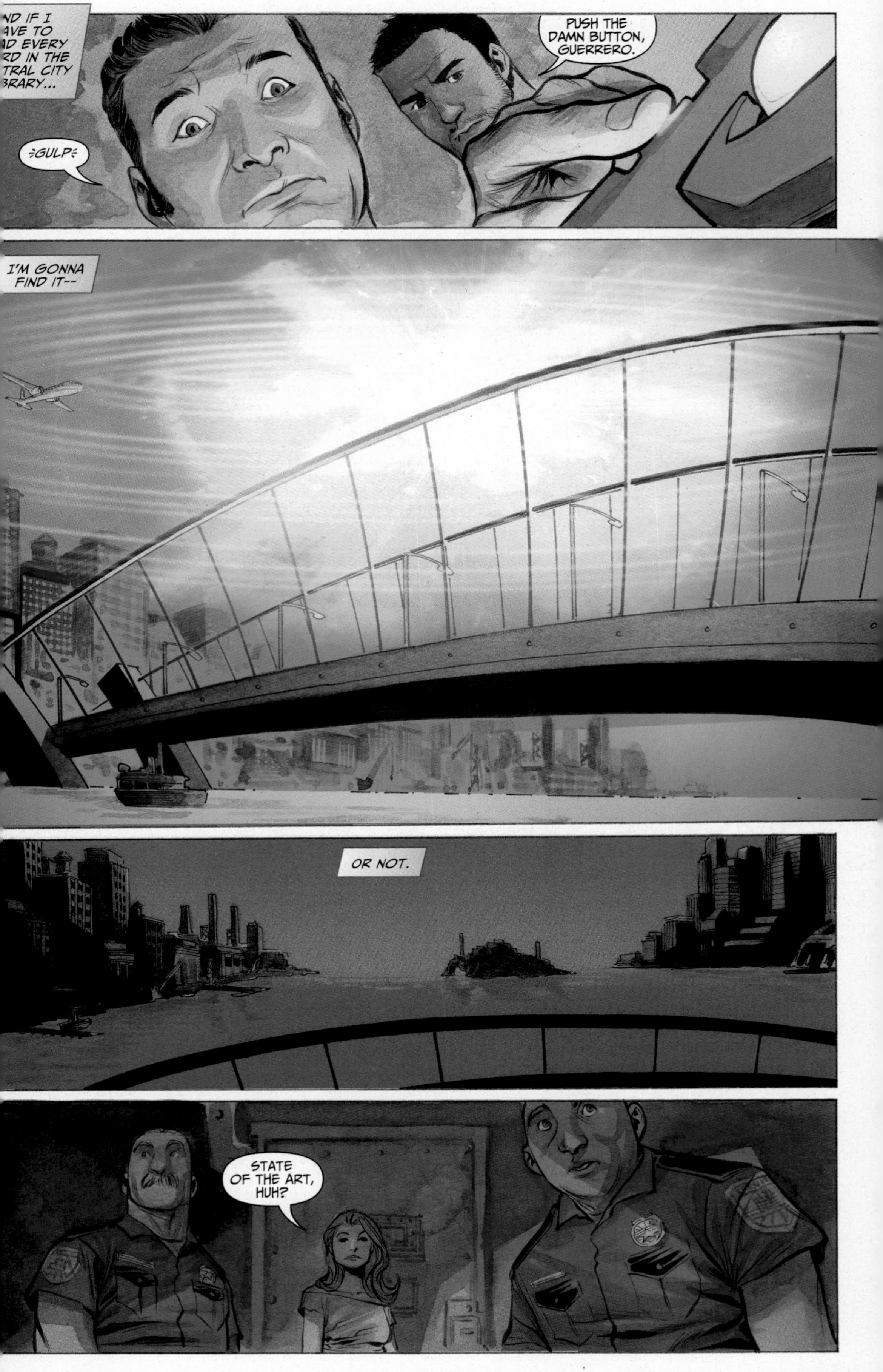
ND IF I
AVE TO
D EVERY
RD IN THE
TRAL CITY
BRARY...
PUSH THE DAMN BUTTON, GUERRERO.
GULP
I'M GONNA FIND IT--
OR NOT.
STATE OF THE ART, HUH?

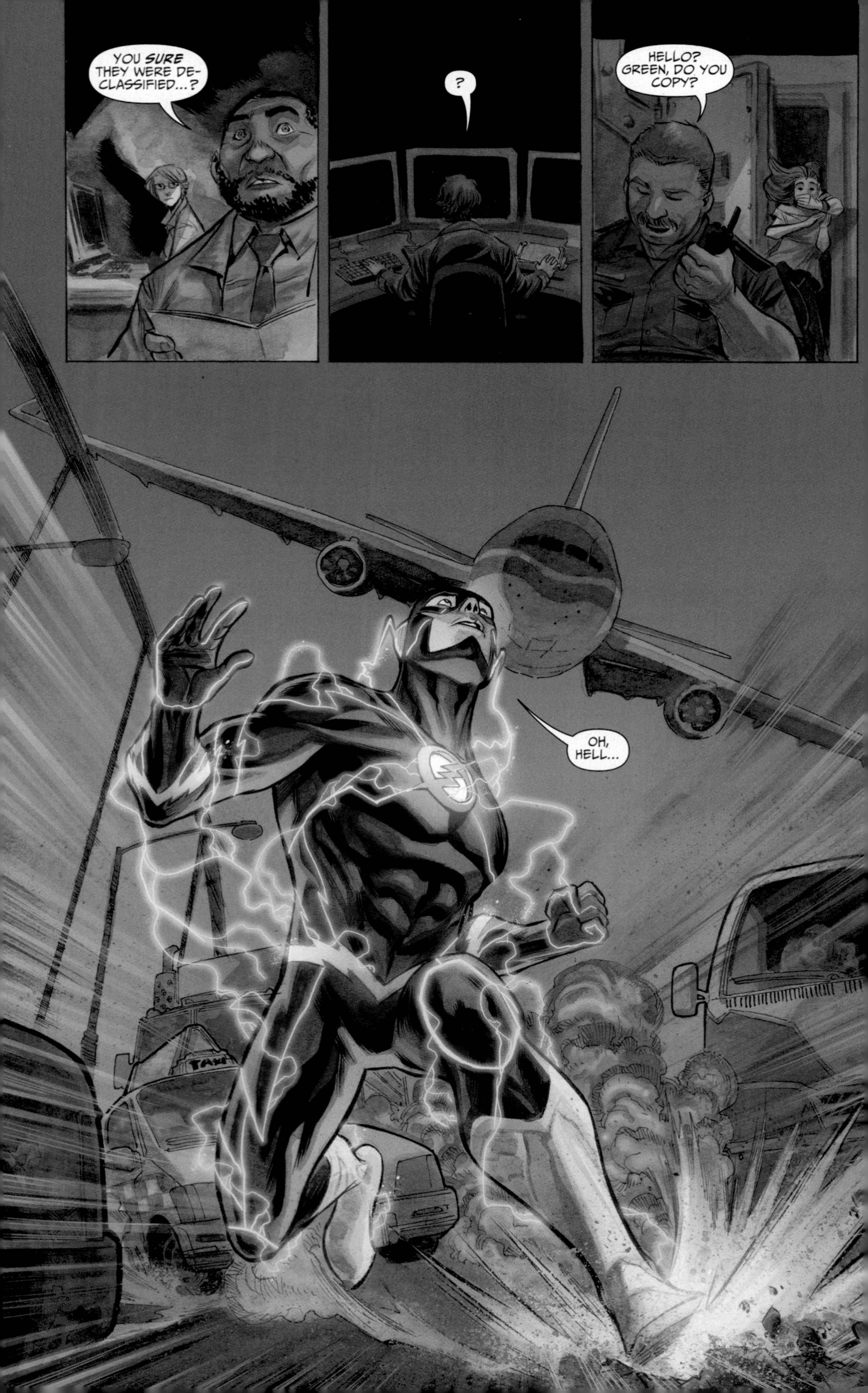
YOU SURE THEY WERE DE-CLASSIFIED...?
?
HELLO? GREEN, DO YOU COPY?
OH, HELL...

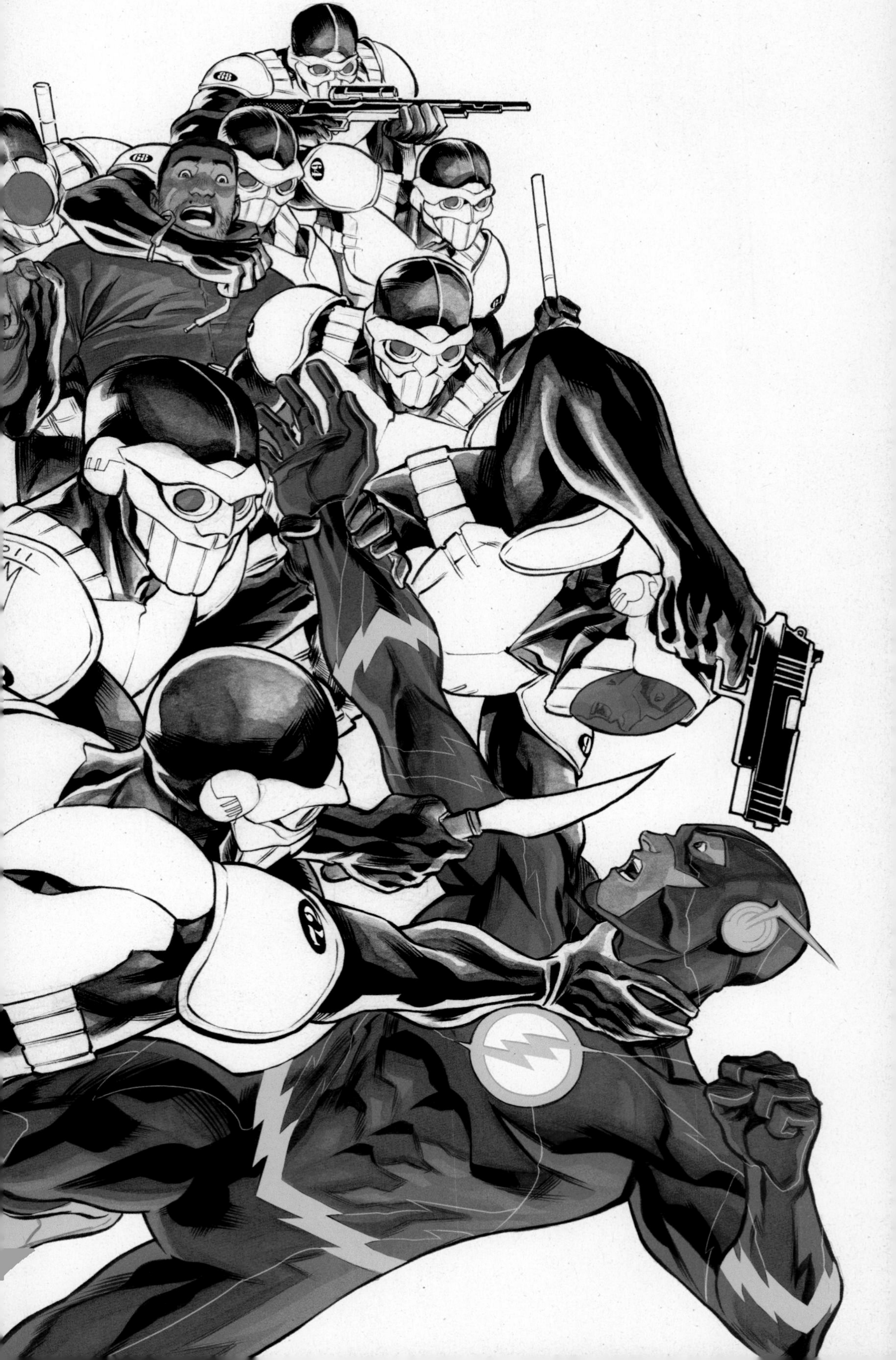

THE FLASH #3

variant cover by JIM LEE, SCOTT WILLIAMS & ALEX SINCLAIR

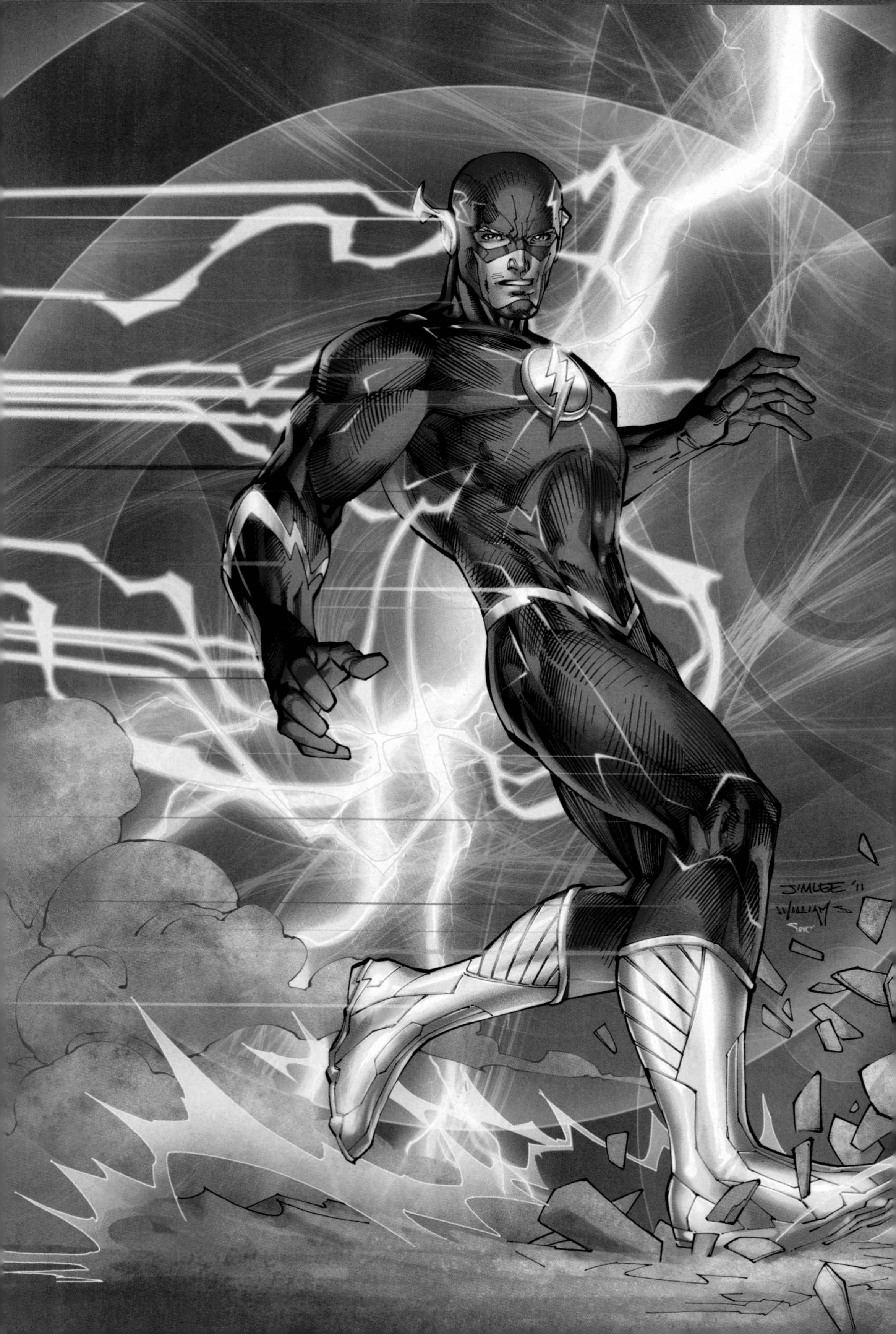
JIMLEE '11
WILLIAMS
SINC

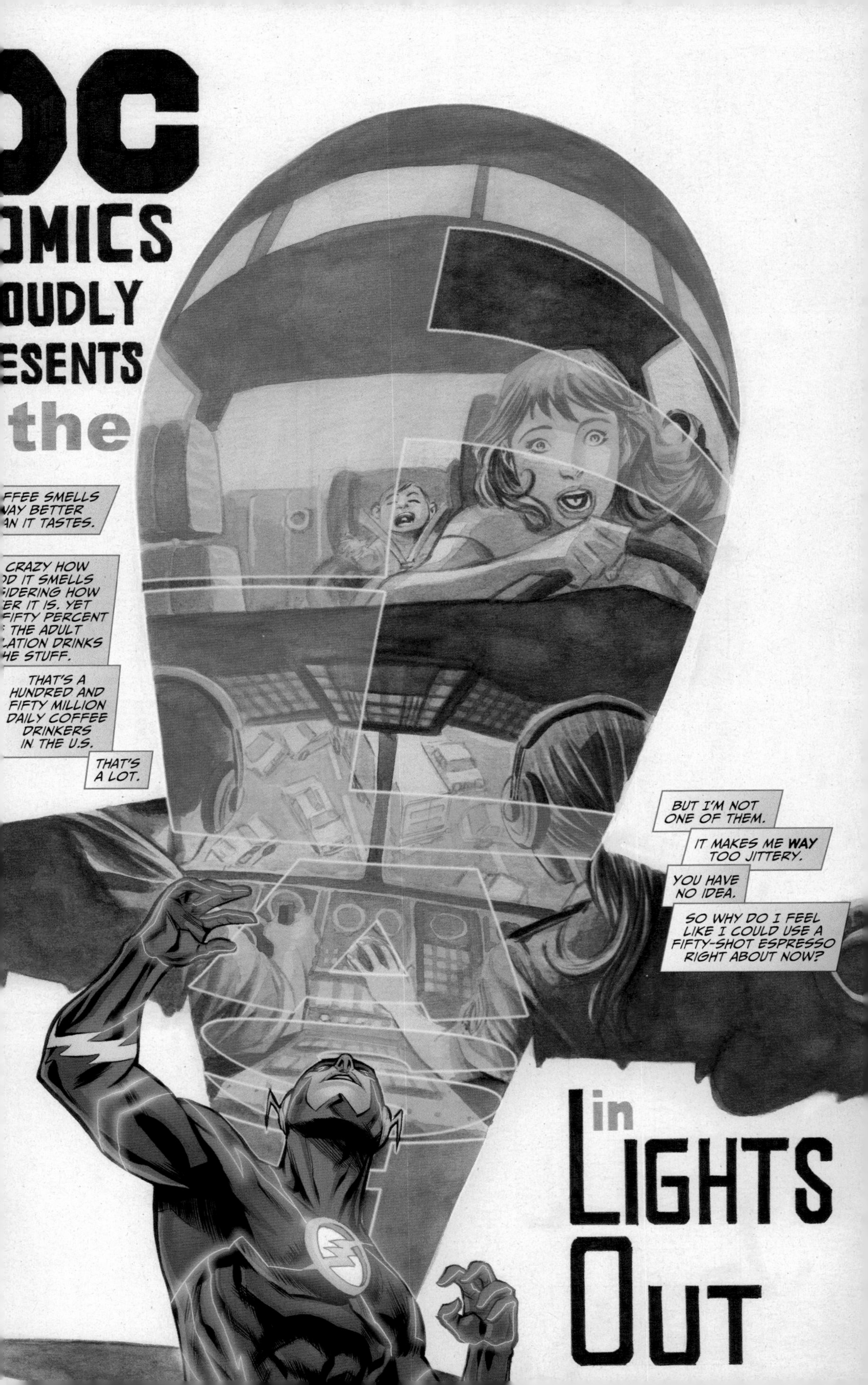

DC
OMICS
OUDLY
ESENTS
the
FFEE SMELLS
WAY BETTER
AN IT TASTES.
CRAZY HOW
OD IT SMELLS
SIDERING HOW
ER IT IS. YET
FIFTY PERCENT
F THE ADULT
LATION DRINKS
HE STUFF.
THAT'S A HUNDRED AND FIFTY MILLION DAILY COFFEE DRINKERS IN THE U.S.
THAT'S A LOT.
BUT I'M NOT ONE OF THEM.
IT MAKES ME WAY TOO JITTERY.
YOU HAVE NO IDEA.
SO WHY DO I FEEL LIKE I COULD USE A FIFTY-SHOT ESPRESSO RIGHT ABOUT NOW?
in
LIGHTS
OUT

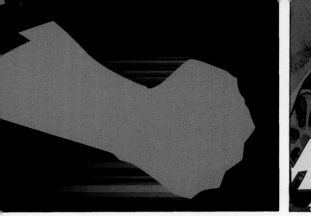

I DON'T KNOW WHY I'M THINKING ABOUT COFFEE.

GUESS I'M A LITTLE A.D.D. SI[N]... I LEARNED THAT MY BRAIN C[AN] TAP INTO THE SPEED FORC[E].

CREATING VORTEXES.

THESE AREN'T THINGS I WAS TAUGHT.

WOOOSH

I DIDN'T GET A MANUAL WITH MY POWERS.

MOST OF THEM I STUMBLED ACROSS AS I FUMBLED MY WAY THROUGH THE EARLY DAYS.

LIKE MY ABILITY TO VIE[W] THROUGH SOLID OBJE[CTS].

HOW'D I LEARN TO DO THAT? TOTAL ACCIDENT.

A QUADRUPLE SHOT OF ESPRESSO OVER ICE, WHILE PULLING AN ALL-NIGHTER IN THE LAB.

THAT WAS MY FIRST AND LAST COFFEE EXPERIENCE.

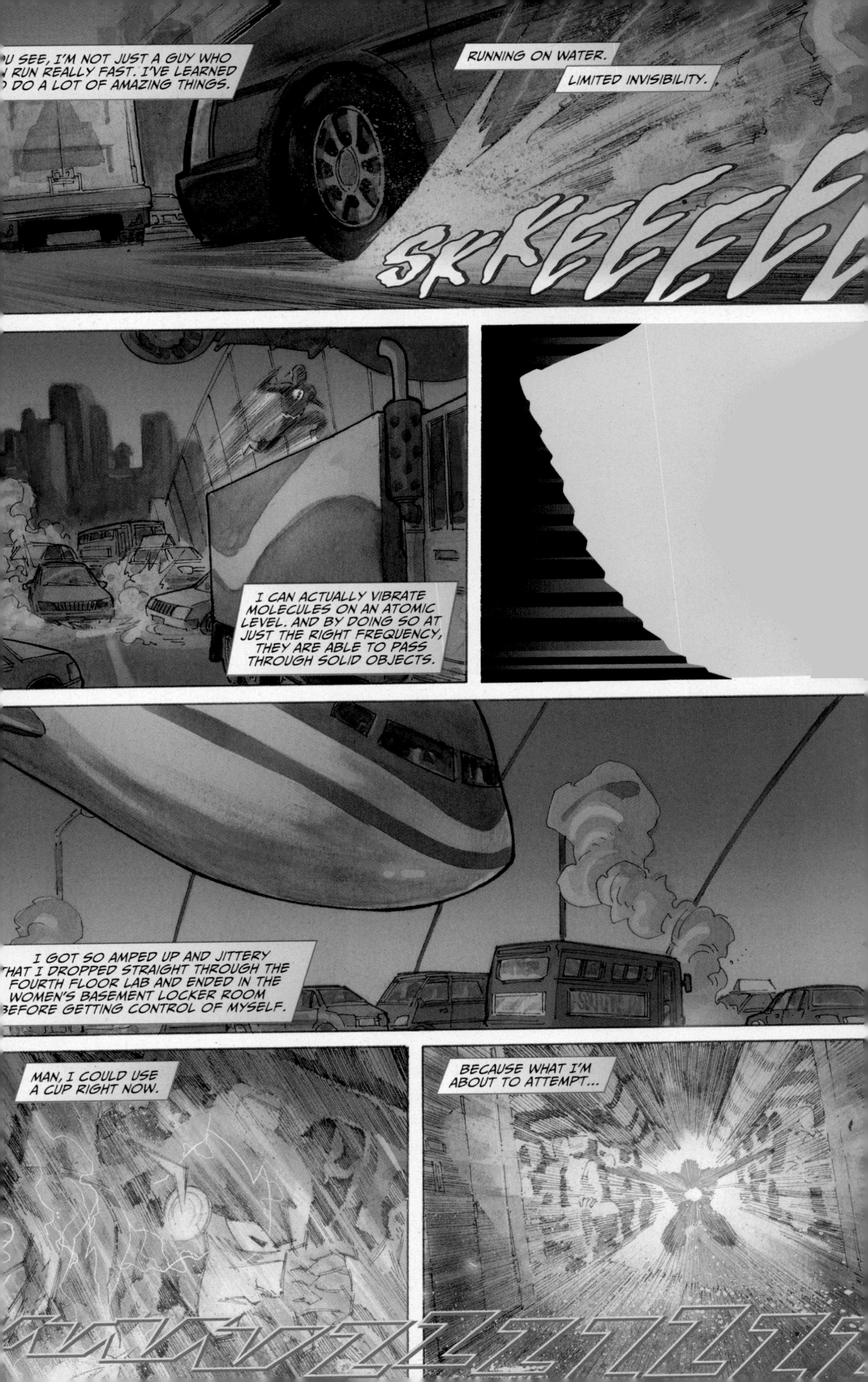

OU SEE, I'M NOT JUST A GUY WHO
N RUN REALLY FAST. I'VE LEARNED
O DO A LOT OF AMAZING THINGS.
RUNNING ON WATER.
LIMITED INVISIBILITY.
SKREEEEE
I CAN ACTUALLY VIBRATE MOLECULES ON AN ATOMIC LEVEL. AND BY DOING SO AT JUST THE RIGHT FREQUENCY, THEY ARE ABLE TO PASS THROUGH SOLID OBJECTS.
I GOT SO AMPED UP AND JITTERY THAT I DROPPED STRAIGHT THROUGH THE FOURTH FLOOR LAB AND ENDED IN THE WOMEN'S BASEMENT LOCKER ROOM BEFORE GETTING CONTROL OF MYSELF.
MAN, I COULD USE A CUP RIGHT NOW.
BECAUSE WHAT I'M ABOUT TO ATTEMPT...

...IS A MIRACLE.

COME ON, BARRY...

KEEP...IT... TOGETHER...

JUST...A LITTLE...

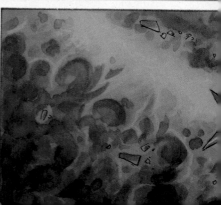

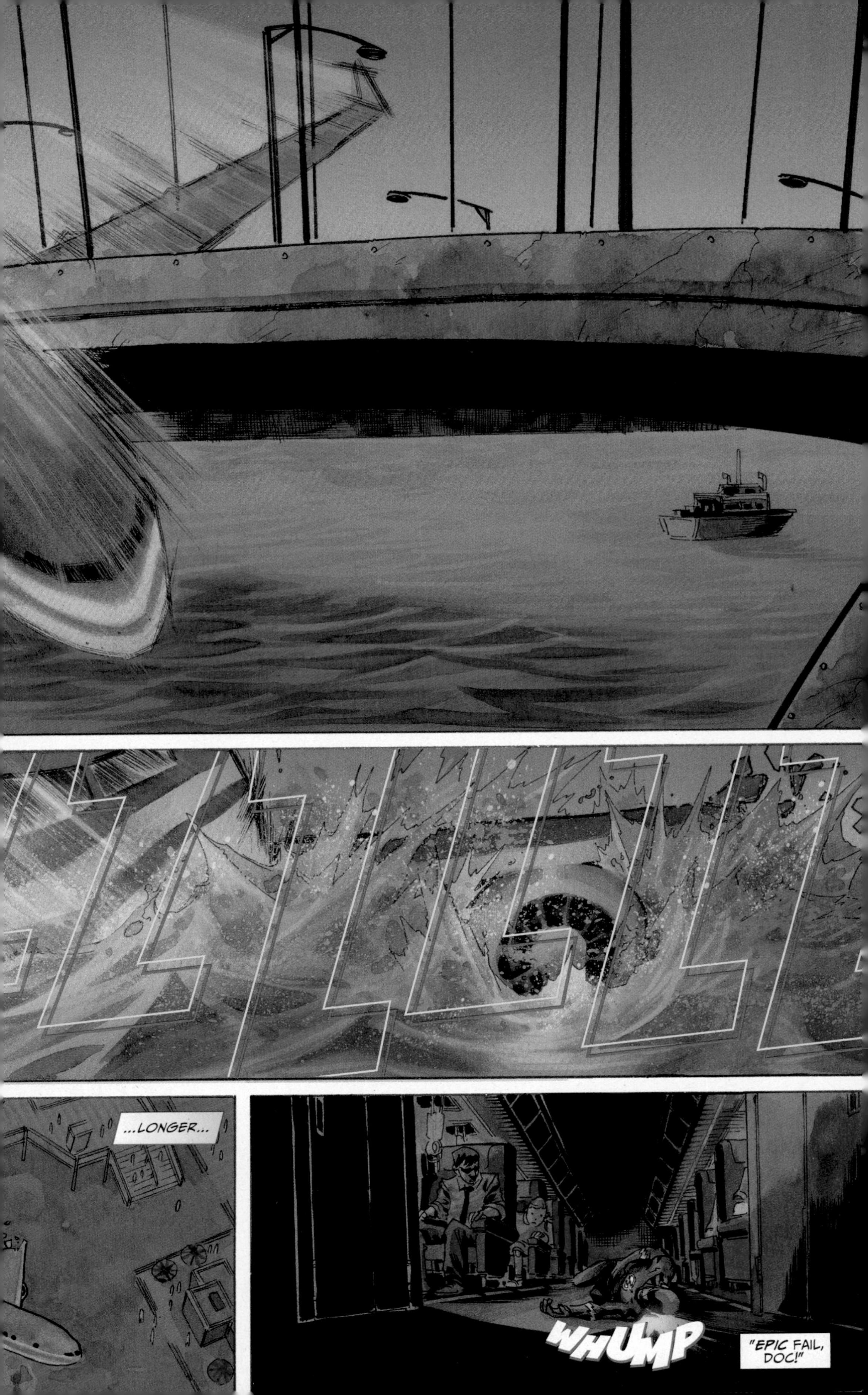
...LONGER...
WHUMP
"EPIC FAIL, DOC!"

WORTHLESS PIECE OF--

NO, DON'T!

BLAM BLAM

DR. GUERRERO WAS OUR BEST CHANCE! WHAT'S WRONG WITH YOU?!

I'M DYING!

SOONER THAN YOU! HE'S HAD A *YEAR*, AND THE DOC DID NOTHING BUT CAUSE THIS *BLACKOUT*! SHOULDN'T BE TOO HARD TO FILL HIS SHOES.

GET YOUR HANDS *OFF* ME!

MURDERERS. AND YOU WONDER WHY I WON'T HELP--

SHUT UP, MANUEL! YOU DON'T GET TO ADD YOUR TWO CENTS! YOU'RE WEAK...

"...YOU'RE NOT ONE OF US."

THIS STINKS!

THAT WOULD BE THE PIG BLADDER GROUND UP INTO A POWDER, LIEUTENANT LAGO.

A HUMAN IN THE FETUS STAGE HAS THE ABILITY TO REGENERATE. BUT SOMEWHERE ALONG THE WAY WE LOSE IT BEFORE WE'RE EVEN BORN.

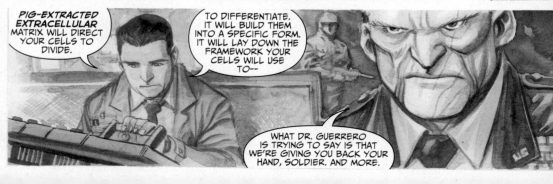

PIG-EXTRACTED EXTRACELLULAR MATRIX WILL DIRECT YOUR CELLS TO DIVIDE.

TO DIFFERENTIATE. IT WILL BUILD THEM INTO A SPECIFIC FORM. IT WILL LAY DOWN THE FRAMEWORK YOUR CELLS WILL USE TO--

WHAT DR. GUERRERO IS TRYING TO SAY IS THAT WE'RE GIVING YOU BACK YOUR HAND, SOLDIER. AND MORE.

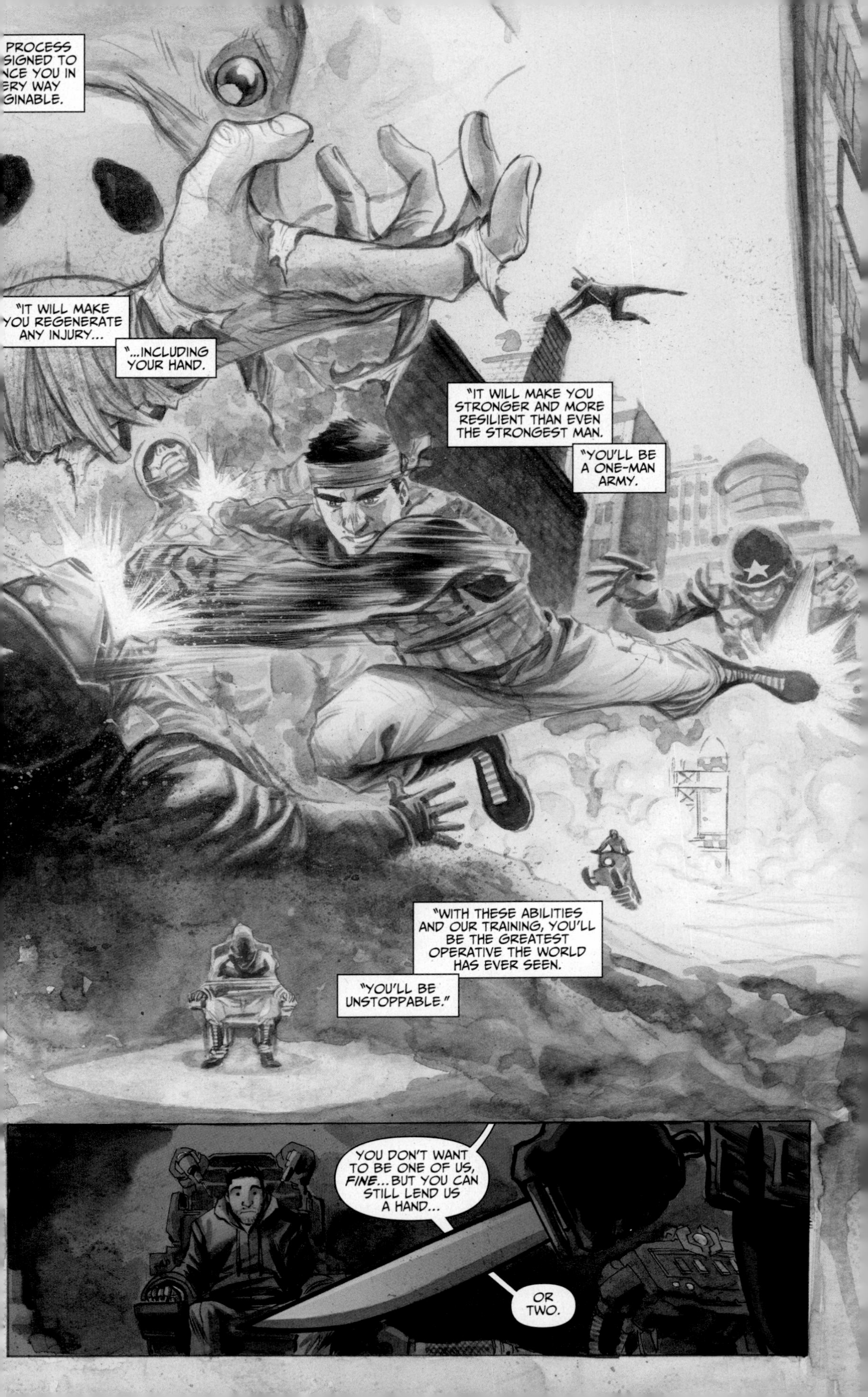
PROCESS
SIGNED TO
NCE YOU IN
ERY WAY
GINABLE.
"IT WILL MAKE YOU REGENERATE ANY INJURY...
"...INCLUDING YOUR HAND.
"IT WILL MAKE YOU STRONGER AND MORE RESILIENT THAN EVEN THE STRONGEST MAN.
"YOU'LL BE A ONE-MAN ARMY.
"WITH THESE ABILITIES AND OUR TRAINING, YOU'LL BE THE GREATEST OPERATIVE THE WORLD HAS EVER SEEN.
"YOU'LL BE UNSTOPPABLE."
YOU DON'T WANT TO BE ONE OF US, *FINE*... BUT YOU CAN STILL LEND US A HAND...
OR TWO.

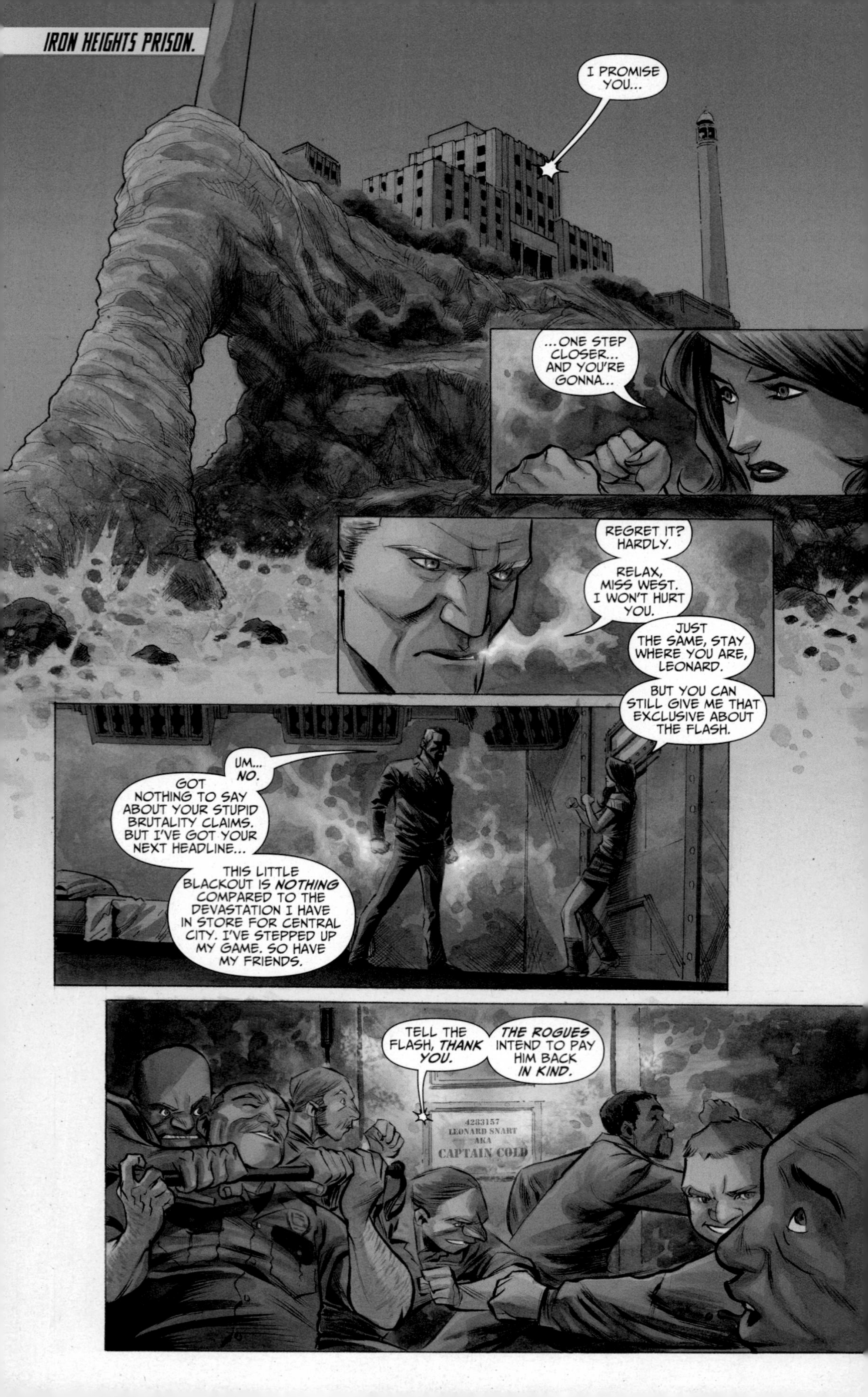
IRON HEIGHTS PRISON.
I PROMISE YOU...
...ONE STEP CLOSER... AND YOU'RE GONNA...
REGRET IT? HARDLY.
RELAX, MISS WEST. I WON'T HURT YOU.
JUST THE SAME, STAY WHERE YOU ARE, LEONARD.
BUT YOU CAN STILL GIVE ME THAT EXCLUSIVE ABOUT THE FLASH.
UM... NO.
GOT NOTHING TO SAY ABOUT YOUR STUPID BRUTALITY CLAIMS. BUT I'VE GOT YOUR NEXT HEADLINE...
THIS LITTLE BLACKOUT IS NOTHING COMPARED TO THE DEVASTATION I HAVE IN STORE FOR CENTRAL CITY. I'VE STEPPED UP MY GAME. SO HAVE MY FRIENDS.
TELL THE FLASH, THANK YOU.
THE ROGUES INTEND TO PAY HIM BACK IN KIND.
4283157 LEONARD SNART AKA CAPTAIN COLD

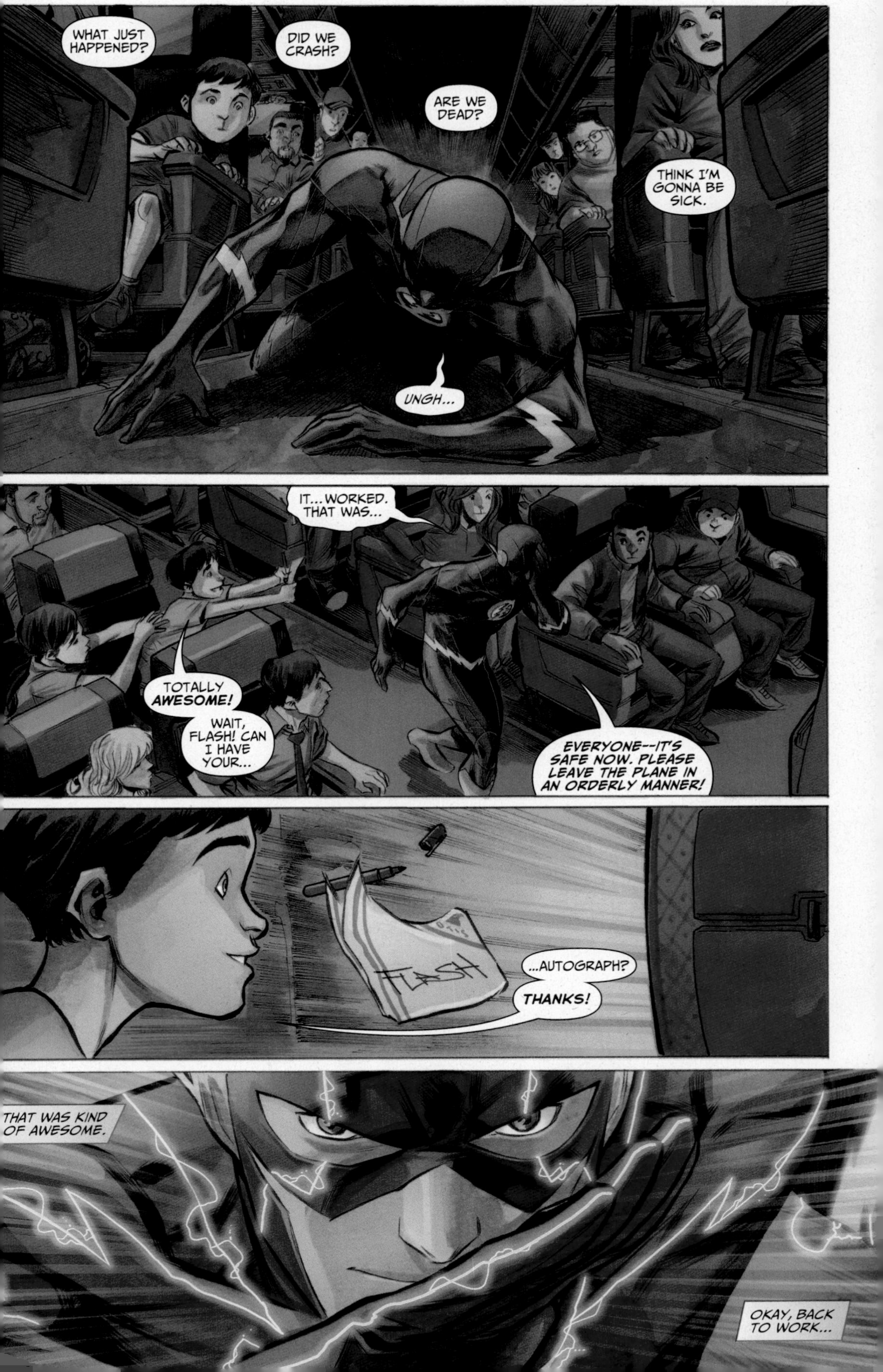
WHAT JUST HAPPENED?
DID WE CRASH?
ARE WE DEAD?
THINK I'M GONNA BE SICK.
UNGH...
IT...WORKED. THAT WAS...
TOTALLY AWESOME!
WAIT, FLASH! CAN I HAVE YOUR...
EVERYONE--IT'S SAFE NOW. PLEASE LEAVE THE PLANE IN AN ORDERLY MANNER!
FLASH
...AUTOGRAPH?
THANKS!
THAT WAS KIND OF AWESOME.
OKAY, BACK TO WORK...

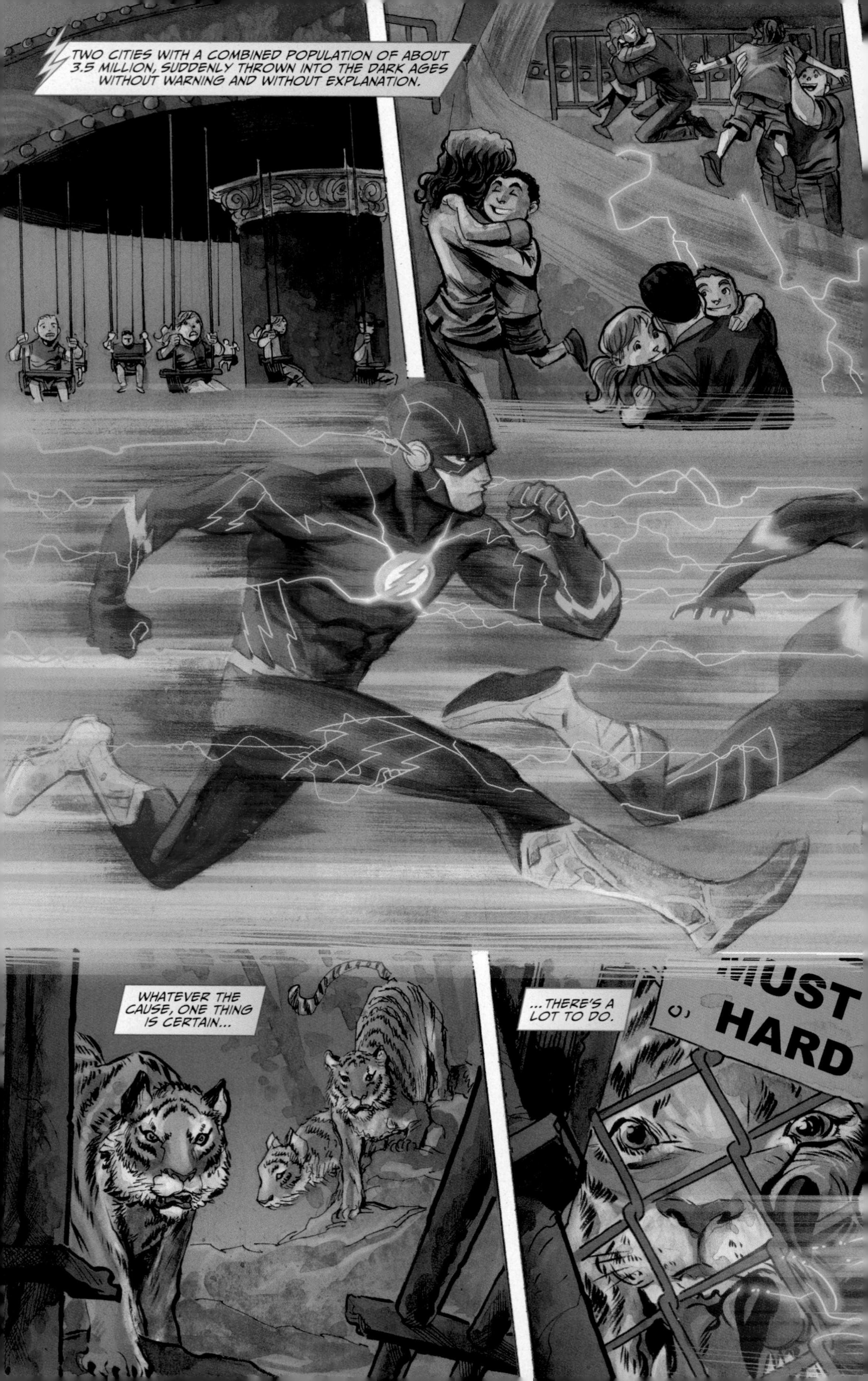

TWO CITIES WITH A COMBINED POPULATION OF ABOUT 3.5 MILLION, SUDDENLY THROWN INTO THE DARK AGES WITHOUT WARNING AND WITHOUT EXPLANATION.
WHATEVER THE CAUSE, ONE THING IS CERTAIN...
...THERE'S A LOT TO DO.
MUST
HARD

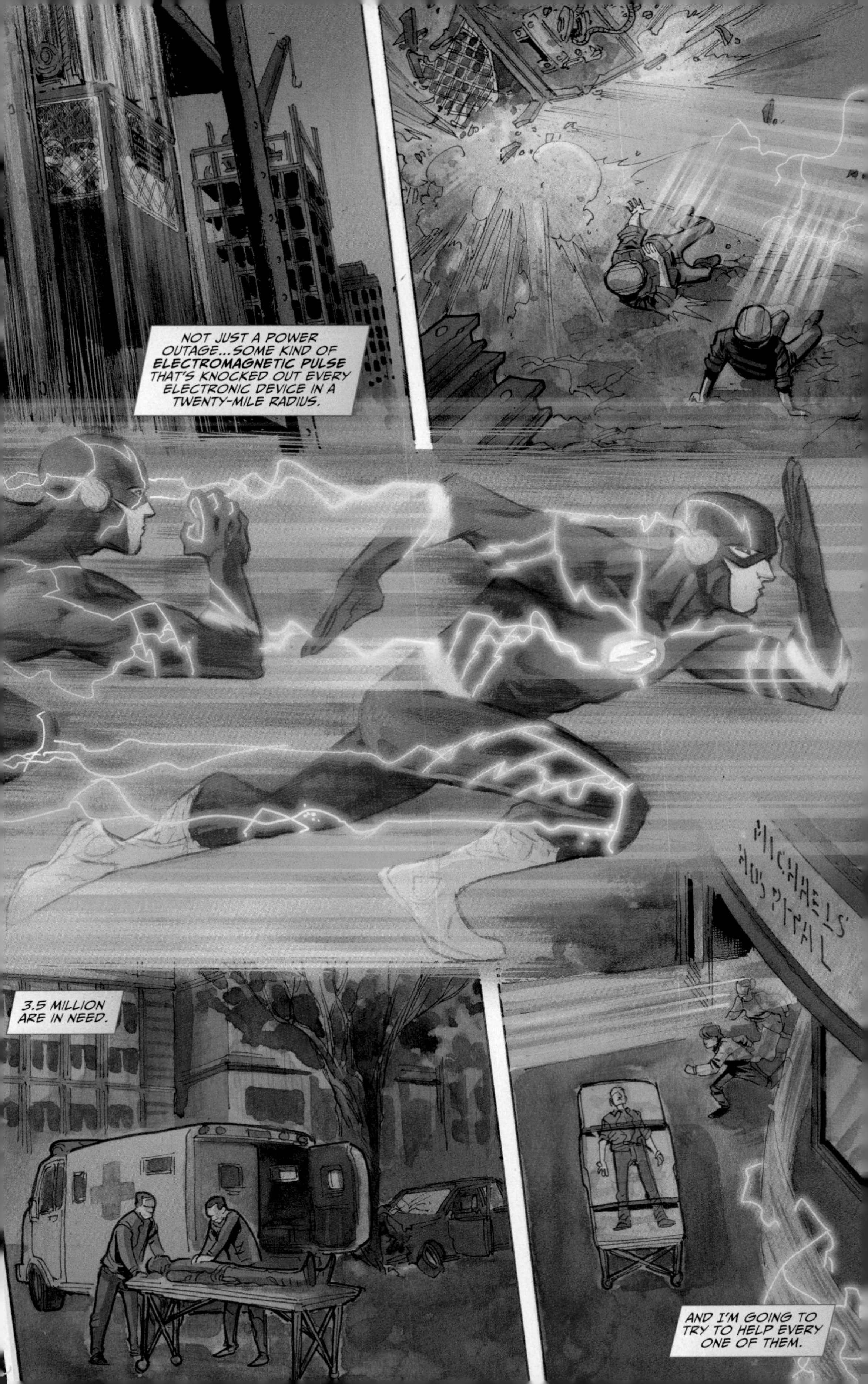
NOT JUST A POWER OUTAGE...SOME KIND OF ELECTROMAGNETIC PULSE THAT'S KNOCKED OUT EVERY ELECTRONIC DEVICE IN A TWENTY-MILE RADIUS.
3.5 MILLION ARE IN NEED.
AND I'M GOING TO TRY TO HELP EVERY ONE OF THEM.

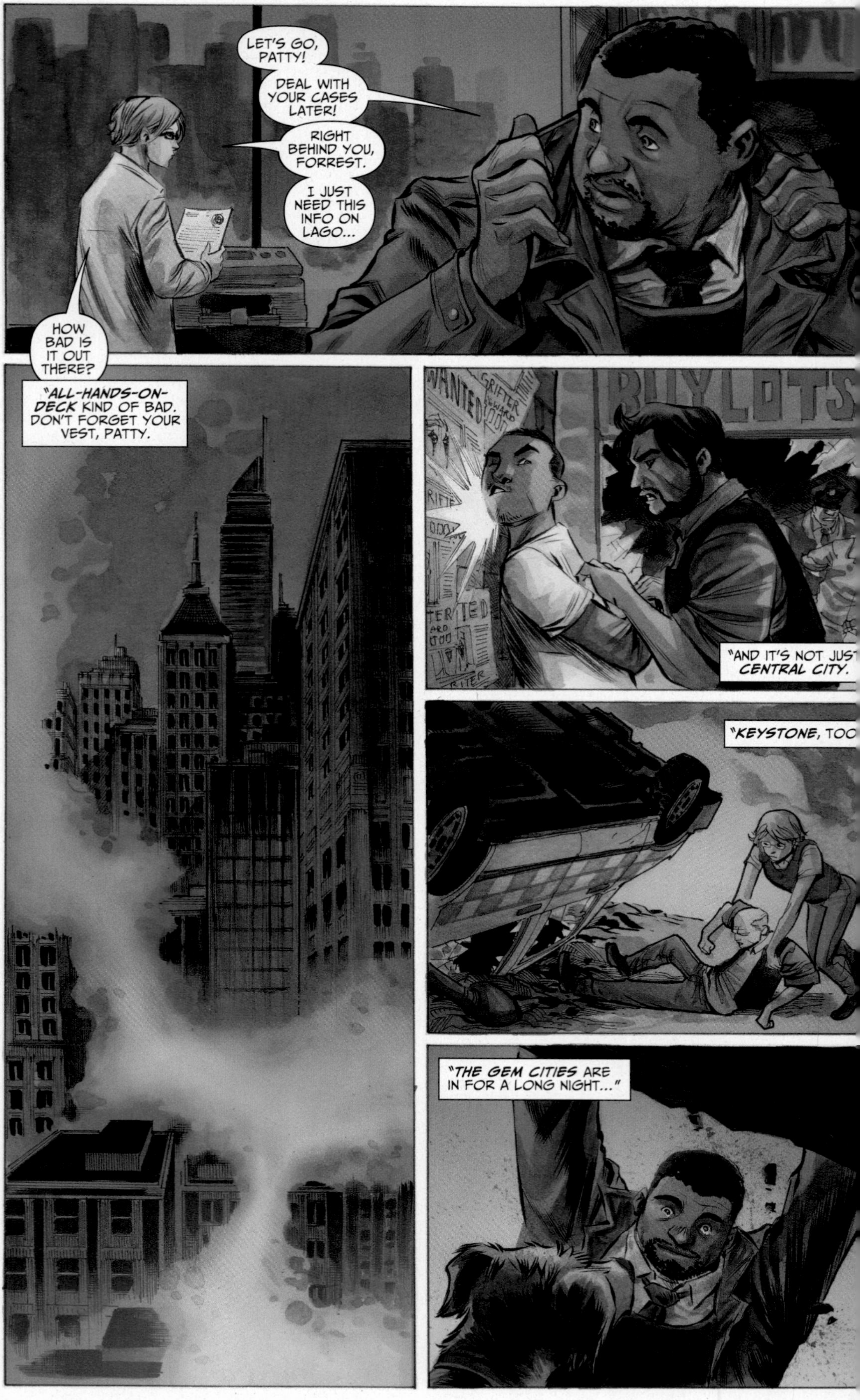
LET'S GO, PATTY!
DEAL WITH YOUR CASES LATER!
RIGHT BEHIND YOU, FORREST.
I JUST NEED THIS INFO ON LAGO...
HOW BAD IS IT OUT THERE?
"ALL-HANDS-ON-DECK KIND OF BAD. DON'T FORGET YOUR VEST, PATTY.
WANTED
GRIFTER
BUYLOTS
"AND IT'S NOT JUST CENTRAL CITY.
"KEYSTONE, TOO
"THE GEM CITIES ARE IN FOR A LONG NIGHT..."

the journal of Darwin Elias:

I'm a man of science, always looking to the future. But as I write this, I can't help but marvel at life's unexpected twists and turns.

Yesterday, I would have typed this on a computer. Yesterday, I'd be inside my luxury car. But today, the keyboard and monitor give way to pen and paper. My 800 horsepower sports car is junk, and my great, great grandfather's <u>Stanley Steam Car</u>, built in 1912, is cutting edge technology.

And all of this because of an <u>Electromagnetic Pulse</u> that has crippled two cities and thrown them back into the <u>Dark Ages</u>.

But even an anomaly like yesterday's E.M.P. blast will leave traces.

And these traces are <u>quantifiable</u>. They are breadcrumbs that will lead me to the <u>truth</u>.

Even if that truth is something no one wants to hear, it must be told.

I'm a man of science, always looking to the future...

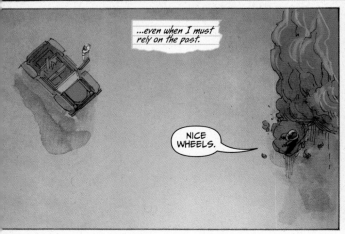

...even when I must rely on the past.

NICE WHEELS.

SAME TO YOU.

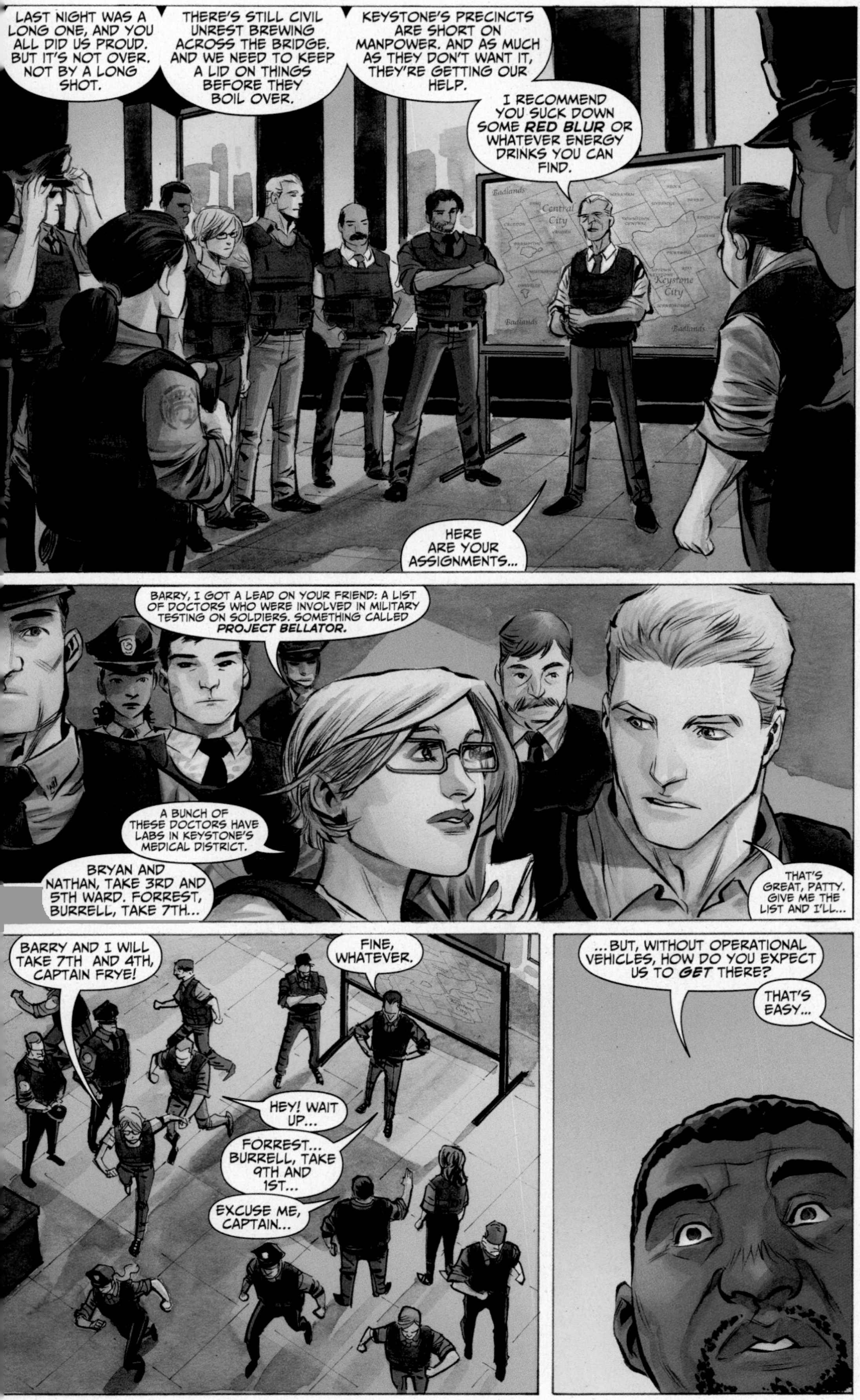
LAST NIGHT WAS A LONG ONE, AND YOU ALL DID US PROUD. BUT IT'S NOT OVER. NOT BY A LONG SHOT.
THERE'S STILL CIVIL UNREST BREWING ACROSS THE BRIDGE. AND WE NEED TO KEEP A LID ON THINGS BEFORE THEY BOIL OVER.
KEYSTONE'S PRECINCTS ARE SHORT ON MANPOWER. AND AS MUCH AS THEY DON'T WANT IT, THEY'RE GETTING OUR HELP.
I RECOMMEND YOU SUCK DOWN SOME RED BLUR OR WHATEVER ENERGY DRINKS YOU CAN FIND.
Badlands
Central City
Keystone City
Badlands
Badlands
HERE ARE YOUR ASSIGNMENTS...
BARRY, I GOT A LEAD ON YOUR FRIEND: A LIST OF DOCTORS WHO WERE INVOLVED IN MILITARY TESTING ON SOLDIERS. SOMETHING CALLED PROJECT BELLATOR.
A BUNCH OF THESE DOCTORS HAVE LABS IN KEYSTONE'S MEDICAL DISTRICT.
BRYAN AND NATHAN, TAKE 3RD AND 5TH WARD. FORREST, BURRELL, TAKE 7TH...
THAT'S GREAT, PATTY. GIVE ME THE LIST AND I'LL...
BARRY AND I WILL TAKE 7TH AND 4TH, CAPTAIN FRYE!
FINE, WHATEVER.
HEY! WAIT UP...
FORREST... BURRELL, TAKE 9TH AND 1ST...
EXCUSE ME, CAPTAIN...
...BUT, WITHOUT OPERATIONAL VEHICLES, HOW DO YOU EXPECT US TO GET THERE?
THAT'S EASY...

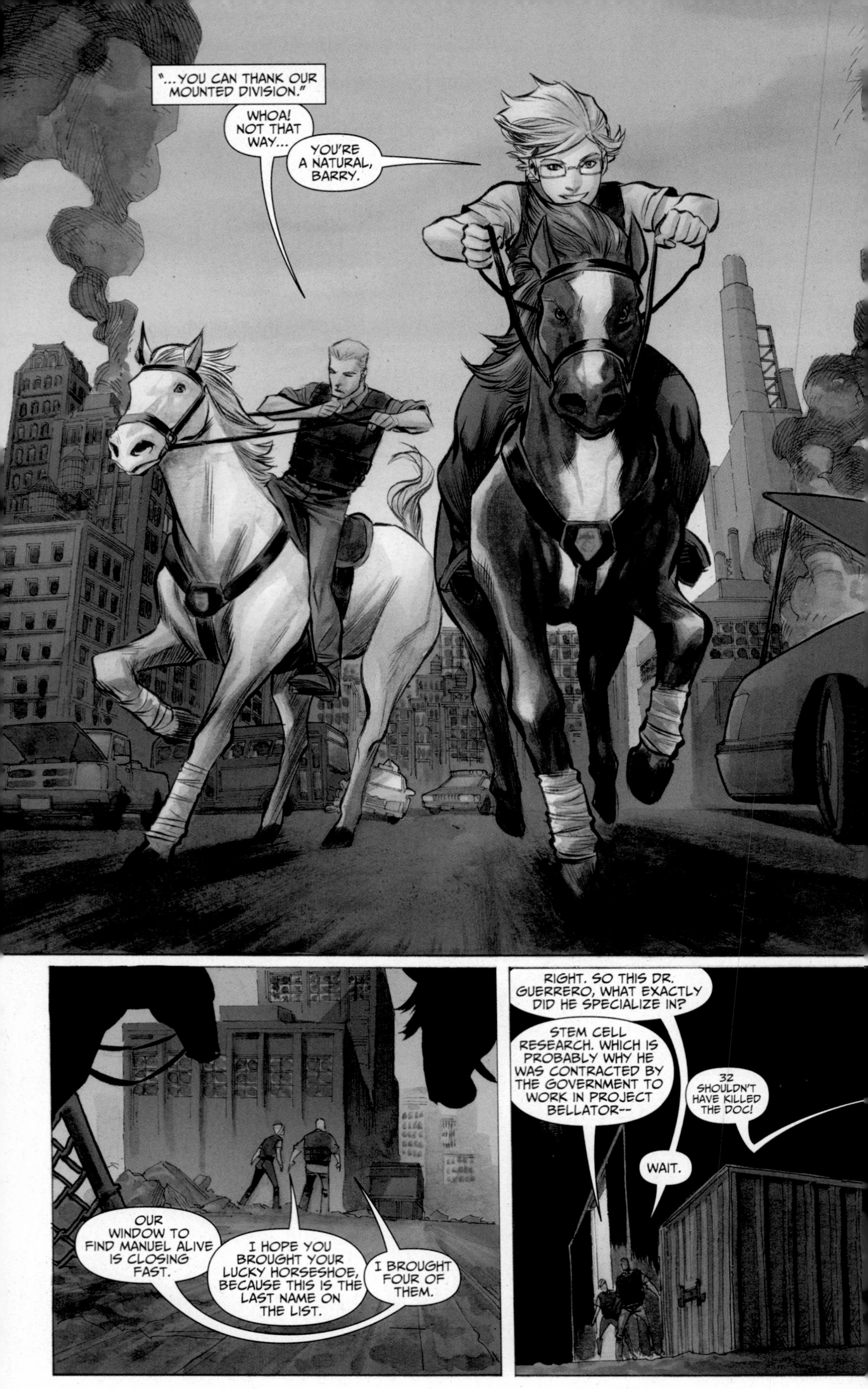
"...YOU CAN THANK OUR MOUNTED DIVISION."
WHOA! NOT THAT WAY...
YOU'RE A NATURAL, BARRY.
OUR WINDOW TO FIND MANUEL ALIVE IS CLOSING FAST.
I HOPE YOU BROUGHT YOUR LUCKY HORSESHOE, BECAUSE THIS IS THE LAST NAME ON THE LIST.
I BROUGHT FOUR OF THEM.
RIGHT. SO THIS DR. GUERRERO, WHAT EXACTLY DID HE SPECIALIZE IN?
STEM CELL RESEARCH. WHICH IS PROBABLY WHY HE WAS CONTRACTED BY THE GOVERNMENT TO WORK IN PROJECT BELLATOR--
WAIT.
32 SHOULDN'T HAVE KILLED THE DOC!

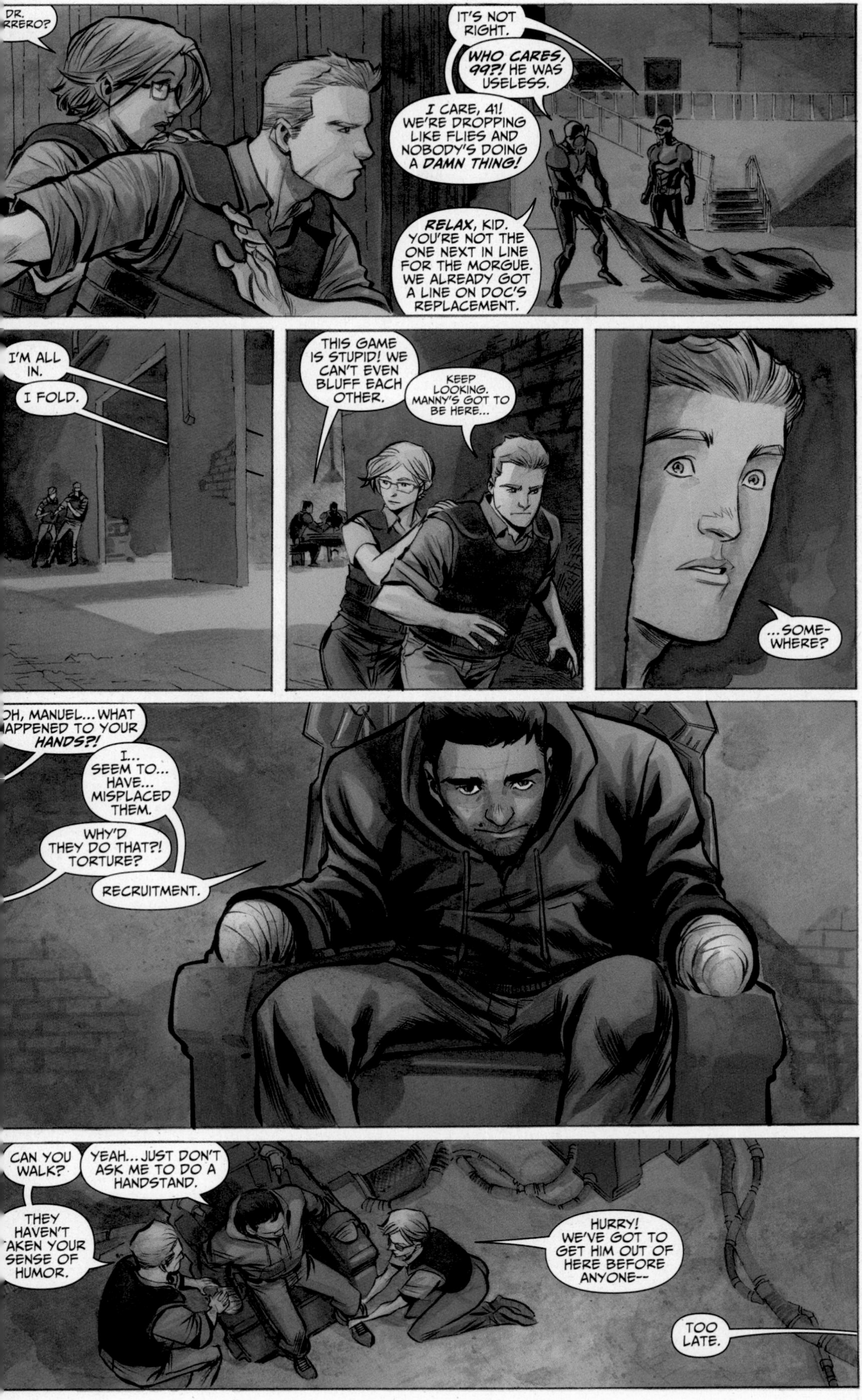
DR. ...RRERO?
IT'S NOT RIGHT.
WHO CARES, 99?! HE WAS USELESS.
I CARE, 41! WE'RE DROPPING LIKE FLIES AND NOBODY'S DOING A DAMN THING!
RELAX, KID. YOU'RE NOT THE ONE NEXT IN LINE FOR THE MORGUE. WE ALREADY GOT A LINE ON DOC'S REPLACEMENT.
I'M ALL IN.
I FOLD.
THIS GAME IS STUPID! WE CAN'T EVEN BLUFF EACH OTHER.
KEEP LOOKING. MANNY'S GOT TO BE HERE...
...SOME-WHERE?
OH, MANUEL... WHAT HAPPENED TO YOUR HANDS?!
I... SEEM TO... HAVE... MISPLACED THEM.
WHY'D THEY DO THAT?! TORTURE?
RECRUITMENT.
CAN YOU WALK?
YEAH... JUST DON'T ASK ME TO DO A HANDSTAND.
THEY HAVEN'T TAKEN YOUR SENSE OF HUMOR.
HURRY! WE'VE GOT TO GET HIM OUT OF HERE BEFORE ANYONE--
TOO LATE.

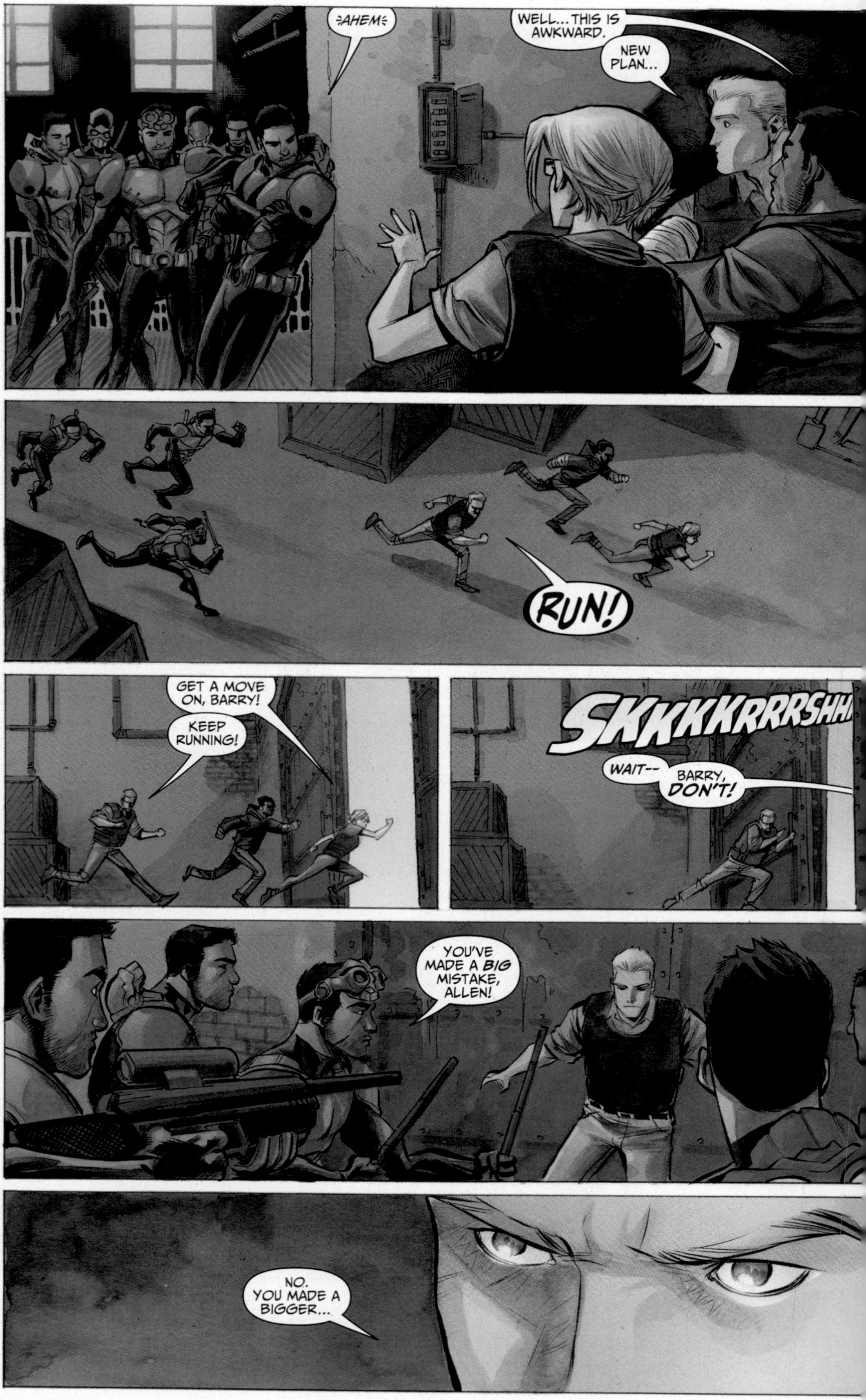

AHEM
WELL... THIS IS AWKWARD.
NEW PLAN...
RUN!
GET A MOVE ON, BARRY!
KEEP RUNNING!
SKKKKRRRSHH
WAIT--
BARRY, DON'T!
YOU'VE MADE A BIG MISTAKE, ALLEN!
NO. YOU MADE A BIGGER...

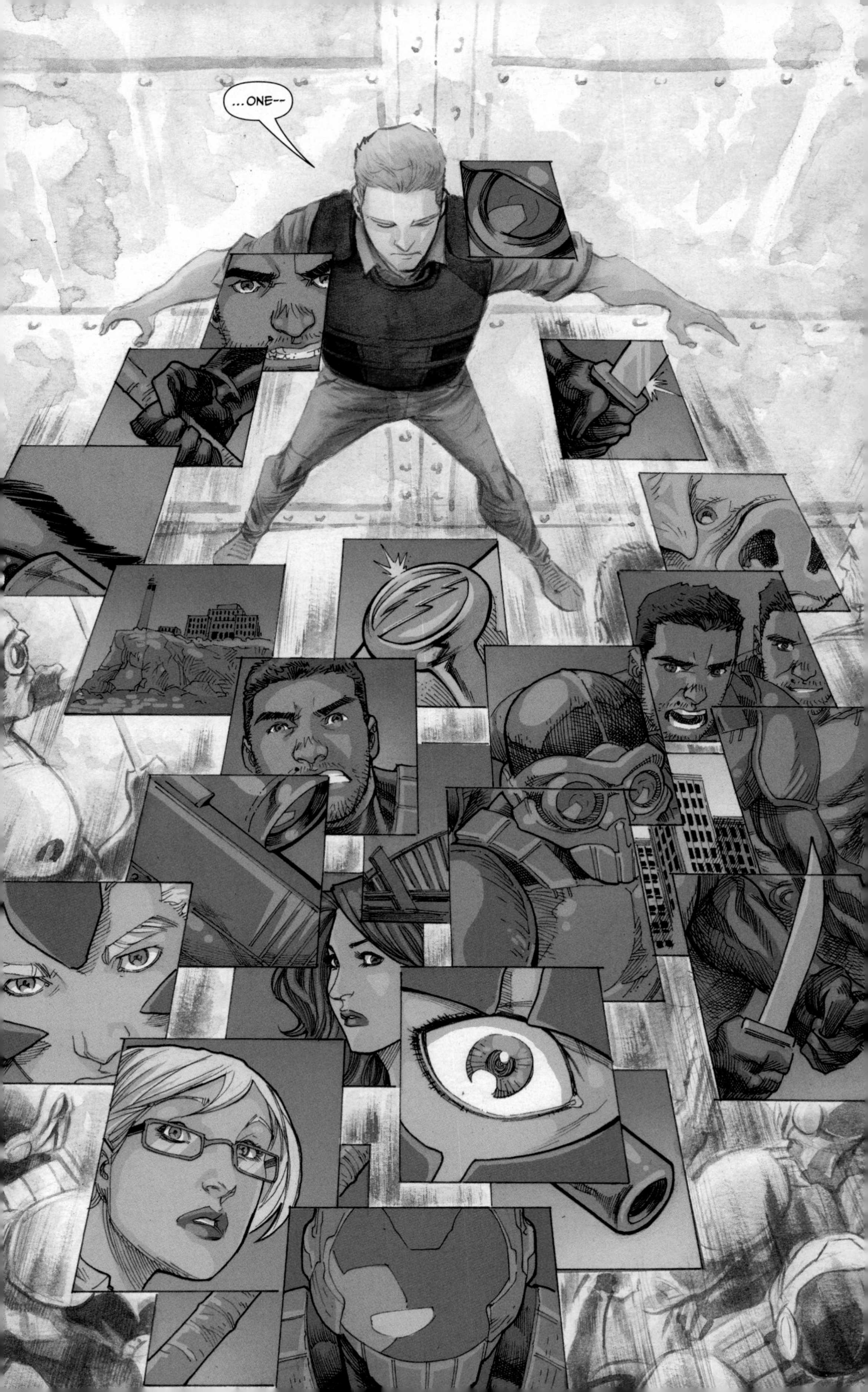
...ONE--

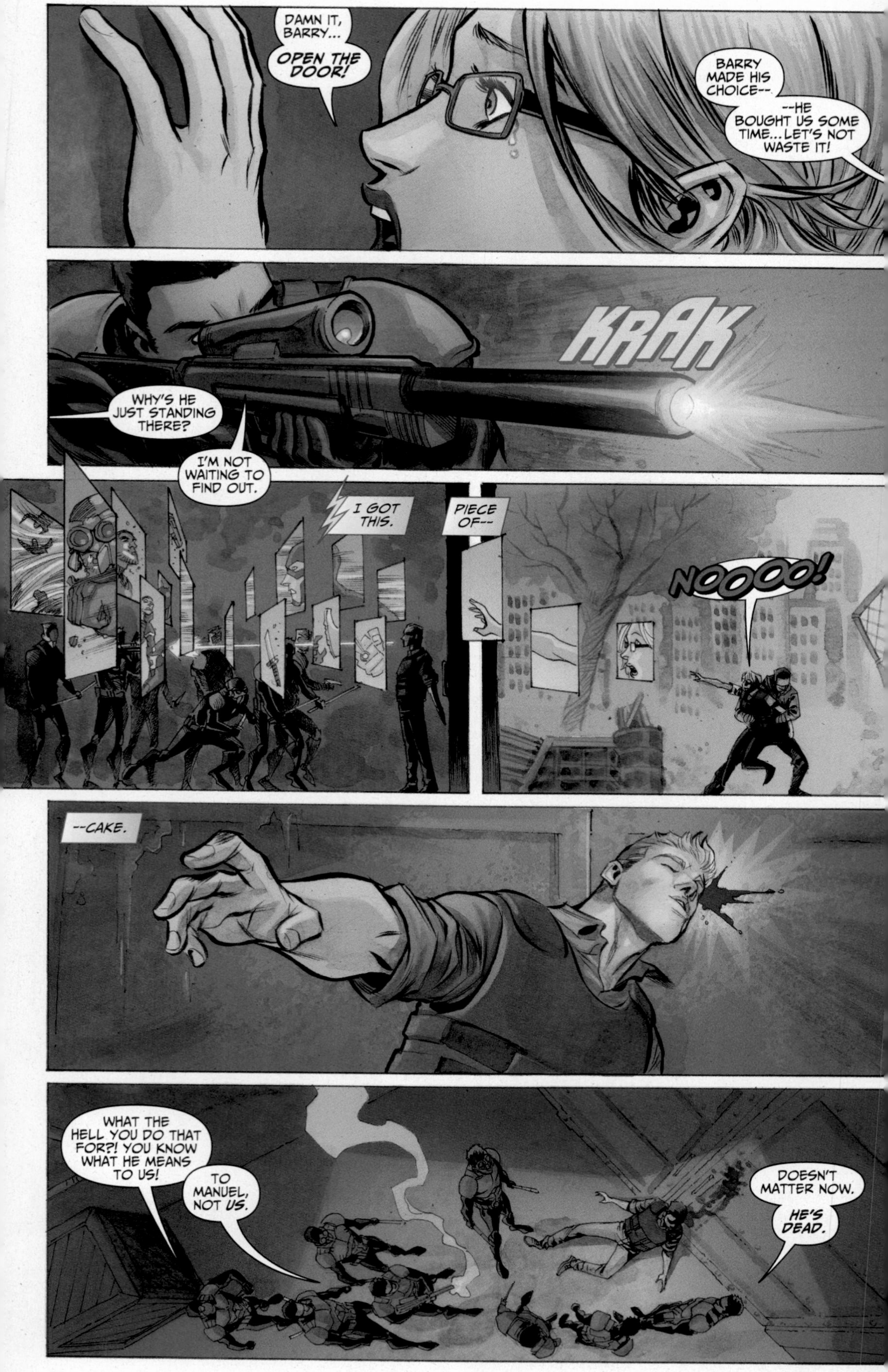
DAMN IT, BARRY... OPEN THE DOOR!
BARRY MADE HIS CHOICE--.
--HE BOUGHT US SOME TIME...LET'S NOT WASTE IT!
KRAK
WHY'S HE JUST STANDING THERE?
I'M NOT WAITING TO FIND OUT.
I GOT THIS.
PIECE OF--
NOOOOO!
--CAKE.
WHAT THE HELL YOU DO THAT FOR?! YOU KNOW WHAT HE MEANS TO US!
TO MANUEL, NOT US.
DOESN'T MATTER NOW.
HE'S DEAD.

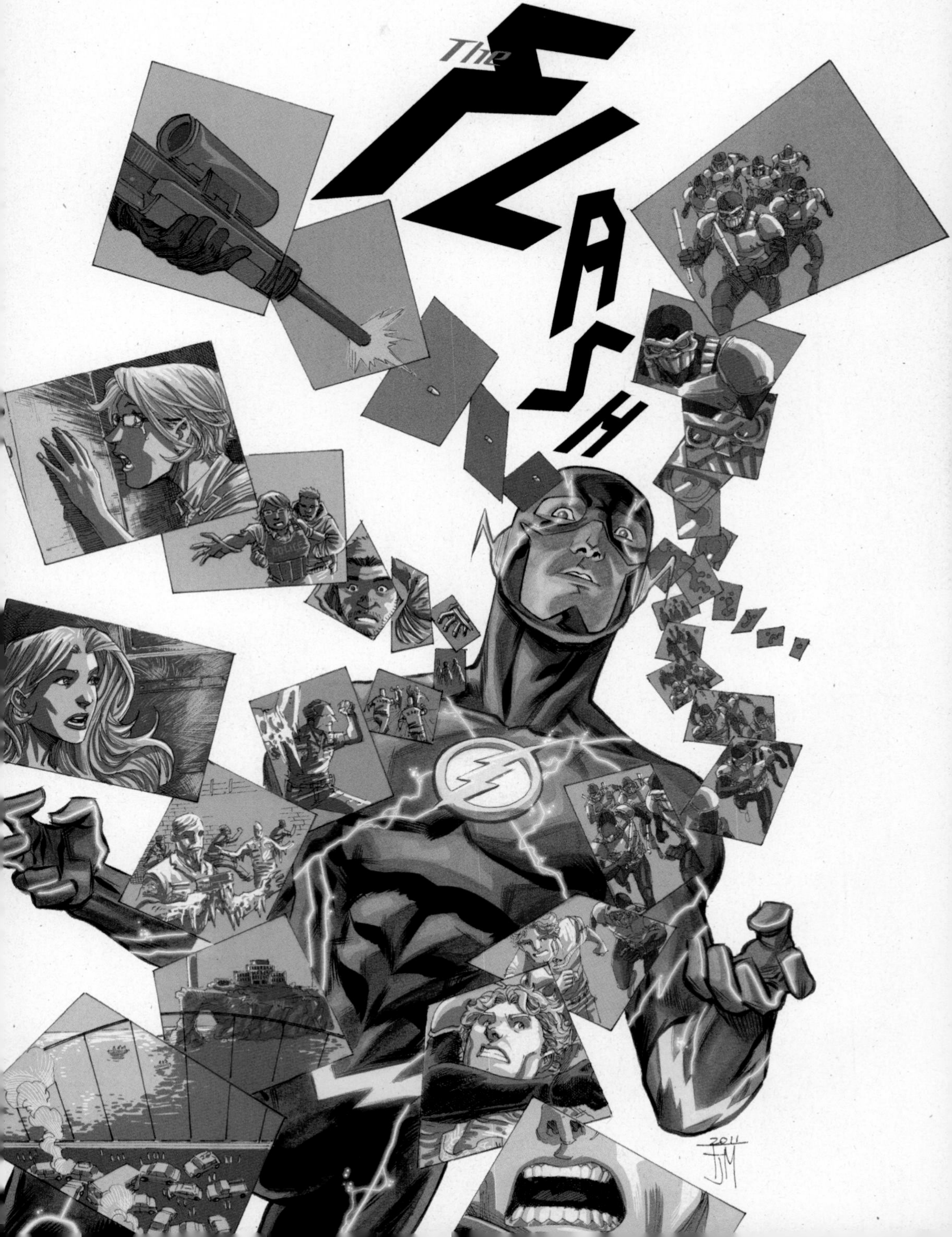
The
FLASH
POLICE
2011

THE FLASH #4
variant cover by ERIC BASALDUA & NEI RUFFINO

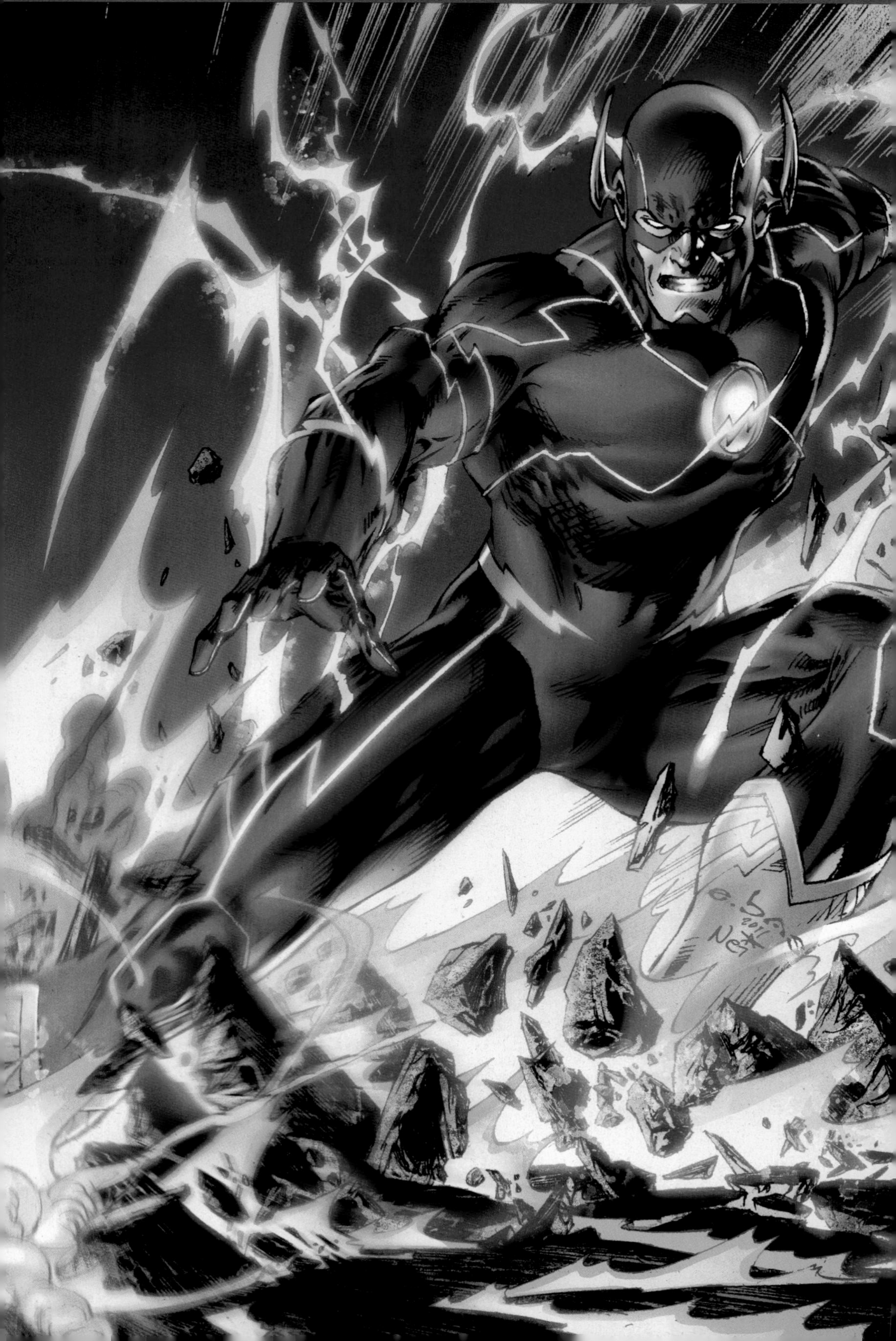

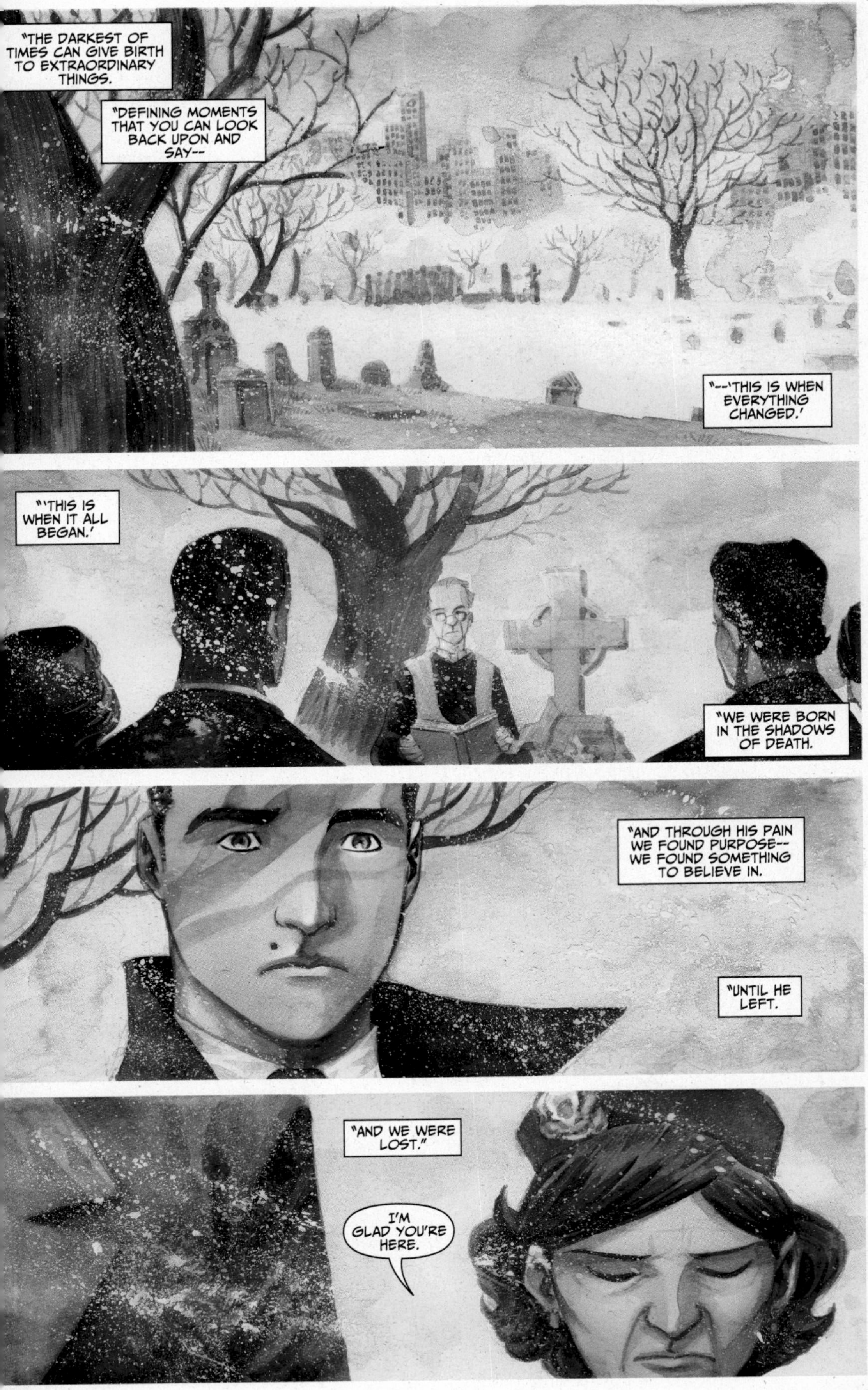
"THE DARKEST OF TIMES CAN GIVE BIRTH TO EXTRAORDINARY THINGS.
"DEFINING MOMENTS THAT YOU CAN LOOK BACK UPON AND SAY--
"--'THIS IS WHEN EVERYTHING CHANGED.'
"'THIS IS WHEN IT ALL BEGAN.'
"WE WERE BORN IN THE SHADOWS OF DEATH.
"AND THROUGH HIS PAIN WE FOUND PURPOSE-- WE FOUND SOMETHING TO BELIEVE IN.
"UNTIL HE LEFT.
"AND WE WERE LOST."
I'M GLAD YOU'RE HERE.

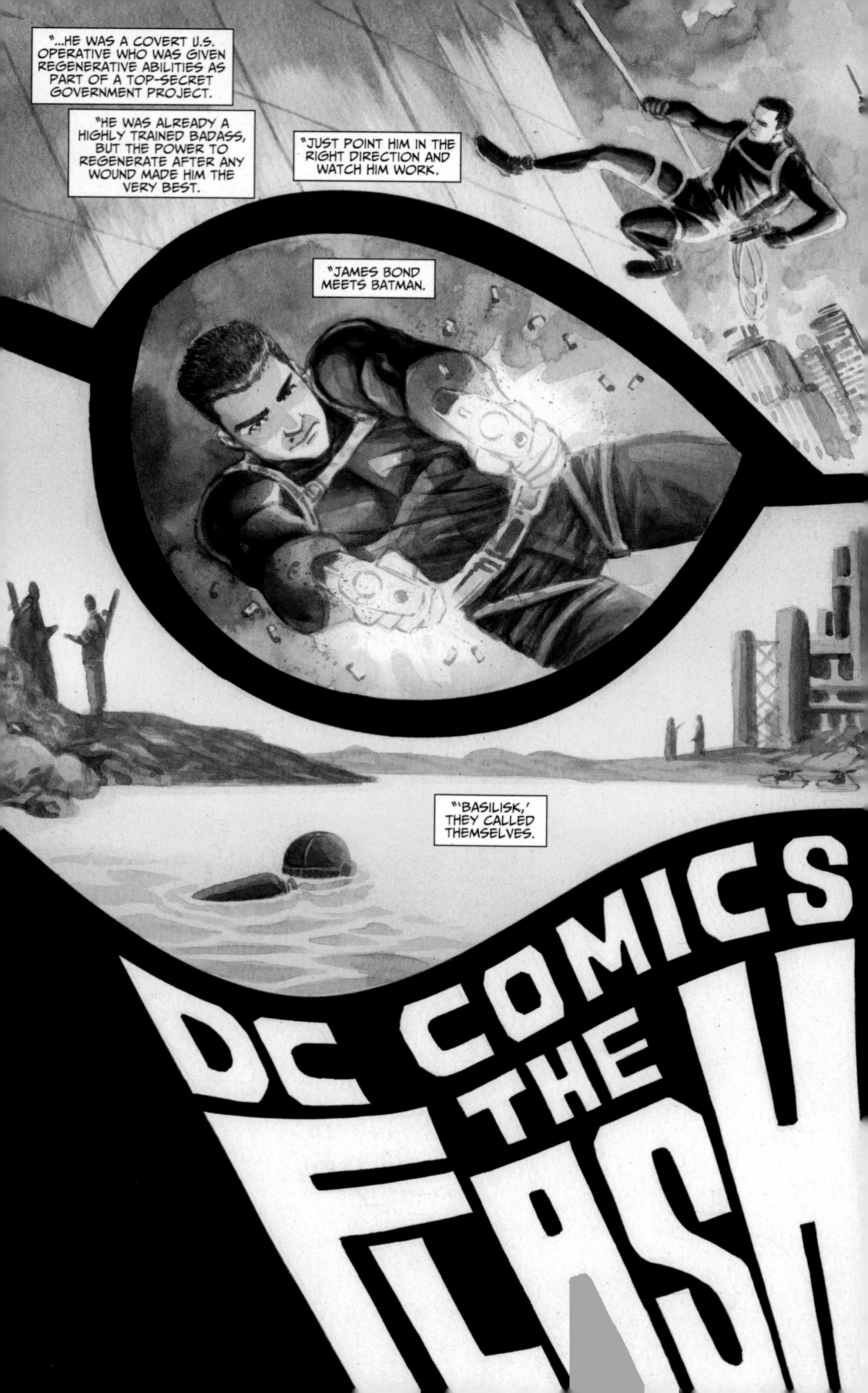
"...HE WAS A COVERT U.S. OPERATIVE WHO WAS GIVEN REGENERATIVE ABILITIES AS PART OF A TOP-SECRET GOVERNMENT PROJECT.
"HE WAS ALREADY A HIGHLY TRAINED BADASS, BUT THE POWER TO REGENERATE AFTER ANY WOUND MADE HIM THE VERY BEST.
"JUST POINT HIM IN THE RIGHT DIRECTION AND WATCH HIM WORK.
"JAMES BOND MEETS BATMAN.
"'BASILISK,' THEY CALLED THEMSELVES.
DC COMICS
THE
FLASH

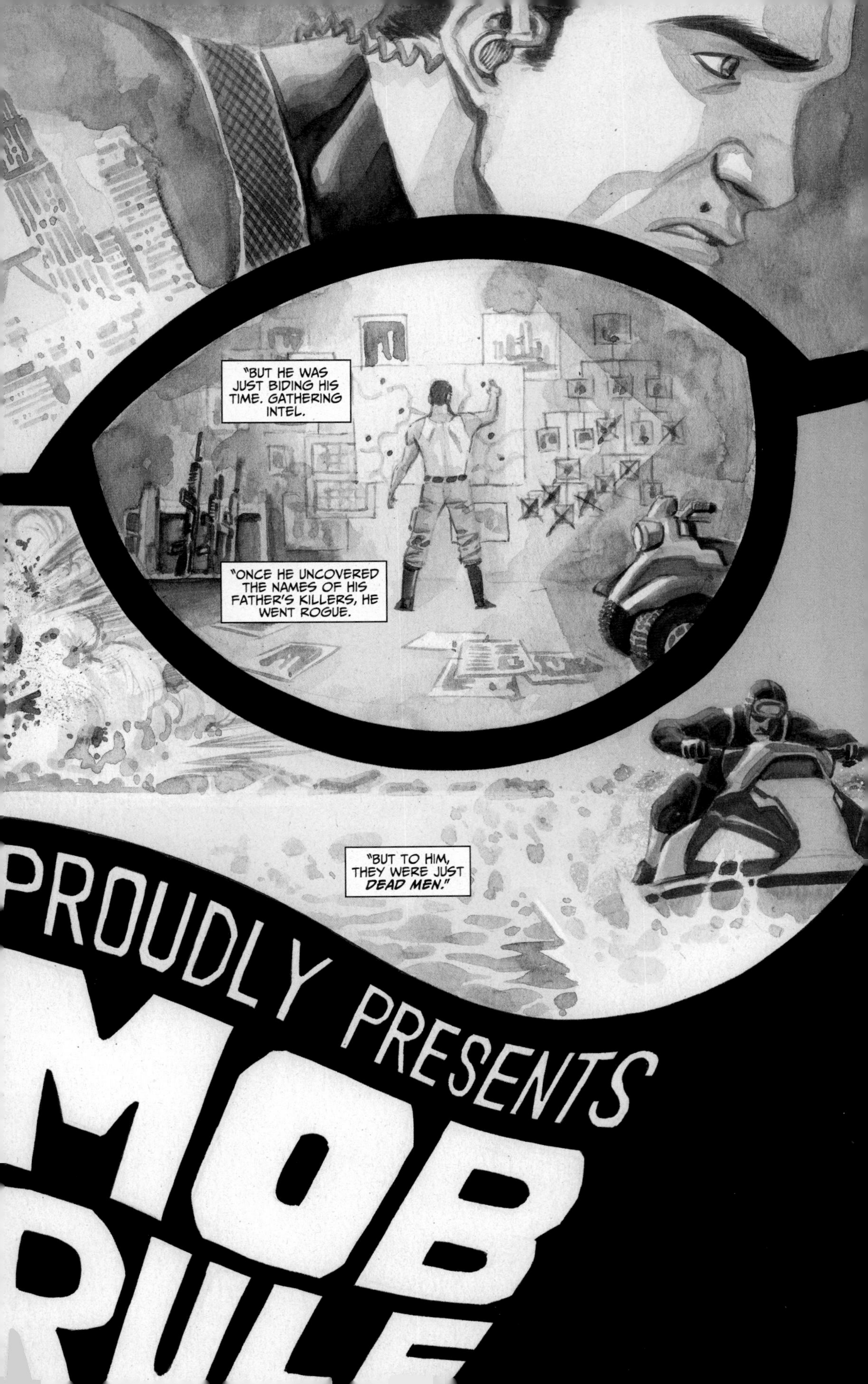
"BUT HE WAS JUST BIDING HIS TIME. GATHERING INTEL.
"ONCE HE UNCOVERED THE NAMES OF HIS FATHER'S KILLERS, HE WENT ROGUE.
"BUT TO HIM, THEY WERE JUST *DEAD MEN.*"
PROUDLY PRESENTS
MOB RULE

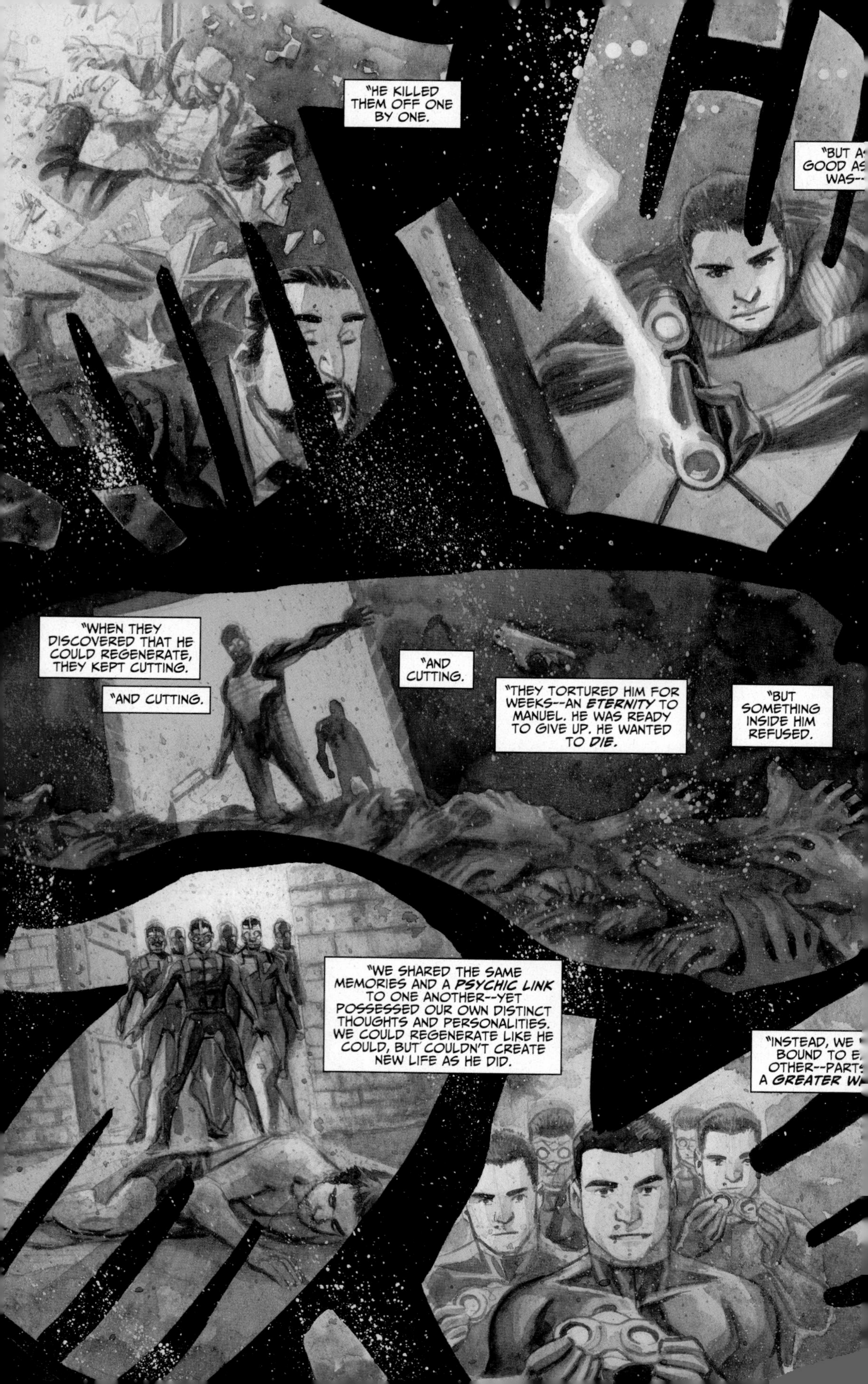
"HE KILLED THEM OFF ONE BY ONE.
"BUT A GOOD AS WAS--
"WHEN THEY DISCOVERED THAT HE COULD REGENERATE, THEY KEPT CUTTING.
"AND CUTTING.
"AND CUTTING.
"THEY TORTURED HIM FOR WEEKS--AN ETERNITY TO MANUEL. HE WAS READY TO GIVE UP. HE WANTED TO DIE.
"BUT SOMETHING INSIDE HIM REFUSED.
"WE SHARED THE SAME MEMORIES AND A PSYCHIC LINK TO ONE ANOTHER--YET POSSESSED OUR OWN DISTINCT THOUGHTS AND PERSONALITIES. WE COULD REGENERATE LIKE HE COULD, BUT COULDN'T CREATE NEW LIFE AS HE DID.
"INSTEAD, WE BOUND TO E OTHER--PARTS A GREATER W

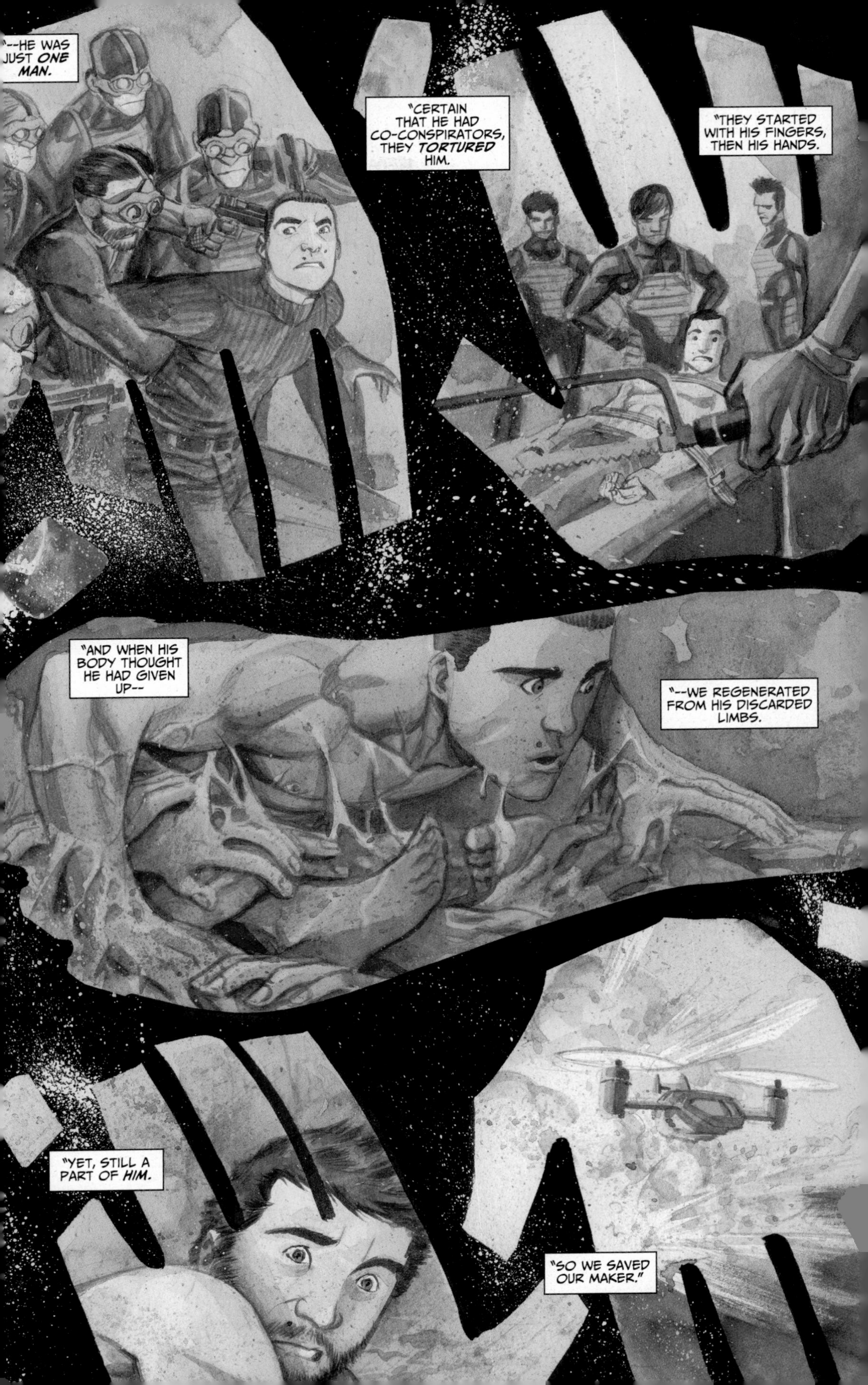
"--HE WAS JUST ONE MAN.
"CERTAIN THAT HE HAD CO-CONSPIRATORS, THEY TORTURED HIM.
"THEY STARTED WITH HIS FINGERS, THEN HIS HANDS.
"AND WHEN HIS BODY THOUGHT HE HAD GIVEN UP--
"--WE REGENERATED FROM HIS DISCARDED LIMBS.
"YET, STILL A PART OF HIM.
"SO WE SAVED OUR MAKER."

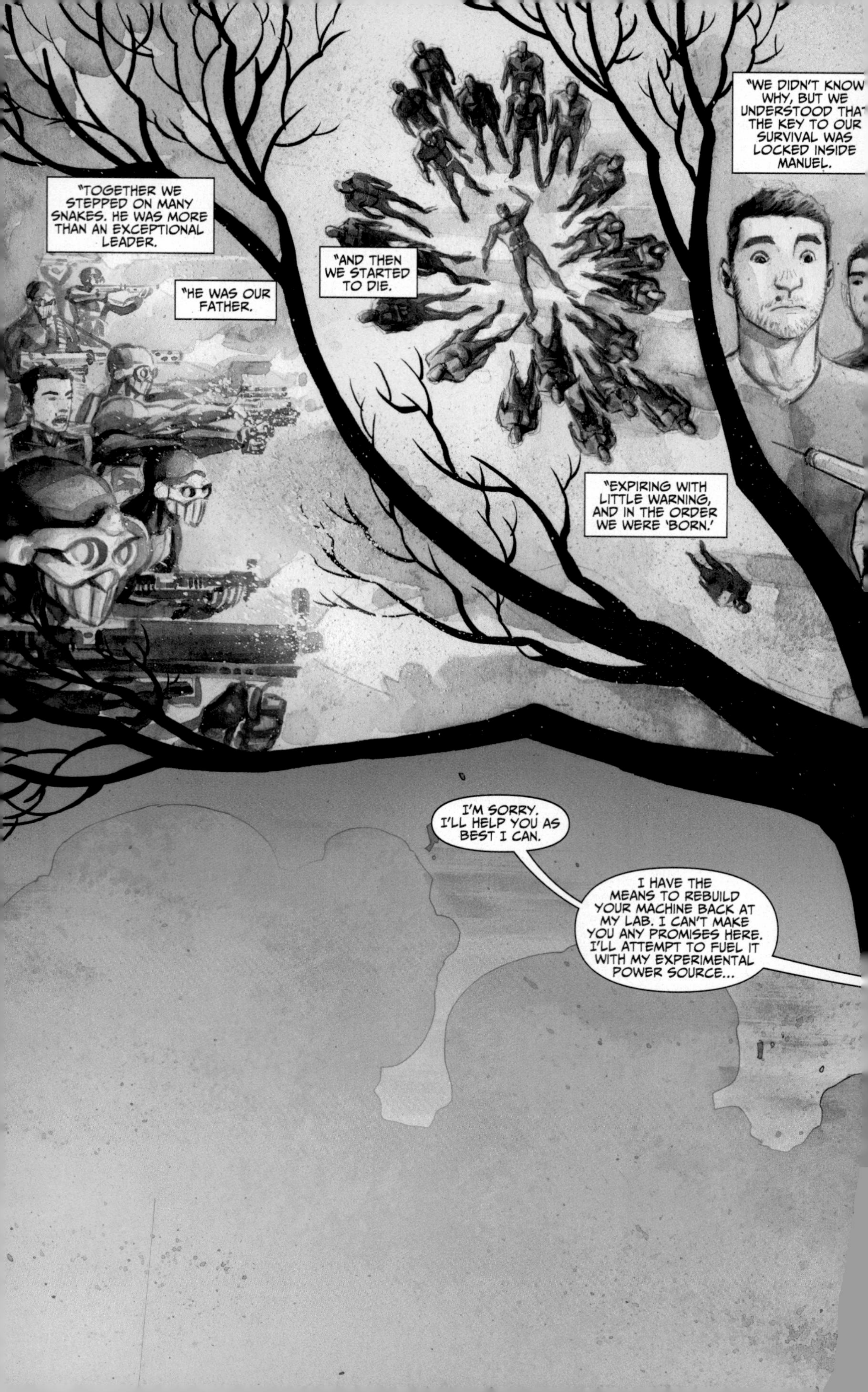
"TOGETHER WE STEPPED ON MANY SNAKES. HE WAS MORE THAN AN EXCEPTIONAL LEADER.
"HE WAS OUR FATHER.
"AND THEN WE STARTED TO DIE.
"EXPIRING WITH LITTLE WARNING, AND IN THE ORDER WE WERE 'BORN.'
"WE DIDN'T KNOW WHY, BUT WE UNDERSTOOD THAT THE KEY TO OUR SURVIVAL WAS LOCKED INSIDE MANUEL.
I'M SORRY. I'LL HELP YOU AS BEST I CAN.
I HAVE THE MEANS TO REBUILD YOUR MACHINE BACK AT MY LAB. I CAN'T MAKE YOU ANY PROMISES HERE. I'LL ATTEMPT TO FUEL IT WITH MY EXPERIMENTAL POWER SOURCE...

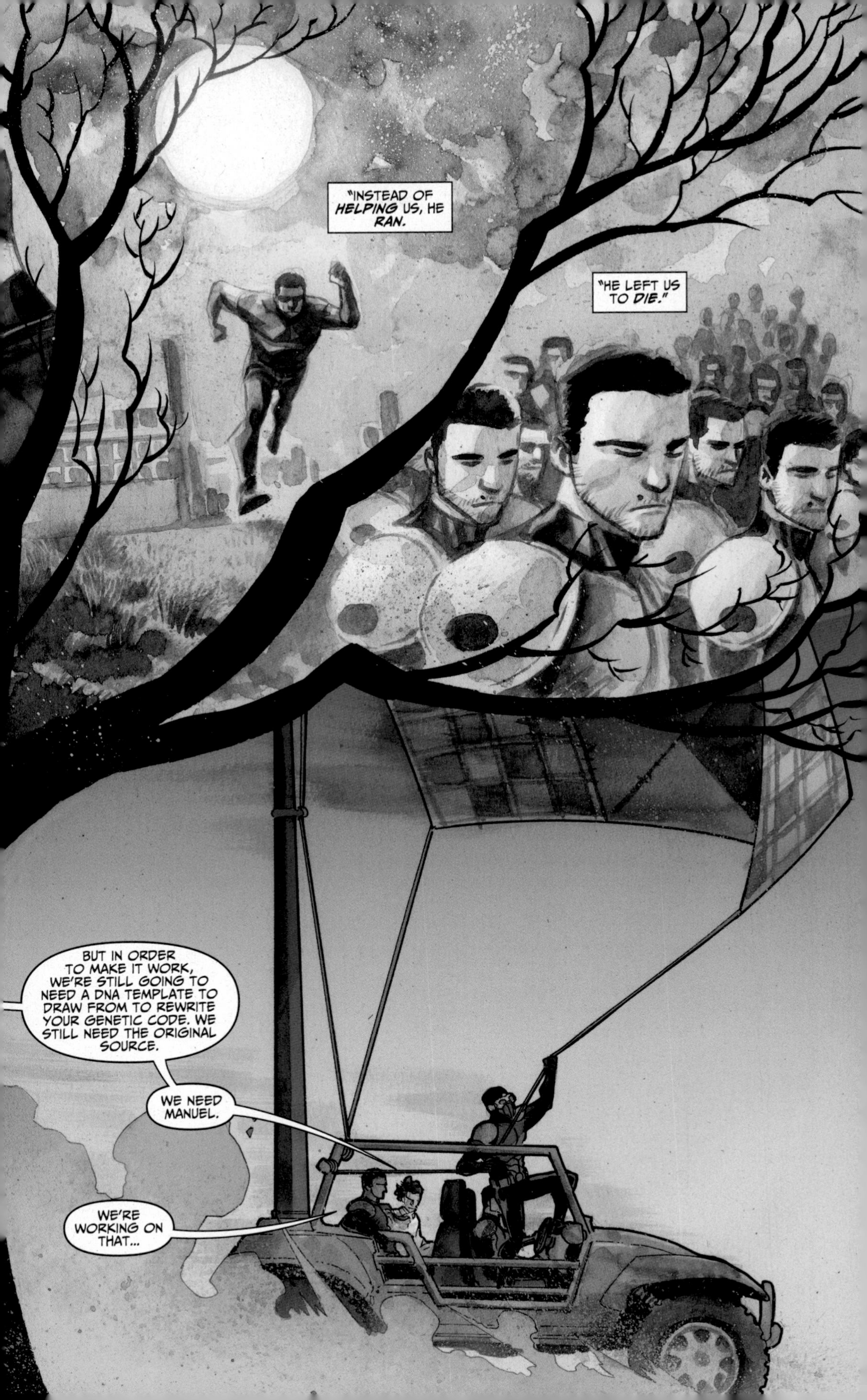
"INSTEAD OF HELPING US, HE RAN.
"HE LEFT US TO DIE."
BUT IN ORDER TO MAKE IT WORK, WE'RE STILL GOING TO NEED A DNA TEMPLATE TO DRAW FROM TO REWRITE YOUR GENETIC CODE. WE STILL NEED THE ORIGINAL SOURCE.
WE NEED MANUEL.
WE'RE WORKING ON THAT...

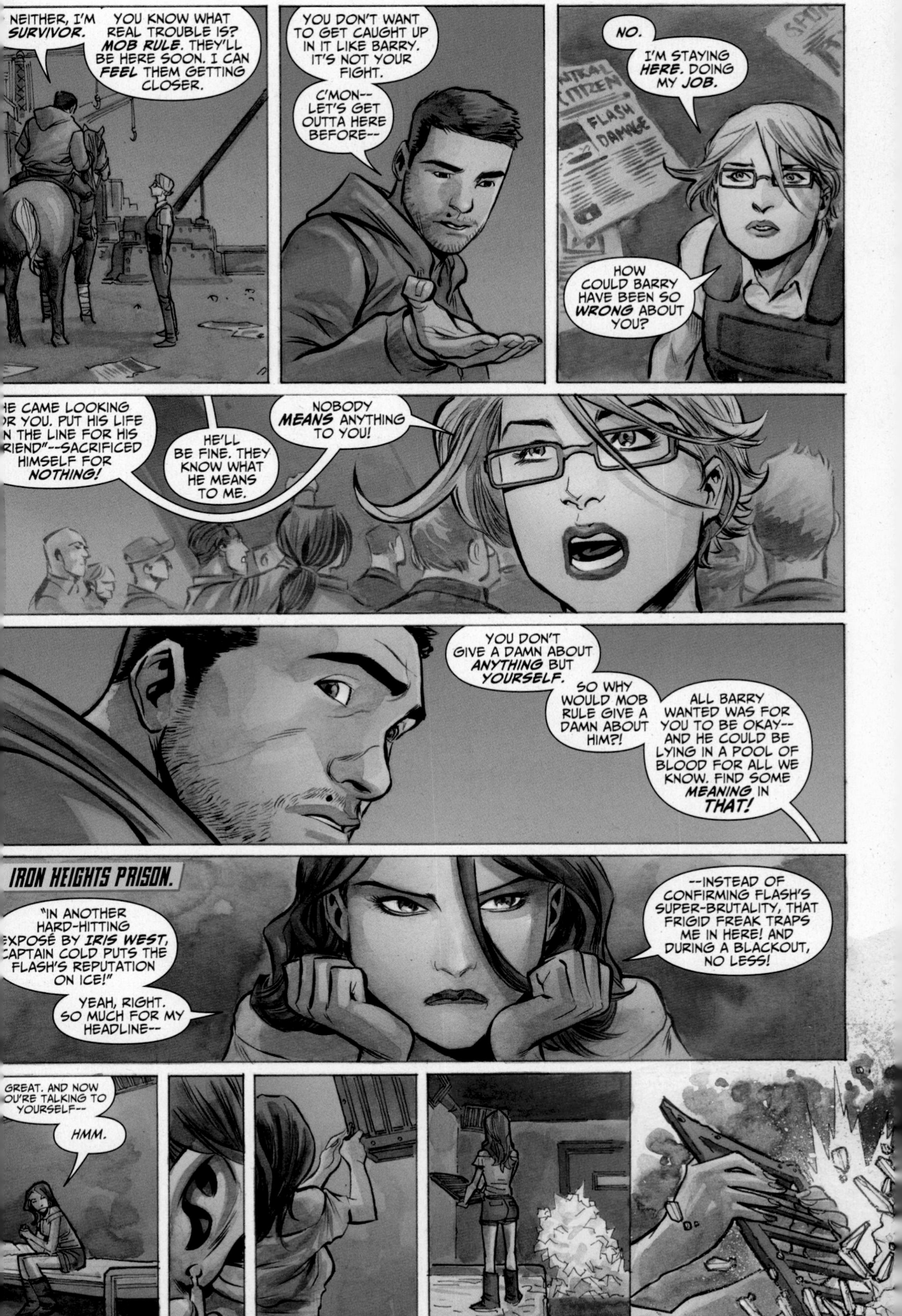
NEITHER, I'M SURVIVOR.
YOU KNOW WHAT REAL TROUBLE IS? MOB RULE. THEY'LL BE HERE SOON. I CAN FEEL THEM GETTING CLOSER.
YOU DON'T WANT TO GET CAUGHT UP IN IT LIKE BARRY. IT'S NOT YOUR FIGHT.
C'MON-- LET'S GET OUTTA HERE BEFORE--
NO.
I'M STAYING HERE. DOING MY JOB.
HOW COULD BARRY HAVE BEEN SO WRONG ABOUT YOU?
FLASH DAMAGE
HE CAME LOOKING FOR YOU. PUT HIS LIFE ON THE LINE FOR HIS "FRIEND"--SACRIFICED HIMSELF FOR NOTHING!
HE'LL BE FINE. THEY KNOW WHAT HE MEANS TO ME.
NOBODY MEANS ANYTHING TO YOU!
YOU DON'T GIVE A DAMN ABOUT ANYTHING BUT YOURSELF.
SO WHY WOULD MOB RULE GIVE A DAMN ABOUT HIM?!
ALL BARRY WANTED WAS FOR YOU TO BE OKAY-- AND HE COULD BE LYING IN A POOL OF BLOOD FOR ALL WE KNOW. FIND SOME MEANING IN THAT!
IRON HEIGHTS PRISON.
"IN ANOTHER HARD-HITTING EXPOSÉ BY IRIS WEST, CAPTAIN COLD PUTS THE FLASH'S REPUTATION ON ICE!"
YEAH, RIGHT. SO MUCH FOR MY HEADLINE--
--INSTEAD OF CONFIRMING FLASH'S SUPER-BRUTALITY, THAT FRIGID FREAK TRAPS ME IN HERE! AND DURING A BLACKOUT, NO LESS!
GREAT. AND NOW YOU'RE TALKING TO YOURSELF--
HMM.

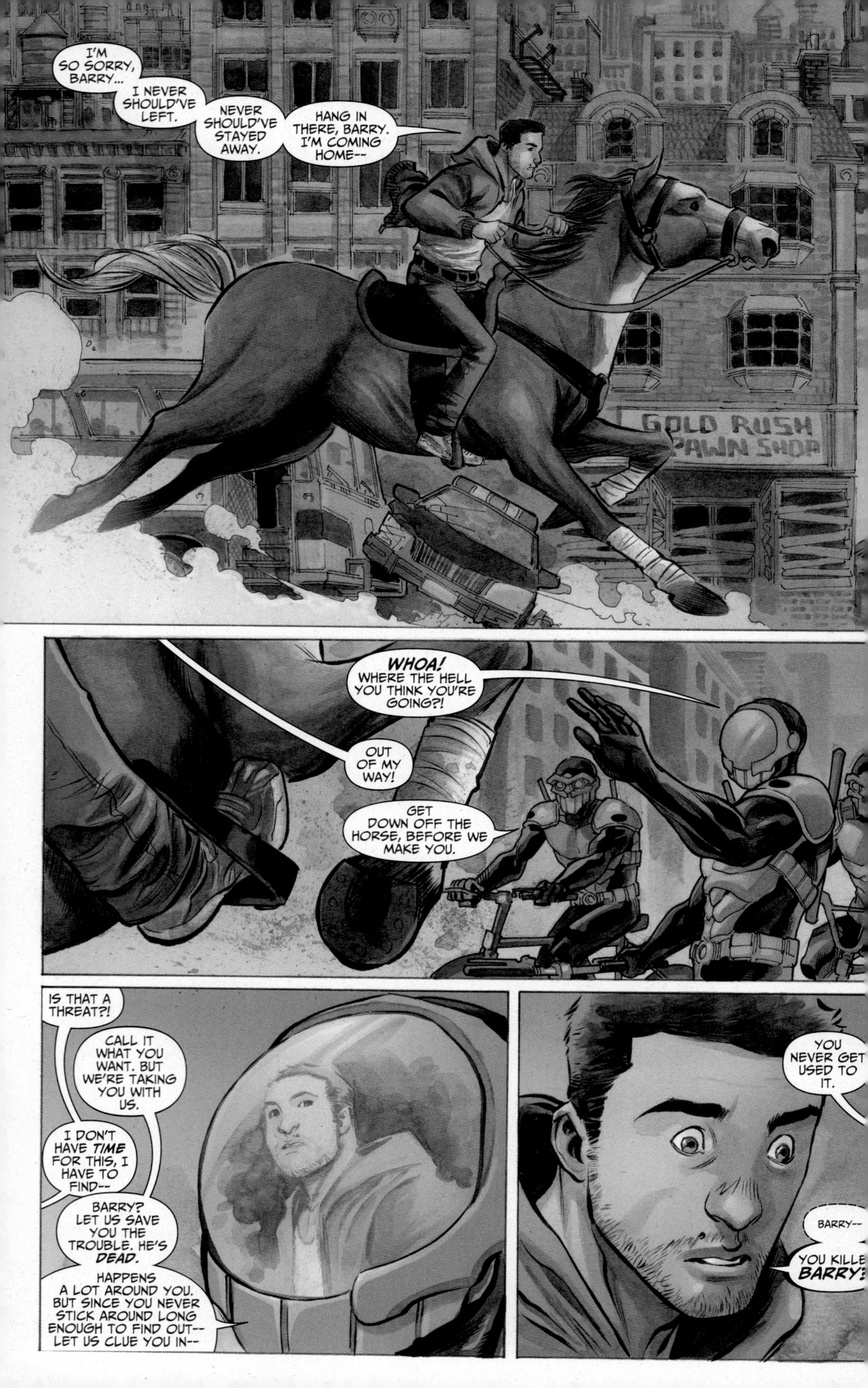
I'M SO SORRY, BARRY...
I NEVER SHOULD'VE LEFT.
NEVER SHOULD'VE STAYED AWAY.
HANG IN THERE, BARRY. I'M COMING HOME--
GOLD RUSH PAWN SHOP
WHOA! WHERE THE HELL YOU THINK YOU'RE GOING?!
OUT OF MY WAY!
GET DOWN OFF THE HORSE, BEFORE WE MAKE YOU.
IS THAT A THREAT?!
CALL IT WHAT YOU WANT. BUT WE'RE TAKING YOU WITH US.
I DON'T HAVE *TIME* FOR THIS, I HAVE TO FIND--
BARRY? LET US SAVE YOU THE TROUBLE. HE'S *DEAD.*
HAPPENS A LOT AROUND YOU. BUT SINCE YOU NEVER STICK AROUND LONG ENOUGH TO FIND OUT-- LET US CLUE YOU IN--
YOU NEVER GET USED TO IT.
BARRY--
YOU KILLE *BARRY*

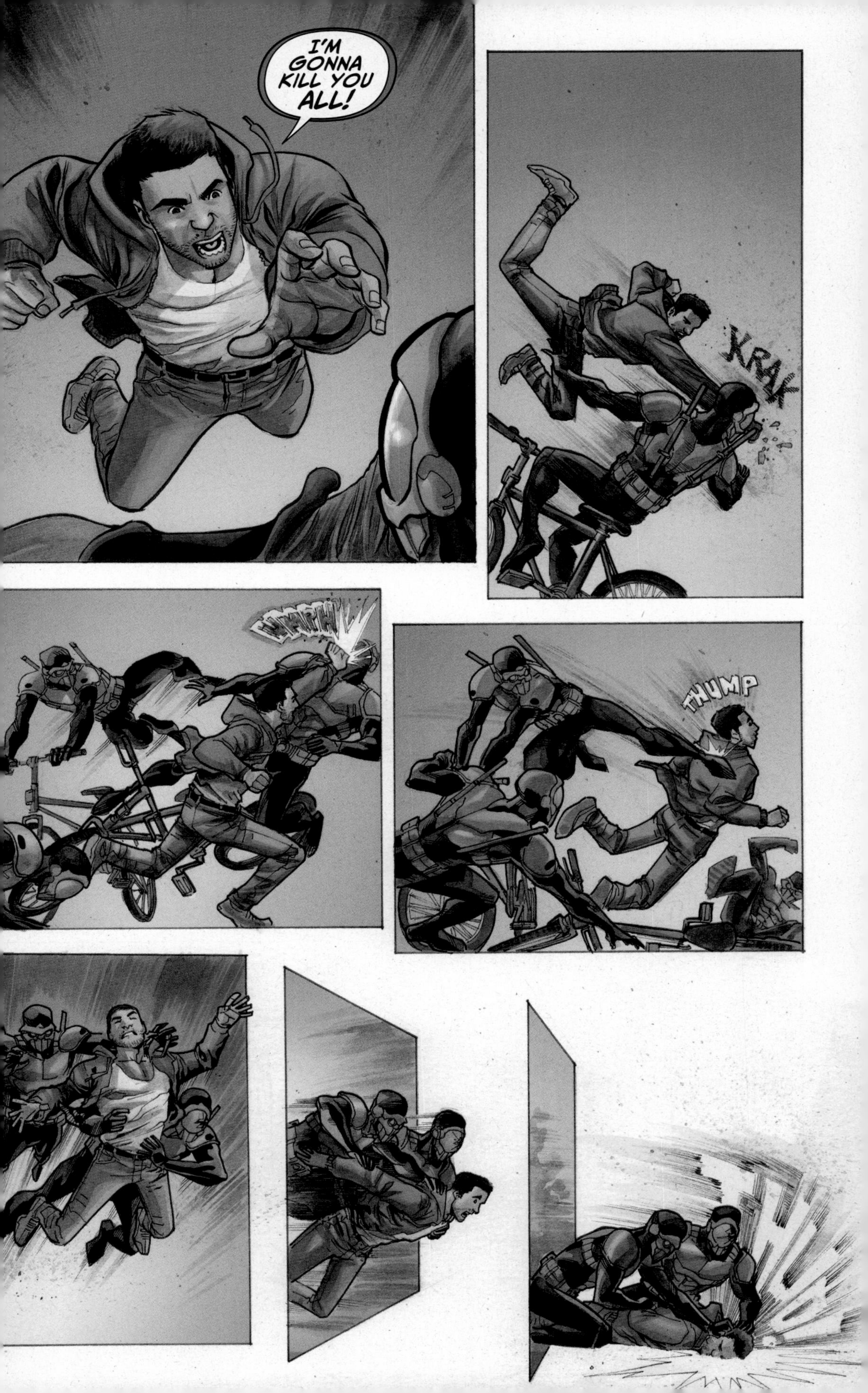
I'M GONNA KILL YOU ALL!
KRAK
THUMP

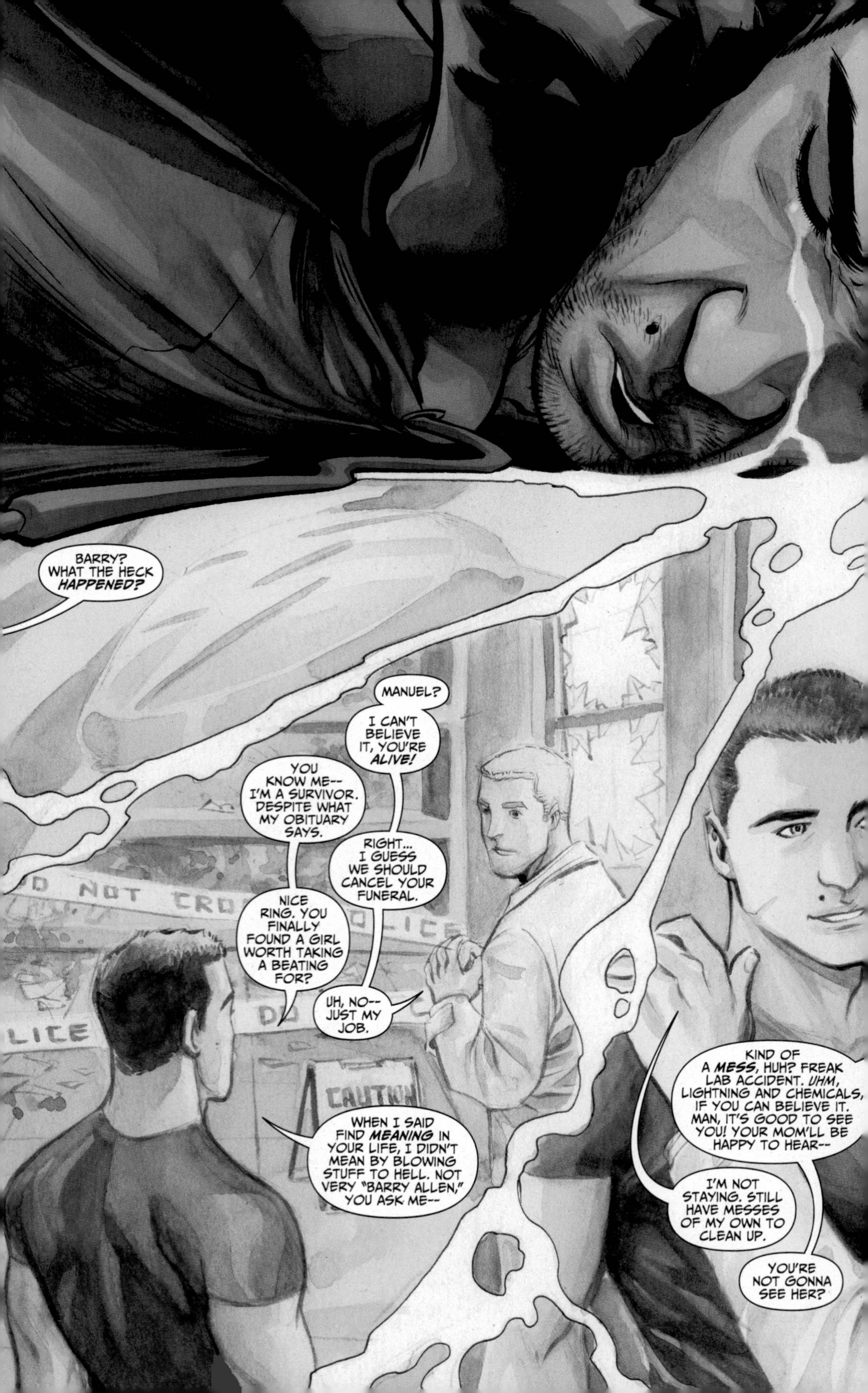
BARRY? WHAT THE HECK *HAPPENED?*
MANUEL?
I CAN'T BELIEVE IT, YOU'RE *ALIVE!*
YOU KNOW ME-- I'M A SURVIVOR. DESPITE WHAT MY OBITUARY SAYS.
RIGHT... I GUESS WE SHOULD CANCEL YOUR FUNERAL.
NICE RING. YOU FINALLY FOUND A GIRL WORTH TAKING A BEATING FOR?
UH, NO-- JUST MY JOB.
DO NOT CRO
POLICE
CAUTION
KIND OF A *MESS*, HUH? FREAK LAB ACCIDENT. *UHM*, LIGHTNING AND CHEMICALS, IF YOU CAN BELIEVE IT. MAN, IT'S GOOD TO SEE YOU! YOUR MOM'LL BE HAPPY TO HEAR--
WHEN I SAID FIND *MEANING* IN YOUR LIFE, I DIDN'T MEAN BY BLOWING STUFF TO HELL. NOT VERY "BARRY ALLEN," YOU ASK ME--
I'M NOT STAYING. STILL HAVE MESSES OF MY OWN TO CLEAN UP.
YOU'RE NOT GONNA SEE HER?

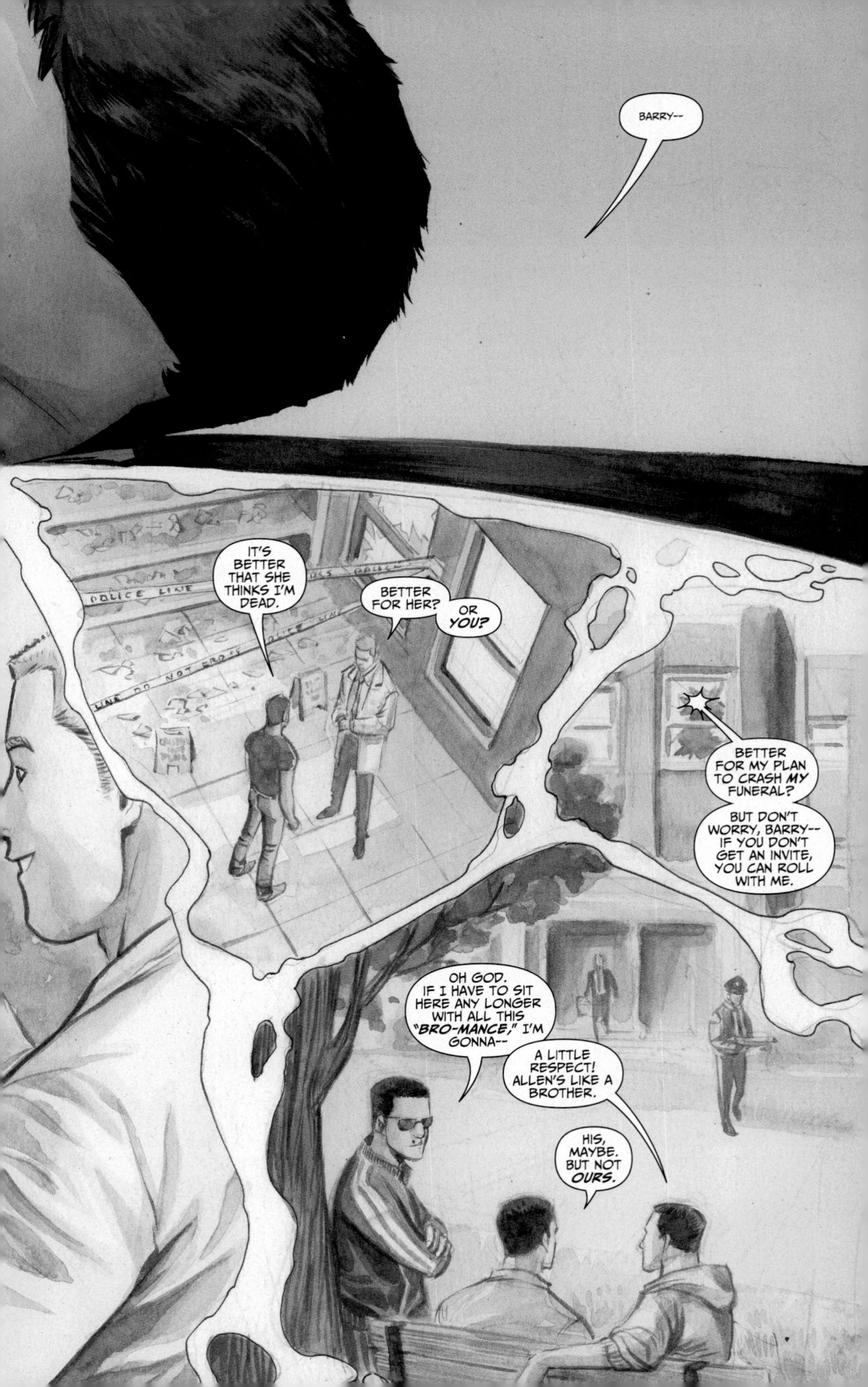
BARRY--
IT'S BETTER THAT SHE THINKS I'M DEAD.
BETTER FOR HER? OR YOU?
BETTER FOR MY PLAN TO CRASH MY FUNERAL?
BUT DON'T WORRY, BARRY-- IF YOU DON'T GET AN INVITE, YOU CAN ROLL WITH ME.
OH GOD. IF I HAVE TO SIT HERE ANY LONGER WITH ALL THIS "BRO-MANCE," I'M GONNA--
A LITTLE RESPECT! ALLEN'S LIKE A BROTHER.
HIS, MAYBE. BUT NOT OURS.
POLICE LINE
DO NOT CROSS

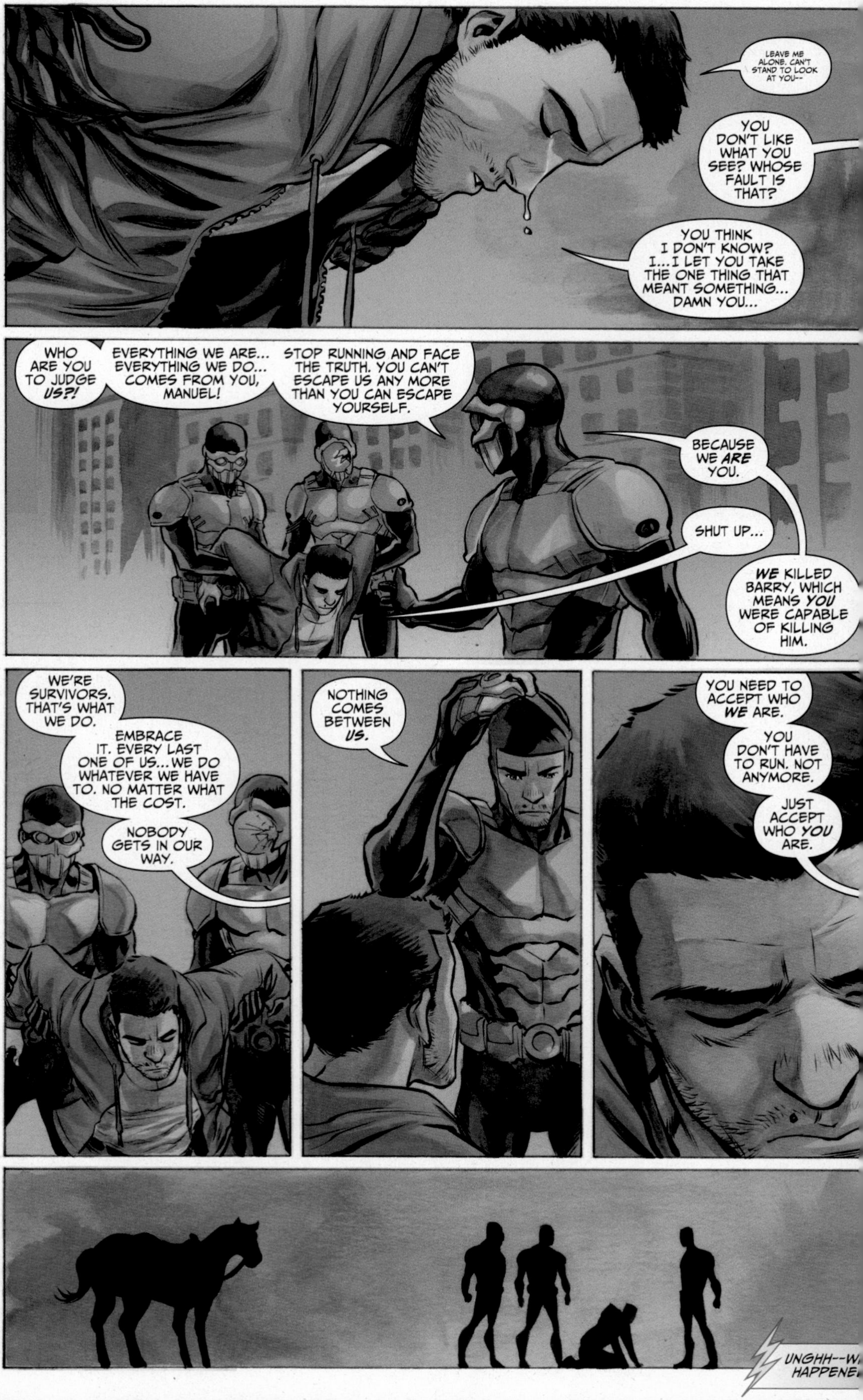
LEAVE ME ALONE. CAN'T STAND TO LOOK AT YOU--
YOU DON'T LIKE WHAT YOU SEE? WHOSE FAULT IS THAT?
YOU THINK I DON'T KNOW? I...I LET YOU TAKE THE ONE THING THAT MEANT SOMETHING... DAMN YOU...
WHO ARE YOU TO JUDGE US?!
EVERYTHING WE ARE... EVERYTHING WE DO... COMES FROM YOU, MANUEL!
STOP RUNNING AND FACE THE TRUTH. YOU CAN'T ESCAPE US ANY MORE THAN YOU CAN ESCAPE YOURSELF.
BECAUSE WE ARE YOU.
SHUT UP...
WE KILLED BARRY, WHICH MEANS YOU WERE CAPABLE OF KILLING HIM.
WE'RE SURVIVORS. THAT'S WHAT WE DO.
EMBRACE IT. EVERY LAST ONE OF US...WE DO WHATEVER WE HAVE TO. NO MATTER WHAT THE COST.
NOBODY GETS IN OUR WAY.
NOTHING COMES BETWEEN US.
YOU NEED TO ACCEPT WHO WE ARE.
YOU DON'T HAVE TO RUN. NOT ANYMORE.
JUST ACCEPT WHO YOU ARE.
UNGHH--W HAPPENE

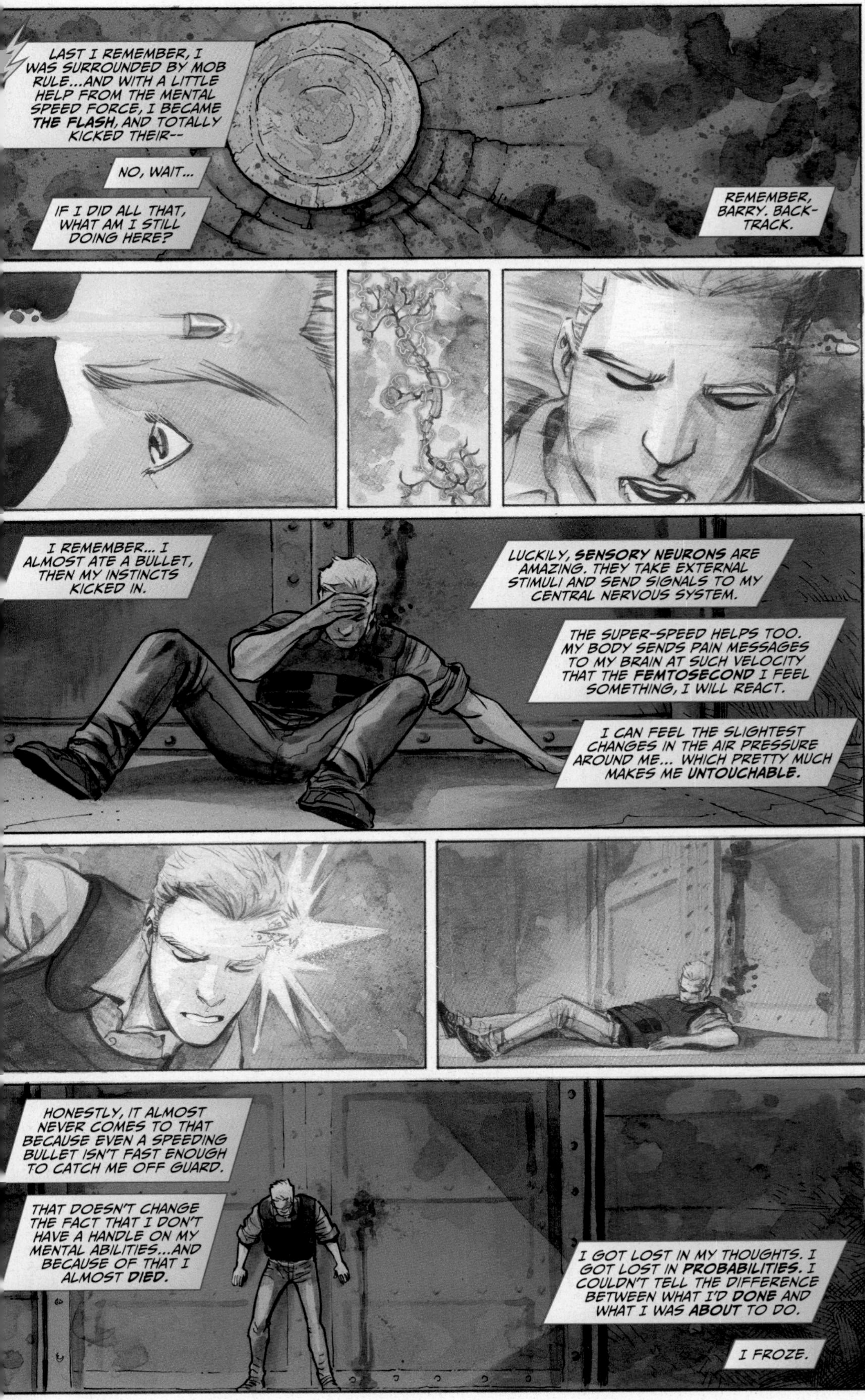
LAST I REMEMBER, I WAS SURROUNDED BY MOB RULE...AND WITH A LITTLE HELP FROM THE MENTAL SPEED FORCE, I BECAME THE FLASH, AND TOTALLY KICKED THEIR--
NO, WAIT...
IF I DID ALL THAT, WHAT AM I STILL DOING HERE?
REMEMBER, BARRY. BACK-TRACK.
I REMEMBER... I ALMOST ATE A BULLET, THEN MY INSTINCTS KICKED IN.
LUCKILY, SENSORY NEURONS ARE AMAZING. THEY TAKE EXTERNAL STIMULI AND SEND SIGNALS TO MY CENTRAL NERVOUS SYSTEM.
THE SUPER-SPEED HELPS TOO. MY BODY SENDS PAIN MESSAGES TO MY BRAIN AT SUCH VELOCITY THAT THE FEMTOSECOND I FEEL SOMETHING, I WILL REACT.
I CAN FEEL THE SLIGHTEST CHANGES IN THE AIR PRESSURE AROUND ME... WHICH PRETTY MUCH MAKES ME UNTOUCHABLE.
HONESTLY, IT ALMOST NEVER COMES TO THAT BECAUSE EVEN A SPEEDING BULLET ISN'T FAST ENOUGH TO CATCH ME OFF GUARD.
THAT DOESN'T CHANGE THE FACT THAT I DON'T HAVE A HANDLE ON MY MENTAL ABILITIES...AND BECAUSE OF THAT I ALMOST DIED.
I GOT LOST IN MY THOUGHTS. I GOT LOST IN PROBABILITIES. I COULDN'T TELL THE DIFFERENCE BETWEEN WHAT I'D DONE AND WHAT I WAS ABOUT TO DO.
I FROZE.

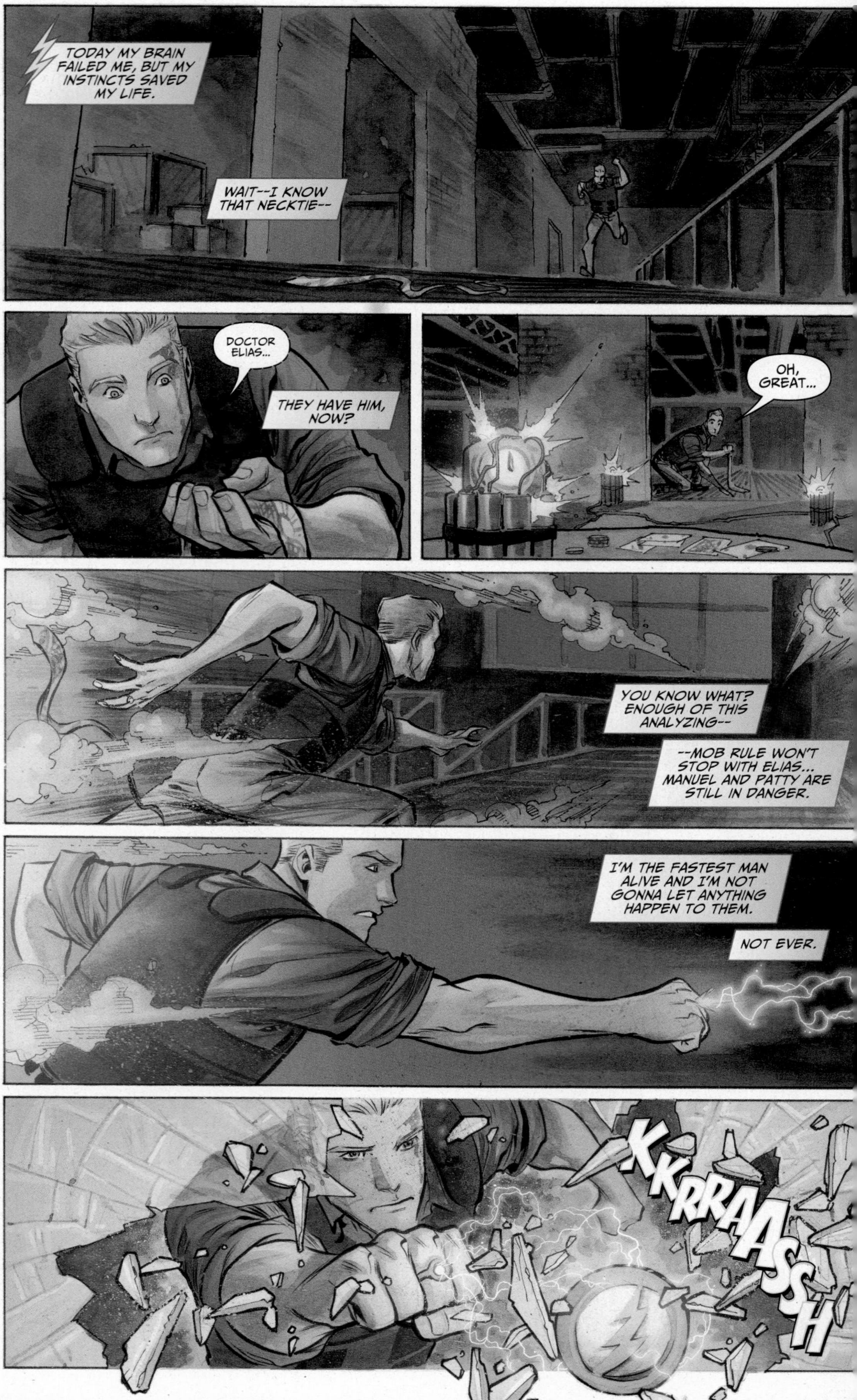
TODAY MY BRAIN FAILED ME, BUT MY INSTINCTS SAVED MY LIFE.
WAIT--I KNOW THAT NECKTIE--
DOCTOR ELIAS...
THEY HAVE HIM, NOW?
OH, GREAT...
YOU KNOW WHAT? ENOUGH OF THIS ANALYZING--
--MOB RULE WON'T STOP WITH ELIAS... MANUEL AND PATTY ARE STILL IN DANGER.
I'M THE FASTEST MAN ALIVE AND I'M NOT GONNA LET ANYTHING HAPPEN TO THEM.
NOT EVER.
KKRRAASSH

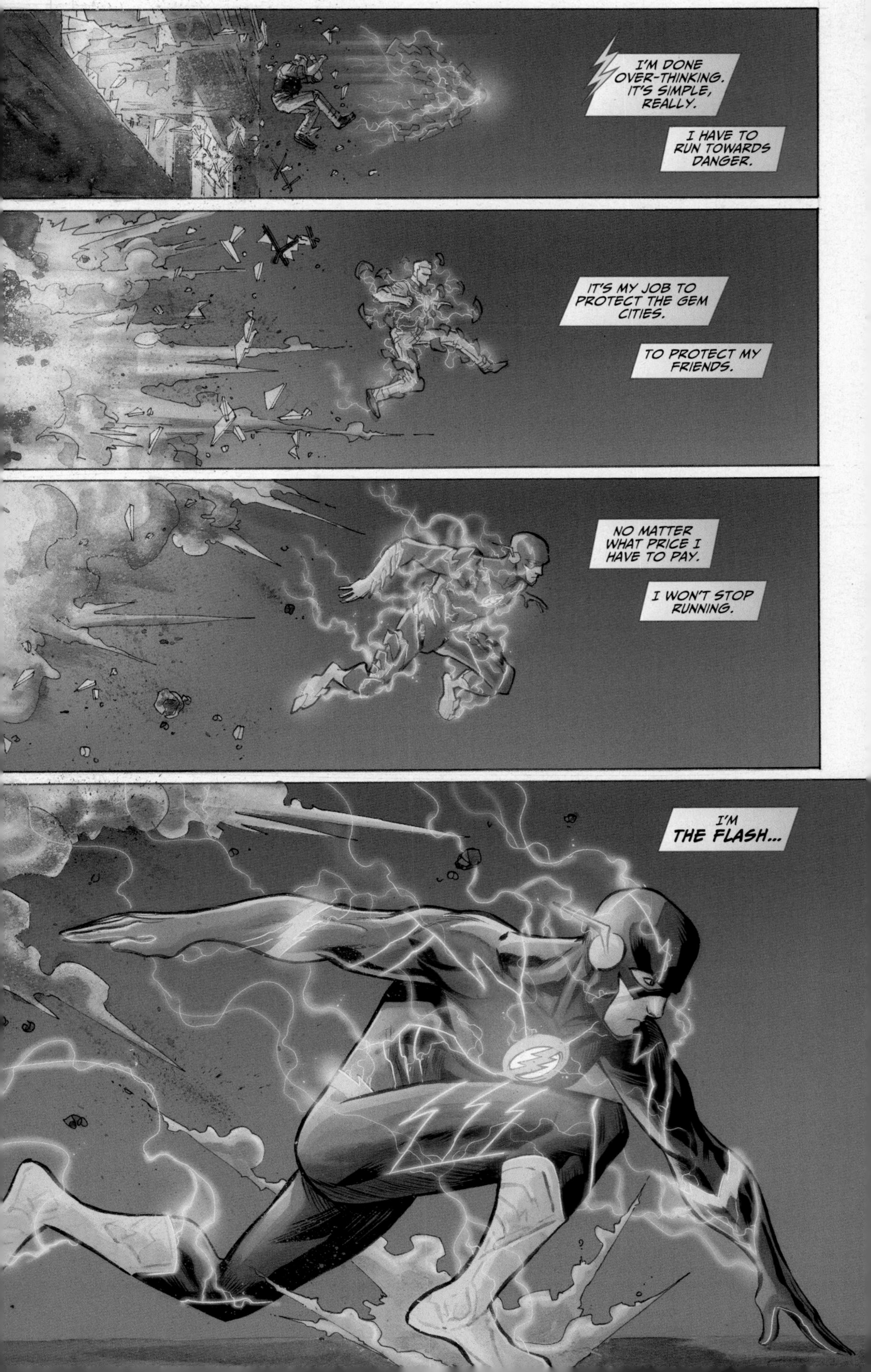
I'M DONE OVER-THINKING. IT'S SIMPLE, REALLY.
I HAVE TO RUN TOWARDS DANGER.
IT'S MY JOB TO PROTECT THE GEM CITIES.
TO PROTECT MY FRIENDS.
NO MATTER WHAT PRICE I HAVE TO PAY.
I WON'T STOP RUNNING.
I'M THE FLASH...

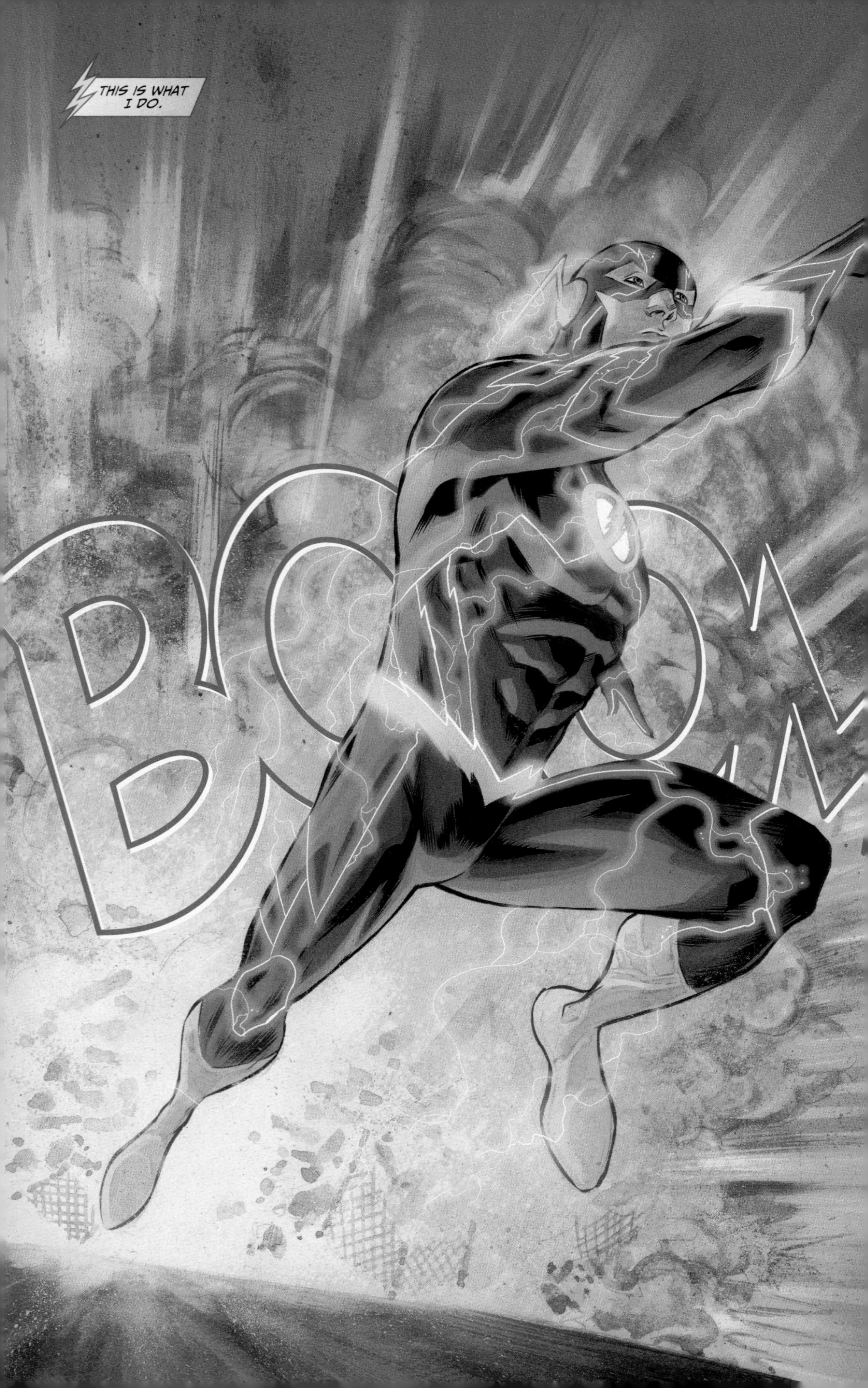
THIS IS WHAT I DO.
BOOM

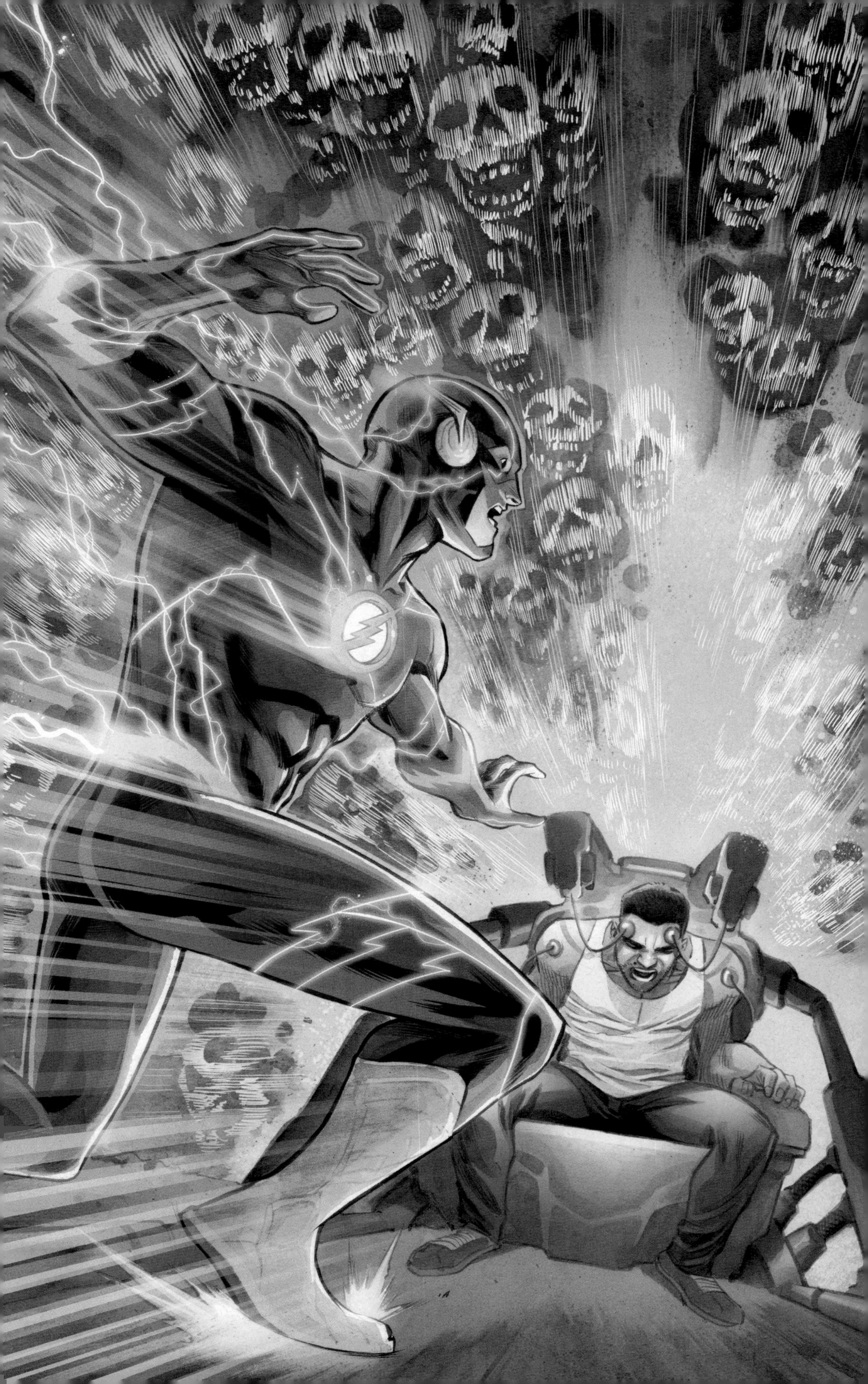

THE FLASH #5

variant cover by GARY FRANK & BRAD ANDERSON

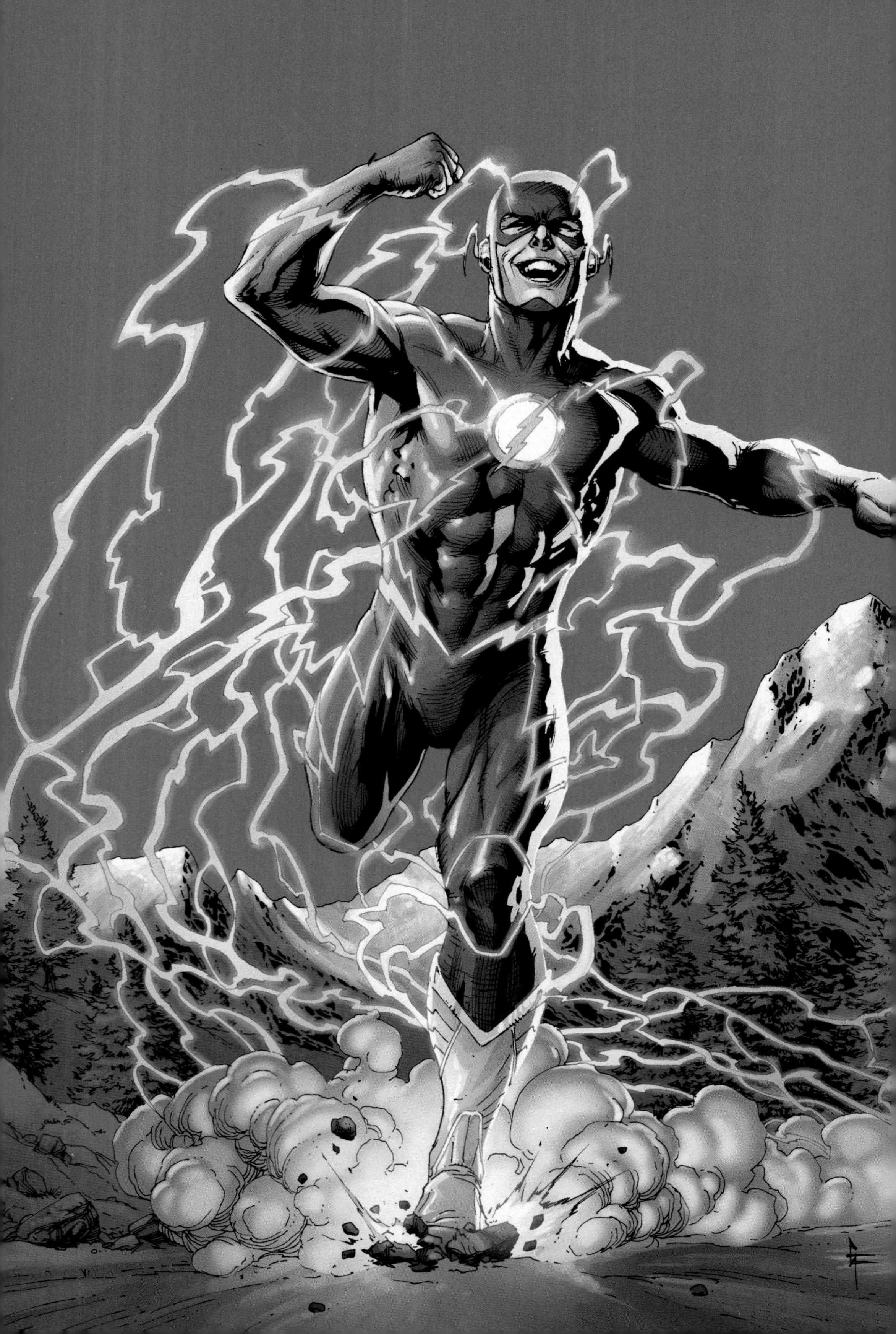

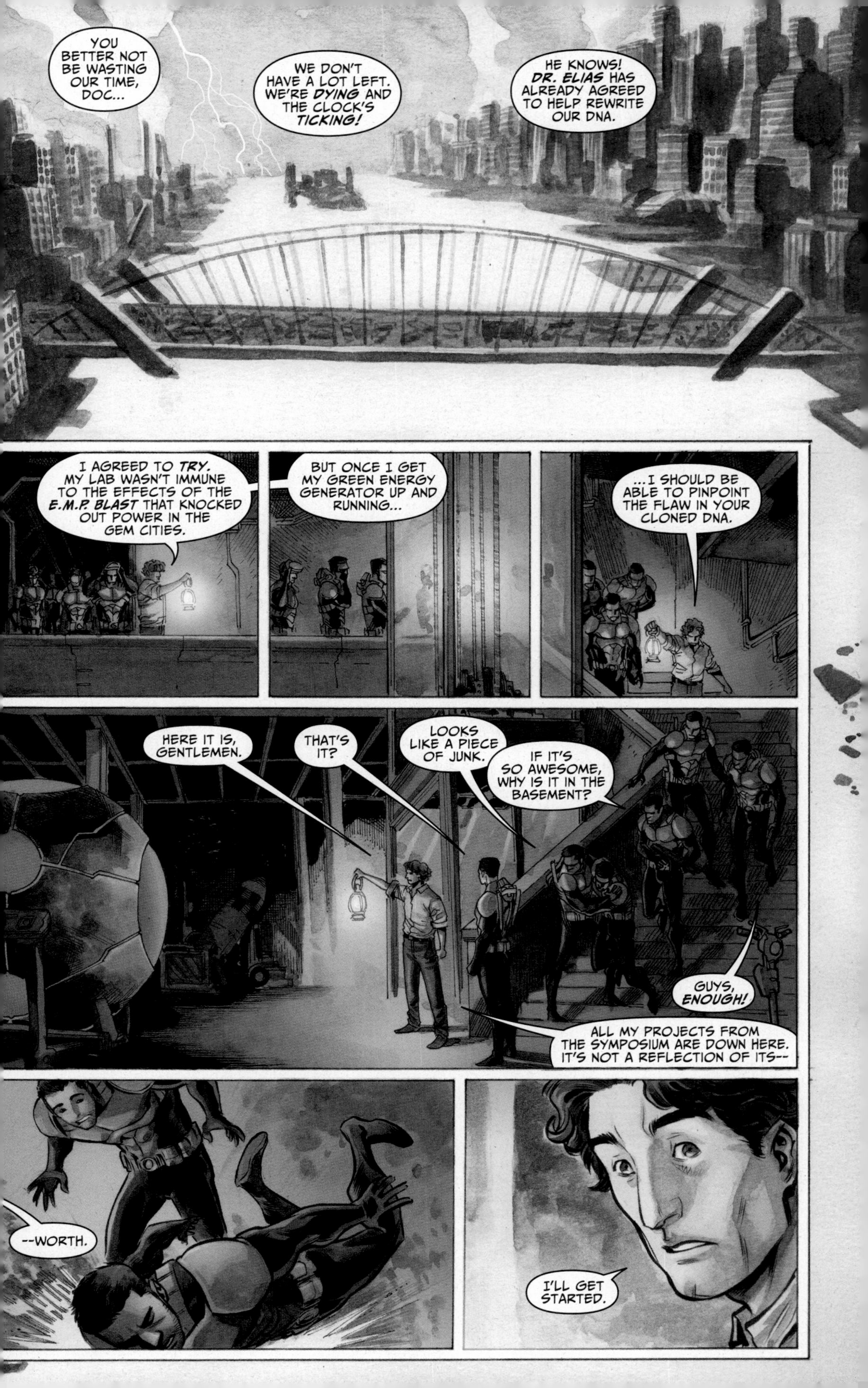
YOU BETTER NOT BE WASTING OUR TIME, DOC...
WE DON'T HAVE A LOT LEFT. WE'RE DYING AND THE CLOCK'S TICKING!
HE KNOWS! DR. ELIAS HAS ALREADY AGREED TO HELP REWRITE OUR DNA.
I AGREED TO TRY. MY LAB WASN'T IMMUNE TO THE EFFECTS OF THE E.M.P. BLAST THAT KNOCKED OUT POWER IN THE GEM CITIES.
BUT ONCE I GET MY GREEN ENERGY GENERATOR UP AND RUNNING...
...I SHOULD BE ABLE TO PINPOINT THE FLAW IN YOUR CLONED DNA.
HERE IT IS, GENTLEMEN.
THAT'S IT?
LOOKS LIKE A PIECE OF JUNK.
IF IT'S SO AWESOME, WHY IS IT IN THE BASEMENT?
GUYS, ENOUGH!
ALL MY PROJECTS FROM THE SYMPOSIUM ARE DOWN HERE. IT'S NOT A REFLECTION OF ITS--
--WORTH.
I'LL GET STARTED.

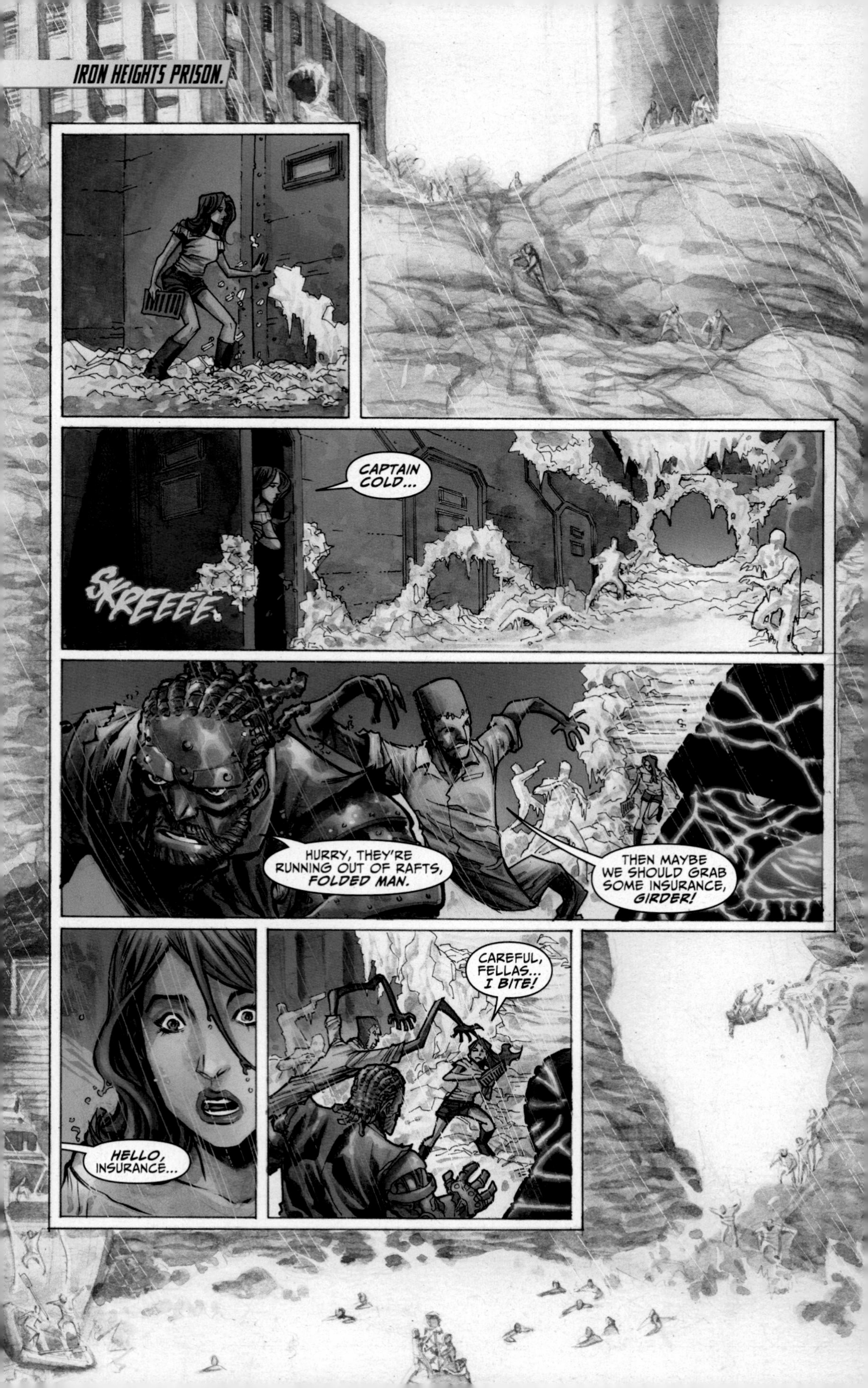
IRON HEIGHTS PRISON.
CAPTAIN COLD...
SKREEEEE
HURRY, THEY'RE RUNNING OUT OF RAFTS, FOLDED MAN.
THEN MAYBE WE SHOULD GRAB SOME INSURANCE, GIRDER!
HELLO, INSURANCE...
CAREFUL, FELLAS... I BITE!

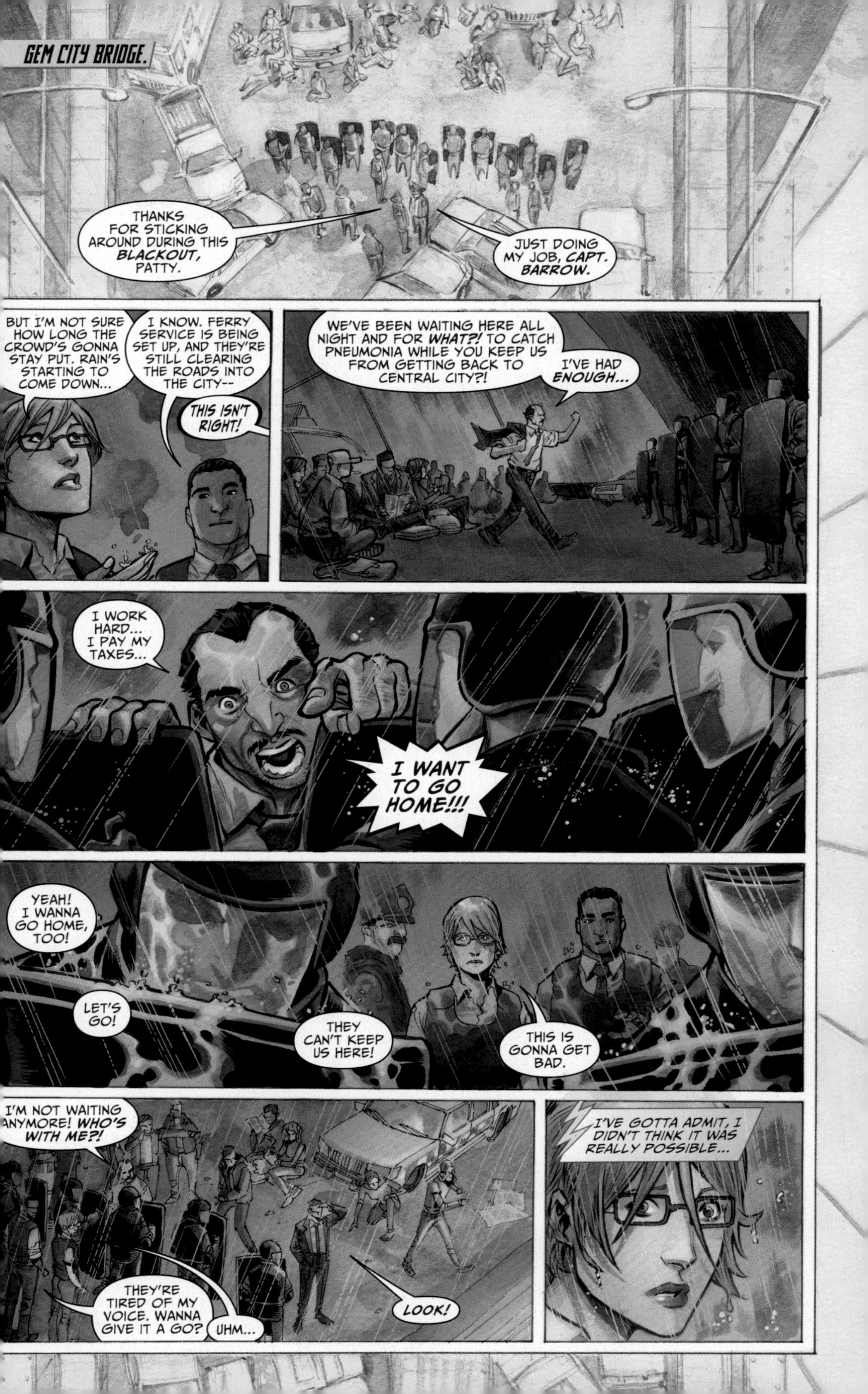
GEM CITY BRIDGE.
THANKS FOR STICKING AROUND DURING THIS BLACKOUT, PATTY.
JUST DOING MY JOB, CAPT. BARROW.
BUT I'M NOT SURE HOW LONG THE CROWD'S GONNA STAY PUT. RAIN'S STARTING TO COME DOWN...
I KNOW. FERRY SERVICE IS BEING SET UP, AND THEY'RE STILL CLEARING THE ROADS INTO THE CITY--
THIS ISN'T RIGHT!
WE'VE BEEN WAITING HERE ALL NIGHT AND FOR WHAT?! TO CATCH PNEUMONIA WHILE YOU KEEP US FROM GETTING BACK TO CENTRAL CITY?!
I'VE HAD ENOUGH...
I WORK HARD... I PAY MY TAXES...
I WANT TO GO HOME!!!
YEAH! I WANNA GO HOME, TOO!
LET'S GO!
THEY CAN'T KEEP US HERE!
THIS IS GONNA GET BAD.
I'M NOT WAITING ANYMORE! WHO'S WITH ME?!
THEY'RE TIRED OF MY VOICE. WANNA GIVE IT A GO?
UHM...
LOOK!
I'VE GOTTA ADMIT, I DIDN'T THINK IT WAS REALLY POSSIBLE...

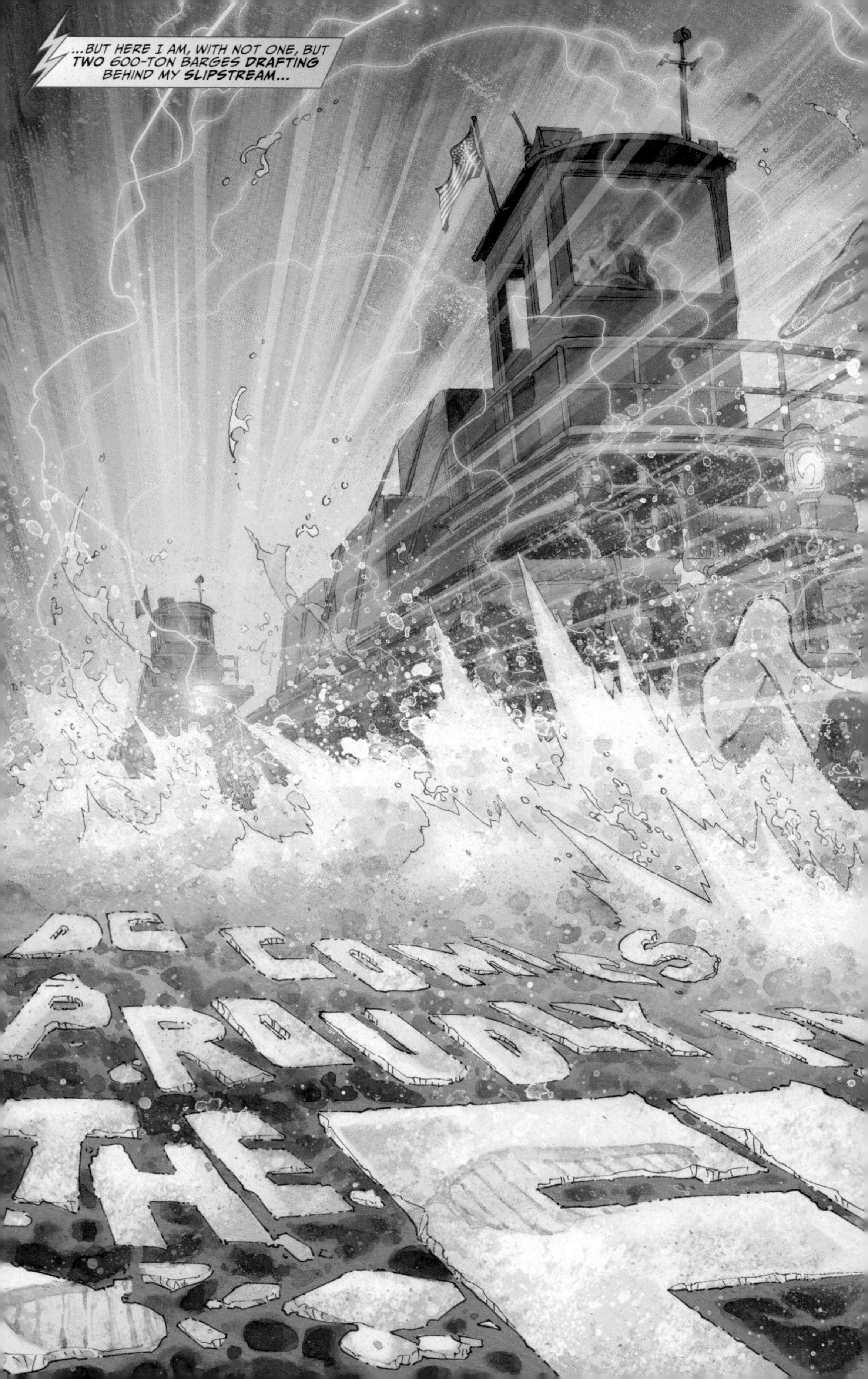
...BUT HERE I AM, WITH NOT ONE, BUT TWO 600-TON BARGES DRAFTING BEHIND MY SLIPSTREAM...
DC COMICS
PROUDLY
THE

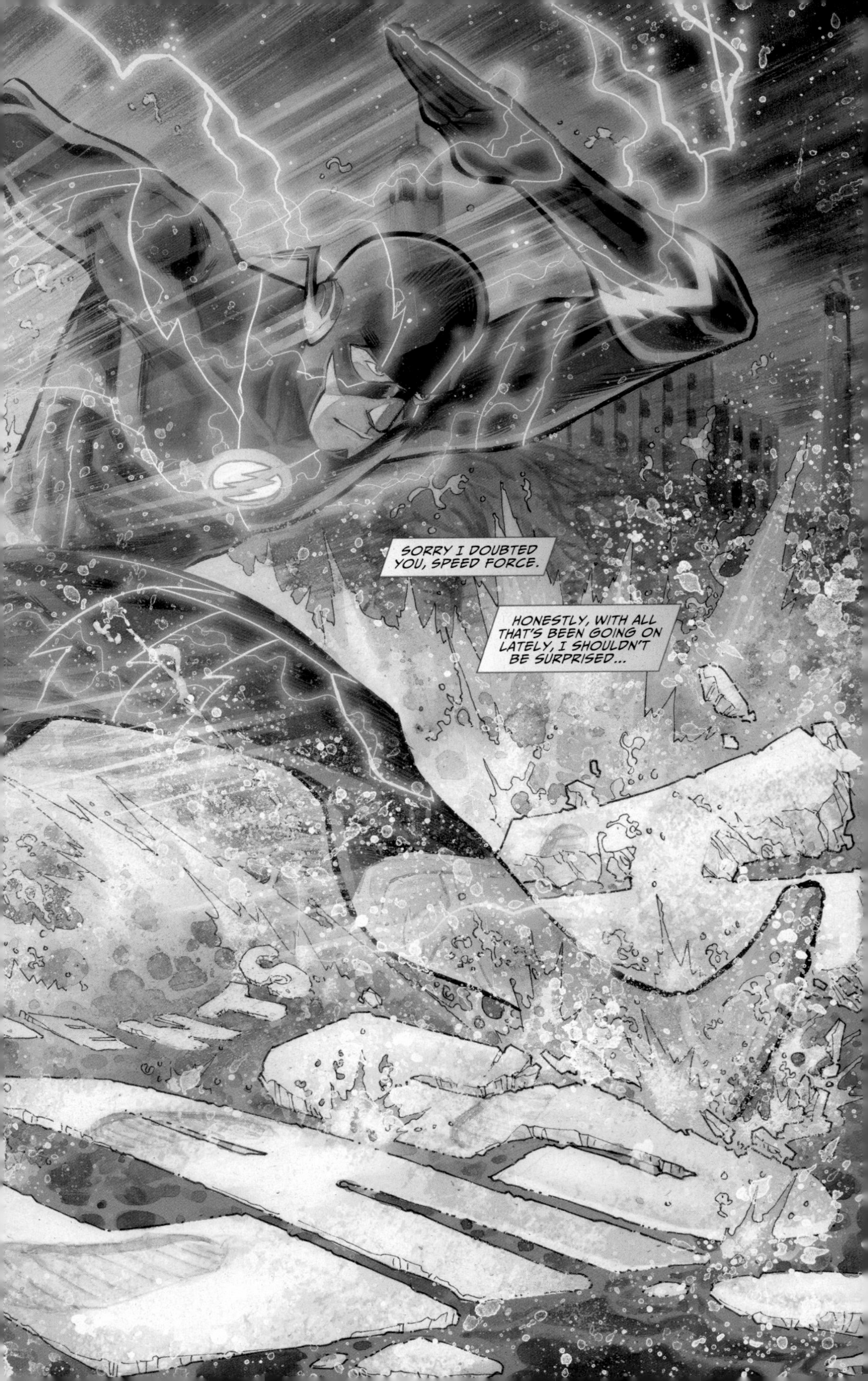
SORRY I DOUBTED YOU, SPEED FORCE.
HONESTLY, WITH ALL THAT'S BEEN GOING ON LATELY, I SHOULDN'T BE SURPRISED...

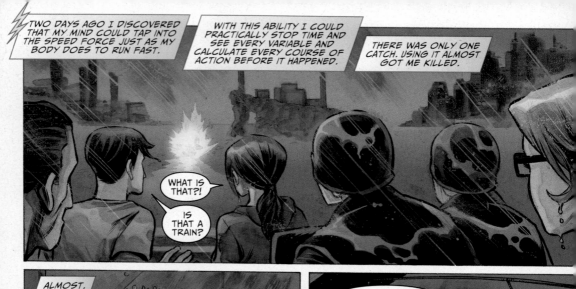

TWO DAYS AGO I DISCOVERED THAT MY MIND COULD TAP INTO THE SPEED FORCE JUST AS MY BODY DOES TO RUN FAST.

WITH THIS ABILITY I COULD PRACTICALLY STOP TIME AND SEE EVERY VARIABLE AND CALCULATE EVERY COURSE OF ACTION BEFORE IT HAPPENED.

THERE WAS ONLY ONE CATCH. USING IT ALMOST GOT ME KILLED.

WHAT IS THAT?!

IS THAT A TRAIN?

ALMOST.

SPECIAL DELIVERY FROM *WAYNE ENTERPRISES!*

OFFICERS, THESE BARGES ARE STOCKED WITH SUPPLIES, GENERATORS AND EMERGENCY VEHICLES. PLEASE SEE THAT THEY GET INTO THE RIGHT HANDS.

FLASH! THEY WON'T LET US CROSS THE BRIDGE!

THE BRIDGE IS SAFE, OFFICERS. IF IT WAS GONNA BLOW UP, IT WOULD'VE DONE IT ALREADY.*

FINALLY!

IT'S ABOUT TIME!

AWESOME!!!!

THERE'S STILL SO MUCH ABOUT MY POWERS THAT I DON'T YET UNDERSTAND.

BUT I'VE GOTTA LEARN IT ON THE FLY. THERE'S A LOT OF WORK TO DO.

BUT IT'S GETTING THERE...

ONE STEP AT A TIME--

THAT ICE...IRON HEIGHTS...

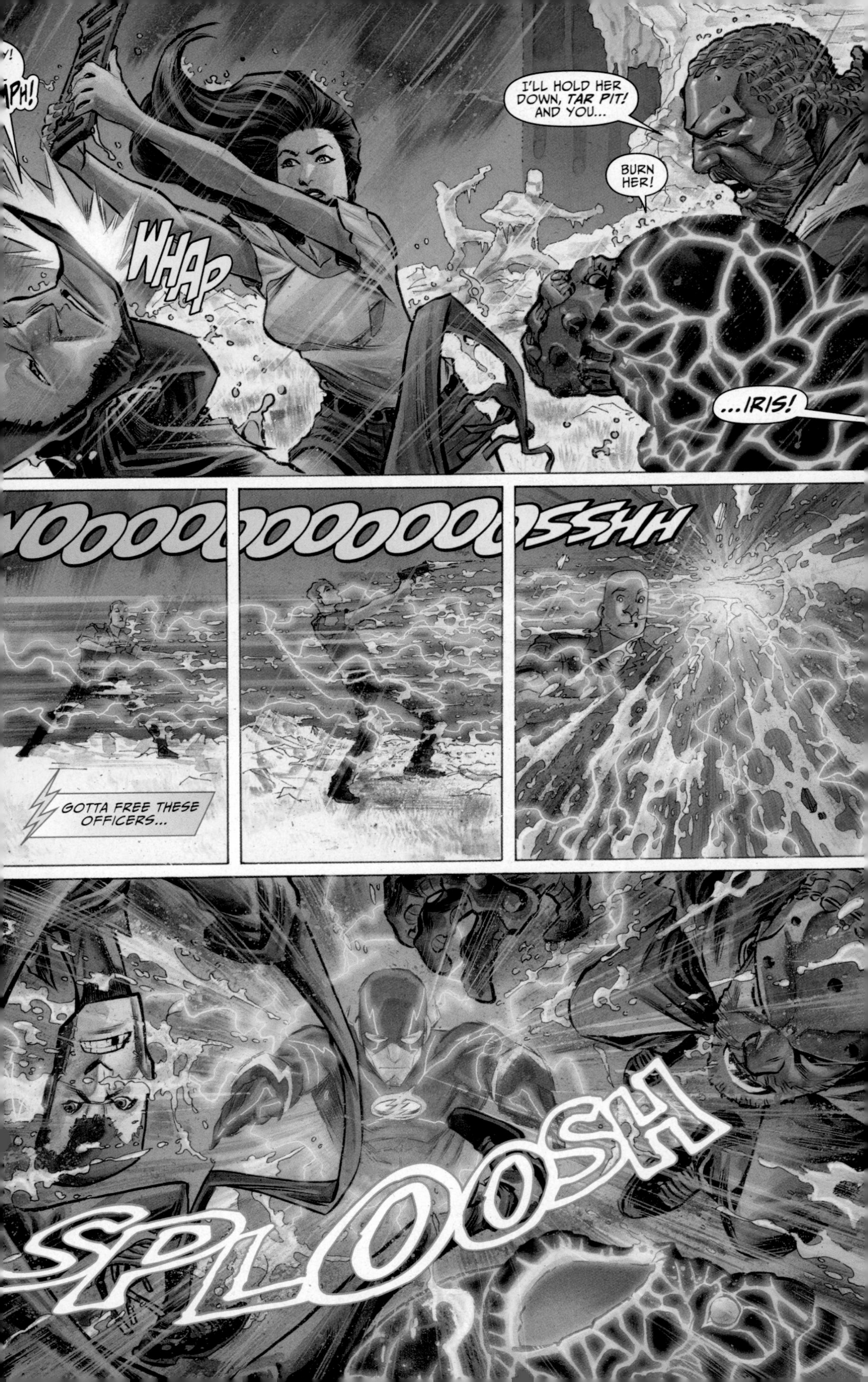

WHAP
I'LL HOLD HER DOWN, *TAR PIT!* AND YOU...
BURN HER!
...IRIS!
OOOOOOOOOOOOOSSHH
GOTTA FREE THESE OFFICERS...
SPLOOSH

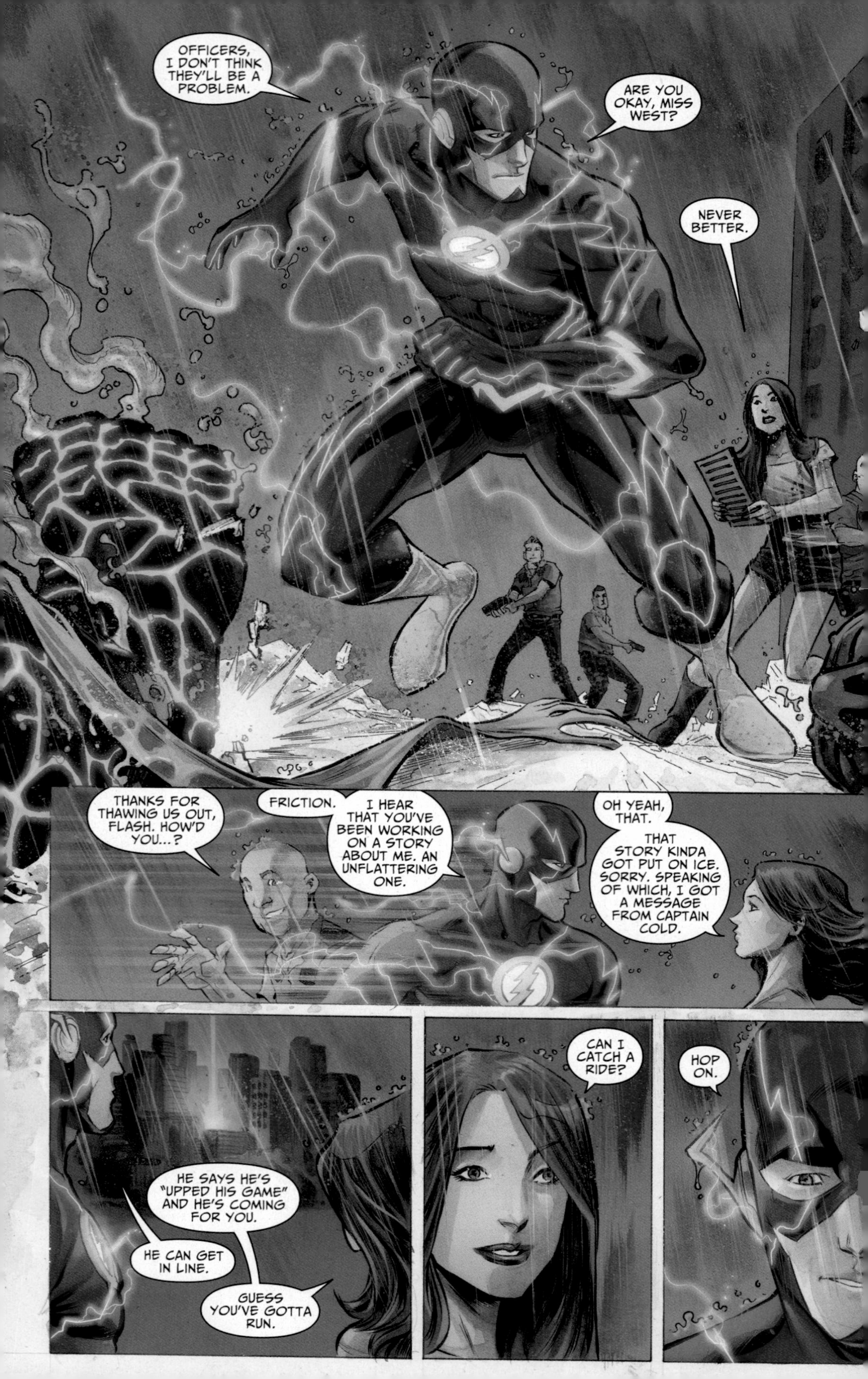
OFFICERS, I DON'T THINK THEY'LL BE A PROBLEM.
ARE YOU OKAY, MISS WEST?
NEVER BETTER.
THANKS FOR THAWING US OUT, FLASH. HOW'D YOU...?
FRICTION.
I HEAR THAT YOU'VE BEEN WORKING ON A STORY ABOUT ME. AN UNFLATTERING ONE.
OH YEAH, THAT.
THAT STORY KINDA GOT PUT ON ICE. SORRY. SPEAKING OF WHICH, I GOT A MESSAGE FROM CAPTAIN COLD.
HE SAYS HE'S "UPPED HIS GAME" AND HE'S COMING FOR YOU.
HE CAN GET IN LINE.
GUESS YOU'VE GOTTA RUN.
CAN I CATCH A RIDE?
HOP ON.

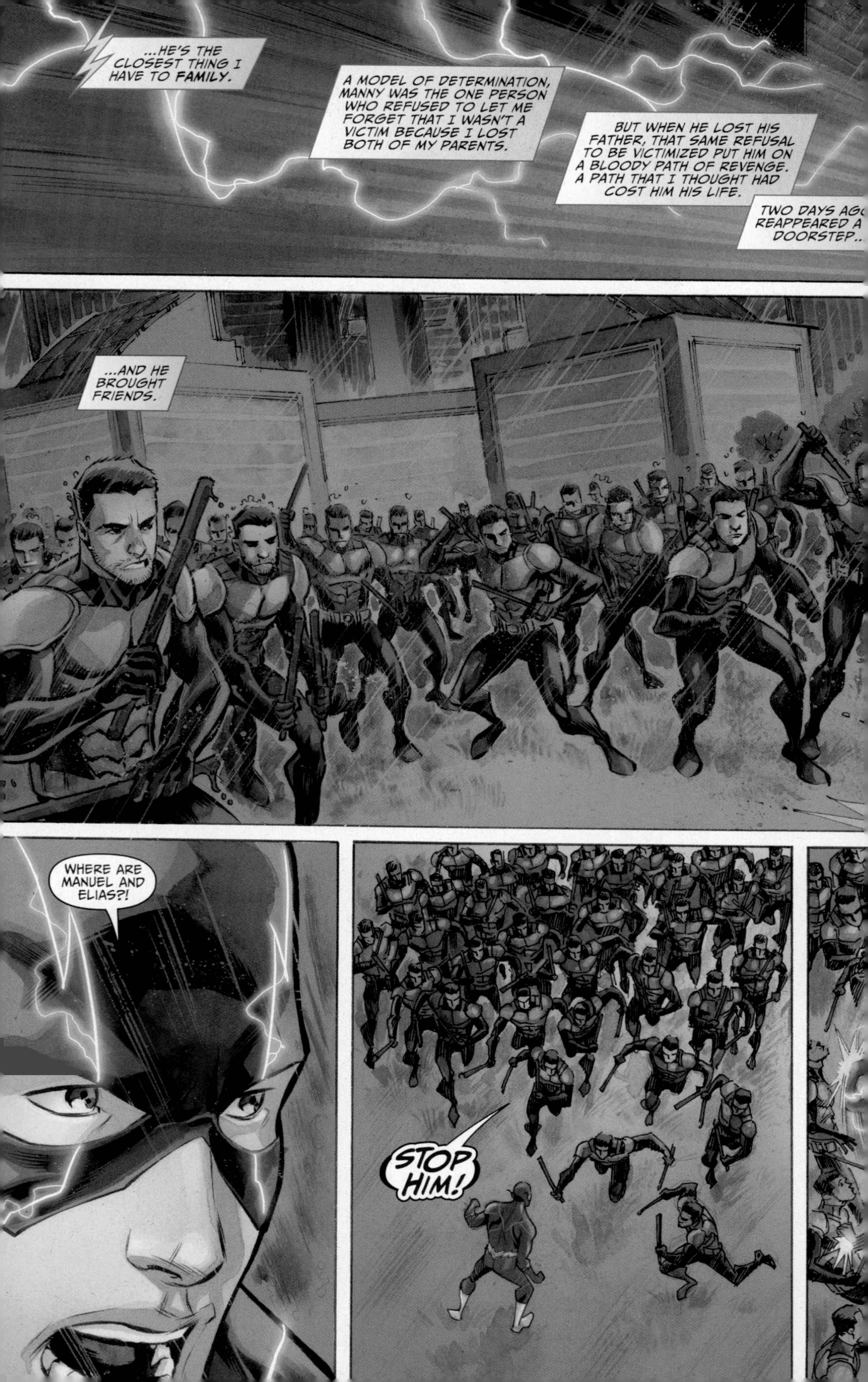
...HE'S THE CLOSEST THING I HAVE TO FAMILY.
A MODEL OF DETERMINATION, MANNY WAS THE ONE PERSON WHO REFUSED TO LET ME FORGET THAT I WASN'T A VICTIM BECAUSE I LOST BOTH OF MY PARENTS.
BUT WHEN HE LOST HIS FATHER, THAT SAME REFUSAL TO BE VICTIMIZED PUT HIM ON A BLOODY PATH OF REVENGE. A PATH THAT I THOUGHT HAD COST HIM HIS LIFE.
TWO DAYS AGO REAPPEARED A DOORSTEP...
...AND HE BROUGHT FRIENDS.
WHERE ARE MANUEL AND ELIAS?!
STOP HIM!

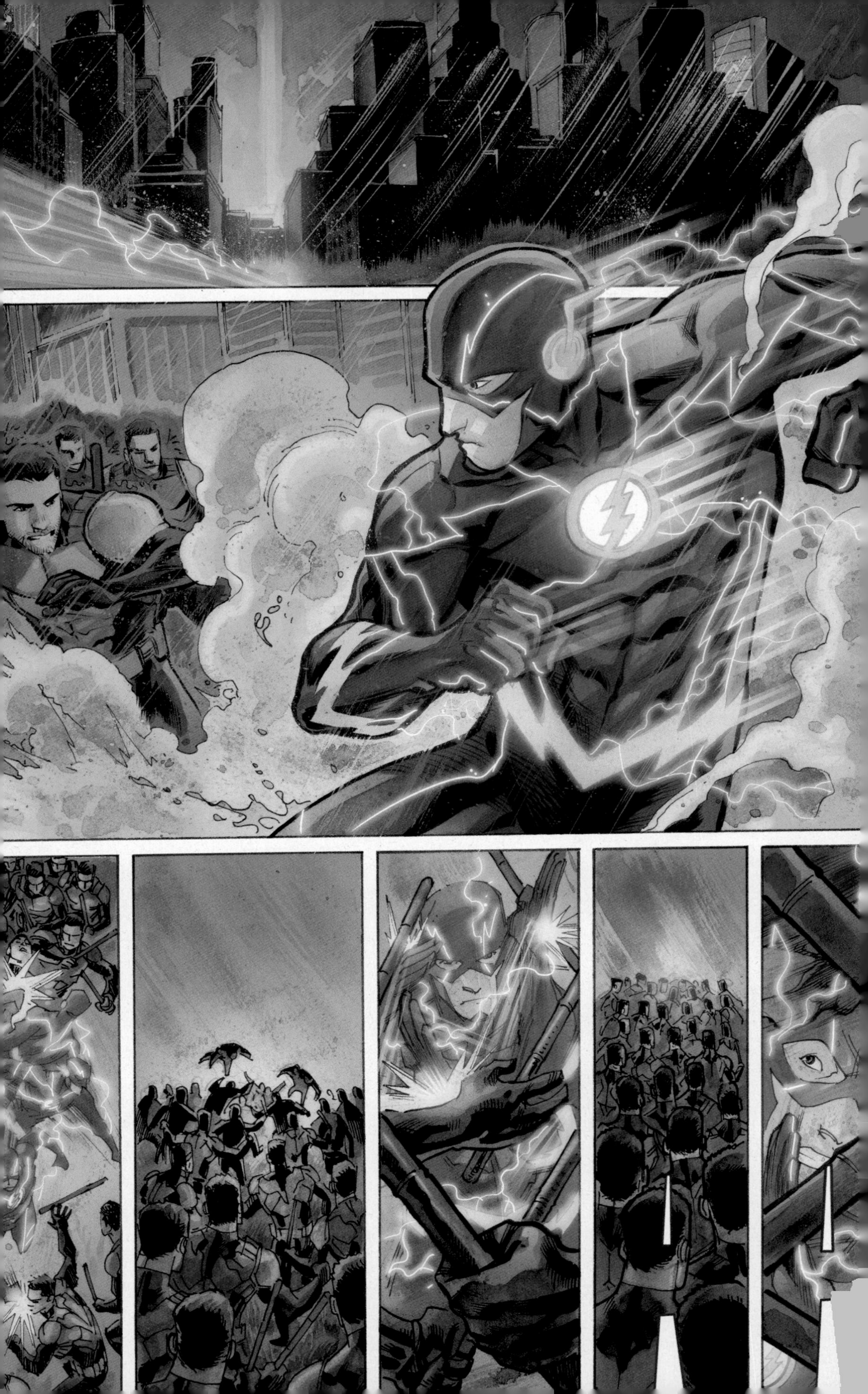

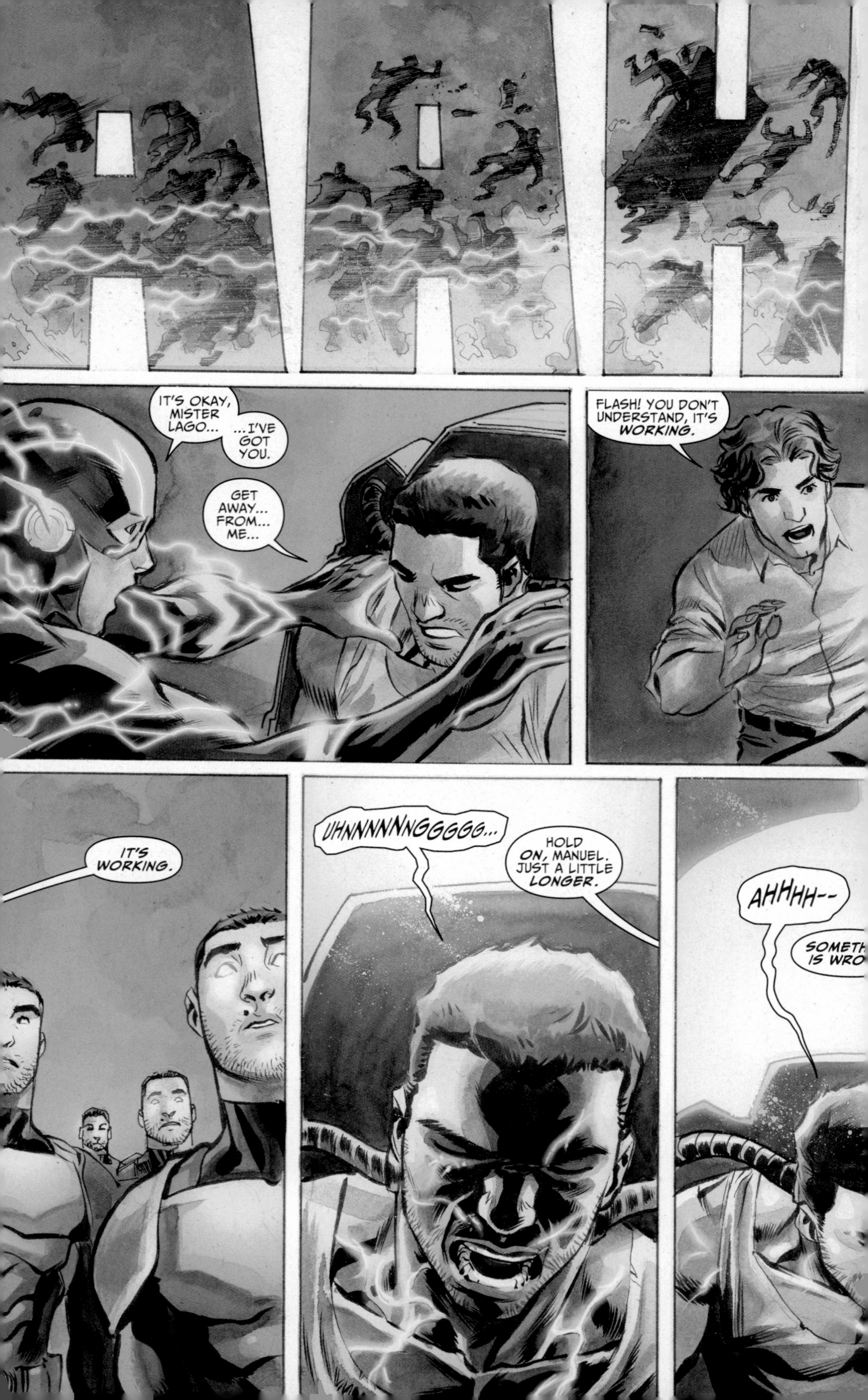
IT'S OKAY, MISTER LAGO...
...I'VE GOT YOU.
GET AWAY... FROM... ME...
FLASH! YOU DON'T UNDERSTAND, IT'S WORKING.
IT'S WORKING.
UHNNNNNNGGGGG...
HOLD ON, MANUEL. JUST A LITTLE LONGER.
AHHHH--
SOMETH IS WRO

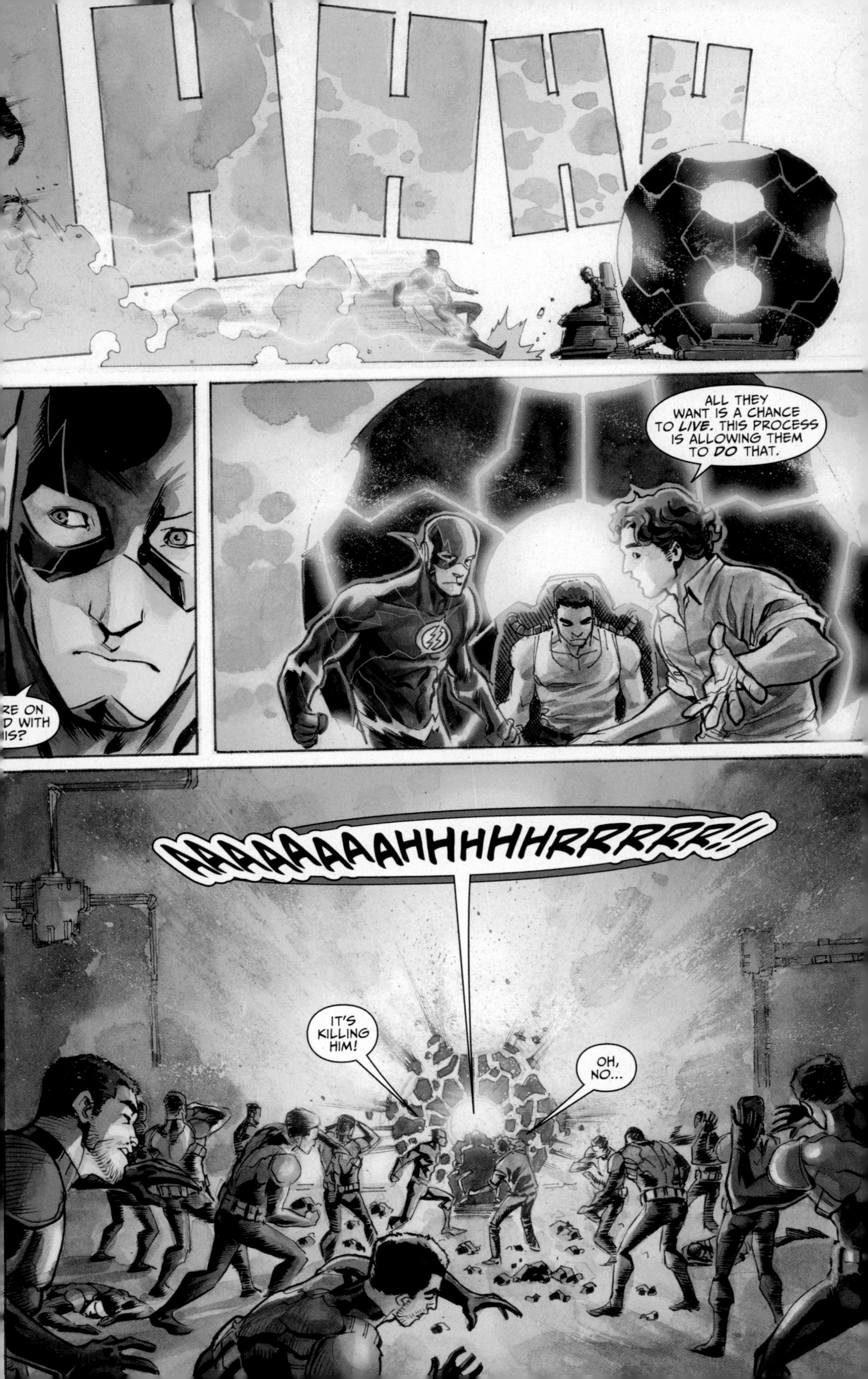
RE ON
D WITH
IS?
ALL THEY WANT IS A CHANCE TO LIVE. THIS PROCESS IS ALLOWING THEM TO DO THAT.
AAAAAAAAHHHHHRRRRRR!!
IT'S KILLING HIM!
OH, NO...

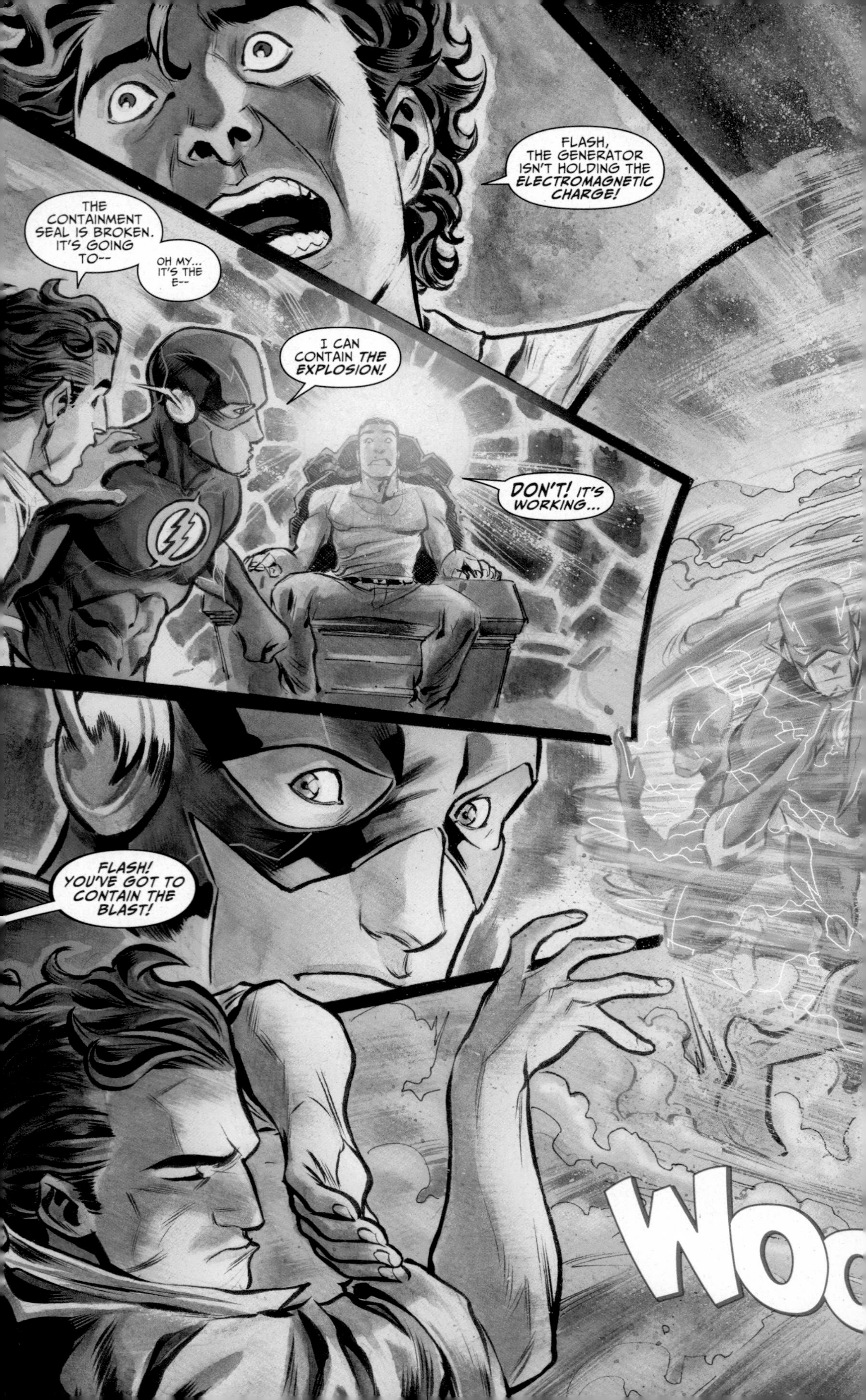

FLASH, THE GENERATOR ISN'T HOLDING THE ELECTROMAGNETIC CHARGE!
THE CONTAINMENT SEAL IS BROKEN. IT'S GOING TO--
OH MY... IT'S THE E--
I CAN CONTAIN THE EXPLOSION!
DON'T! IT'S WORKING...
FLASH! YOU'VE GOT TO CONTAIN THE BLAST!
WOO

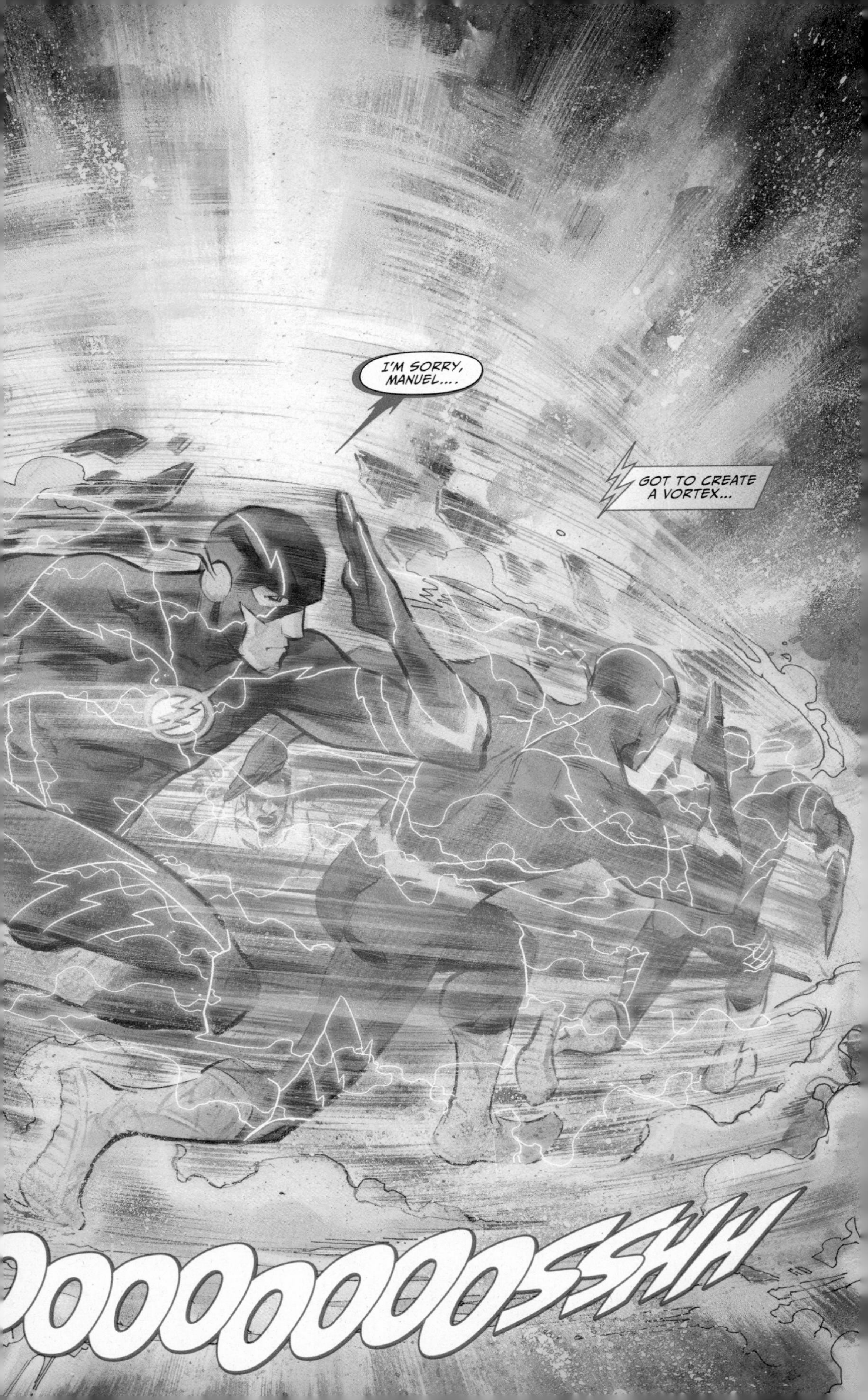
I'M SORRY, MANUEL....
GOT TO CREATE A VORTEX...
OOOOOOOOOOSSH

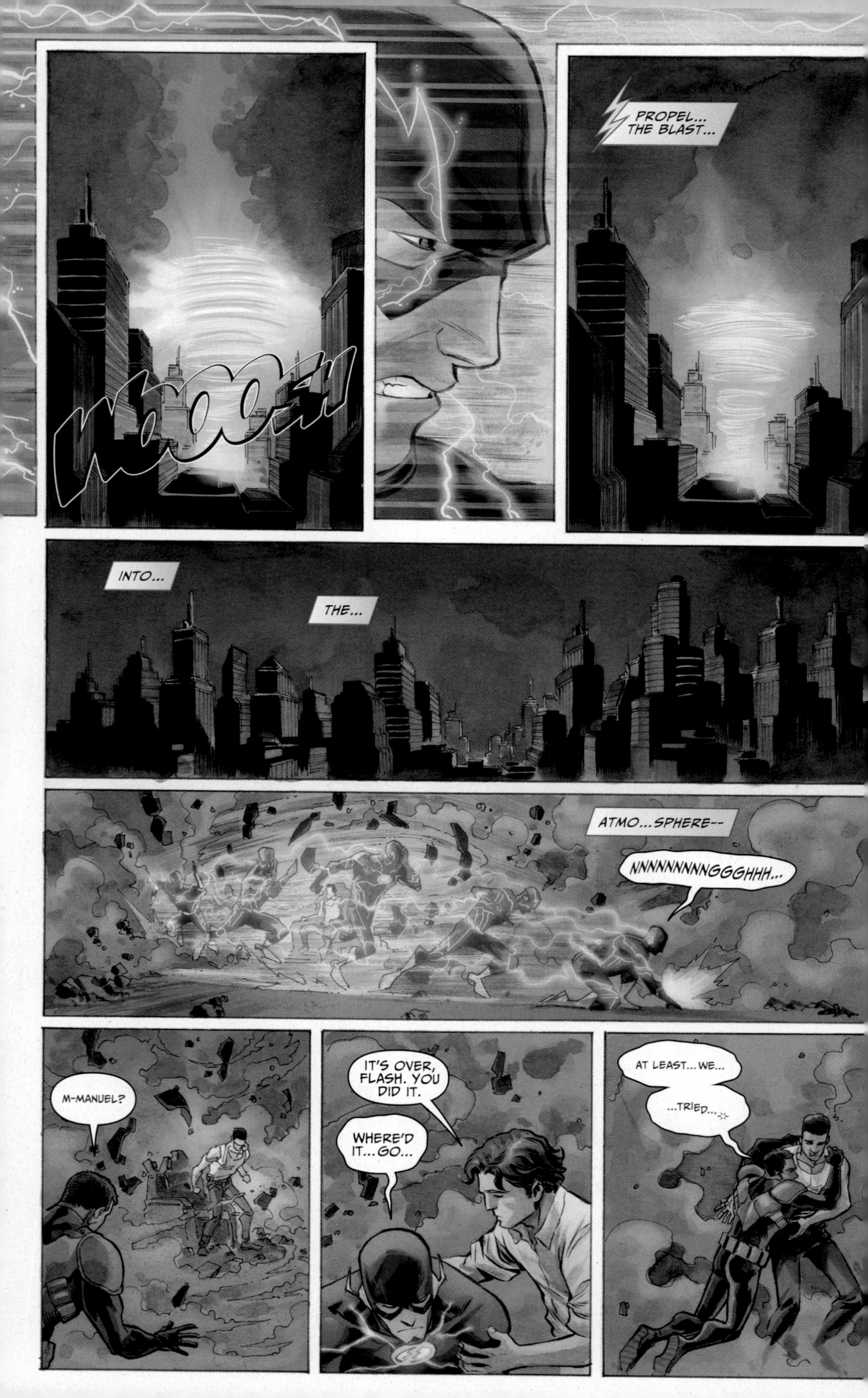
WOOSH
PROPEL... THE BLAST...
INTO...
THE...
ATMO...SPHERE--
NNNNNNNNNGGGHHH...
M-MANUEL?
IT'S OVER, FLASH. YOU DID IT.
WHERE'D IT... GO...
AT LEAST... WE...
...TRIED...

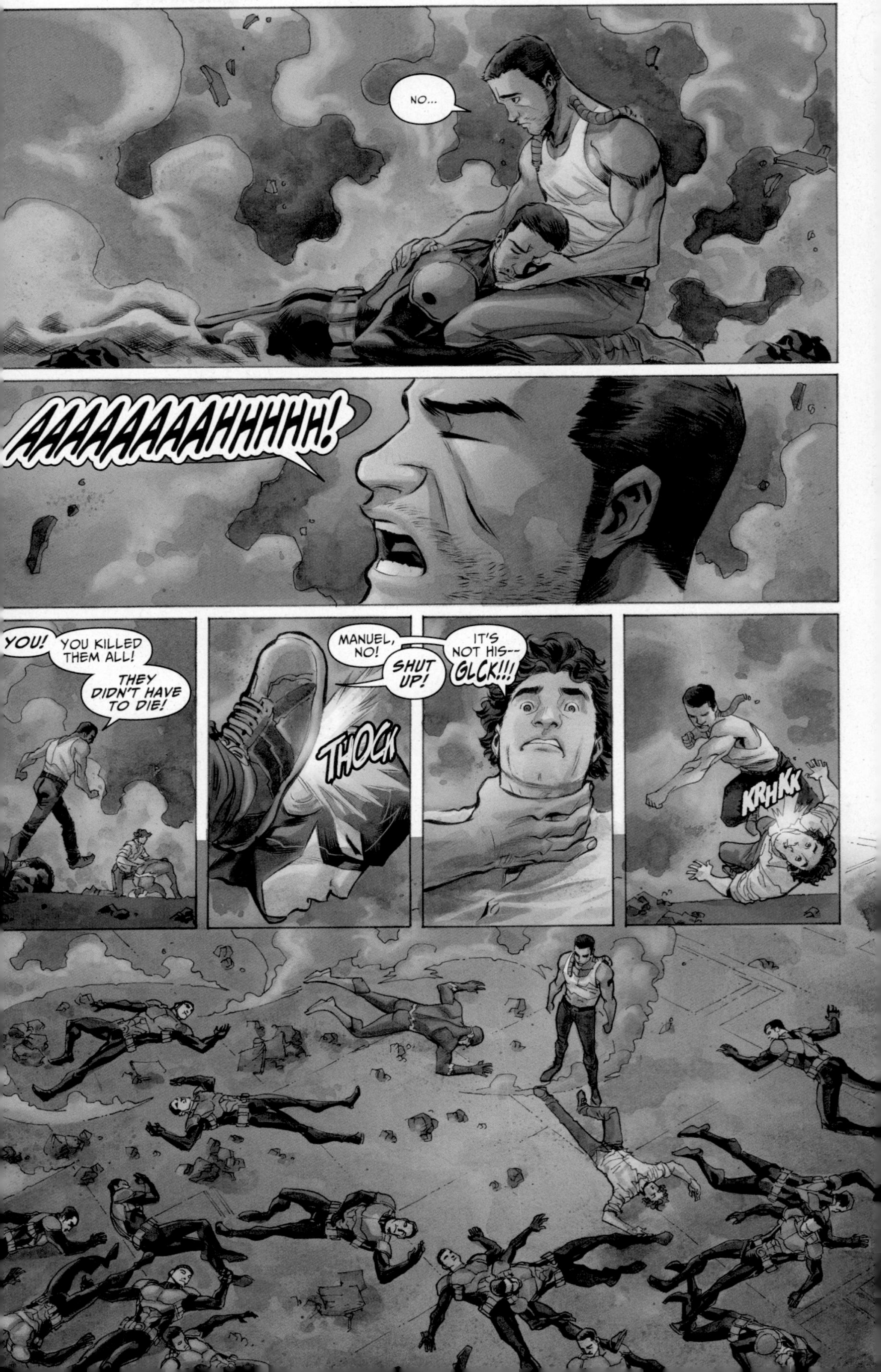
NO...
AAAAAAAAAHHHHH!
YOU!
YOU KILLED THEM ALL!
THEY DIDN'T HAVE TO DIE!
MANUEL, NO!
SHUT UP!
THOCK
IT'S NOT HIS--
GLCK!!!
KRHKK

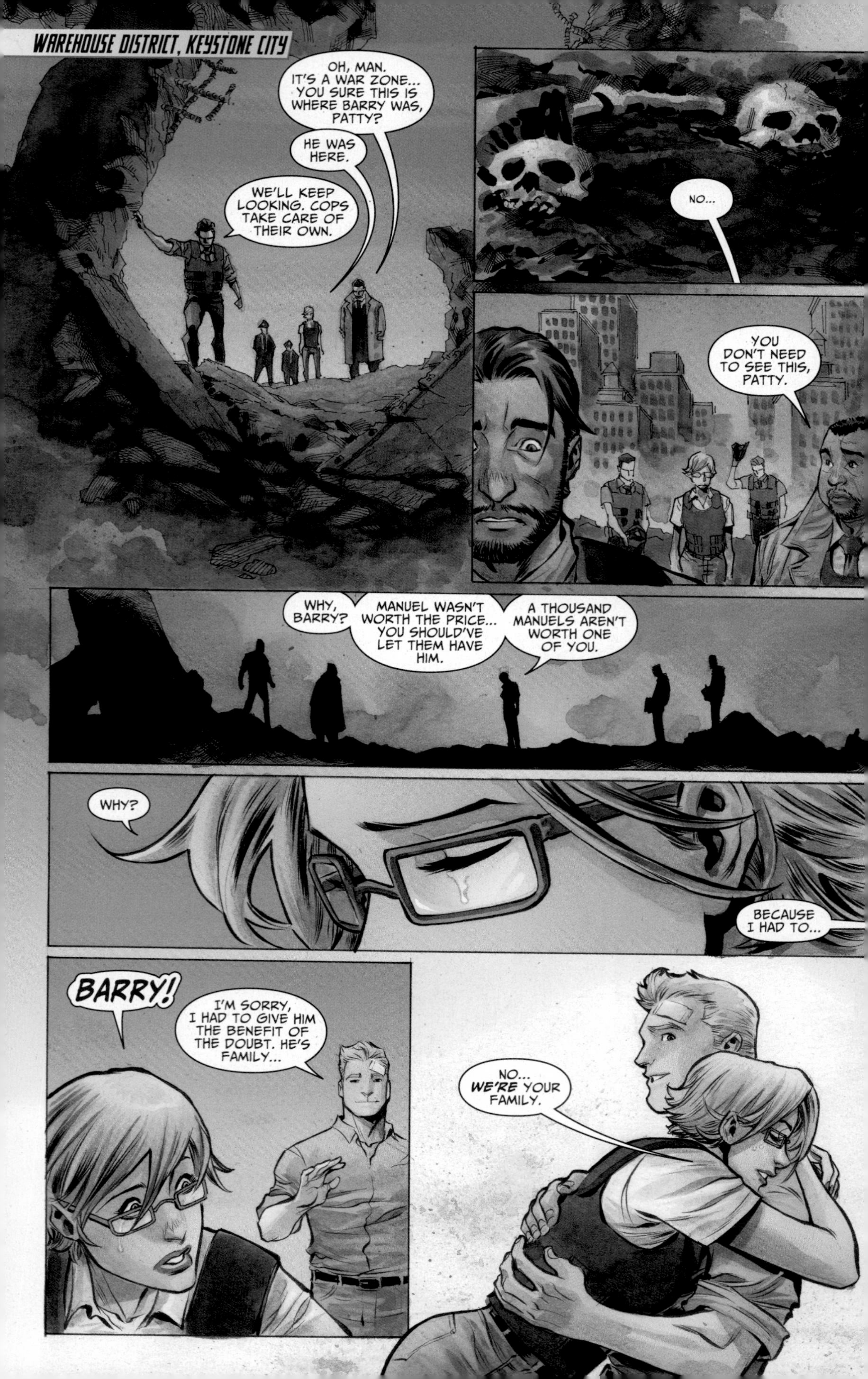
WAREHOUSE DISTRICT, KEYSTONE CITY
OH, MAN. IT'S A WAR ZONE... YOU SURE THIS IS WHERE BARRY WAS, PATTY?
HE WAS HERE.
WE'LL KEEP LOOKING. COPS TAKE CARE OF THEIR OWN.
NO...
YOU DON'T NEED TO SEE THIS, PATTY.
WHY, BARRY?
MANUEL WASN'T WORTH THE PRICE... YOU SHOULD'VE LET THEM HAVE HIM.
A THOUSAND MANUELS AREN'T WORTH ONE OF YOU.
WHY?
BECAUSE I HAD TO...
BARRY!
I'M SORRY, I HAD TO GIVE HIM THE BENEFIT OF THE DOUBT. HE'S FAMILY...
NO... WE'RE YOUR FAMILY.

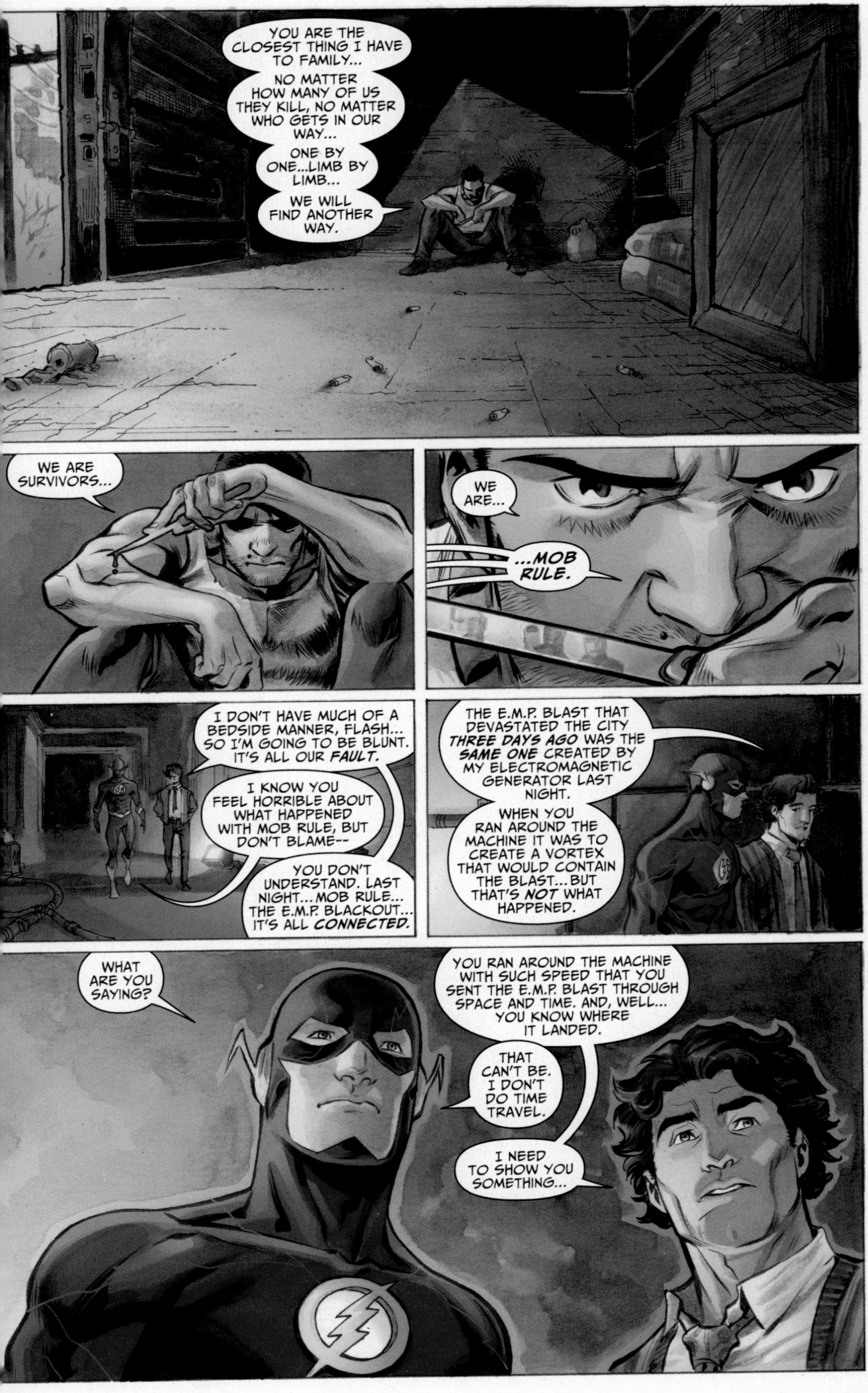
YOU ARE THE CLOSEST THING I HAVE TO FAMILY...
NO MATTER HOW MANY OF US THEY KILL, NO MATTER WHO GETS IN OUR WAY...
ONE BY ONE...LIMB BY LIMB...
WE WILL FIND ANOTHER WAY.
WE ARE SURVIVORS...
WE ARE...
...MOB RULE.
I DON'T HAVE MUCH OF A BEDSIDE MANNER, FLASH... SO I'M GOING TO BE BLUNT. IT'S ALL OUR FAULT.
I KNOW YOU FEEL HORRIBLE ABOUT WHAT HAPPENED WITH MOB RULE, BUT DON'T BLAME--
YOU DON'T UNDERSTAND. LAST NIGHT...MOB RULE... THE E.M.P. BLACKOUT... IT'S ALL CONNECTED.
THE E.M.P. BLAST THAT DEVASTATED THE CITY THREE DAYS AGO WAS THE SAME ONE CREATED BY MY ELECTROMAGNETIC GENERATOR LAST NIGHT.
WHEN YOU RAN AROUND THE MACHINE IT WAS TO CREATE A VORTEX THAT WOULD CONTAIN THE BLAST...BUT THAT'S NOT WHAT HAPPENED.
WHAT ARE YOU SAYING?
YOU RAN AROUND THE MACHINE WITH SUCH SPEED THAT YOU SENT THE E.M.P. BLAST THROUGH SPACE AND TIME. AND, WELL... YOU KNOW WHERE IT LANDED.
THAT CAN'T BE. I DON'T DO TIME TRAVEL.
I NEED TO SHOW YOU SOMETHING...

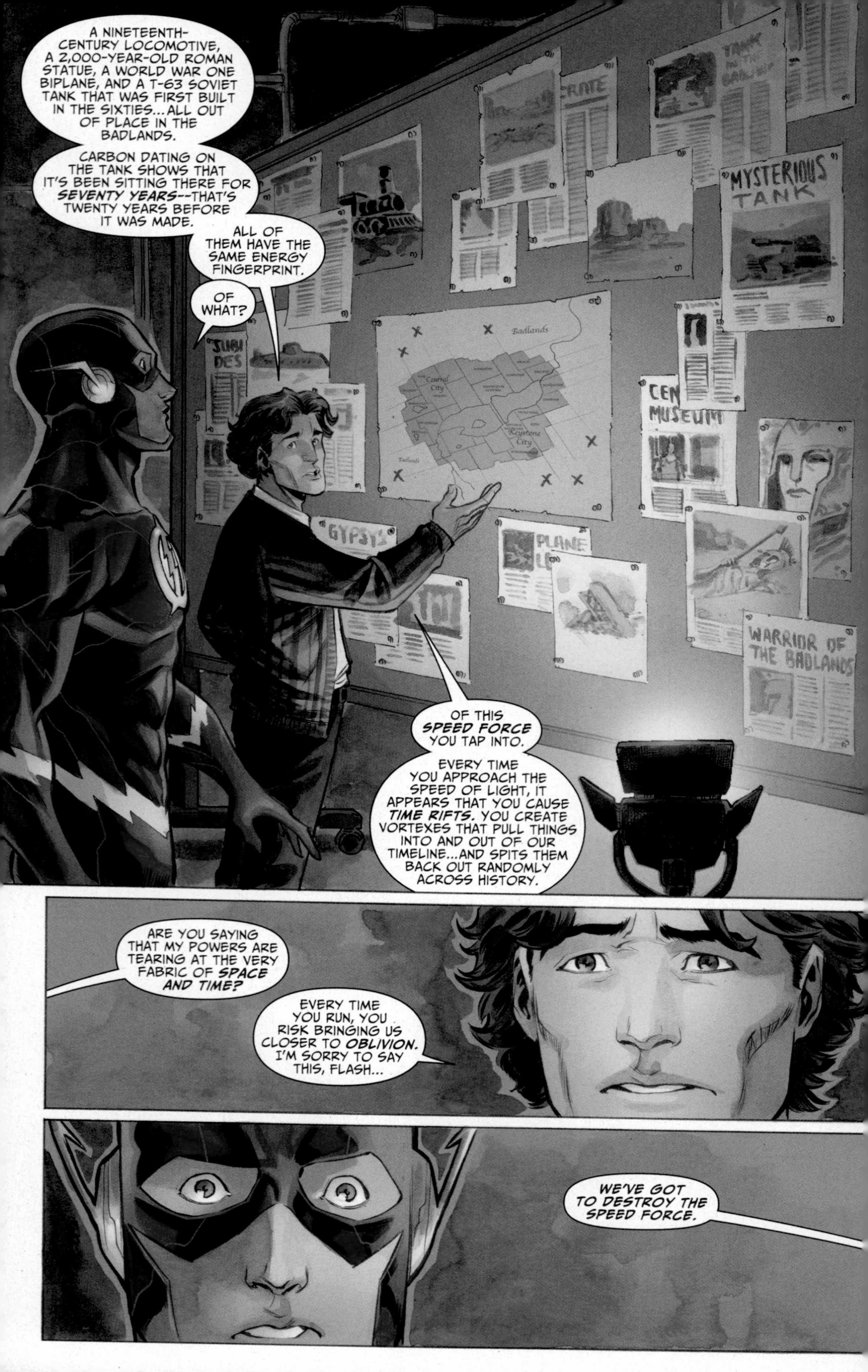
A NINETEENTH-CENTURY LOCOMOTIVE, A 2,000-YEAR-OLD ROMAN STATUE, A WORLD WAR ONE BIPLANE, AND A T-63 SOVIET TANK THAT WAS FIRST BUILT IN THE SIXTIES...ALL OUT OF PLACE IN THE BADLANDS.
CARBON DATING ON THE TANK SHOWS THAT IT'S BEEN SITTING THERE FOR ***SEVENTY YEARS***--THAT'S TWENTY YEARS BEFORE IT WAS MADE.
ALL OF THEM HAVE THE SAME ENERGY FINGERPRINT.
OF WHAT?
MYSTERIOUS TANK
Badlands
Central City
Keystone City
Badlands
CEN MUSEUM
WARRIOR OF THE BADLANDS
OF THIS ***SPEED FORCE*** YOU TAP INTO.
EVERY TIME YOU APPROACH THE SPEED OF LIGHT, IT APPEARS THAT YOU CAUSE ***TIME RIFTS.*** YOU CREATE VORTEXES THAT PULL THINGS INTO AND OUT OF OUR TIMELINE...AND SPITS THEM BACK OUT RANDOMLY ACROSS HISTORY.
ARE YOU SAYING THAT MY POWERS ARE TEARING AT THE VERY FABRIC OF ***SPACE AND TIME?***
EVERY TIME YOU RUN, YOU RISK BRINGING US CLOSER TO ***OBLIVION.*** I'M SORRY TO SAY THIS, FLASH...
WE'VE GOT TO DESTROY THE SPEED FORCE.

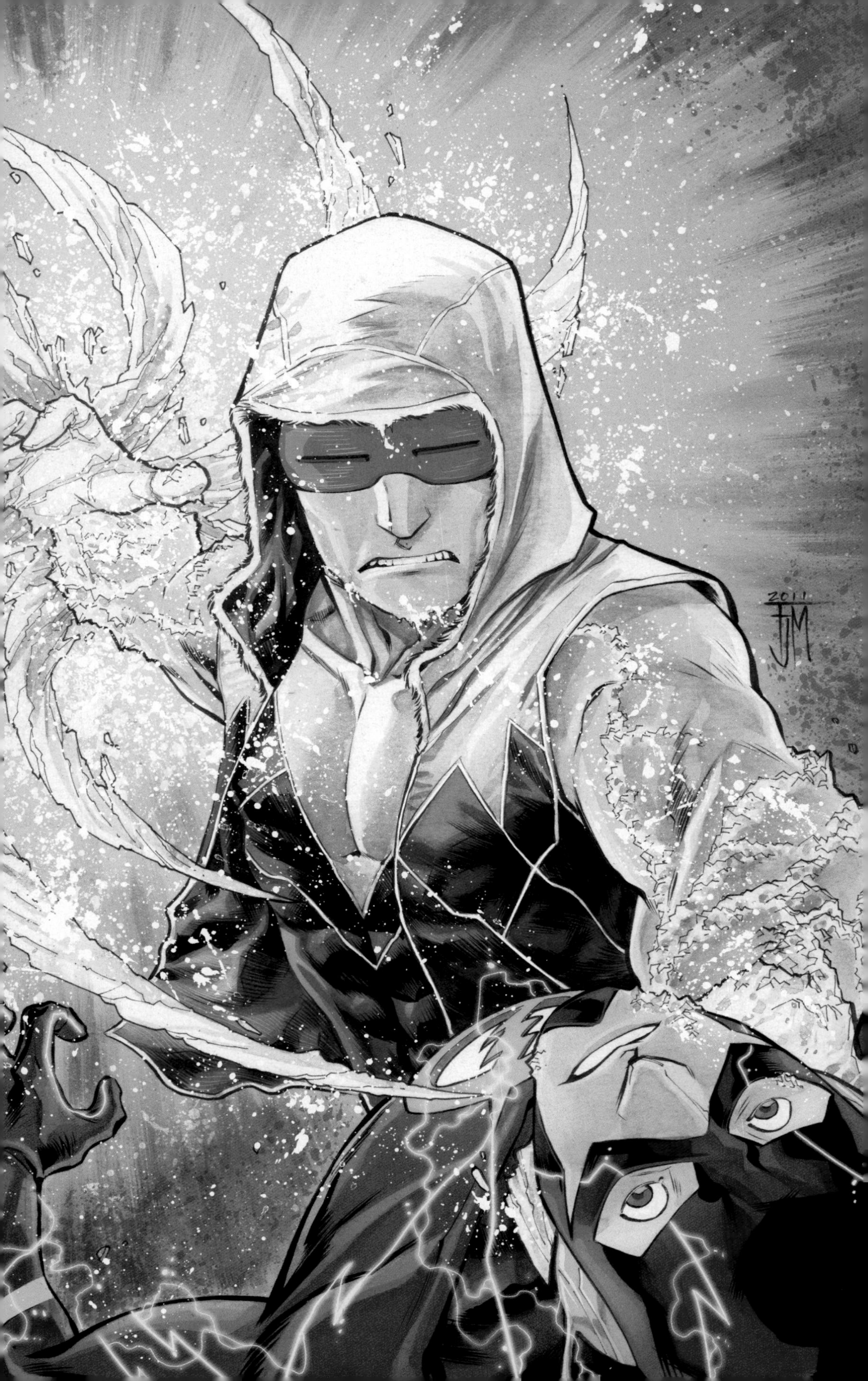

THE FLASH #6
variant cover by MIKE CHOI

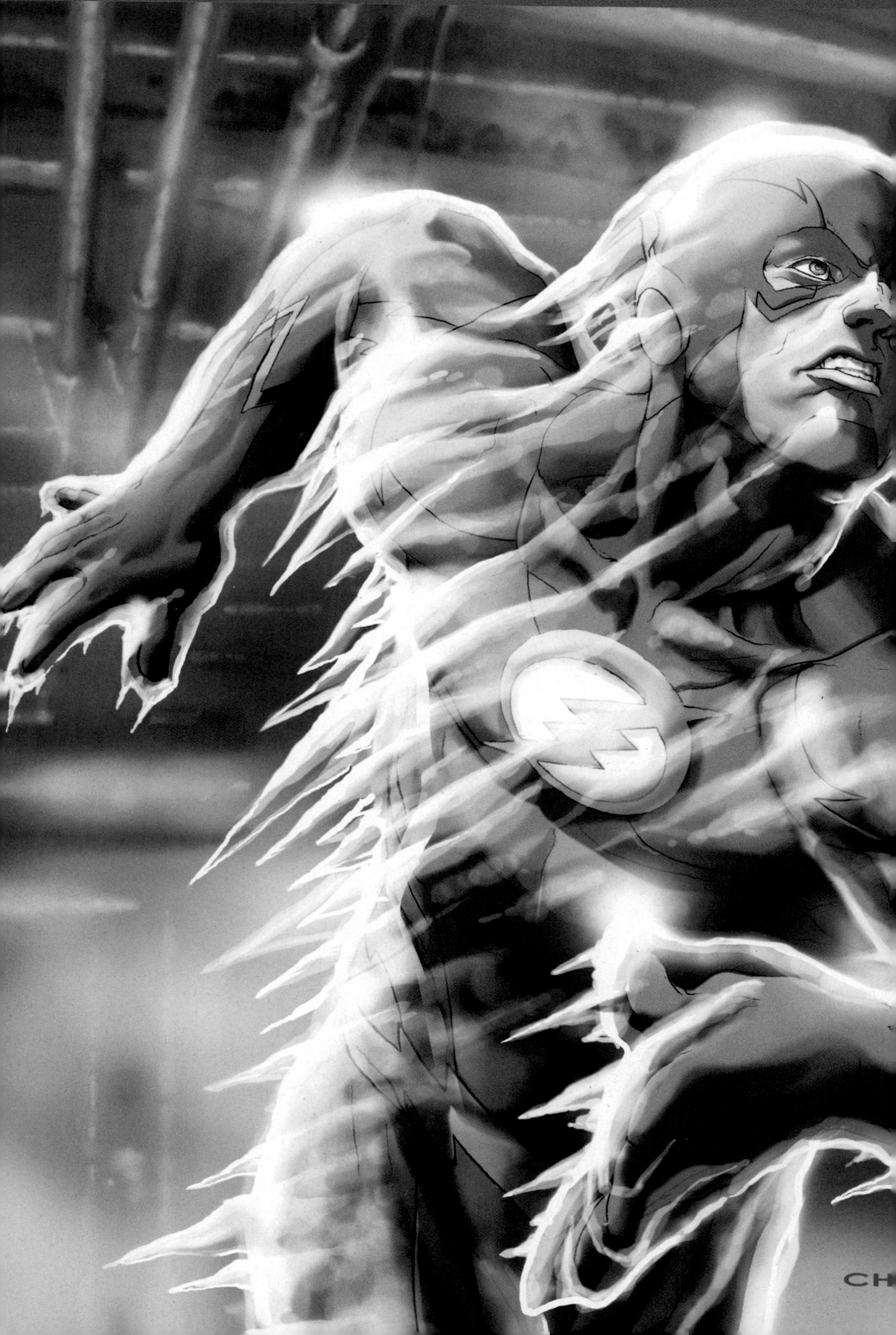
CH

NOW.

IN THE FIVE YEARS I'VE BEEN THE FLASH, I'VE FACED MANY ADVERSARIES...

BUT NONE AS PERSISTENT AS CAPTAIN COLD. NO MATTER HOW MANY TIMES I PUT HIM DOWN, HE'D ALWAYS GET BACK UP FOR THE NEXT BIG SCORE.

LOOKING FOR STRENGTH IN NUMBERS, HE ORGANIZED A GROUP OF LOCAL THUGS. THEY CALLED THEMSELVES THE ROGUES.

I TOOK THEM DOWN, TOO.

THE THING ABOUT CAPTAIN COLD WAS, NO MATTER WHAT, HE WAS ALWAYS ABOUT THE SCORE. GET IN, GRAB, AND GET OUT. HE RESPECTED THE RULES OF THIS CAT AND MOUSE GAME.

HE'D DO ANYTHING TO WIN; HOWEVER, HIS SENSE OF HONOR ALWAYS PREVENTED HIM FROM USING HIS FREEZE PISTOLS FOR MURDER.

BUT THAT'S NOT WHAT I SEE TODAY...

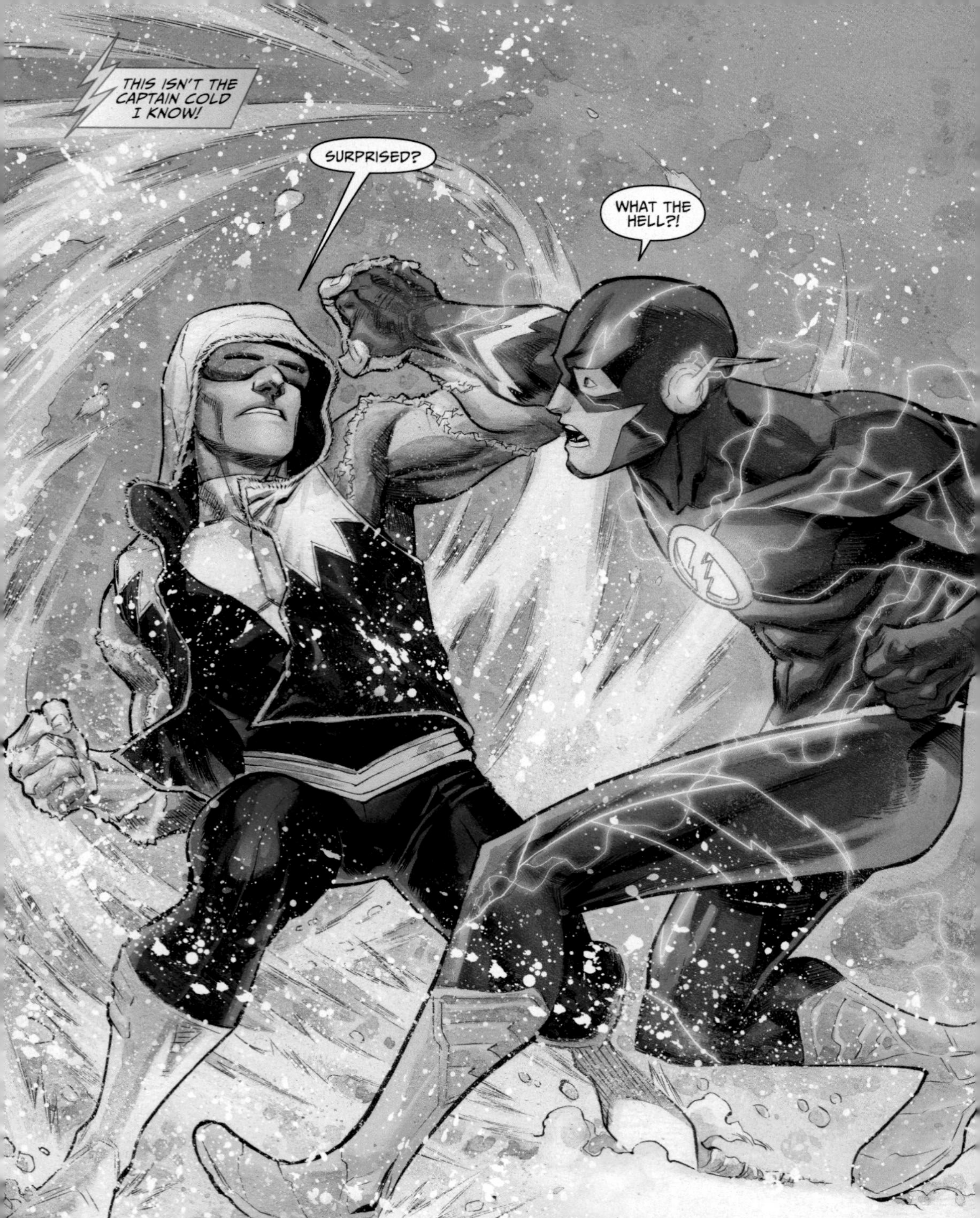
THIS ISN'T THE CAPTAIN COLD I KNOW!
SURPRISED?
WHAT THE HELL?!
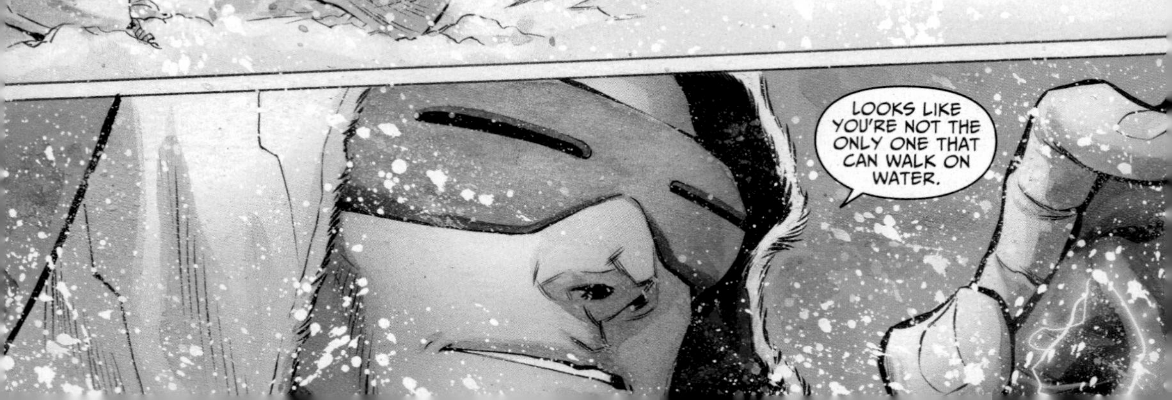
LOOKS LIKE YOU'RE NOT THE ONLY ONE THAT CAN WALK ON WATER.

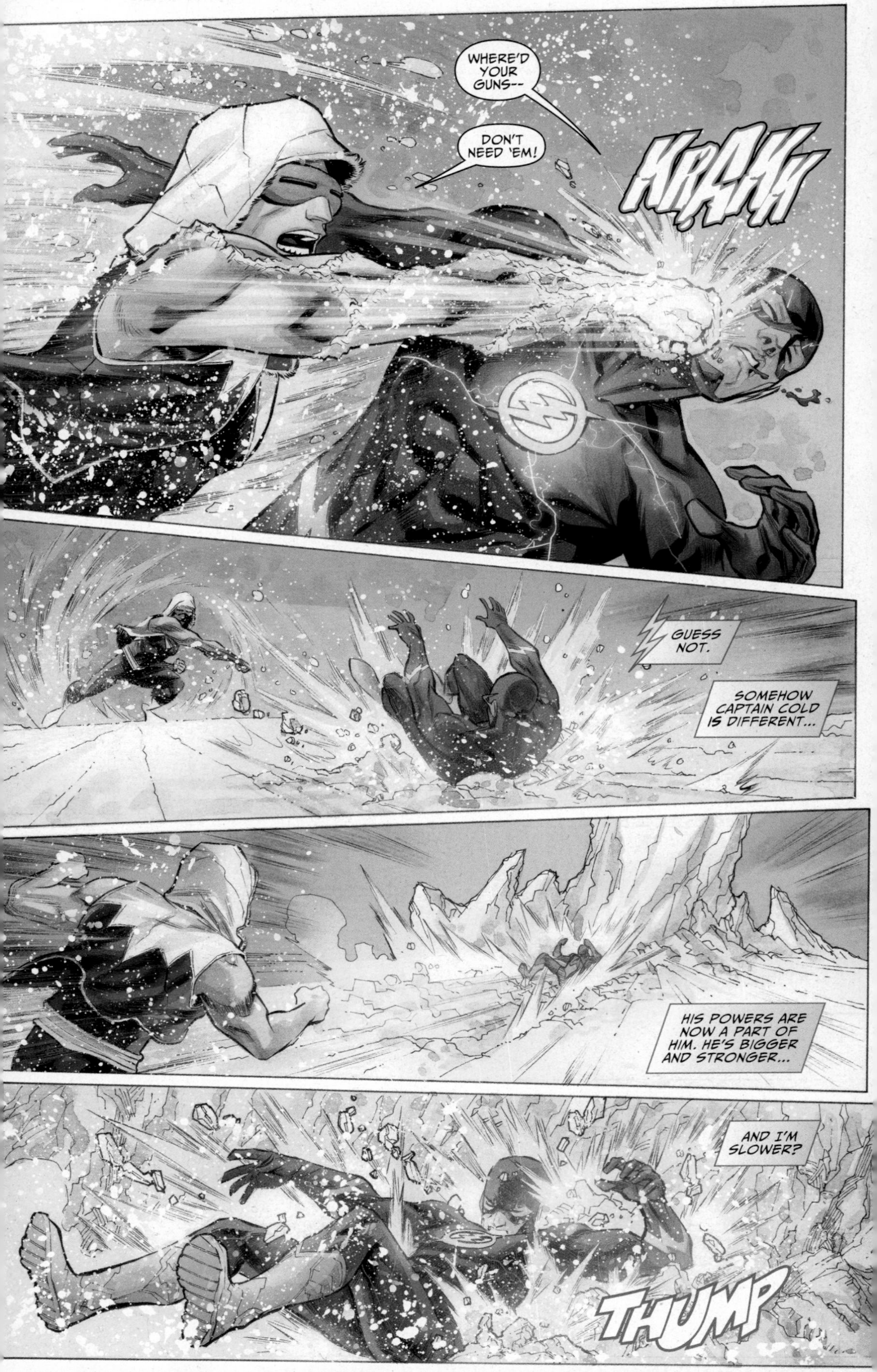
WHERE'D YOUR GUNS--
DON'T NEED 'EM!
KRAKK
GUESS NOT.
SOMEHOW CAPTAIN COLD IS DIFFERENT...
HIS POWERS ARE NOW A PART OF HIM. HE'S BIGGER AND STRONGER...
AND I'M SLOWER?
THUMP

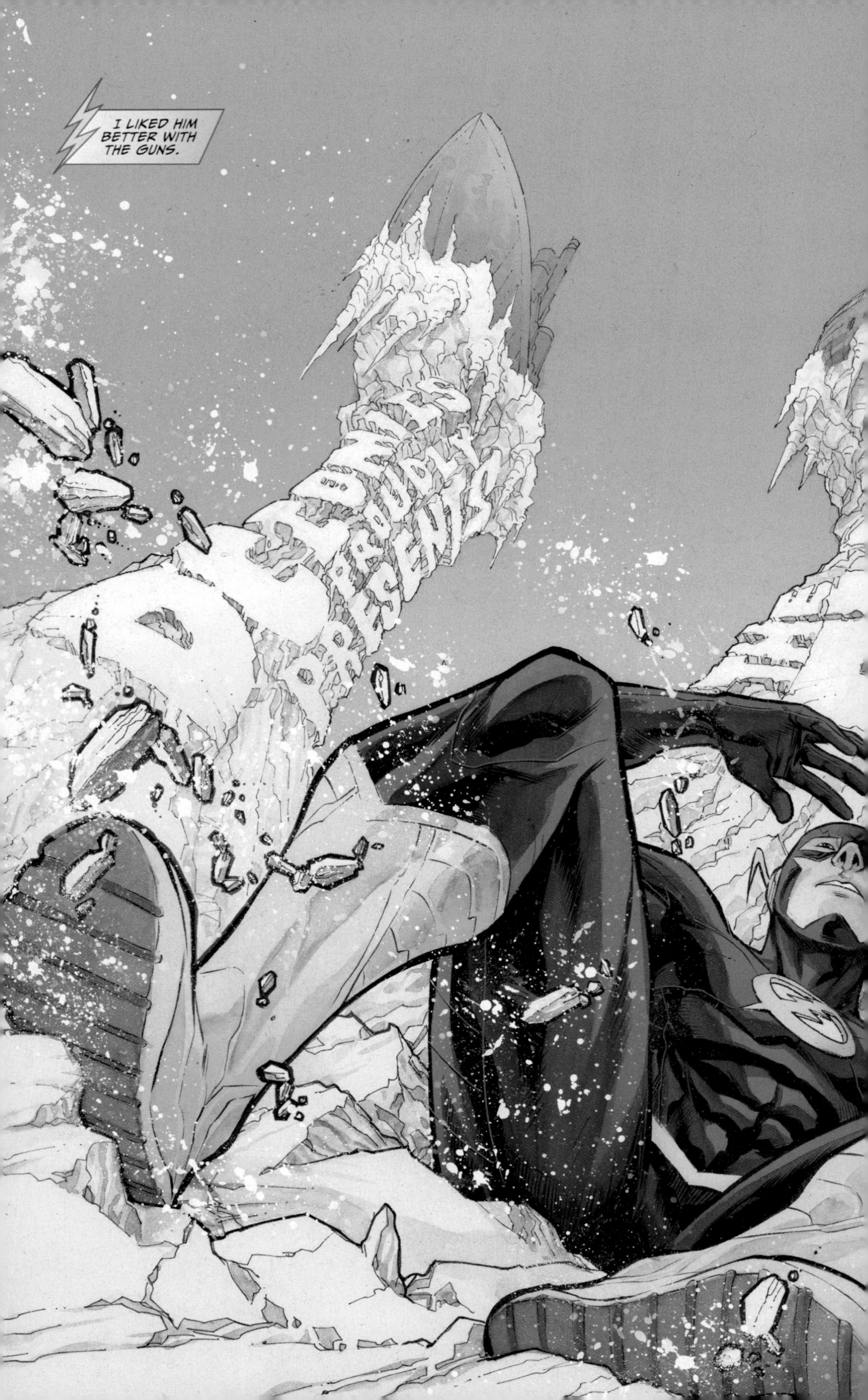
I LIKED HIM BETTER WITH THE GUNS.

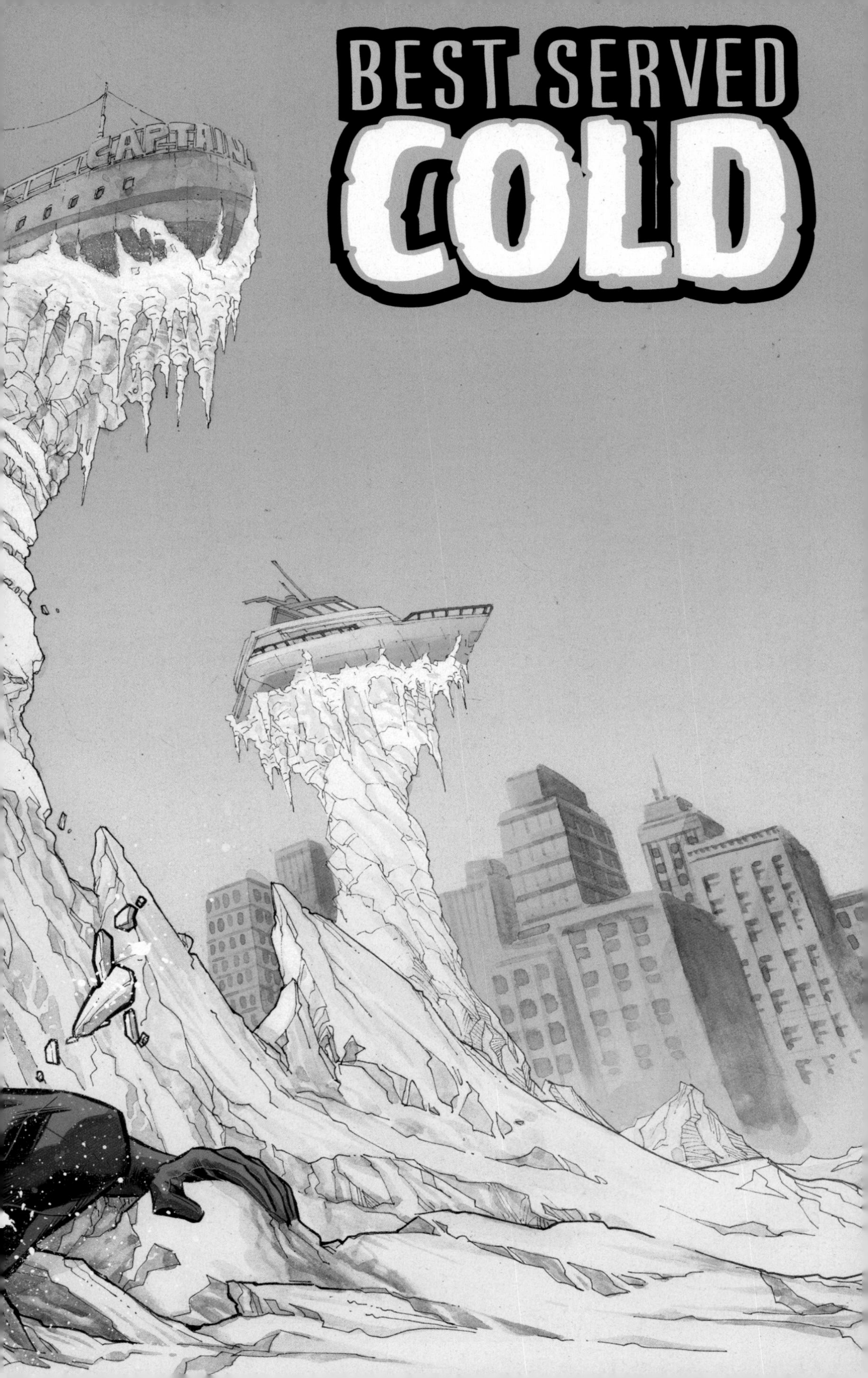
BEST SERVED
COLD
CAPTAIN

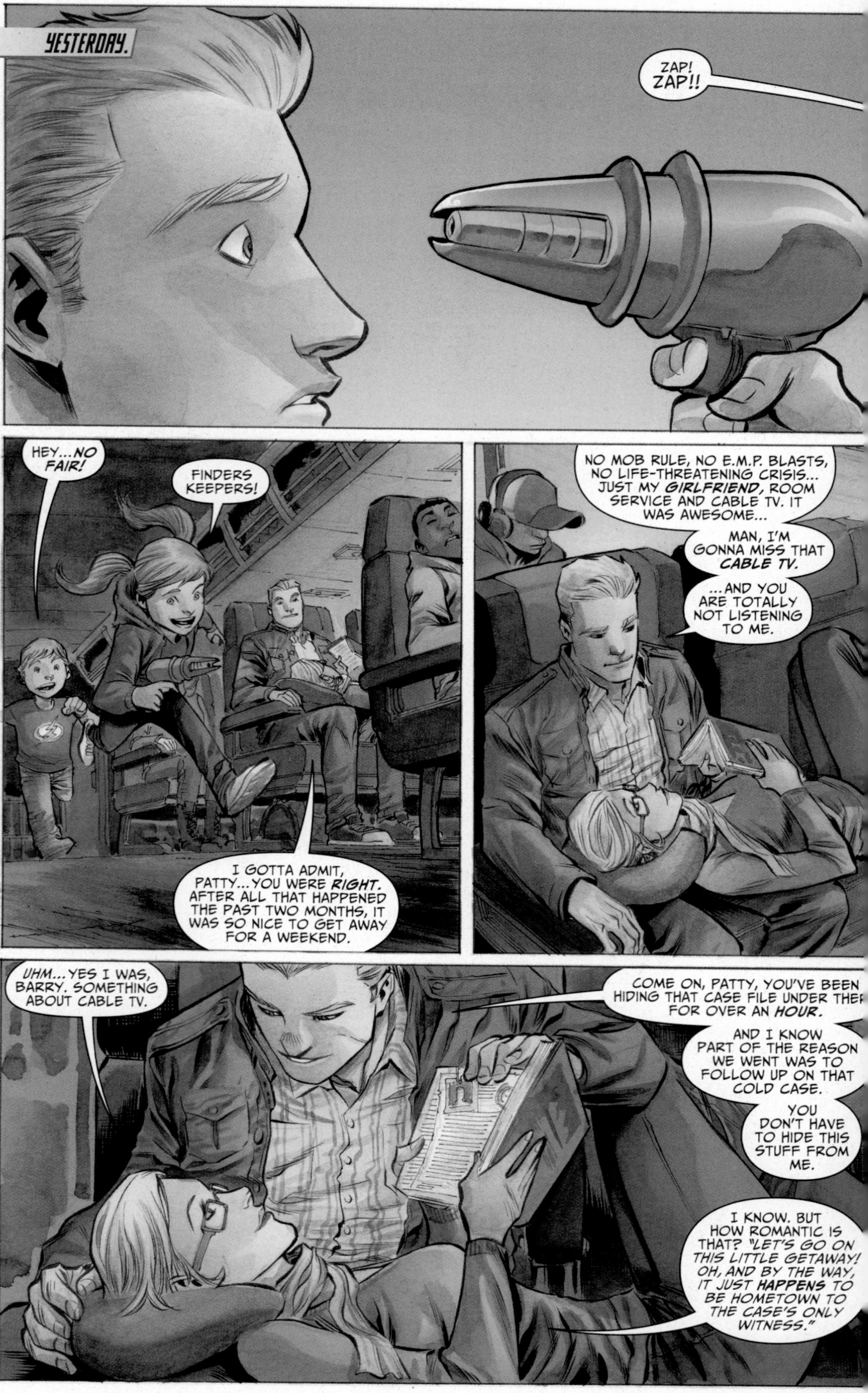
YESTERDAY.
ZAP! ZAP!!
HEY...NO FAIR!
FINDERS KEEPERS!
I GOTTA ADMIT, PATTY...YOU WERE RIGHT. AFTER ALL THAT HAPPENED THE PAST TWO MONTHS, IT WAS SO NICE TO GET AWAY FOR A WEEKEND.
NO MOB RULE, NO E.M.P. BLASTS, NO LIFE-THREATENING CRISIS... JUST MY GIRLFRIEND, ROOM SERVICE AND CABLE TV. IT WAS AWESOME...
MAN, I'M GONNA MISS THAT CABLE TV.
...AND YOU ARE TOTALLY NOT LISTENING TO ME.
UHM...YES I WAS, BARRY. SOMETHING ABOUT CABLE TV.
COME ON, PATTY, YOU'VE BEEN HIDING THAT CASE FILE UNDER THER FOR OVER AN HOUR.
AND I KNOW PART OF THE REASON WE WENT WAS TO FOLLOW UP ON THAT COLD CASE.
YOU DON'T HAVE TO HIDE THIS STUFF FROM ME.
I KNOW. BUT HOW ROMANTIC IS THAT? "LET'S GO ON THIS LITTLE GETAWAY! OH, AND BY THE WAY, IT JUST HAPPENS TO BE HOMETOWN TO THE CASE'S ONLY WITNESS."

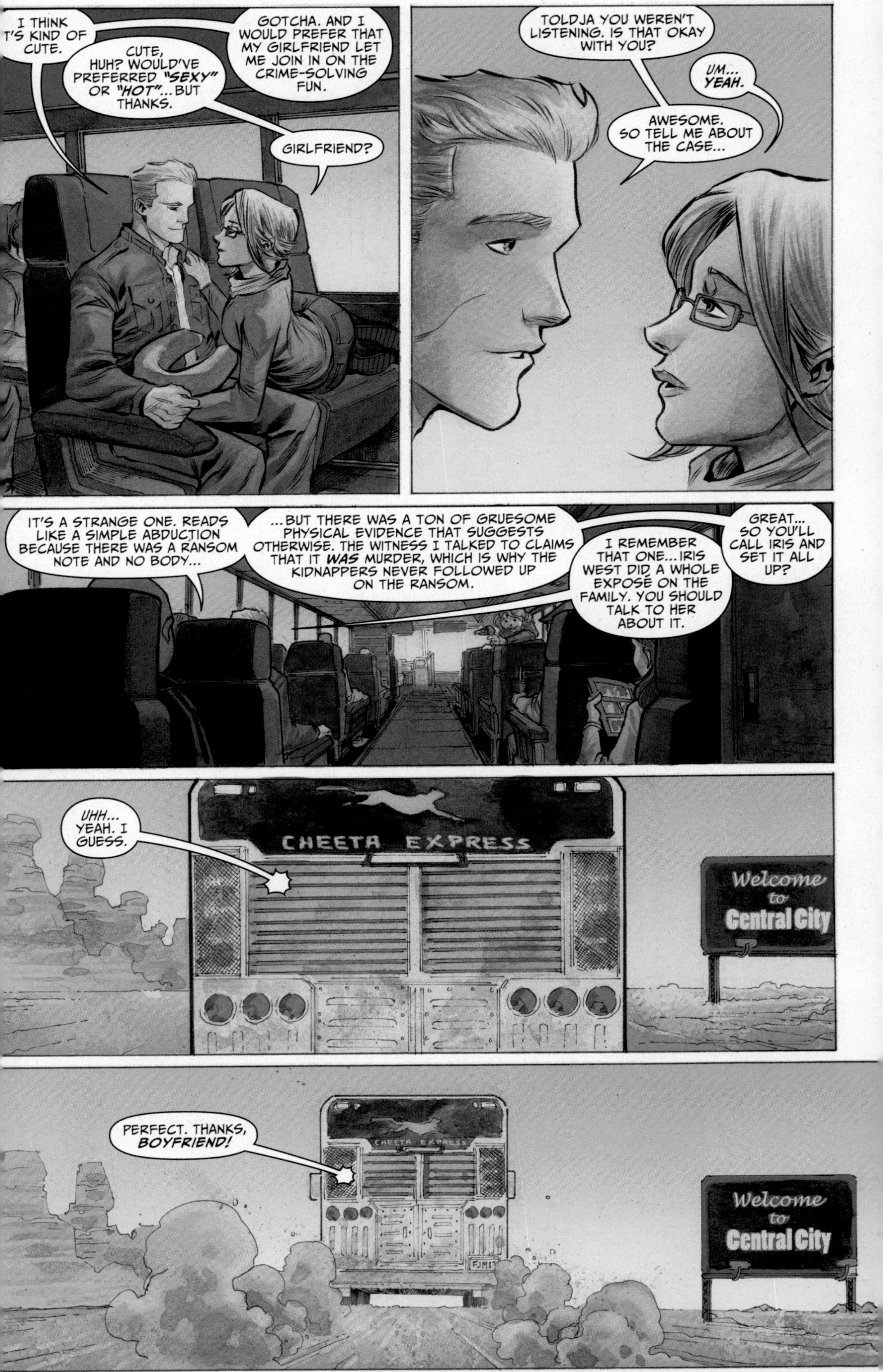
I THINK IT'S KIND OF CUTE.
CUTE, HUH? WOULD'VE PREFERRED "SEXY" OR "HOT"...BUT THANKS.
GOTCHA. AND I WOULD PREFER THAT MY GIRLFRIEND LET ME JOIN IN ON THE CRIME-SOLVING FUN.
GIRLFRIEND?
TOLDJA YOU WEREN'T LISTENING. IS THAT OKAY WITH YOU?
UM... YEAH.
AWESOME. SO TELL ME ABOUT THE CASE...
IT'S A STRANGE ONE. READS LIKE A SIMPLE ABDUCTION BECAUSE THERE WAS A RANSOM NOTE AND NO BODY...
...BUT THERE WAS A TON OF GRUESOME PHYSICAL EVIDENCE THAT SUGGESTS OTHERWISE. THE WITNESS I TALKED TO CLAIMS THAT IT WAS MURDER, WHICH IS WHY THE KIDNAPPERS NEVER FOLLOWED UP ON THE RANSOM.
I REMEMBER THAT ONE...IRIS WEST DID A WHOLE EXPOSÉ ON THE FAMILY. YOU SHOULD TALK TO HER ABOUT IT.
GREAT... SO YOU'LL CALL IRIS AND SET IT ALL UP?
UHH... YEAH. I GUESS.
CHEETA EXPRESS
Welcome to Central City
PERFECT. THANKS, BOYFRIEND!
CHEETA EXPRESS
Welcome to Central City

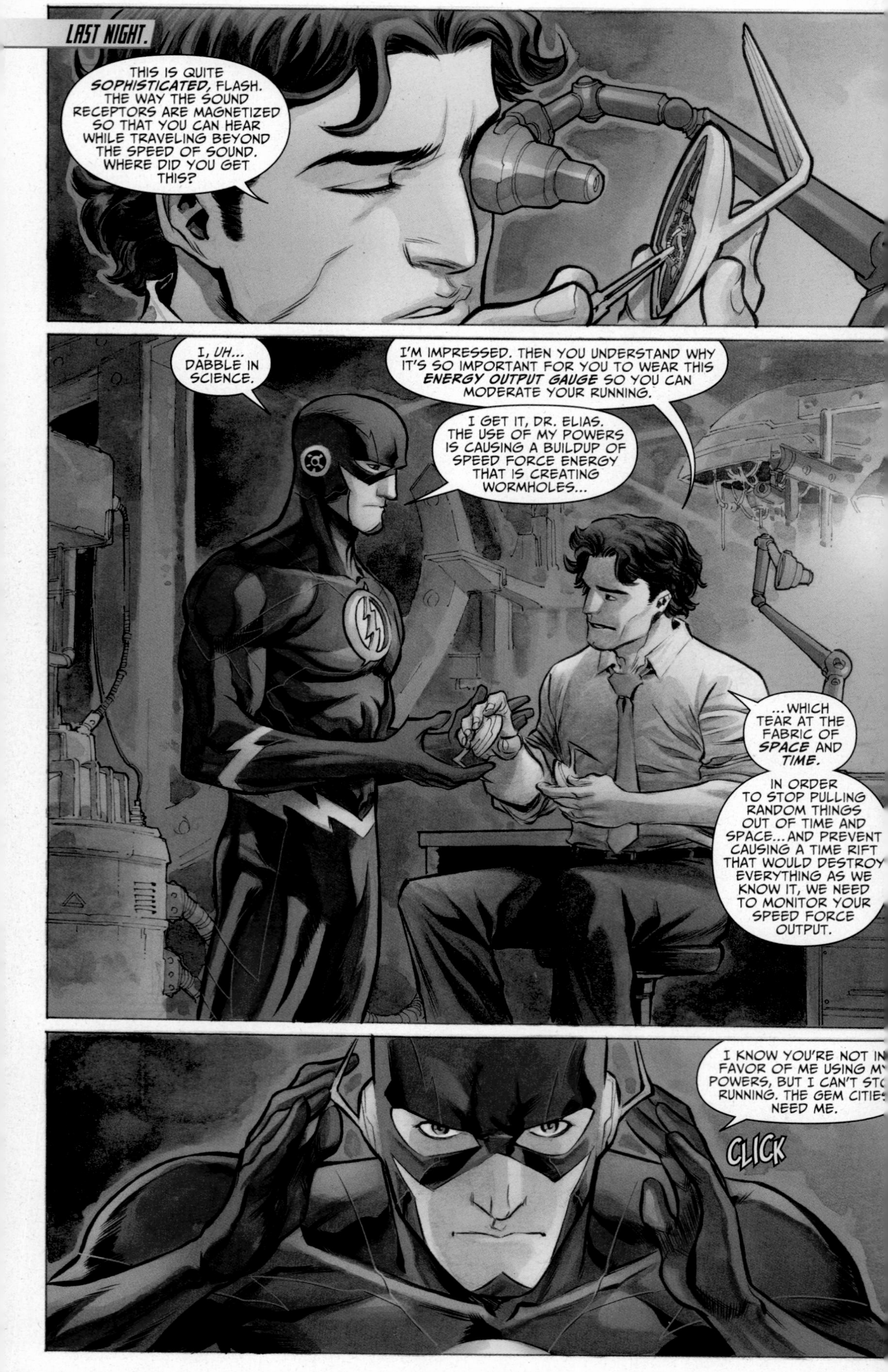
LAST NIGHT.
THIS IS QUITE SOPHISTICATED, FLASH. THE WAY THE SOUND RECEPTORS ARE MAGNETIZED SO THAT YOU CAN HEAR WHILE TRAVELING BEYOND THE SPEED OF SOUND. WHERE DID YOU GET THIS?
I, UH... DABBLE IN SCIENCE.
I'M IMPRESSED. THEN YOU UNDERSTAND WHY IT'S SO IMPORTANT FOR YOU TO WEAR THIS ENERGY OUTPUT GAUGE SO YOU CAN MODERATE YOUR RUNNING.
I GET IT, DR. ELIAS. THE USE OF MY POWERS IS CAUSING A BUILDUP OF SPEED FORCE ENERGY THAT IS CREATING WORMHOLES...
...WHICH TEAR AT THE FABRIC OF SPACE AND TIME.
IN ORDER TO STOP PULLING RANDOM THINGS OUT OF TIME AND SPACE...AND PREVENT CAUSING A TIME RIFT THAT WOULD DESTROY EVERYTHING AS WE KNOW IT, WE NEED TO MONITOR YOUR SPEED FORCE OUTPUT.
I KNOW YOU'RE NOT IN FAVOR OF ME USING MY POWERS, BUT I CAN'T STOP RUNNING. THE GEM CITIES NEED ME.
CLICK

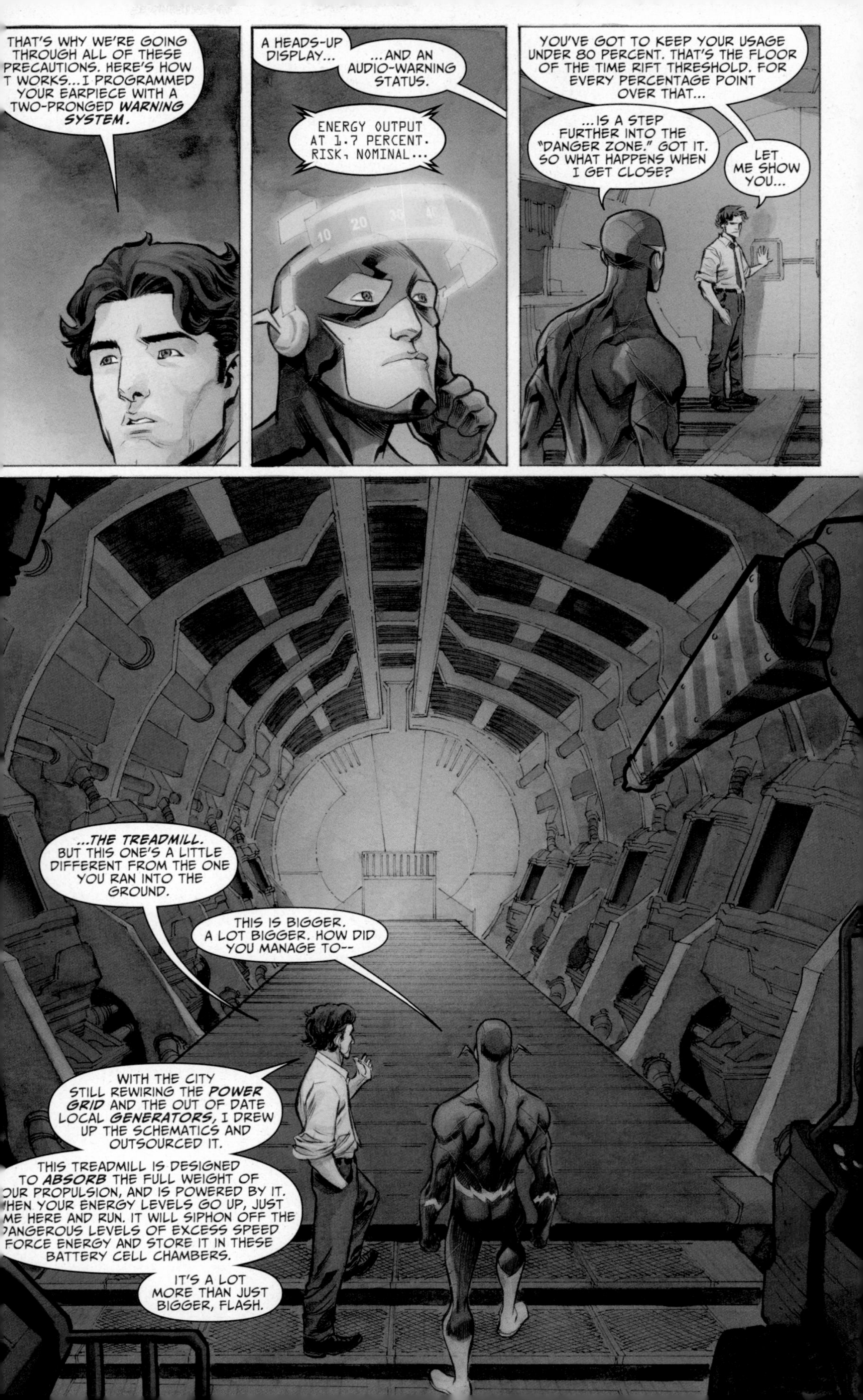
THAT'S WHY WE'RE GOING THROUGH ALL OF THESE PRECAUTIONS. HERE'S HOW IT WORKS...I PROGRAMMED YOUR EARPIECE WITH A TWO-PRONGED WARNING SYSTEM.
A HEADS-UP DISPLAY...
...AND AN AUDIO-WARNING STATUS.
ENERGY OUTPUT AT 1.7 PERCENT. RISK, NOMINAL...
10 20 30 40
YOU'VE GOT TO KEEP YOUR USAGE UNDER 80 PERCENT. THAT'S THE FLOOR OF THE TIME RIFT THRESHOLD. FOR EVERY PERCENTAGE POINT OVER THAT...
...IS A STEP FURTHER INTO THE "DANGER ZONE." GOT IT. SO WHAT HAPPENS WHEN I GET CLOSE?
LET ME SHOW YOU...
...THE TREADMILL. BUT THIS ONE'S A LITTLE DIFFERENT FROM THE ONE YOU RAN INTO THE GROUND.
THIS IS BIGGER. A LOT BIGGER. HOW DID YOU MANAGE TO--
WITH THE CITY STILL REWIRING THE POWER GRID AND THE OUT OF DATE LOCAL GENERATORS, I DREW UP THE SCHEMATICS AND OUTSOURCED IT.
THIS TREADMILL IS DESIGNED TO ABSORB THE FULL WEIGHT OF OUR PROPULSION, AND IS POWERED BY IT. WHEN YOUR ENERGY LEVELS GO UP, JUST COME HERE AND RUN. IT WILL SIPHON OFF THE DANGEROUS LEVELS OF EXCESS SPEED FORCE ENERGY AND STORE IT IN THESE BATTERY CELL CHAMBERS.
IT'S A LOT MORE THAN JUST BIGGER, FLASH.

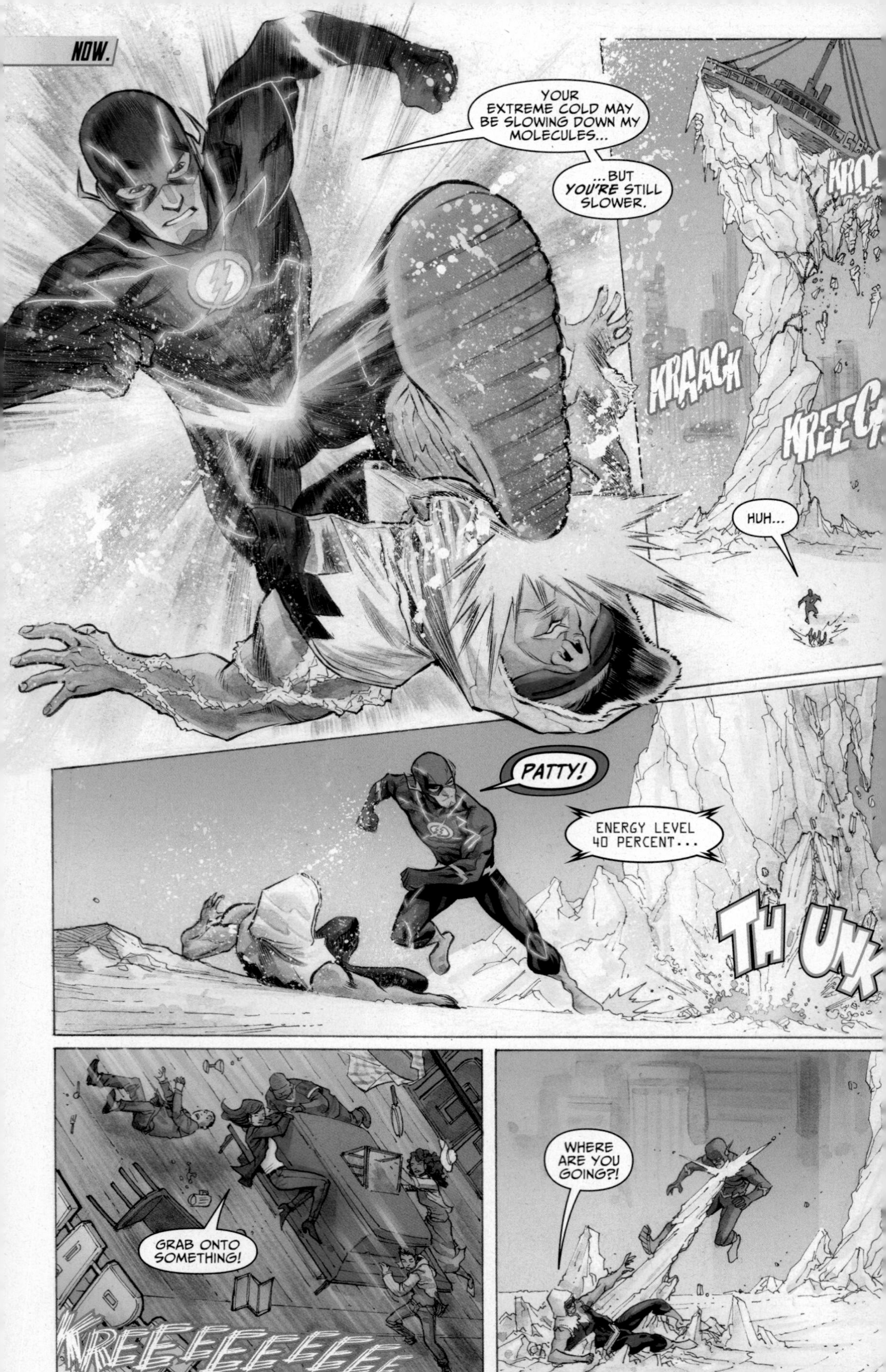
NOW.
YOUR EXTREME COLD MAY BE SLOWING DOWN MY MOLECULES...
...BUT YOU'RE STILL SLOWER.
KROO
KRAACK
KREEC
HUH...
PATTY!
ENERGY LEVEL 40 PERCENT...
THUNK
GRAB ONTO SOMETHING!
KREEEEEEEEEE
WHERE ARE YOU GOING?!

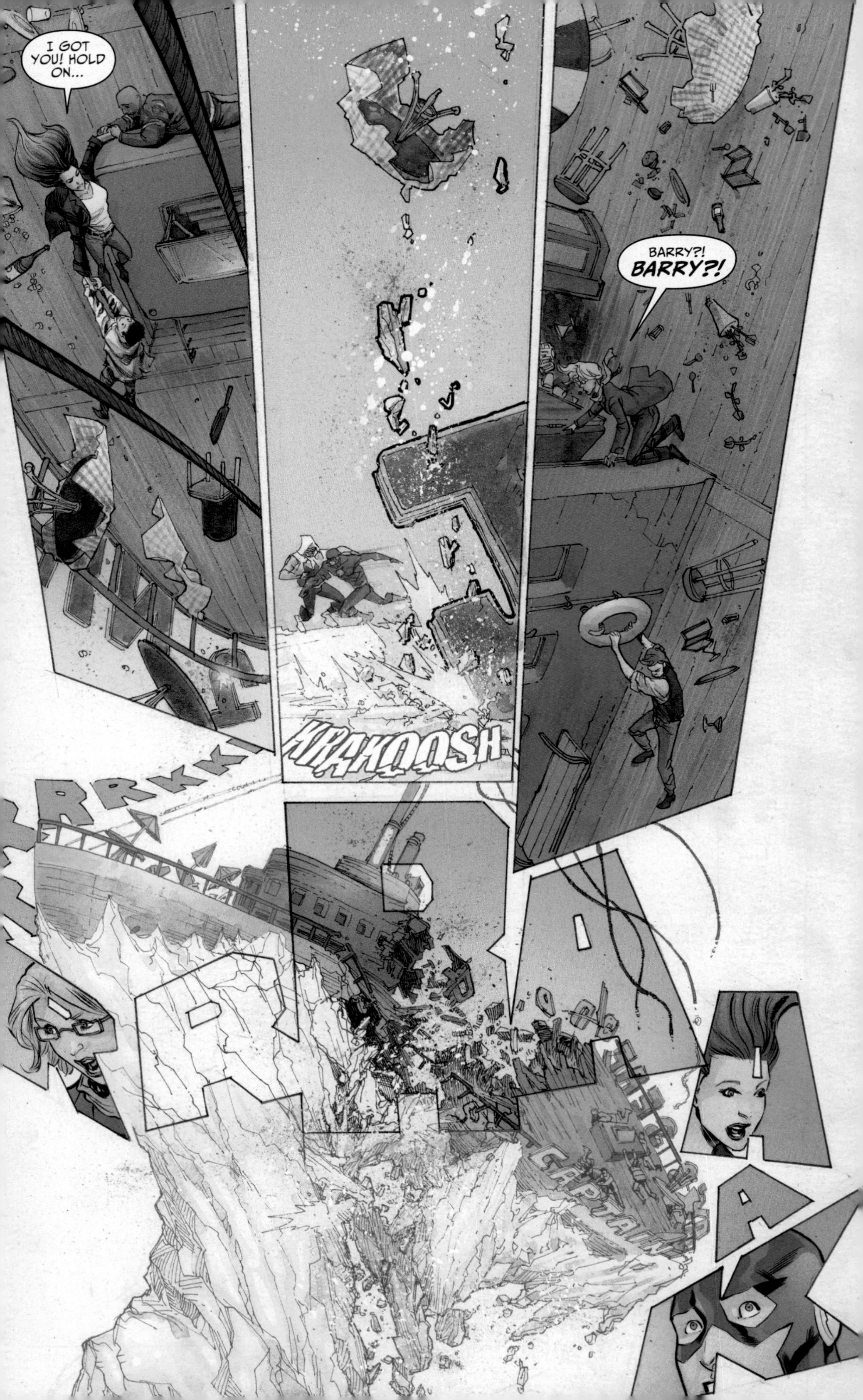
I GOT YOU! HOLD ON...
BARRY?! BARRY?!
KRAKOOSH

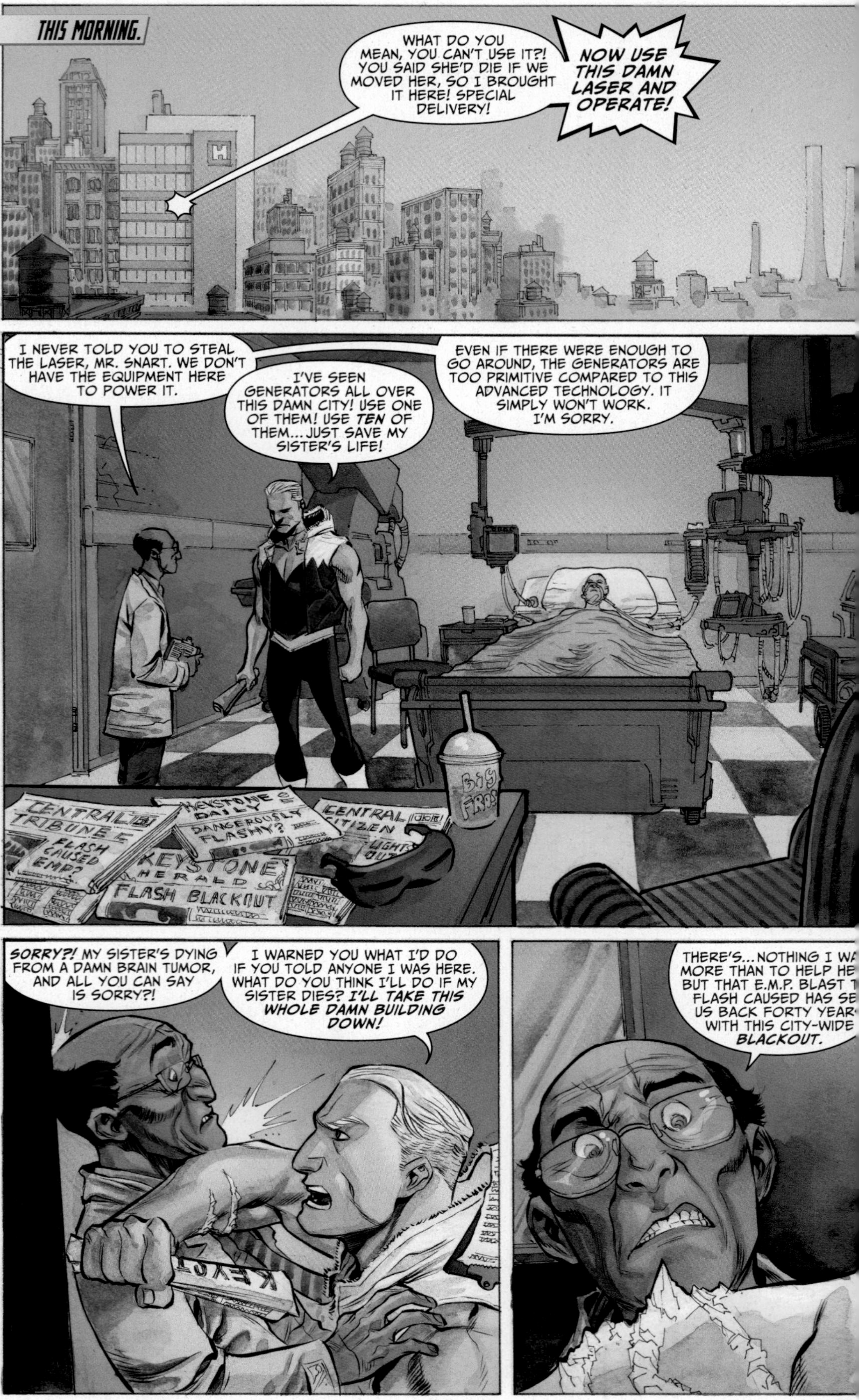
THIS MORNING.
WHAT DO YOU MEAN, YOU CAN'T USE IT?! YOU SAID SHE'D DIE IF WE MOVED HER, SO I BROUGHT IT HERE! SPECIAL DELIVERY!
NOW USE THIS DAMN LASER AND OPERATE!
I NEVER TOLD YOU TO STEAL THE LASER, MR. SNART. WE DON'T HAVE THE EQUIPMENT HERE TO POWER IT.
I'VE SEEN GENERATORS ALL OVER THIS DAMN CITY! USE ONE OF THEM! USE TEN OF THEM... JUST SAVE MY SISTER'S LIFE!
EVEN IF THERE WERE ENOUGH TO GO AROUND, THE GENERATORS ARE TOO PRIMITIVE COMPARED TO THIS ADVANCED TECHNOLOGY. IT SIMPLY WON'T WORK. I'M SORRY.
CENTRAL TRIBUNE
FLASH CAUSED EMP?
KEYSTONE DAILY
DANGEROUSLY FLASHY?
CENTRAL CITIZEN
KEYSTONE HERALD
FLASH BLACKOUT
BIG FROS
SORRY?! MY SISTER'S DYING FROM A DAMN BRAIN TUMOR, AND ALL YOU CAN SAY IS SORRY?!
I WARNED YOU WHAT I'D DO IF YOU TOLD ANYONE I WAS HERE. WHAT DO YOU THINK I'LL DO IF MY SISTER DIES? I'LL TAKE THIS WHOLE DAMN BUILDING DOWN!
THERE'S... NOTHING I WA MORE THAN TO HELP HE BUT THAT E.M.P. BLAST T FLASH CAUSED HAS SE US BACK FORTY YEAR WITH THIS CITY-WIDE BLACKOUT.

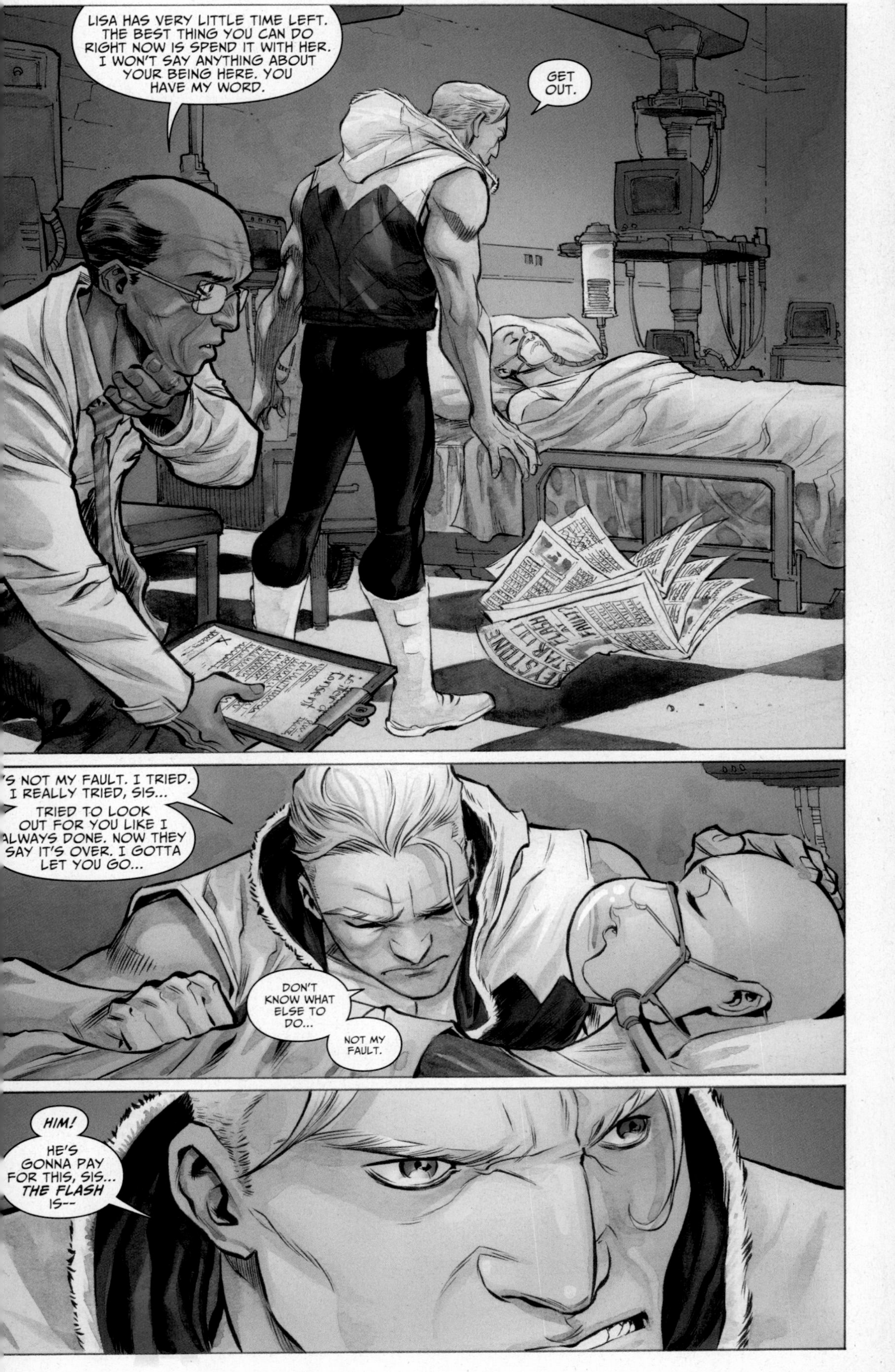
LISA HAS VERY LITTLE TIME LEFT. THE BEST THING YOU CAN DO RIGHT NOW IS SPEND IT WITH HER. I WON'T SAY ANYTHING ABOUT YOUR BEING HERE. YOU HAVE MY WORD.
GET OUT.
'S NOT MY FAULT. I TRIED. I REALLY TRIED, SIS...
TRIED TO LOOK OUT FOR YOU LIKE I ALWAYS DONE. NOW THEY SAY IT'S OVER. I GOTTA LET YOU GO...
DON'T KNOW WHAT ELSE TO DO...
NOT MY FAULT.
HIM!
HE'S GONNA PAY FOR THIS, SIS... *THE FLASH* IS--

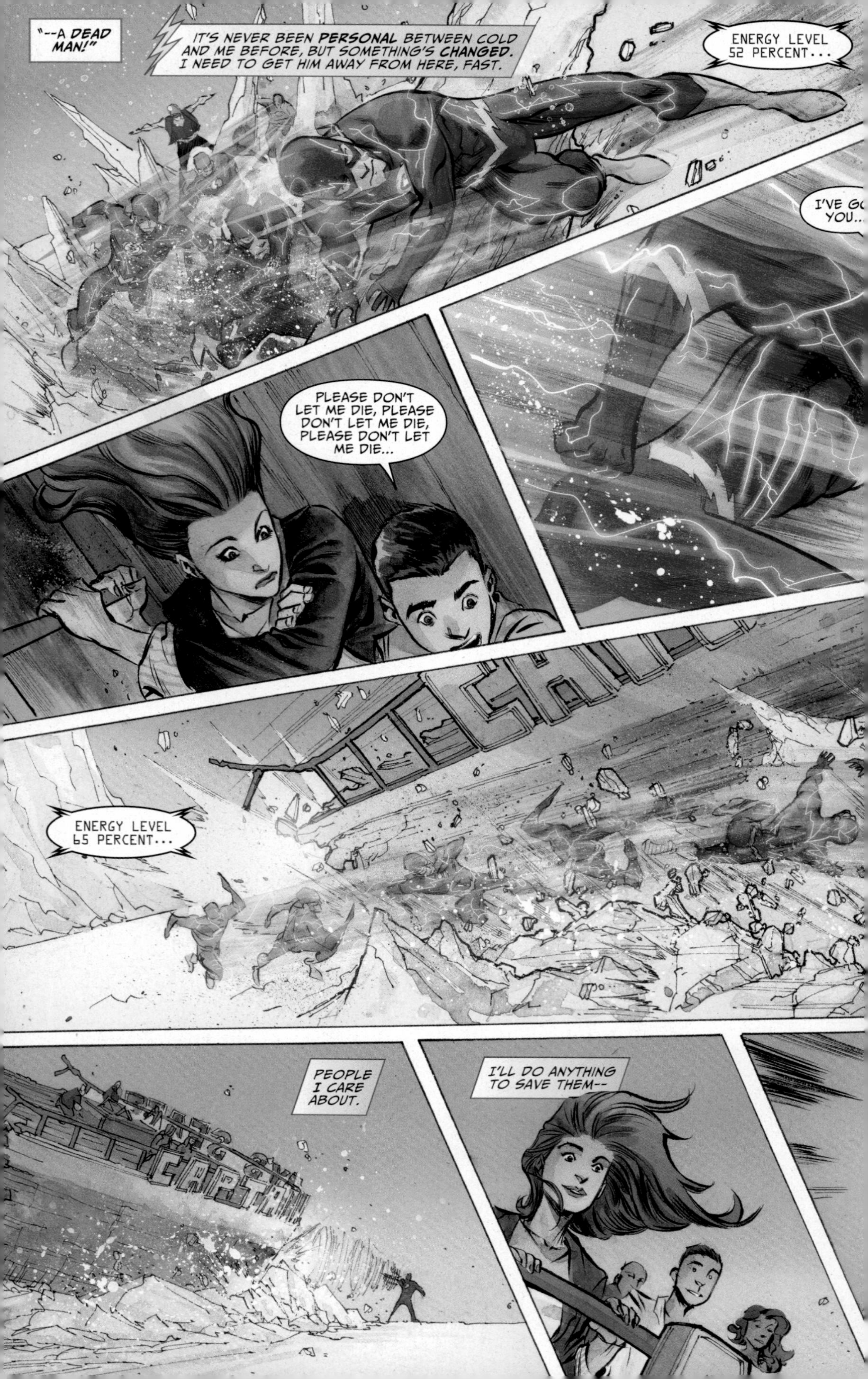
"--A DEAD MAN!"
IT'S NEVER BEEN PERSONAL BETWEEN COLD AND ME BEFORE, BUT SOMETHING'S CHANGED. I NEED TO GET HIM AWAY FROM HERE, FAST.
ENERGY LEVEL 52 PERCENT...
I'VE GO YOU...
PLEASE DON'T LET ME DIE, PLEASE DON'T LET ME DIE, PLEASE DON'T LET ME DIE...
ENERGY LEVEL 65 PERCENT...
PEOPLE I CARE ABOUT.
I'LL DO ANYTHING TO SAVE THEM--

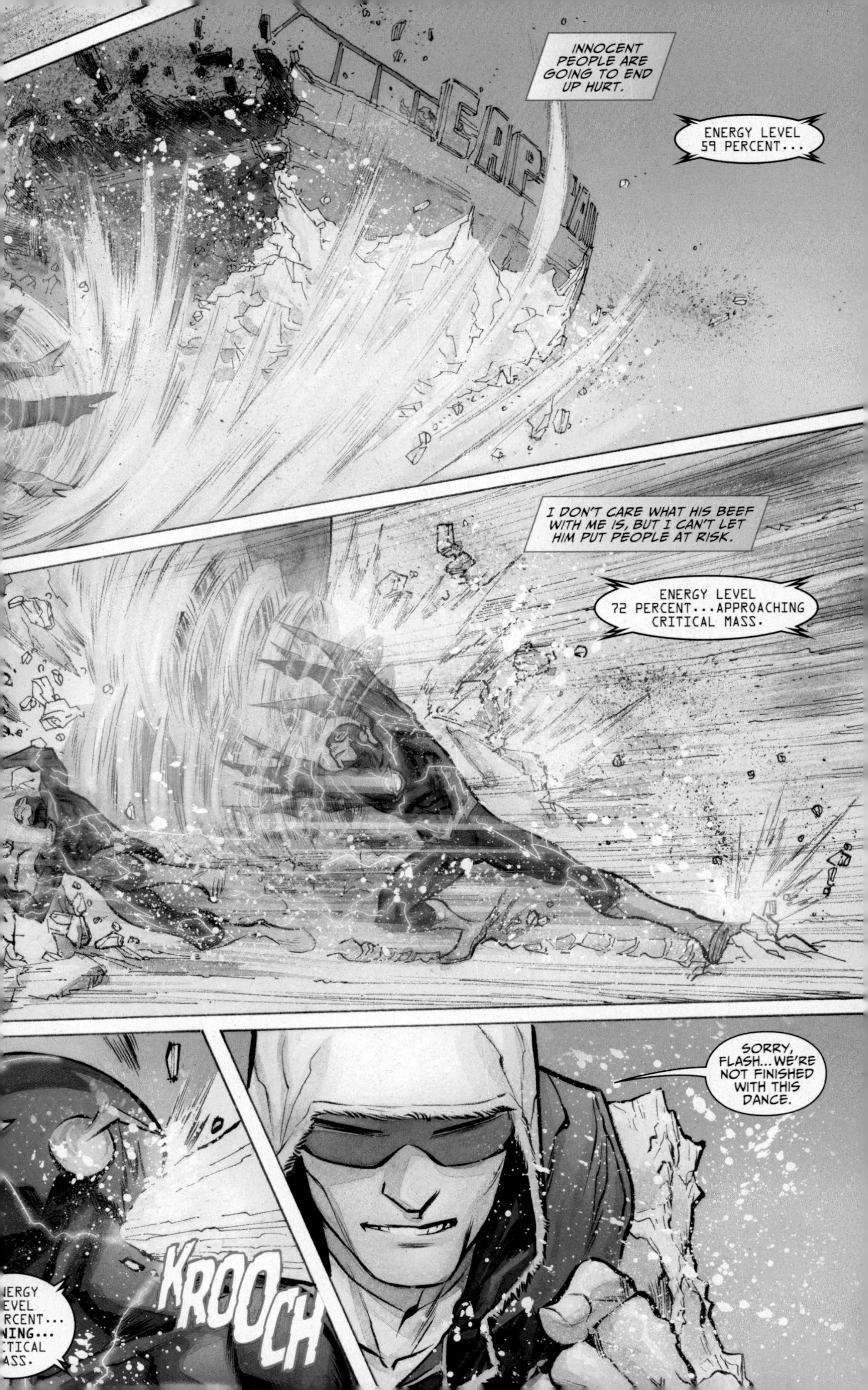
INNOCENT PEOPLE ARE GOING TO END UP HURT.
ENERGY LEVEL 59 PERCENT...
I DON'T CARE WHAT HIS BEEF WITH ME IS, BUT I CAN'T LET HIM PUT PEOPLE AT RISK.
ENERGY LEVEL 72 PERCENT...APPROACHING CRITICAL MASS.
SORRY, FLASH...WE'RE NOT FINISHED WITH THIS DANCE.
ERGY EVEL RCENT... NING... TICAL ASS.
KROOCH

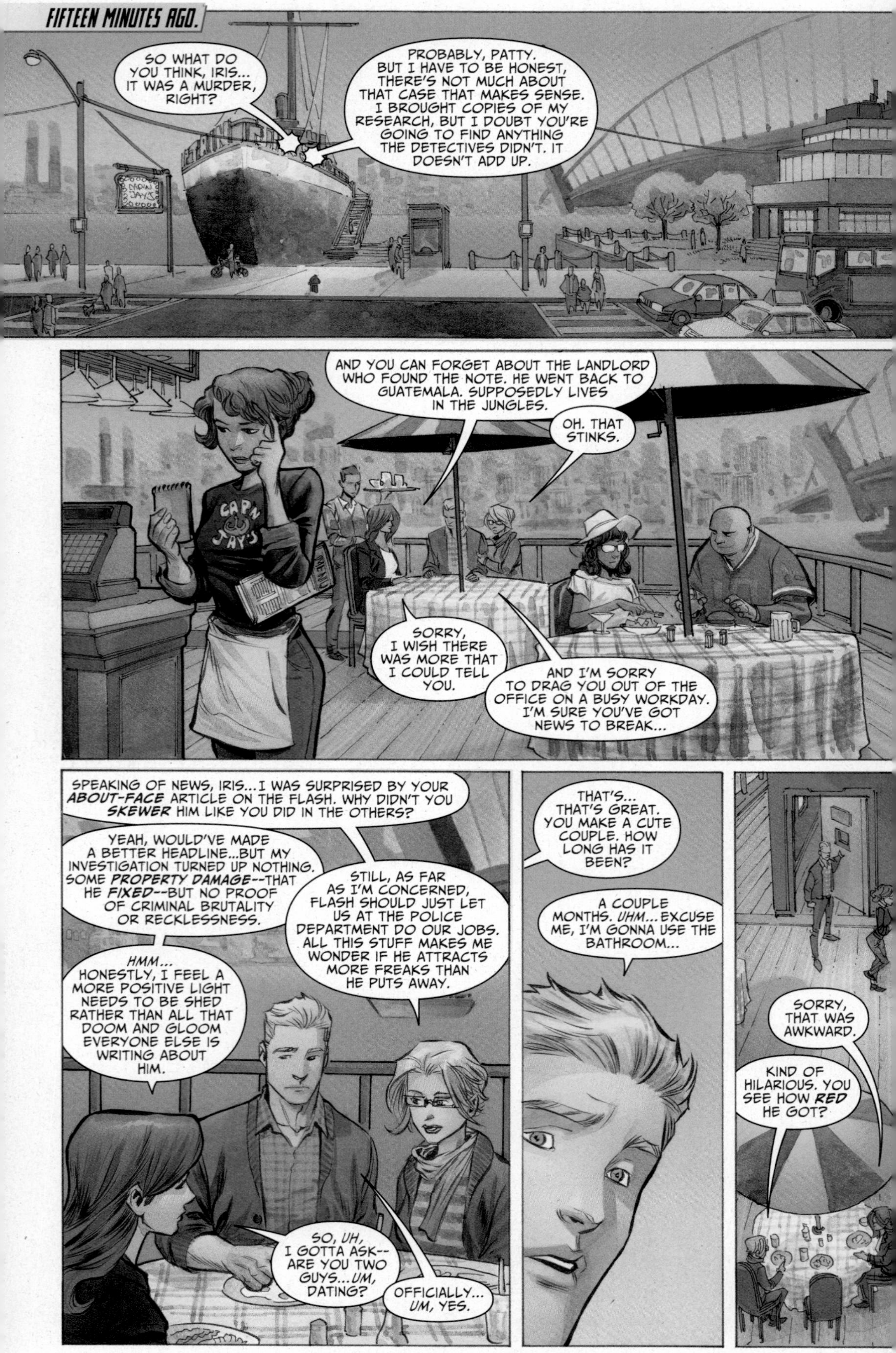
FIFTEEN MINUTES AGO.
SO WHAT DO YOU THINK, IRIS... IT WAS A MURDER, RIGHT?
CAP'N JAY'S
PROBABLY, PATTY. BUT I HAVE TO BE HONEST, THERE'S NOT MUCH ABOUT THAT CASE THAT MAKES SENSE. I BROUGHT COPIES OF MY RESEARCH, BUT I DOUBT YOU'RE GOING TO FIND ANYTHING THE DETECTIVES DIDN'T. IT DOESN'T ADD UP.
AND YOU CAN FORGET ABOUT THE LANDLORD WHO FOUND THE NOTE. HE WENT BACK TO GUATEMALA. SUPPOSEDLY LIVES IN THE JUNGLES.
OH. THAT STINKS.
CAP'N JAY'S
SORRY, I WISH THERE WAS MORE THAT I COULD TELL YOU.
AND I'M SORRY TO DRAG YOU OUT OF THE OFFICE ON A BUSY WORKDAY. I'M SURE YOU'VE GOT NEWS TO BREAK...
SPEAKING OF NEWS, IRIS... I WAS SURPRISED BY YOUR *ABOUT-FACE* ARTICLE ON THE FLASH. WHY DIDN'T YOU *SKEWER* HIM LIKE YOU DID IN THE OTHERS?
YEAH, WOULD'VE MADE A BETTER HEADLINE...BUT MY INVESTIGATION TURNED UP NOTHING. SOME *PROPERTY DAMAGE*--THAT HE *FIXED*--BUT NO PROOF OF CRIMINAL BRUTALITY OR RECKLESSNESS.
STILL, AS FAR AS I'M CONCERNED, FLASH SHOULD JUST LET US AT THE POLICE DEPARTMENT DO OUR JOBS. ALL THIS STUFF MAKES ME WONDER IF HE ATTRACTS MORE FREAKS THAN HE PUTS AWAY.
HMM... HONESTLY, I FEEL A MORE POSITIVE LIGHT NEEDS TO BE SHED RATHER THAN ALL THAT DOOM AND GLOOM EVERYONE ELSE IS WRITING ABOUT HIM.
SO, UH, I GOTTA ASK-- ARE YOU TWO GUYS...*UM*, DATING?
OFFICIALLY... *UM*, YES.
THAT'S... THAT'S GREAT. YOU MAKE A CUTE COUPLE. HOW LONG HAS IT BEEN?
A COUPLE MONTHS. *UHM*... EXCUSE ME, I'M GONNA USE THE BATHROOM...
SORRY, THAT WAS AWKWARD.
KIND OF HILARIOUS. YOU SEE HOW *RED* HE GOT?

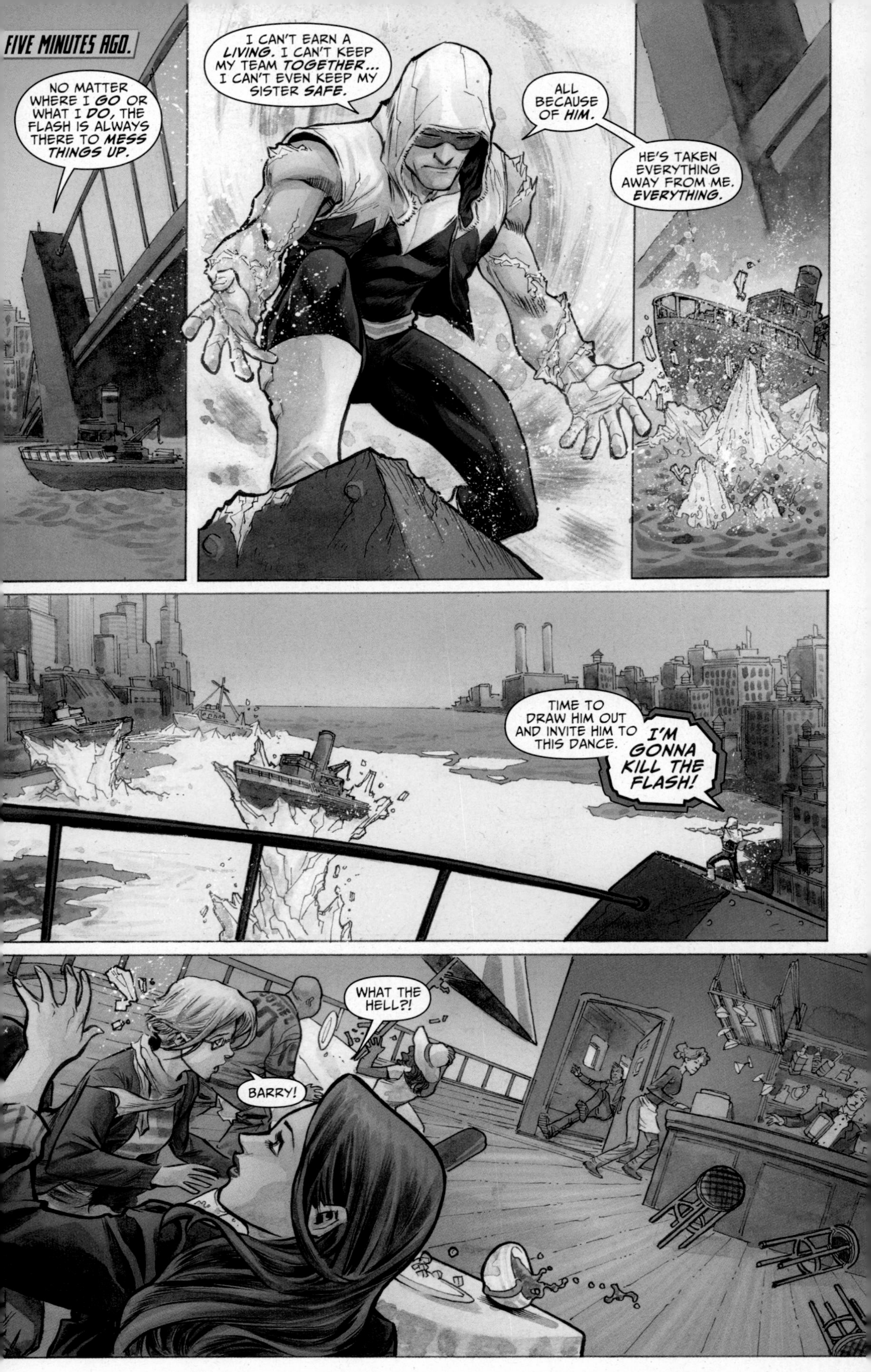
FIVE MINUTES AGO.
NO MATTER WHERE I GO OR WHAT I DO, THE FLASH IS ALWAYS THERE TO MESS THINGS UP.
I CAN'T EARN A LIVING. I CAN'T KEEP MY TEAM TOGETHER... I CAN'T EVEN KEEP MY SISTER SAFE.
ALL BECAUSE OF HIM.
HE'S TAKEN EVERYTHING AWAY FROM ME. EVERYTHING.
TIME TO DRAW HIM OUT AND INVITE HIM TO THIS DANCE.
I'M GONNA KILL THE FLASH!
WHAT THE HELL?!
BARRY!

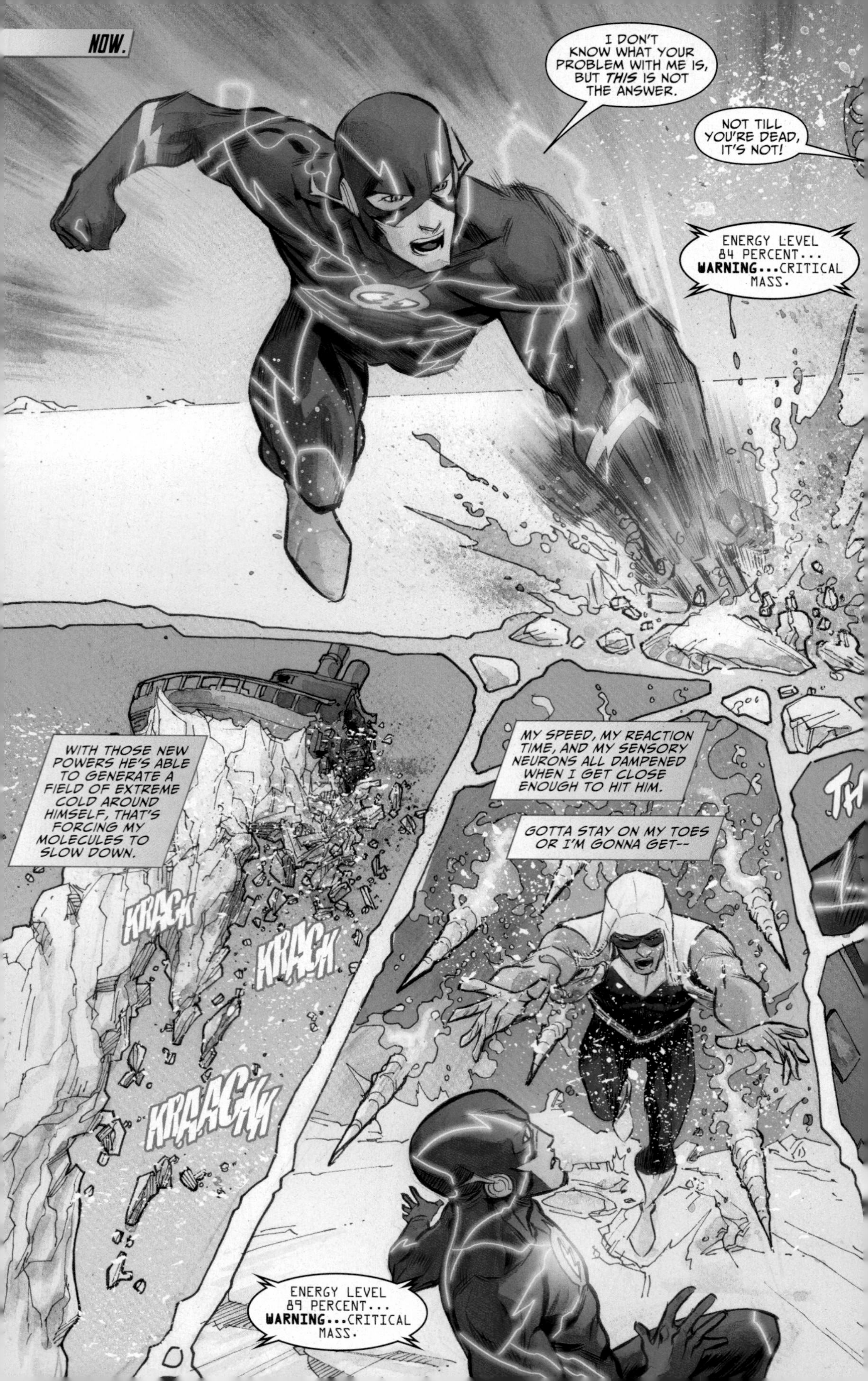

NOW.
I DON'T KNOW WHAT YOUR PROBLEM WITH ME IS, BUT THIS IS NOT THE ANSWER.
NOT TILL YOU'RE DEAD, IT'S NOT!
ENERGY LEVEL 84 PERCENT... WARNING...CRITICAL MASS.
WITH THOSE NEW POWERS HE'S ABLE TO GENERATE A FIELD OF EXTREME COLD AROUND HIMSELF, THAT'S FORCING MY MOLECULES TO SLOW DOWN.
KRACK
KRACK
KRAACKK
MY SPEED, MY REACTION TIME, AND MY SENSORY NEURONS ALL DAMPENED WHEN I GET CLOSE ENOUGH TO HIT HIM.
GOTTA STAY ON MY TOES OR I'M GONNA GET--
ENERGY LEVEL 89 PERCENT... WARNING...CRITICAL MASS.

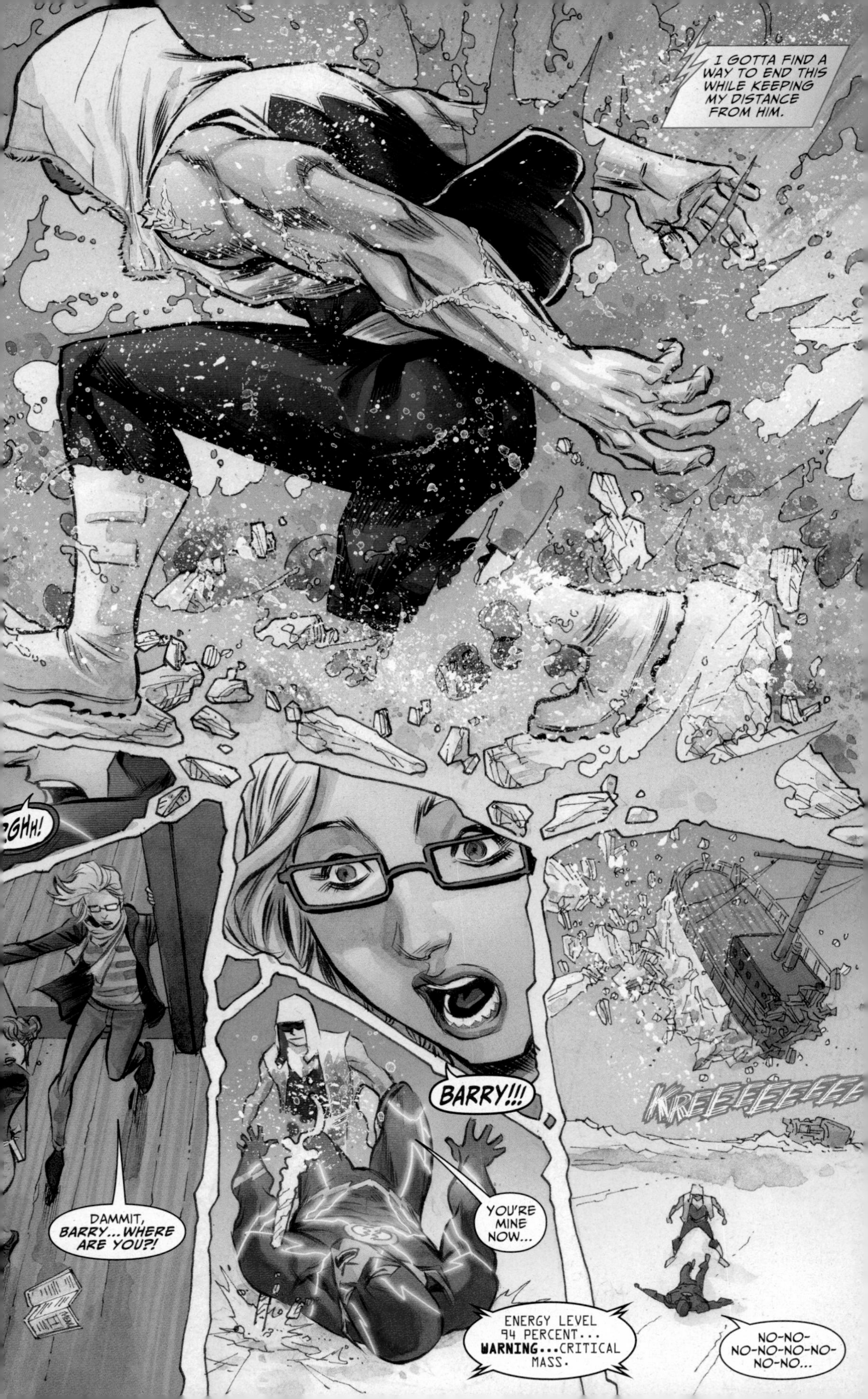
I GOTTA FIND A WAY TO END THIS WHILE KEEPING MY DISTANCE FROM HIM.
GHH!
DAMMIT, BARRY...WHERE ARE YOU?!
BARRY!!!
KREEEEEEEE
YOU'RE MINE NOW...
ENERGY LEVEL 94 PERCENT... WARNING...CRITICAL MASS.
NO-NO-NO-NO-NO-NO-NO-NO...

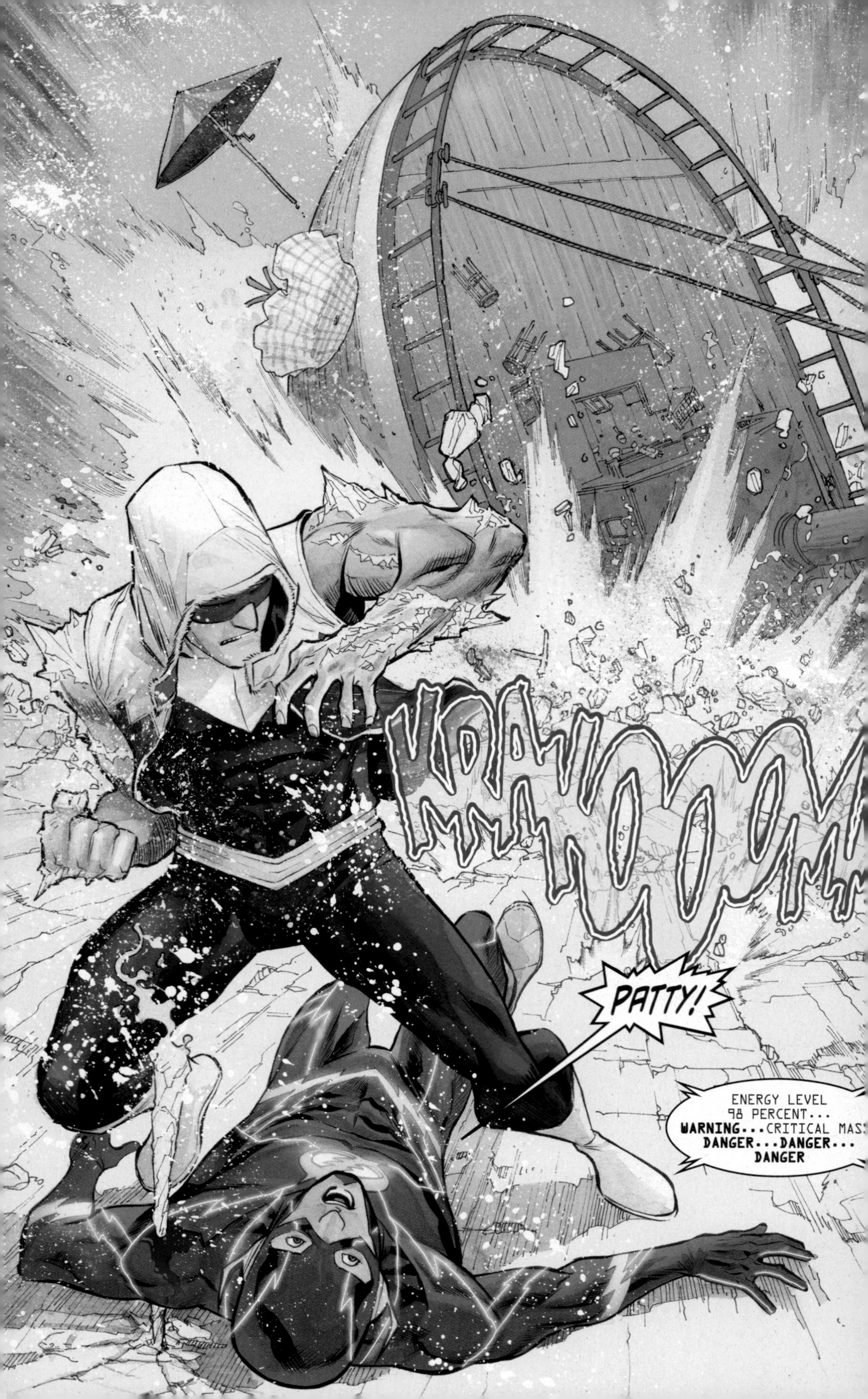
PATTY!
ENERGY LEVEL 98 PERCENT... WARNING...CRITICAL MAS
DANGER...DANGER... DANGER

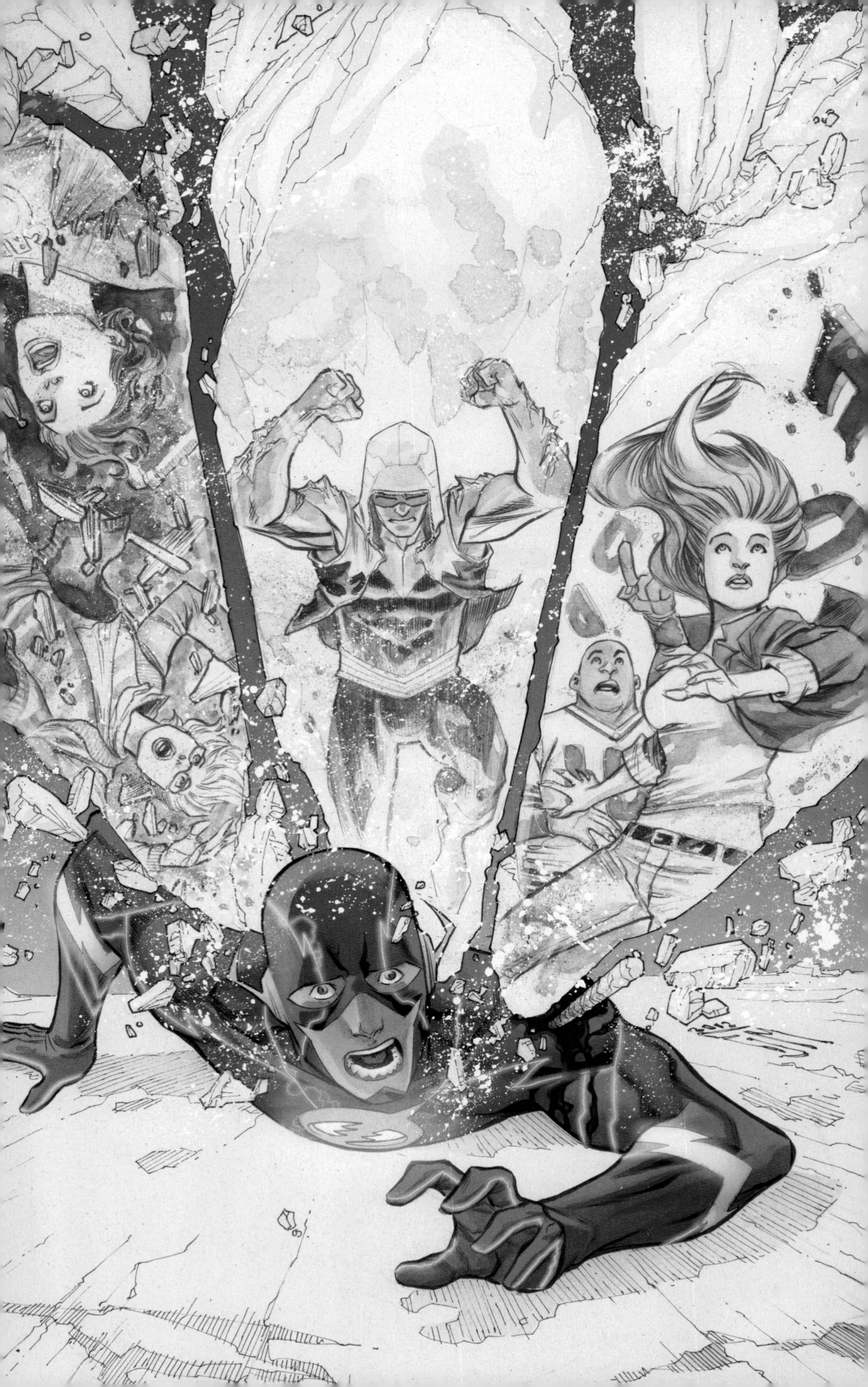

THE FLASH #7
variant cover by DALE KEOWN

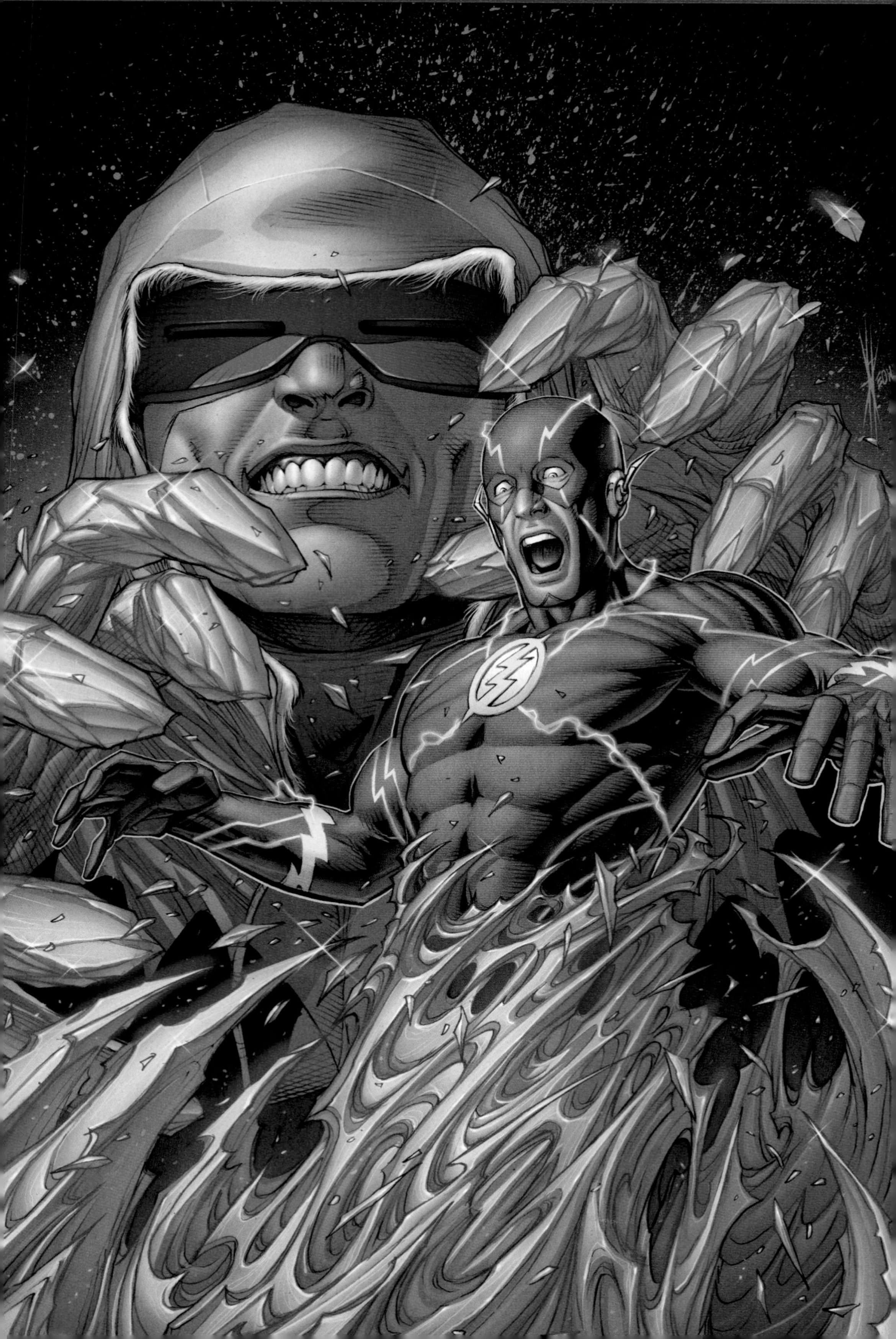

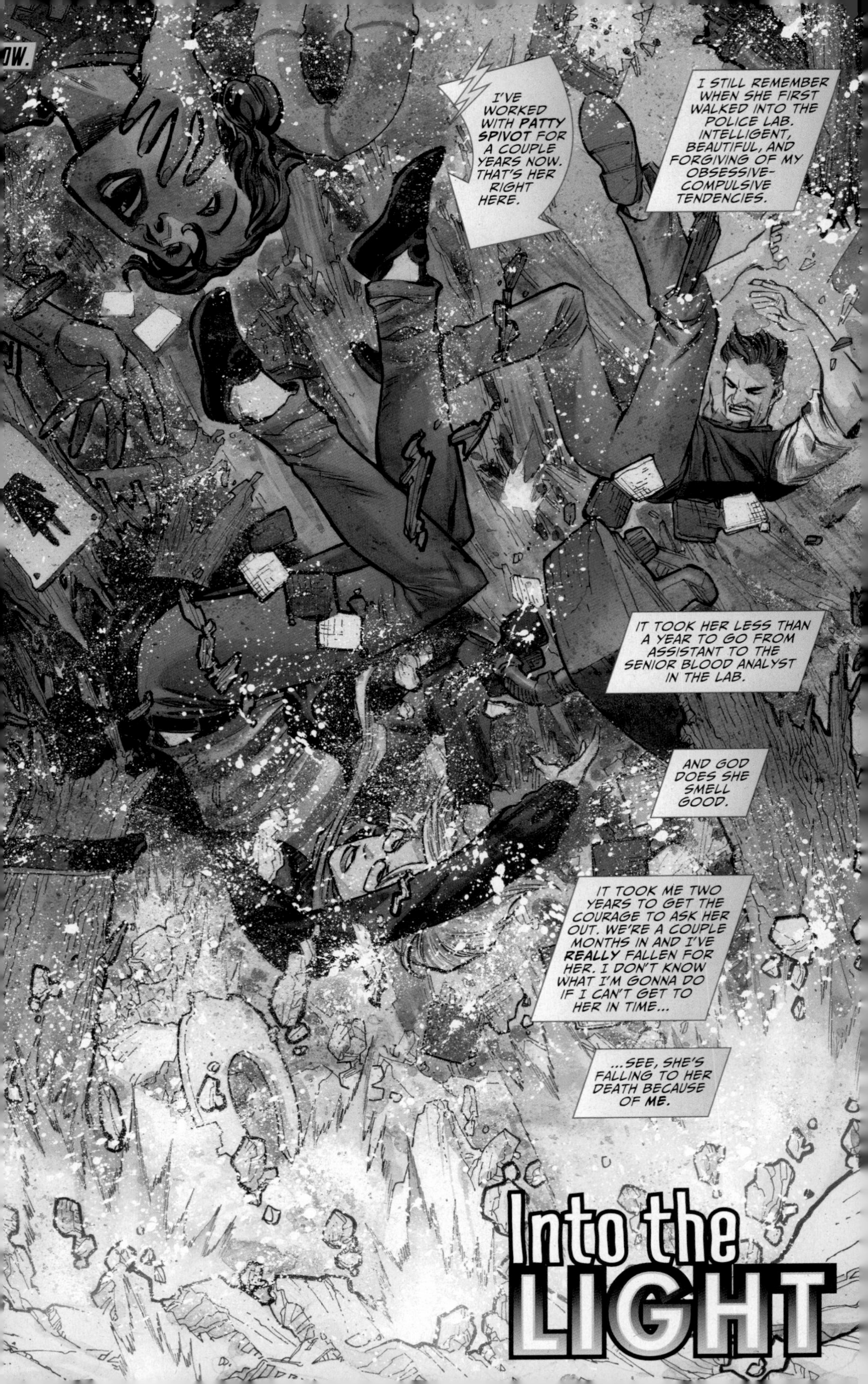
OW.
I'VE WORKED WITH PATTY SPIVOT FOR A COUPLE YEARS NOW. THAT'S HER RIGHT HERE.
I STILL REMEMBER WHEN SHE FIRST WALKED INTO THE POLICE LAB. INTELLIGENT, BEAUTIFUL, AND FORGIVING OF MY OBSESSIVE-COMPULSIVE TENDENCIES.
IT TOOK HER LESS THAN A YEAR TO GO FROM ASSISTANT TO THE SENIOR BLOOD ANALYST IN THE LAB.
AND GOD DOES SHE SMELL GOOD.
IT TOOK ME TWO YEARS TO GET THE COURAGE TO ASK HER OUT. WE'RE A COUPLE MONTHS IN AND I'VE REALLY FALLEN FOR HER. I DON'T KNOW WHAT I'M GONNA DO IF I CAN'T GET TO HER IN TIME...
...SEE, SHE'S FALLING TO HER DEATH BECAUSE OF ME.
Into the LIGHT

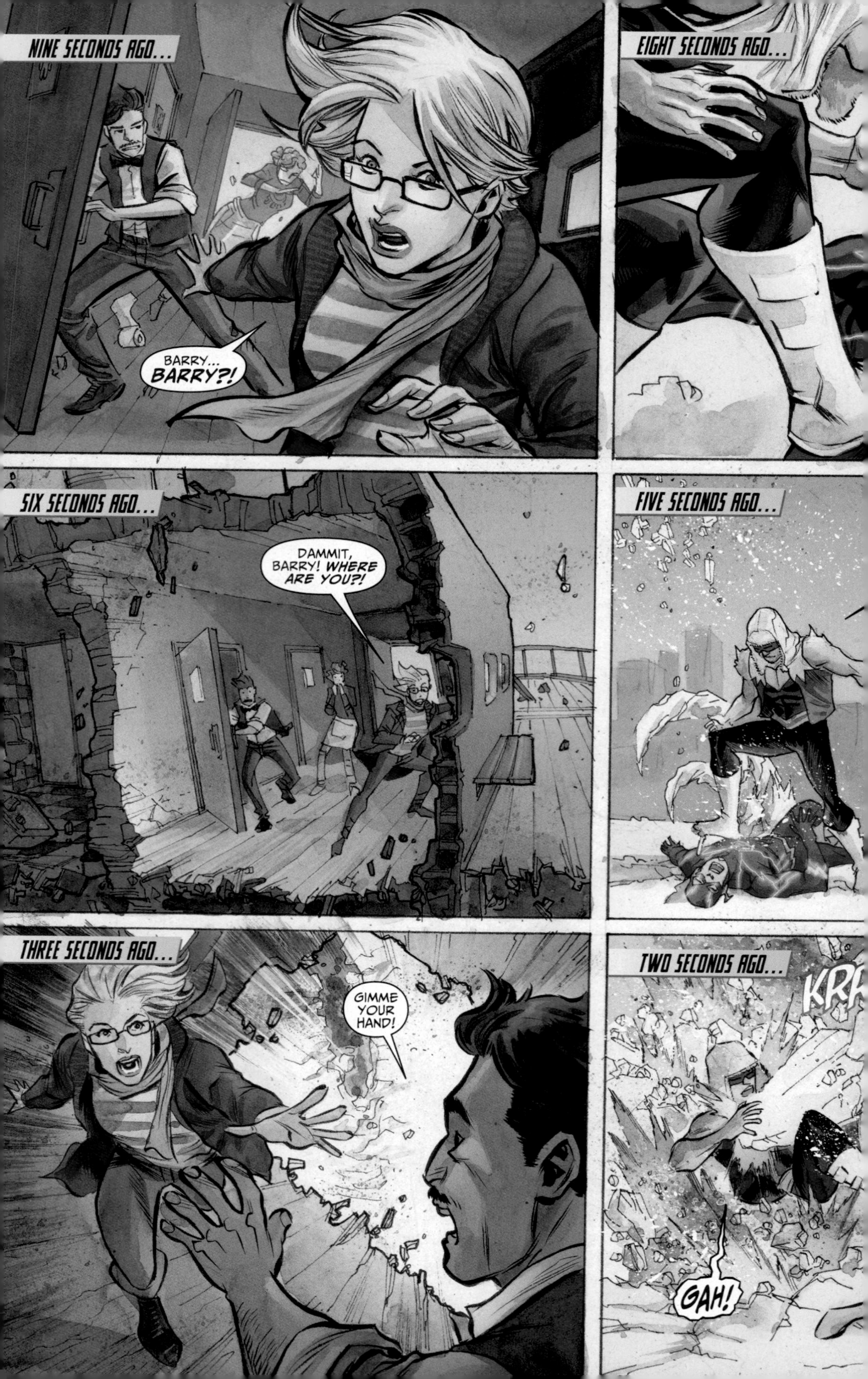
NINE SECONDS AGO...
BARRY... BARRY?!
EIGHT SECONDS AGO...
SIX SECONDS AGO...
DAMMIT, BARRY! WHERE ARE YOU?!
FIVE SECONDS AGO...
THREE SECONDS AGO...
GIMME YOUR HAND!
TWO SECONDS AGO...
GAH!

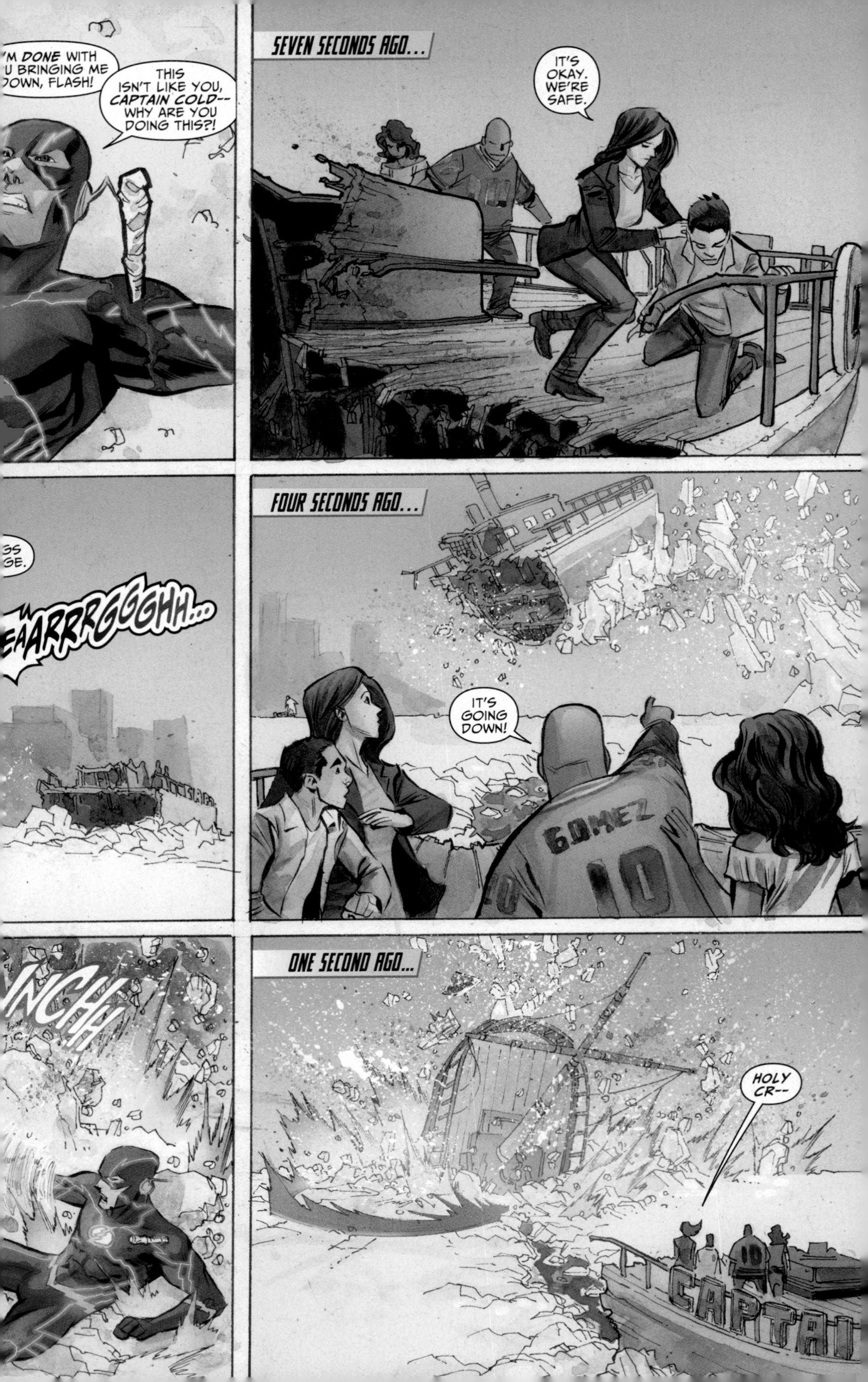

'M DONE WITH
U BRINGING ME
DOWN, FLASH!
THIS ISN'T LIKE YOU, CAPTAIN COLD-- WHY ARE YOU DOING THIS?!
SEVEN SECONDS AGO...
IT'S OKAY. WE'RE SAFE.
GS
GE.
EAARRRGGGHH...
FOUR SECONDS AGO...
IT'S GOING DOWN!
GOMEZ
10
NCHH
ONE SECOND AGO...
HOLY CR--
CAPTAI

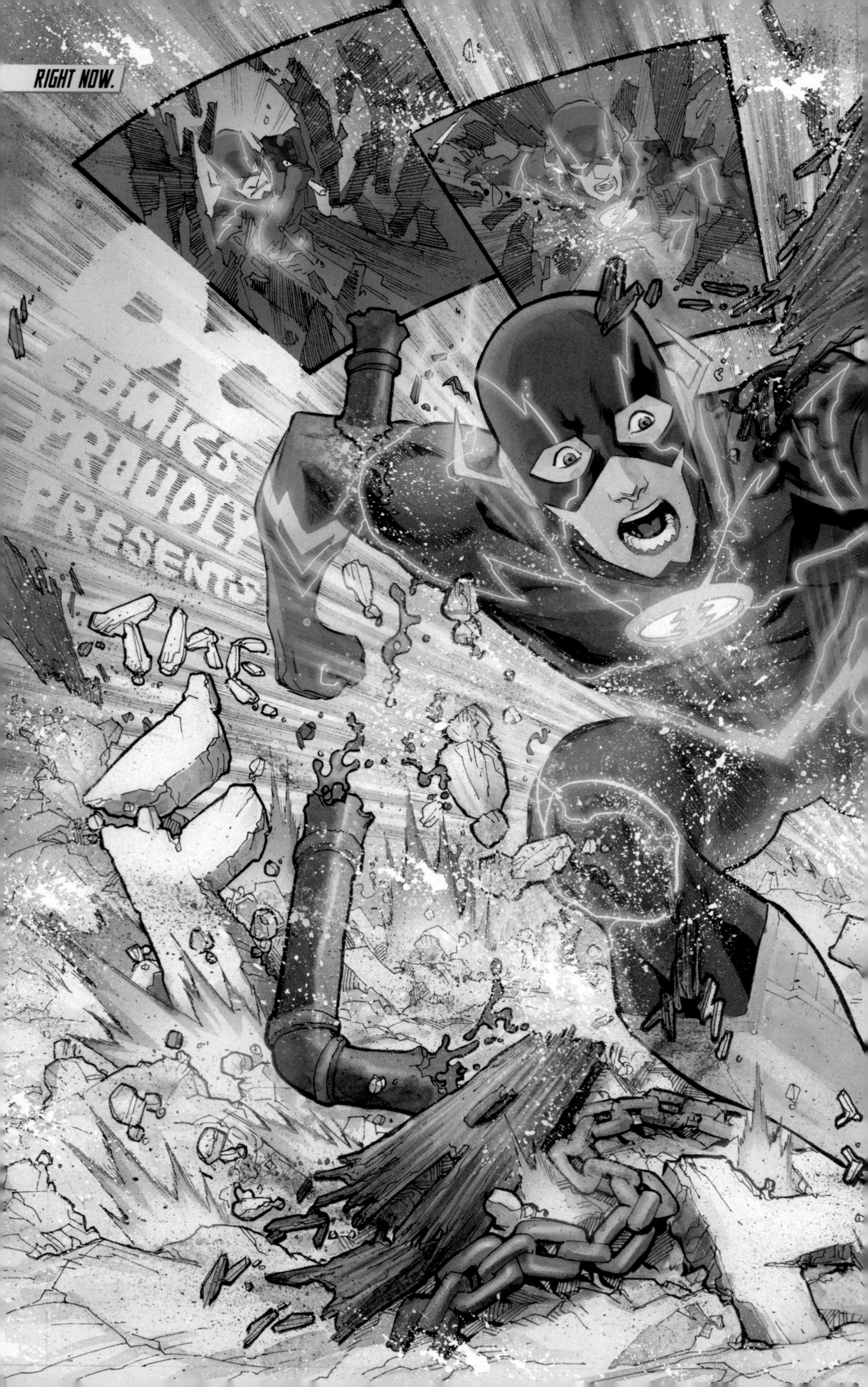
RIGHT NOW.
PROUDLY
PRESENTS
THE

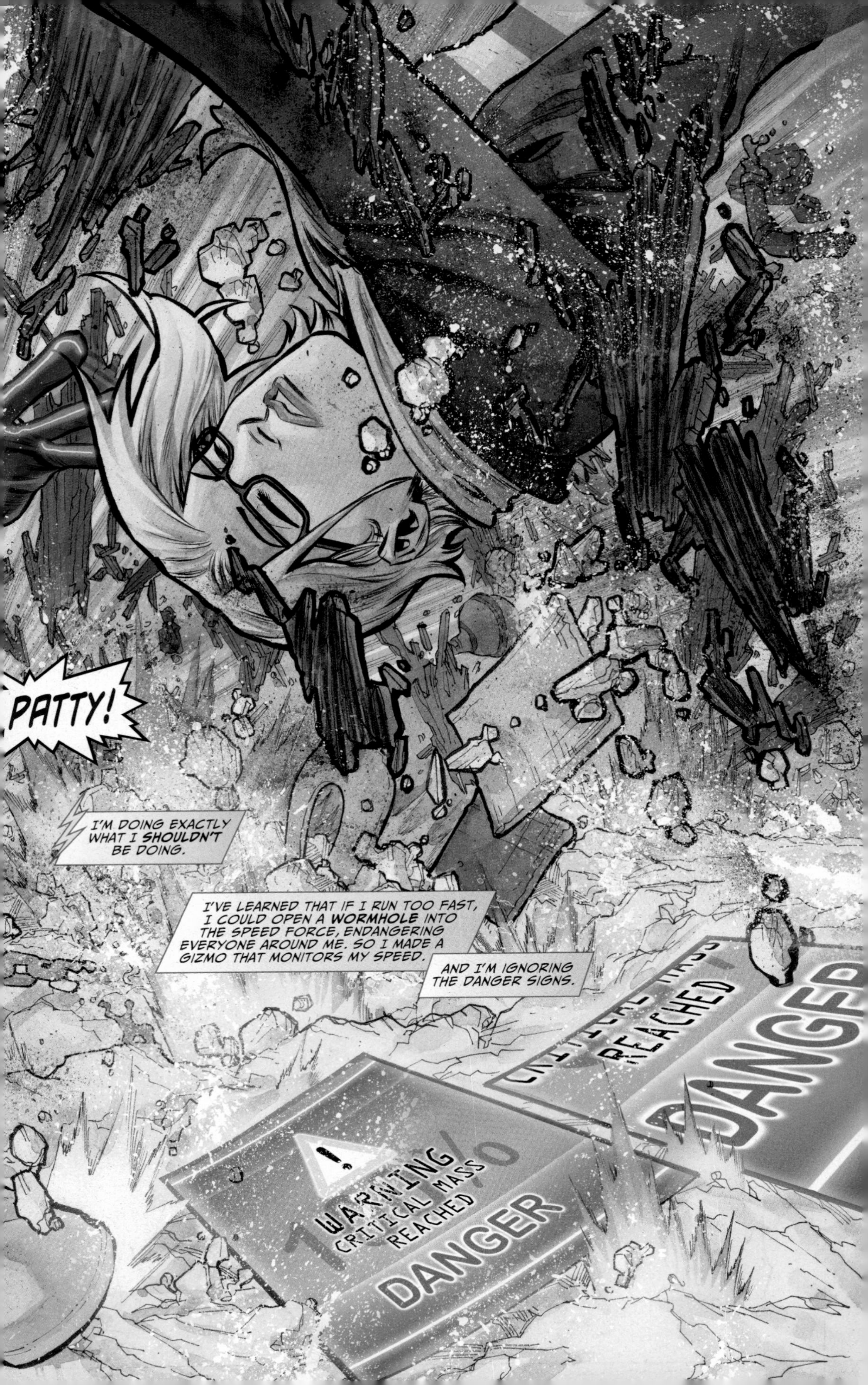
PATTY!
I'M DOING EXACTLY WHAT I SHOULDN'T BE DOING.
I'VE LEARNED THAT IF I RUN TOO FAST, I COULD OPEN A WORMHOLE INTO THE SPEED FORCE, ENDANGERING EVERYONE AROUND ME. SO I MADE A GIZMO THAT MONITORS MY SPEED.
AND I'M IGNORING THE DANGER SIGNS.
REACHED
DANGER
WARNING
CRITICAL MASS
REACHED
DANGER

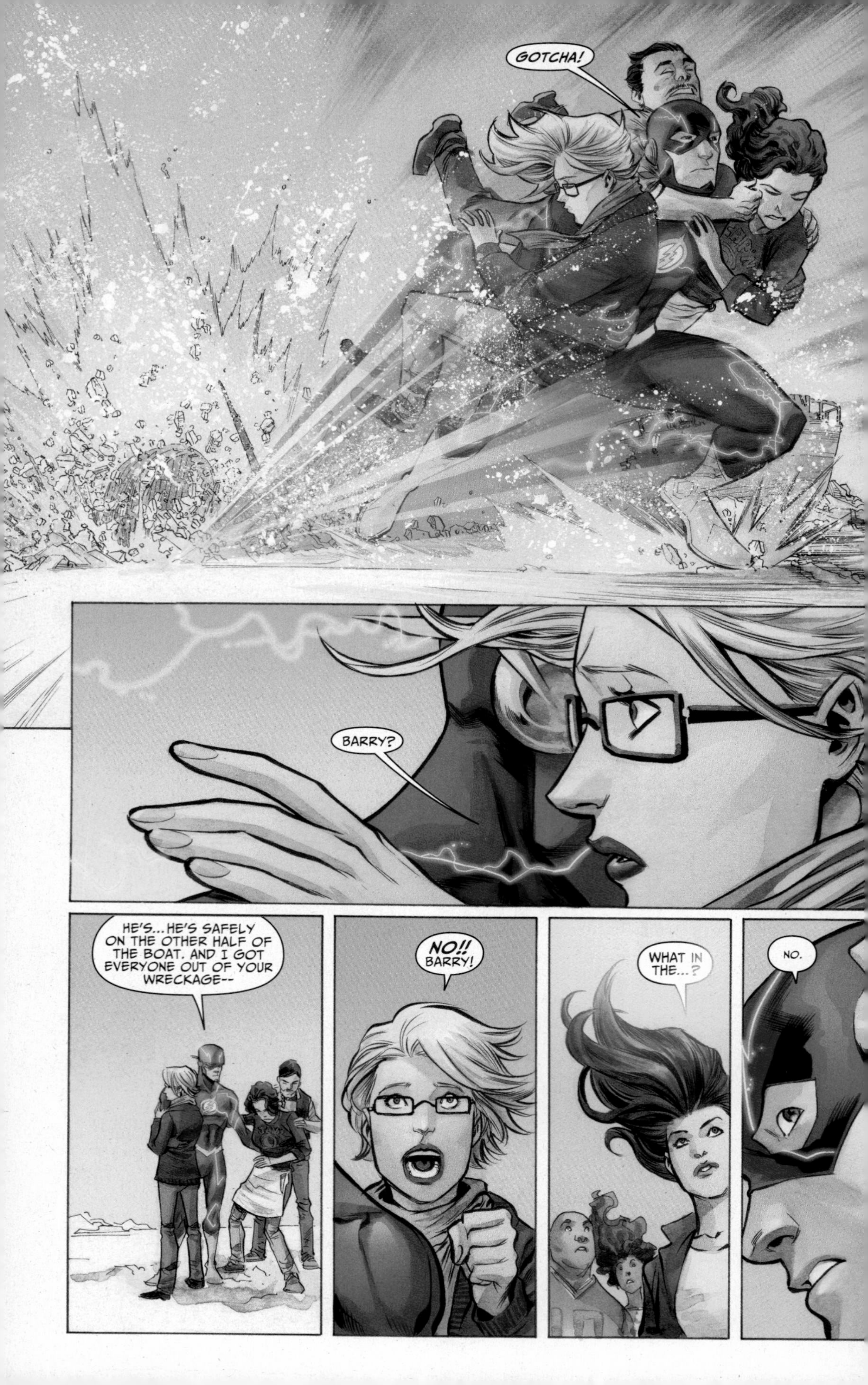
GOTCHA!
BARRY?
HE'S...HE'S SAFELY ON THE OTHER HALF OF THE BOAT. AND I GOT EVERYONE OUT OF YOUR WRECKAGE--
NO!! BARRY!
WHAT IN THE...?
NO.

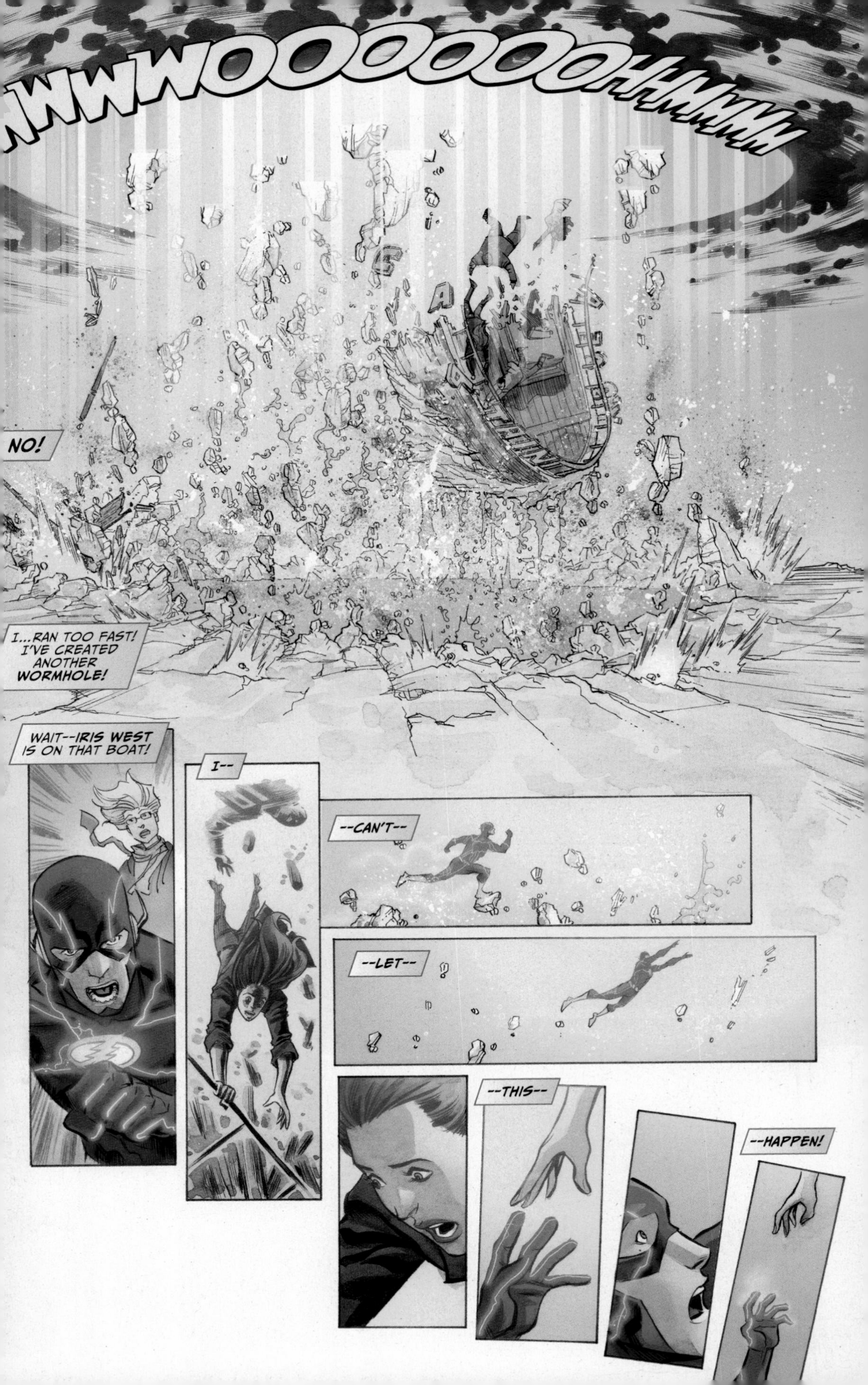
WWWOOOOOOOHMMMM
NO!
I...RAN TOO FAST! I'VE CREATED ANOTHER WORMHOLE!
WAIT--IRIS WEST IS ON THAT BOAT!
I--
--CAN'T--
--LET--
--THIS--
--HAPPEN!

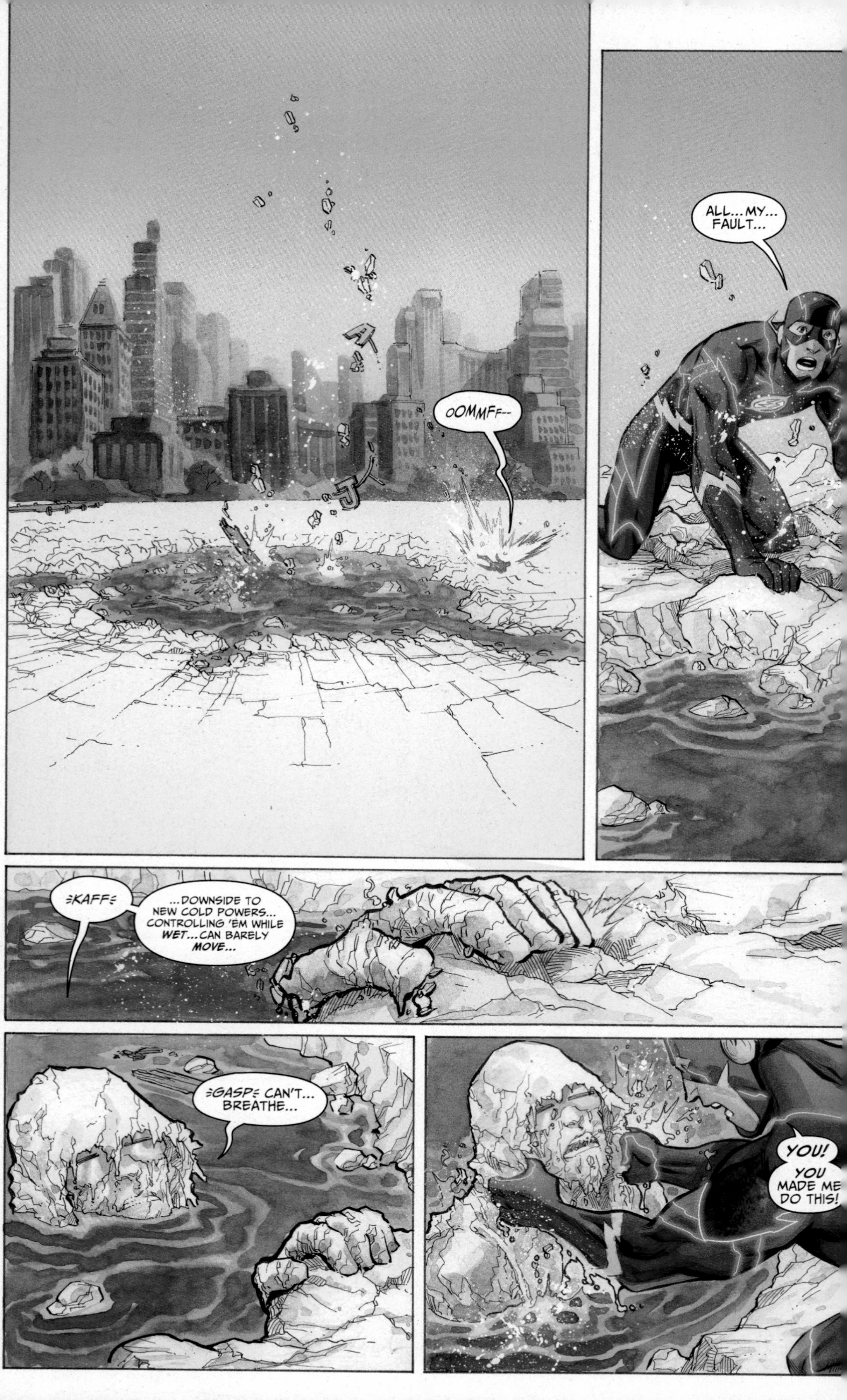

OOMMFF--
ALL... MY... FAULT...
=KAFF=
...DOWNSIDE TO NEW COLD POWERS... CONTROLLING 'EM WHILE WET...CAN BARELY MOVE...
=GASP= CAN'T... BREATHE...
YOU! YOU MADE ME DO THIS!

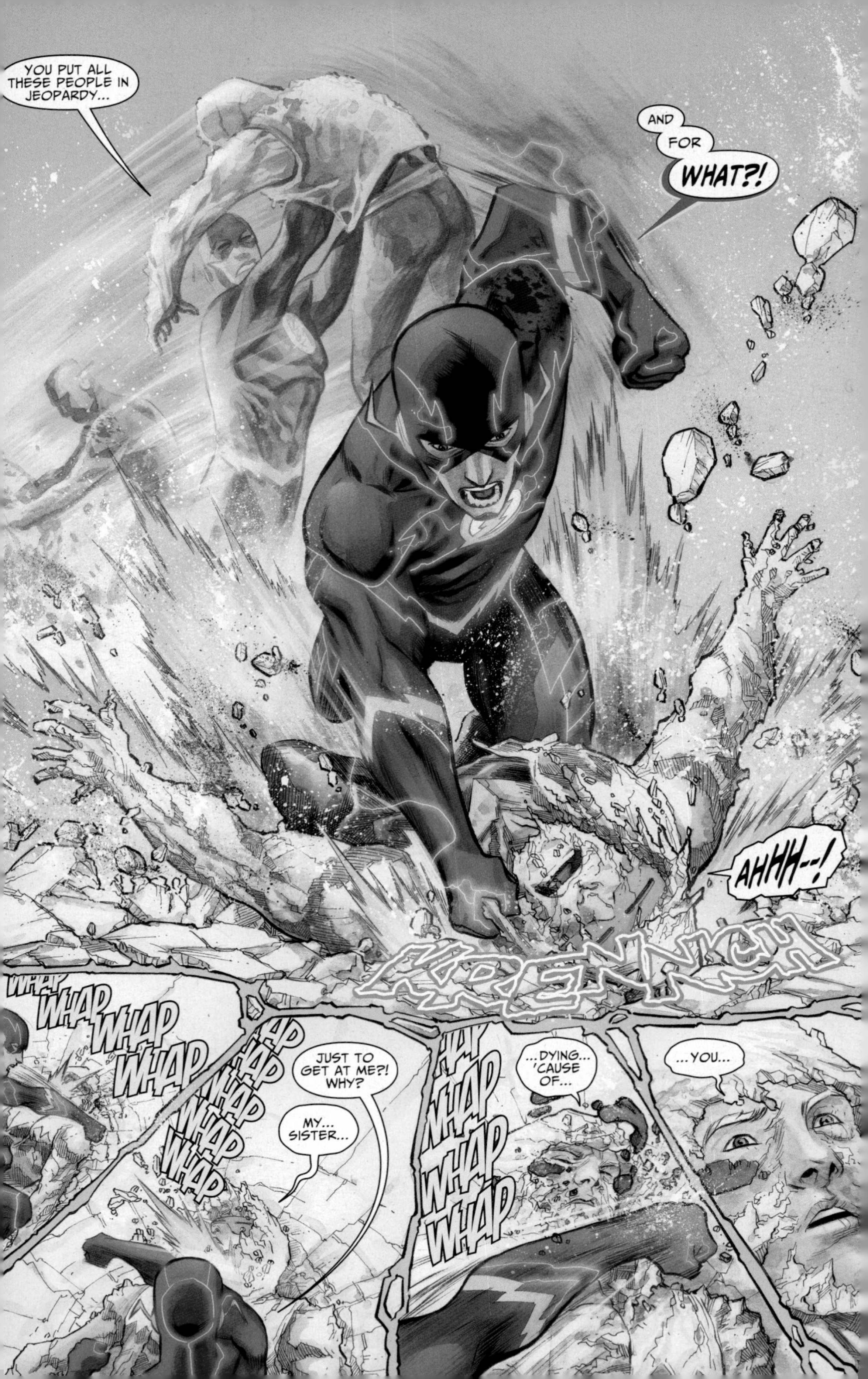

YOU PUT ALL THESE PEOPLE IN JEOPARDY...
AND FOR WHAT?!
AHHH--!
KRRENNCH
WHAP WHAP WHAP WHAP
JUST TO GET AT ME?! WHY?
MY... SISTER...
...DYING... 'CAUSE OF...
...YOU...

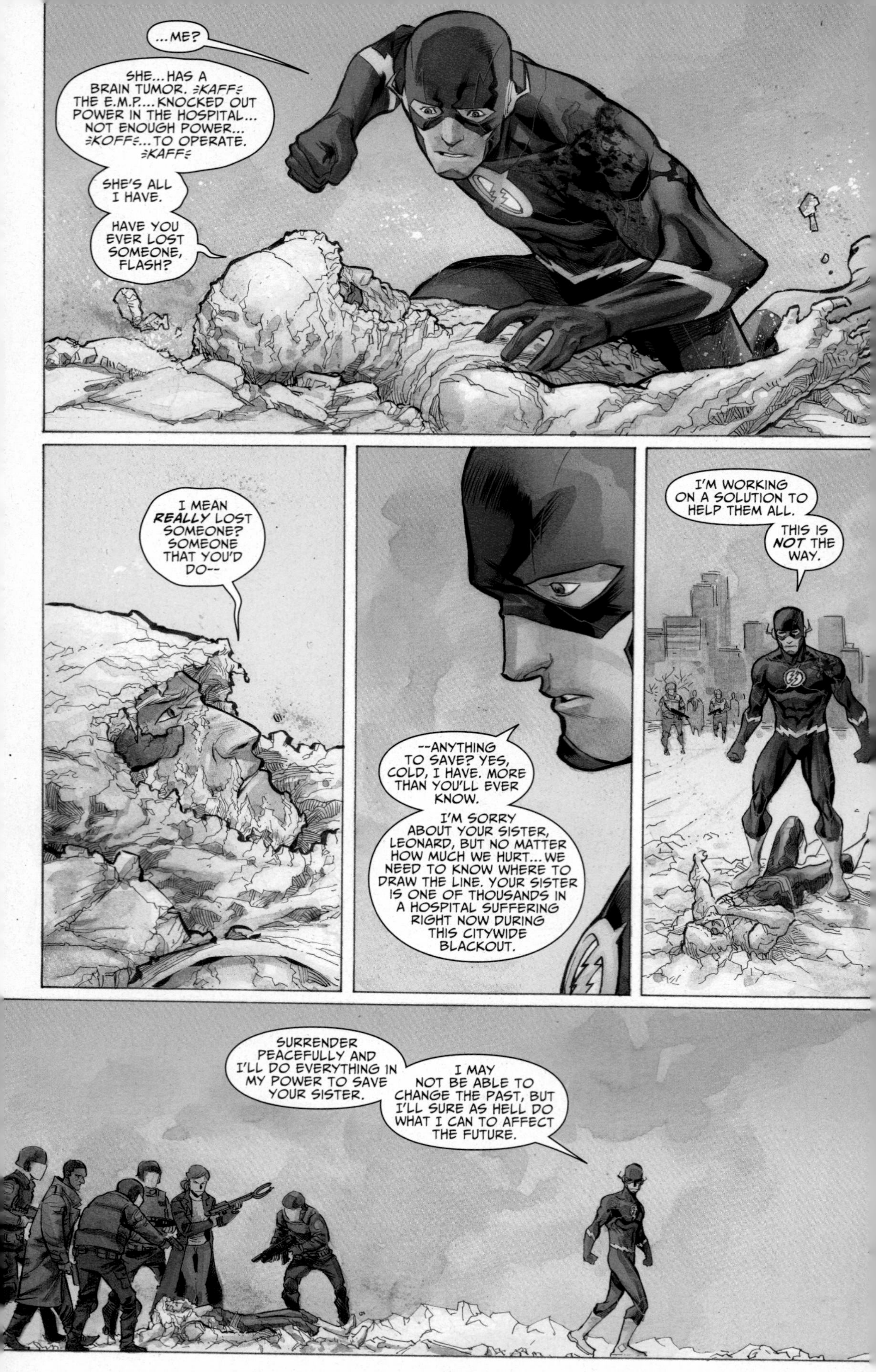
...ME?
SHE...HAS A BRAIN TUMOR. KAFF THE E.M.P....KNOCKED OUT POWER IN THE HOSPITAL... NOT ENOUGH POWER... KOFF...TO OPERATE. KAFF
SHE'S ALL I HAVE.
HAVE YOU EVER LOST SOMEONE, FLASH?
I MEAN REALLY LOST SOMEONE? SOMEONE THAT YOU'D DO--
--ANYTHING TO SAVE? YES, COLD, I HAVE. MORE THAN YOU'LL EVER KNOW.
I'M SORRY ABOUT YOUR SISTER, LEONARD, BUT NO MATTER HOW MUCH WE HURT...WE NEED TO KNOW WHERE TO DRAW THE LINE. YOUR SISTER IS ONE OF THOUSANDS IN A HOSPITAL SUFFERING RIGHT NOW DURING THIS CITYWIDE BLACKOUT.
I'M WORKING ON A SOLUTION TO HELP THEM ALL.
THIS IS NOT THE WAY.
SURRENDER PEACEFULLY AND I'LL DO EVERYTHING IN MY POWER TO SAVE YOUR SISTER.
I MAY NOT BE ABLE TO CHANGE THE PAST, BUT I'LL SURE AS HELL DO WHAT I CAN TO AFFECT THE FUTURE.

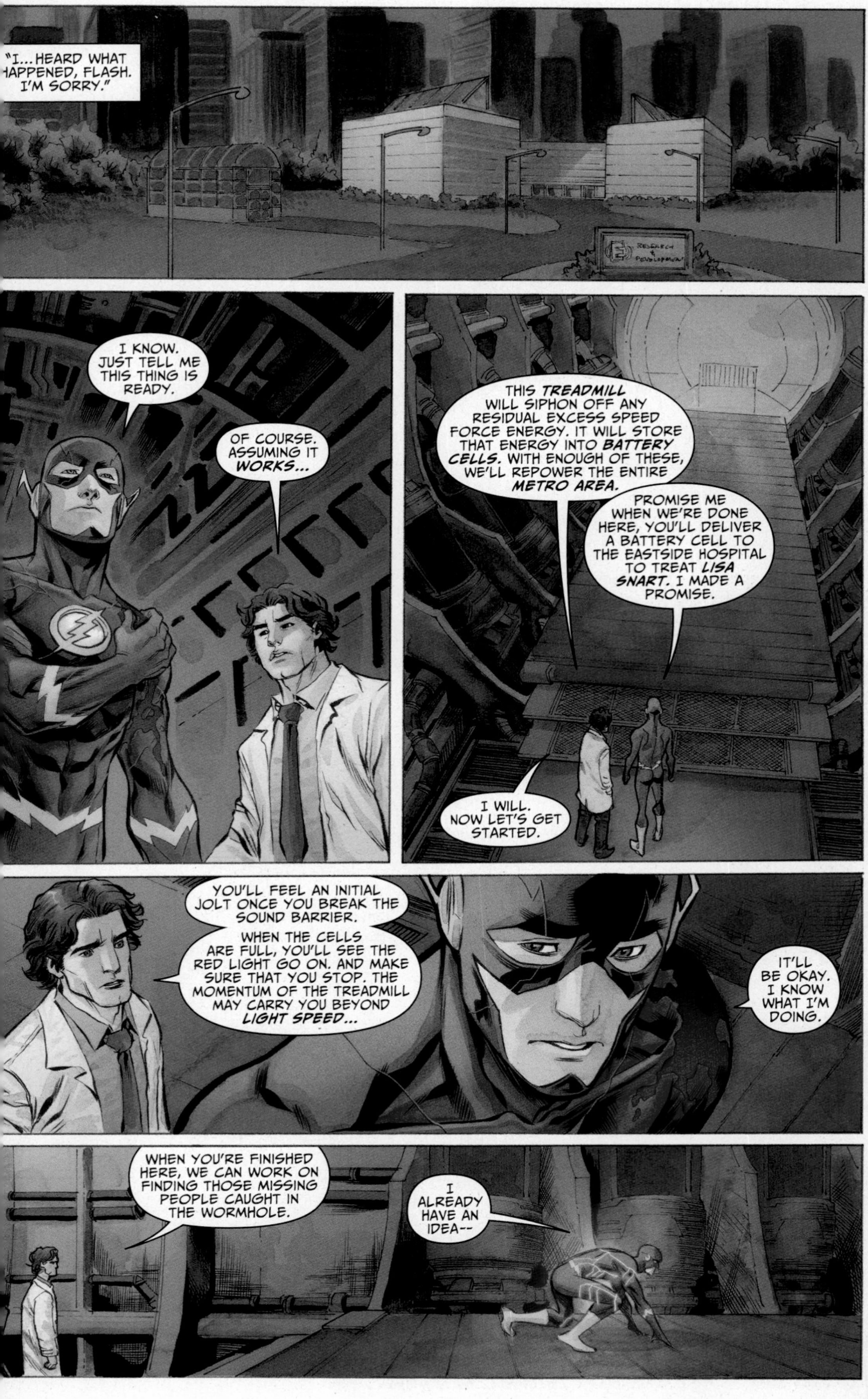
"I... HEARD WHAT HAPPENED, FLASH. I'M SORRY."
RESEARCH & DEVELOPMENT
I KNOW. JUST TELL ME THIS THING IS READY.
OF COURSE. ASSUMING IT WORKS...
THIS TREADMILL WILL SIPHON OFF ANY RESIDUAL EXCESS SPEED FORCE ENERGY. IT WILL STORE THAT ENERGY INTO BATTERY CELLS. WITH ENOUGH OF THESE, WE'LL REPOWER THE ENTIRE METRO AREA.
PROMISE ME WHEN WE'RE DONE HERE, YOU'LL DELIVER A BATTERY CELL TO THE EASTSIDE HOSPITAL TO TREAT LISA SNART. I MADE A PROMISE.
I WILL. NOW LET'S GET STARTED.
YOU'LL FEEL AN INITIAL JOLT ONCE YOU BREAK THE SOUND BARRIER.
WHEN THE CELLS ARE FULL, YOU'LL SEE THE RED LIGHT GO ON. AND MAKE SURE THAT YOU STOP. THE MOMENTUM OF THE TREADMILL MAY CARRY YOU BEYOND LIGHT SPEED...
IT'LL BE OKAY. I KNOW WHAT I'M DOING.
WHEN YOU'RE FINISHED HERE, WE CAN WORK ON FINDING THOSE MISSING PEOPLE CAUGHT IN THE WORMHOLE.
I ALREADY HAVE AN IDEA--

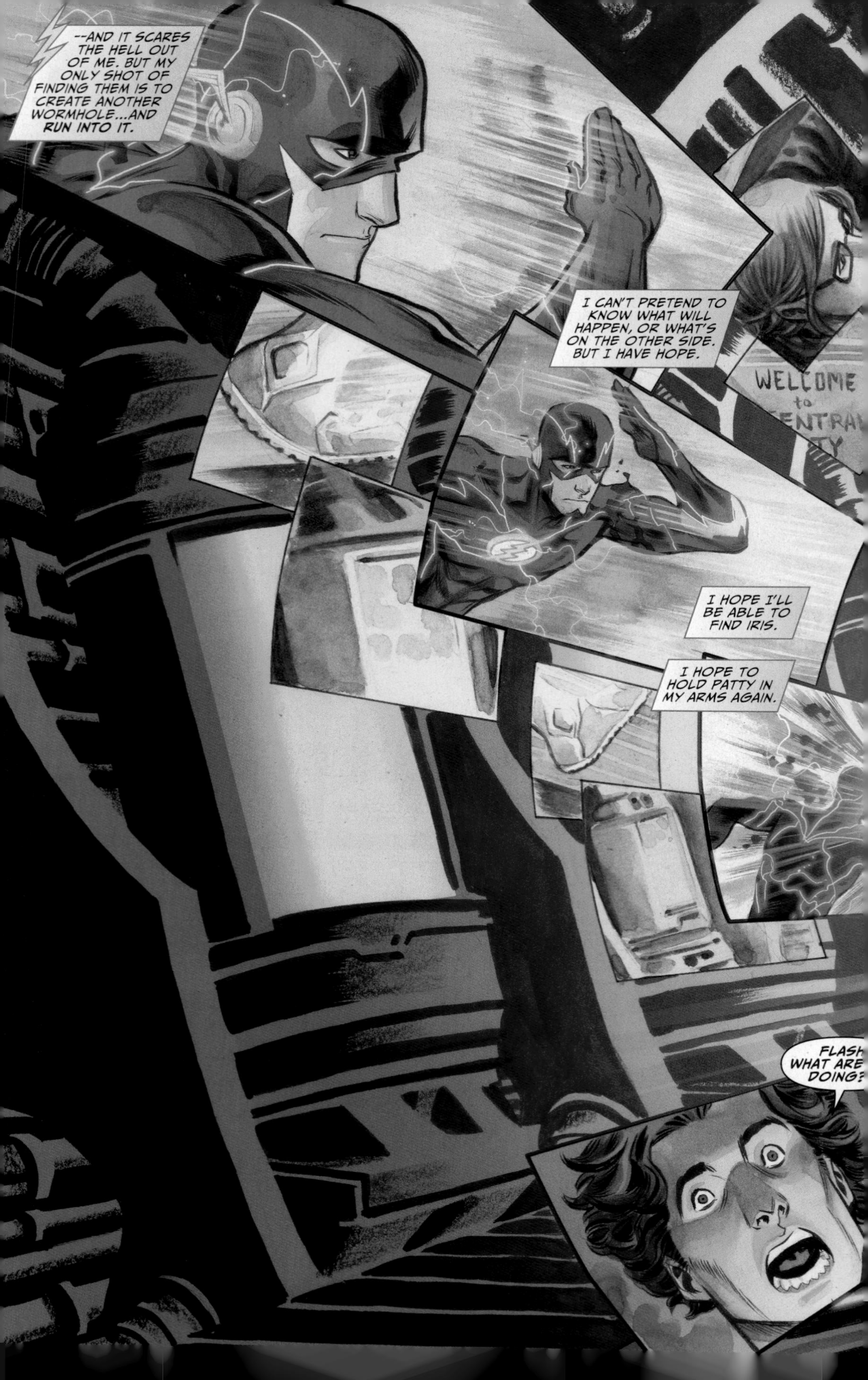
--AND IT SCARES THE HELL OUT OF ME. BUT MY ONLY SHOT OF FINDING THEM IS TO CREATE ANOTHER WORMHOLE...AND RUN INTO IT.
I CAN'T PRETEND TO KNOW WHAT WILL HAPPEN, OR WHAT'S ON THE OTHER SIDE. BUT I HAVE HOPE.
WELCOME to
I HOPE I'LL BE ABLE TO FIND IRIS.
I HOPE TO HOLD PATTY IN MY ARMS AGAIN.

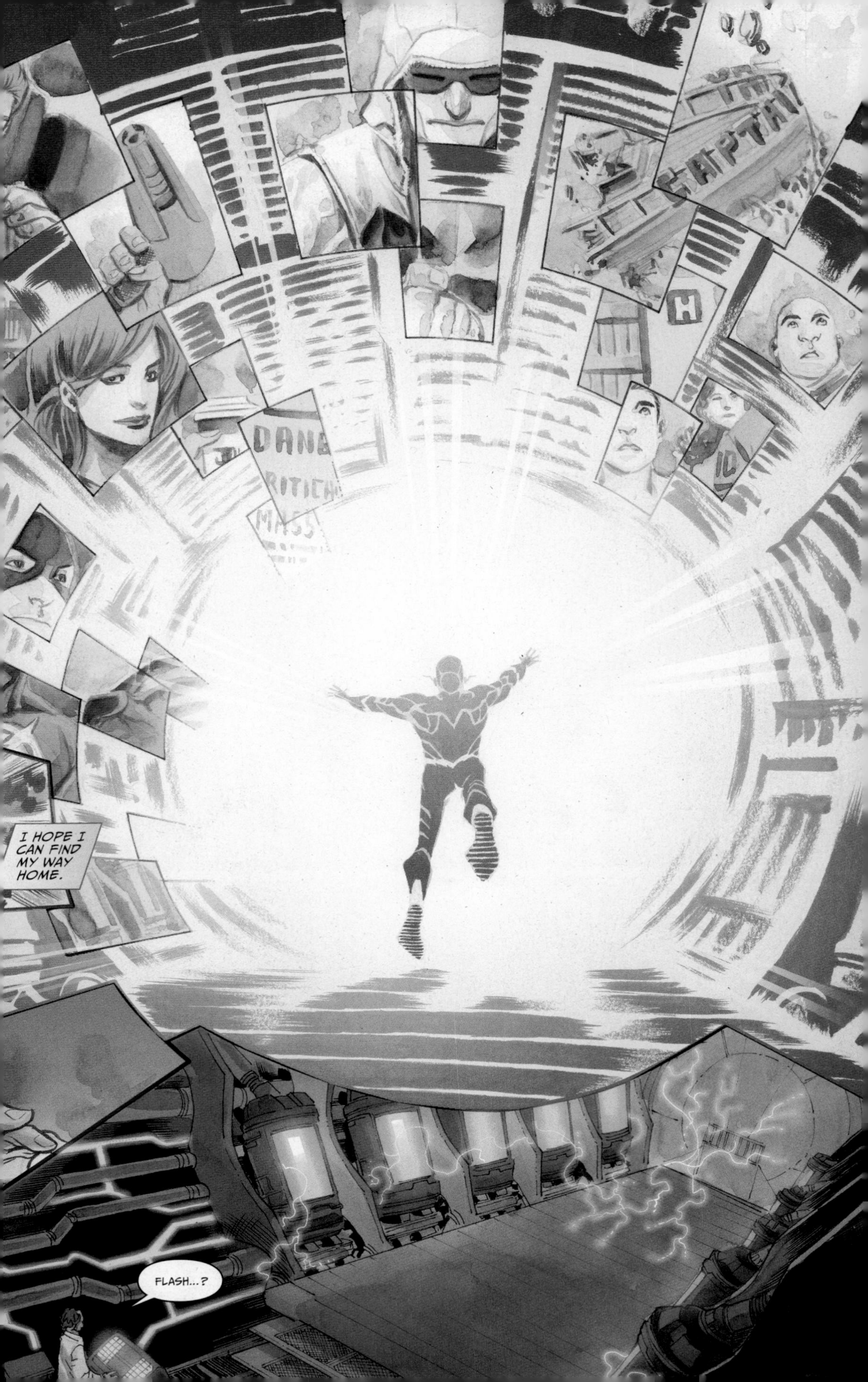
I HOPE I CAN FIND MY WAY HOME.
FLASH...?

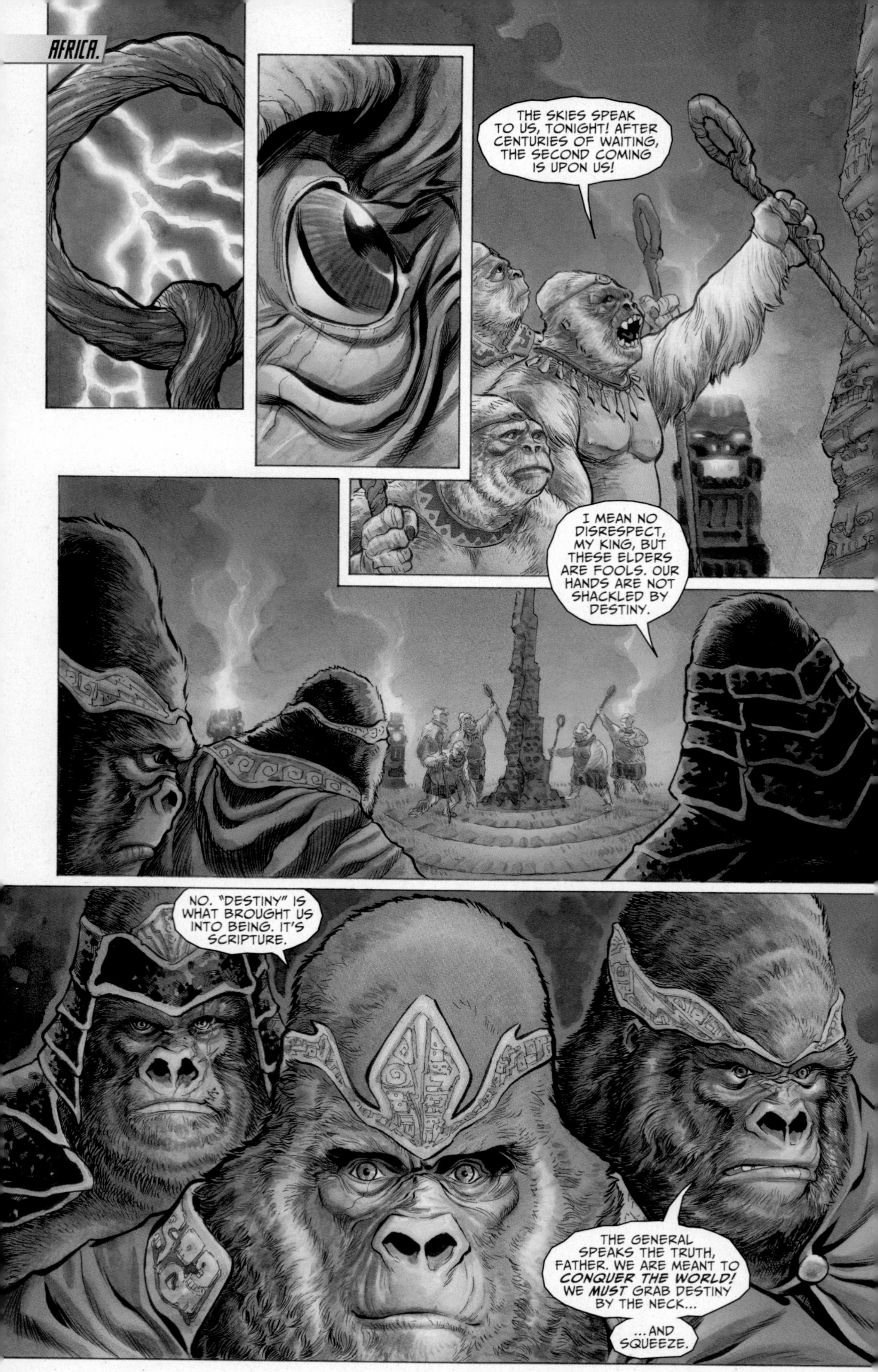
AFRICA.
THE SKIES SPEAK TO US, TONIGHT! AFTER CENTURIES OF WAITING, THE SECOND COMING IS UPON US!
I MEAN NO DISRESPECT, MY KING, BUT THESE ELDERS ARE FOOLS. OUR HANDS ARE NOT SHACKLED BY DESTINY.
NO. "DESTINY" IS WHAT BROUGHT US INTO BEING. IT'S SCRIPTURE.
THE GENERAL SPEAKS THE TRUTH, FATHER. WE ARE MEANT TO ***CONQUER THE WORLD!*** WE ***MUST*** GRAB DESTINY BY THE NECK...
...AND SQUEEZE.

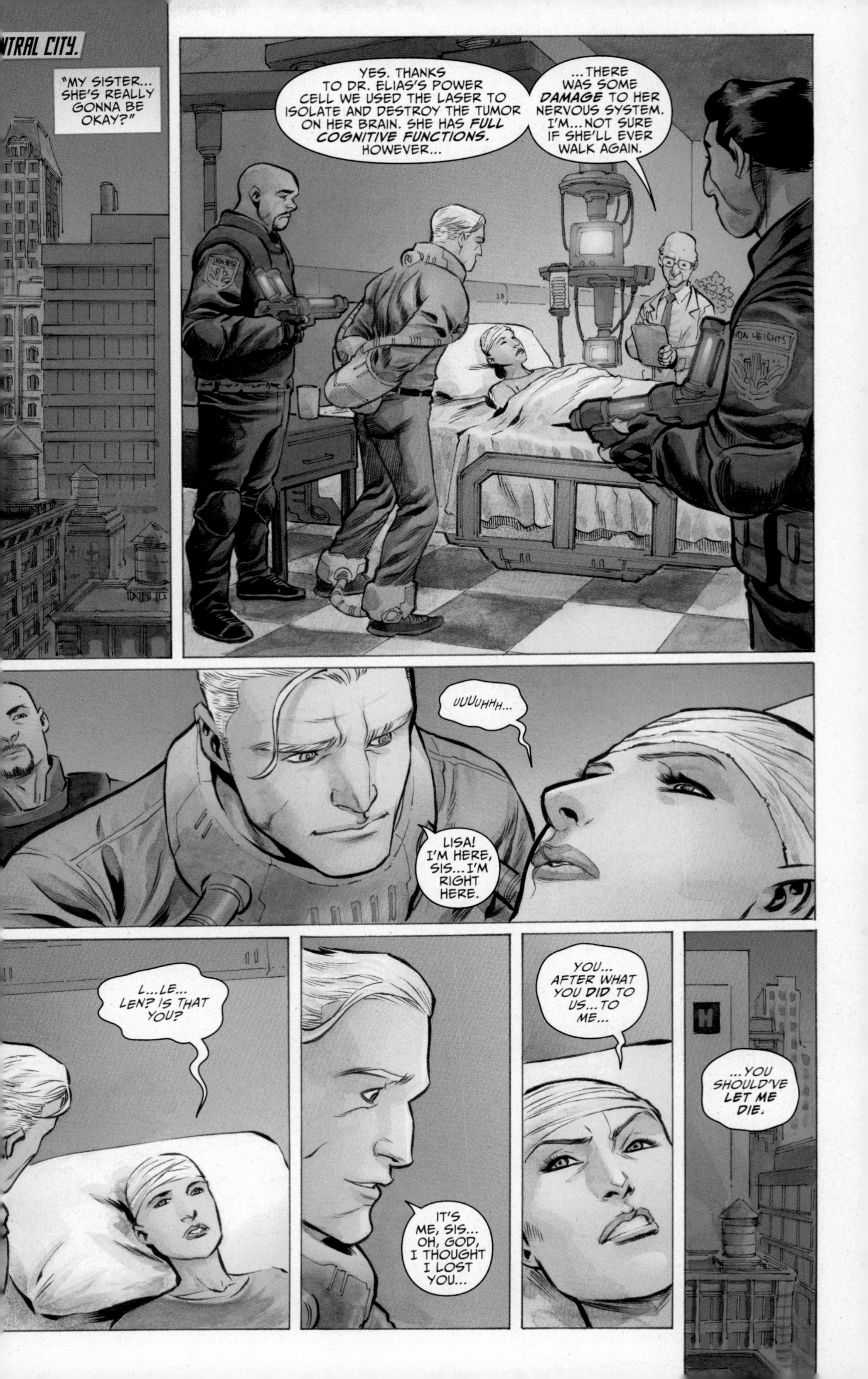
NTRAL CITY.
"MY SISTER... SHE'S REALLY GONNA BE OKAY?"
YES. THANKS TO DR. ELIAS'S POWER CELL WE USED THE LASER TO ISOLATE AND DESTROY THE TUMOR ON HER BRAIN. SHE HAS FULL COGNITIVE FUNCTIONS. HOWEVER...
...THERE WAS SOME DAMAGE TO HER NERVOUS SYSTEM. I'M...NOT SURE IF SHE'LL EVER WALK AGAIN.
UUUUHHH...
LISA! I'M HERE, SIS...I'M RIGHT HERE.
L...LE... LEN? IS THAT YOU?
IT'S ME, SIS... OH, GOD, I THOUGHT I LOST YOU...
YOU... AFTER WHAT YOU DID TO US...TO ME...
...YOU SHOULD'VE LET ME DIE.

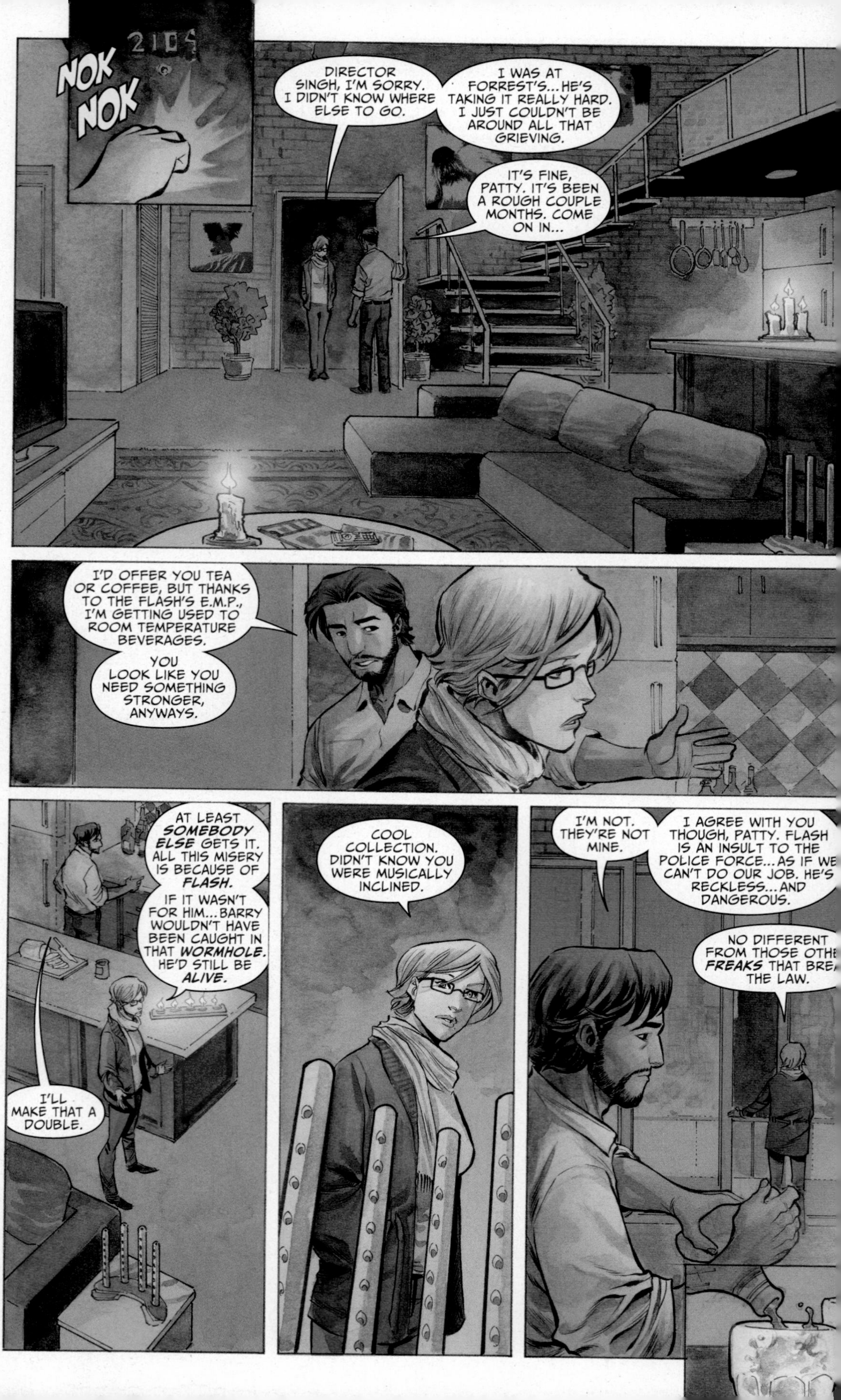
NOK NOK
2105
DIRECTOR SINGH, I'M SORRY. I DIDN'T KNOW WHERE ELSE TO GO.
I WAS AT FORREST'S... HE'S TAKING IT REALLY HARD. I JUST COULDN'T BE AROUND ALL THAT GRIEVING.
IT'S FINE, PATTY. IT'S BEEN A ROUGH COUPLE MONTHS. COME ON IN...
I'D OFFER YOU TEA OR COFFEE, BUT THANKS TO THE FLASH'S E.M.P., I'M GETTING USED TO ROOM TEMPERATURE BEVERAGES.
YOU LOOK LIKE YOU NEED SOMETHING STRONGER, ANYWAYS.
I'LL MAKE THAT A DOUBLE.
AT LEAST SOMEBODY ELSE GETS IT. ALL THIS MISERY IS BECAUSE OF FLASH.
IF IT WASN'T FOR HIM... BARRY WOULDN'T HAVE BEEN CAUGHT IN THAT WORMHOLE. HE'D STILL BE ALIVE.
COOL COLLECTION. DIDN'T KNOW YOU WERE MUSICALLY INCLINED.
I'M NOT. THEY'RE NOT MINE.
I AGREE WITH YOU THOUGH, PATTY. FLASH IS AN INSULT TO THE POLICE FORCE... AS IF WE CAN'T DO OUR JOB. HE'S RECKLESS... AND DANGEROUS.
NO DIFFERENT FROM THOSE OTHE FREAKS THAT BRE THE LAW.

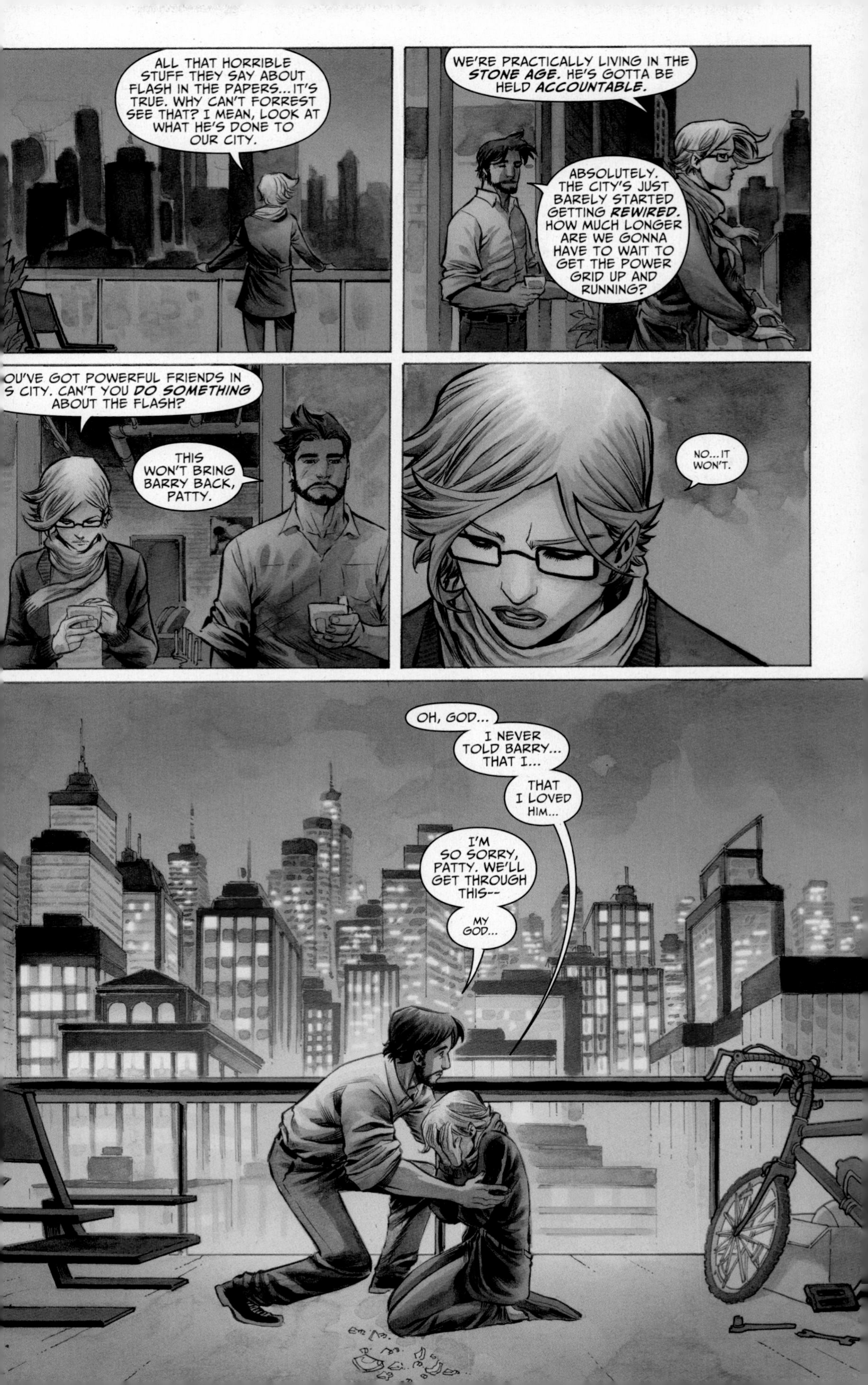
ALL THAT HORRIBLE STUFF THEY SAY ABOUT FLASH IN THE PAPERS...IT'S TRUE. WHY CAN'T FORREST SEE THAT? I MEAN, LOOK AT WHAT HE'S DONE TO OUR CITY.
WE'RE PRACTICALLY LIVING IN THE STONE AGE. HE'S GOTTA BE HELD ACCOUNTABLE.
ABSOLUTELY. THE CITY'S JUST BARELY STARTED GETTING REWIRED. HOW MUCH LONGER ARE WE GONNA HAVE TO WAIT TO GET THE POWER GRID UP AND RUNNING?
OU'VE GOT POWERFUL FRIENDS IN S CITY. CAN'T YOU DO SOMETHING ABOUT THE FLASH?
THIS WON'T BRING BARRY BACK, PATTY.
NO...IT WON'T.
OH, GOD...
I NEVER TOLD BARRY... THAT I...
THAT I LOVED HIM...
I'M SO SORRY, PATTY. WE'LL GET THROUGH THIS--
MY GOD...

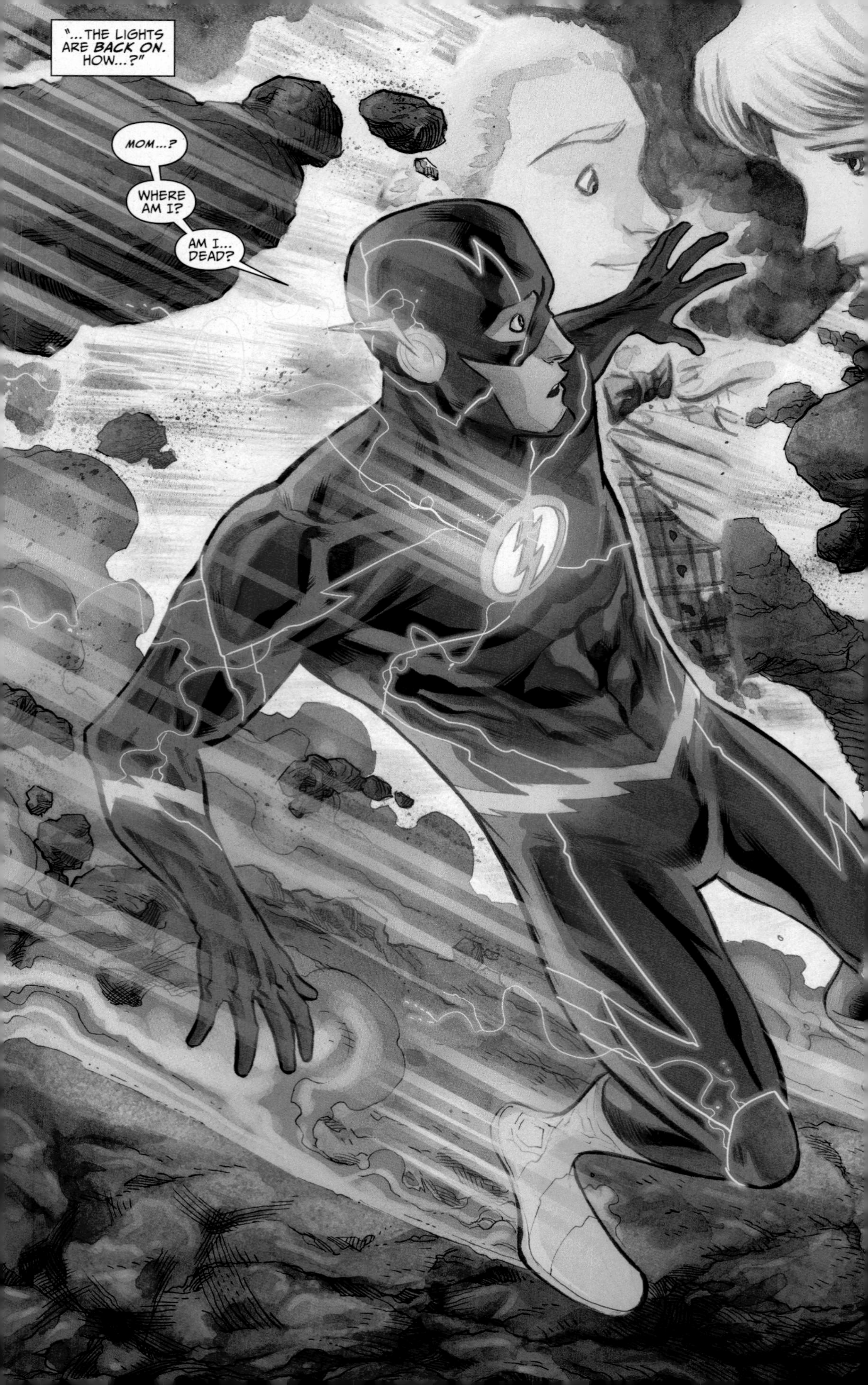
"...THE LIGHTS ARE BACK ON. HOW...?"
MOM...?
WHERE AM I?
AM I... DEAD?

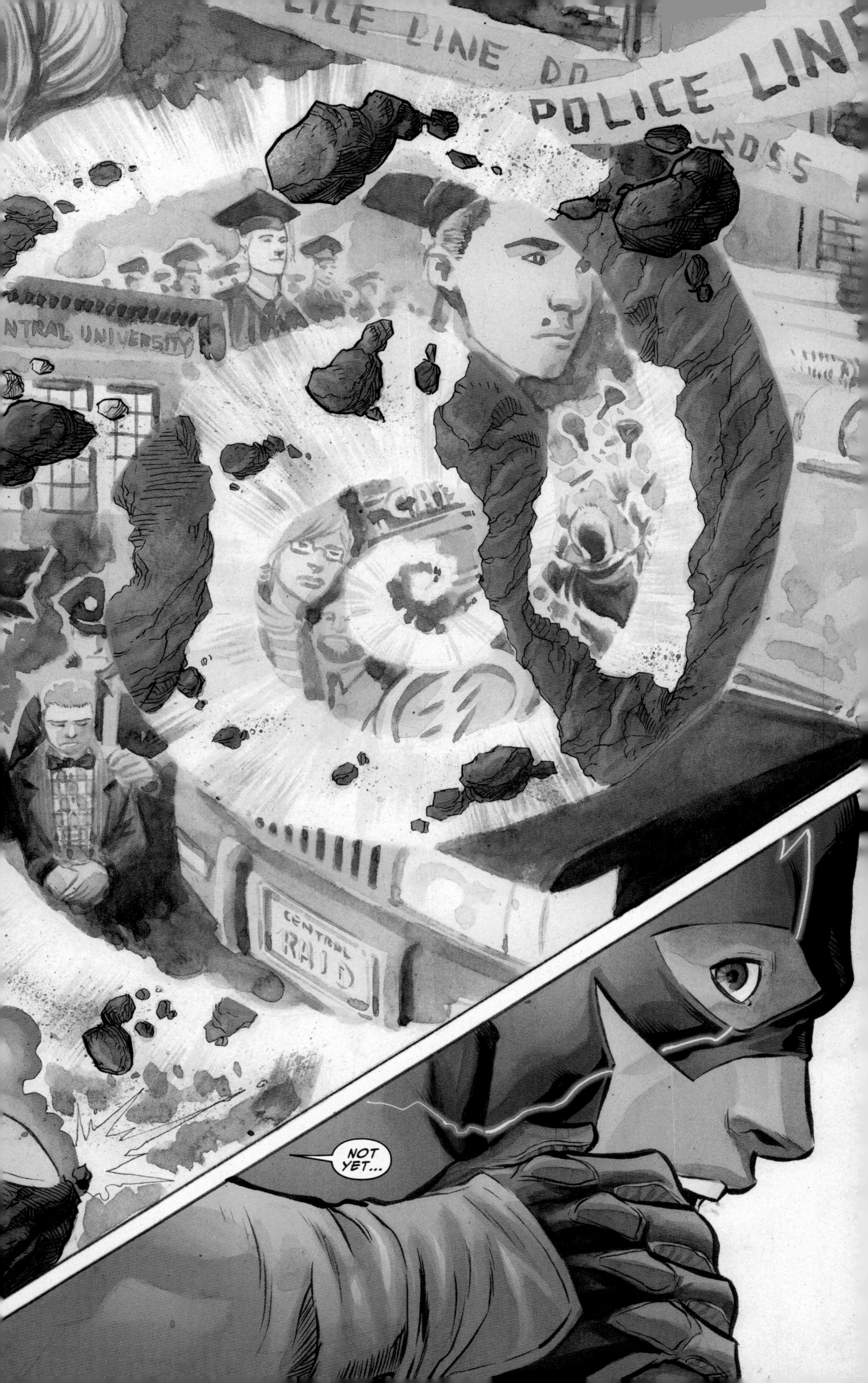
NOT YET...

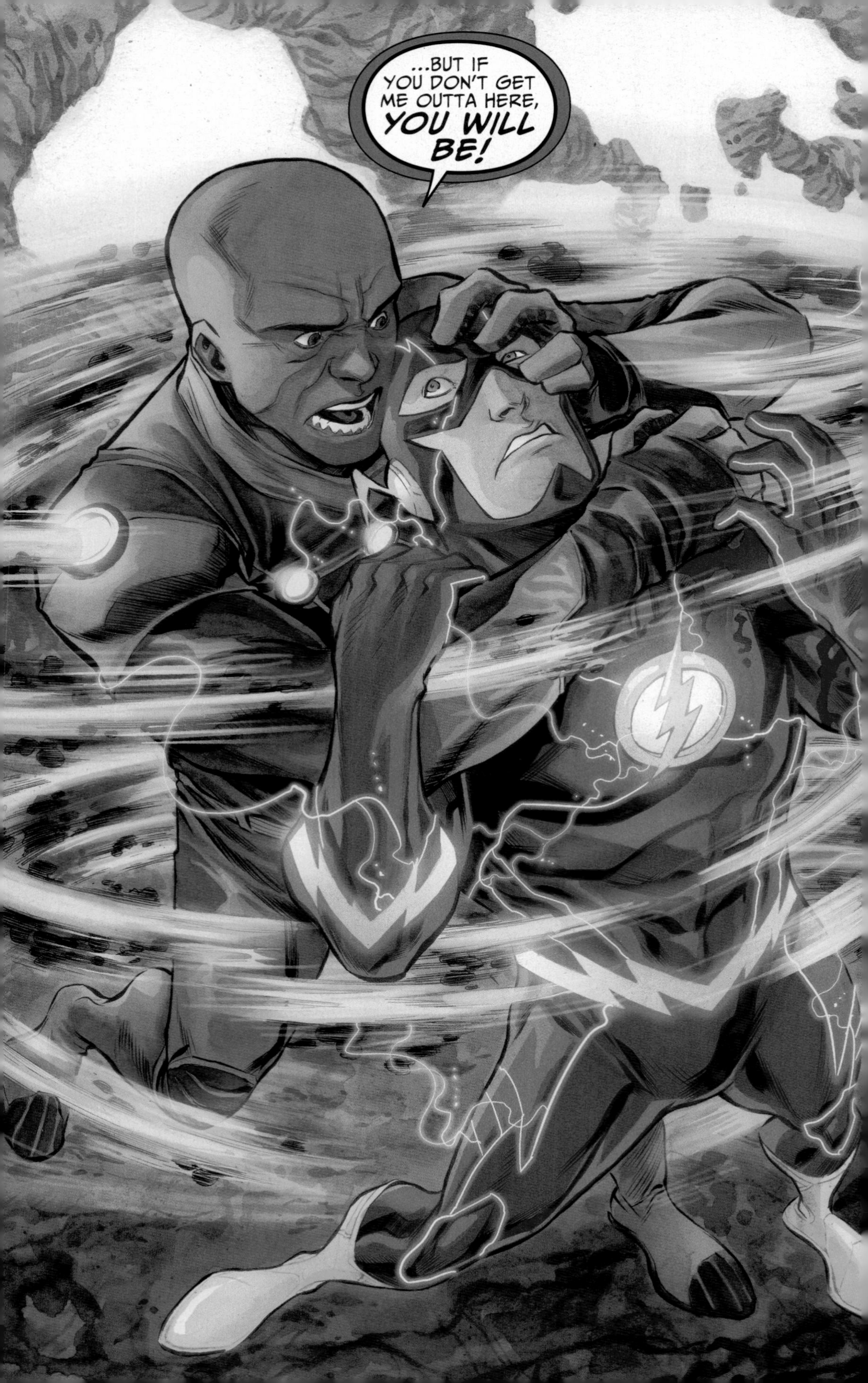
...BUT IF YOU DON'T GET ME OUTTA HERE, YOU WILL BE!

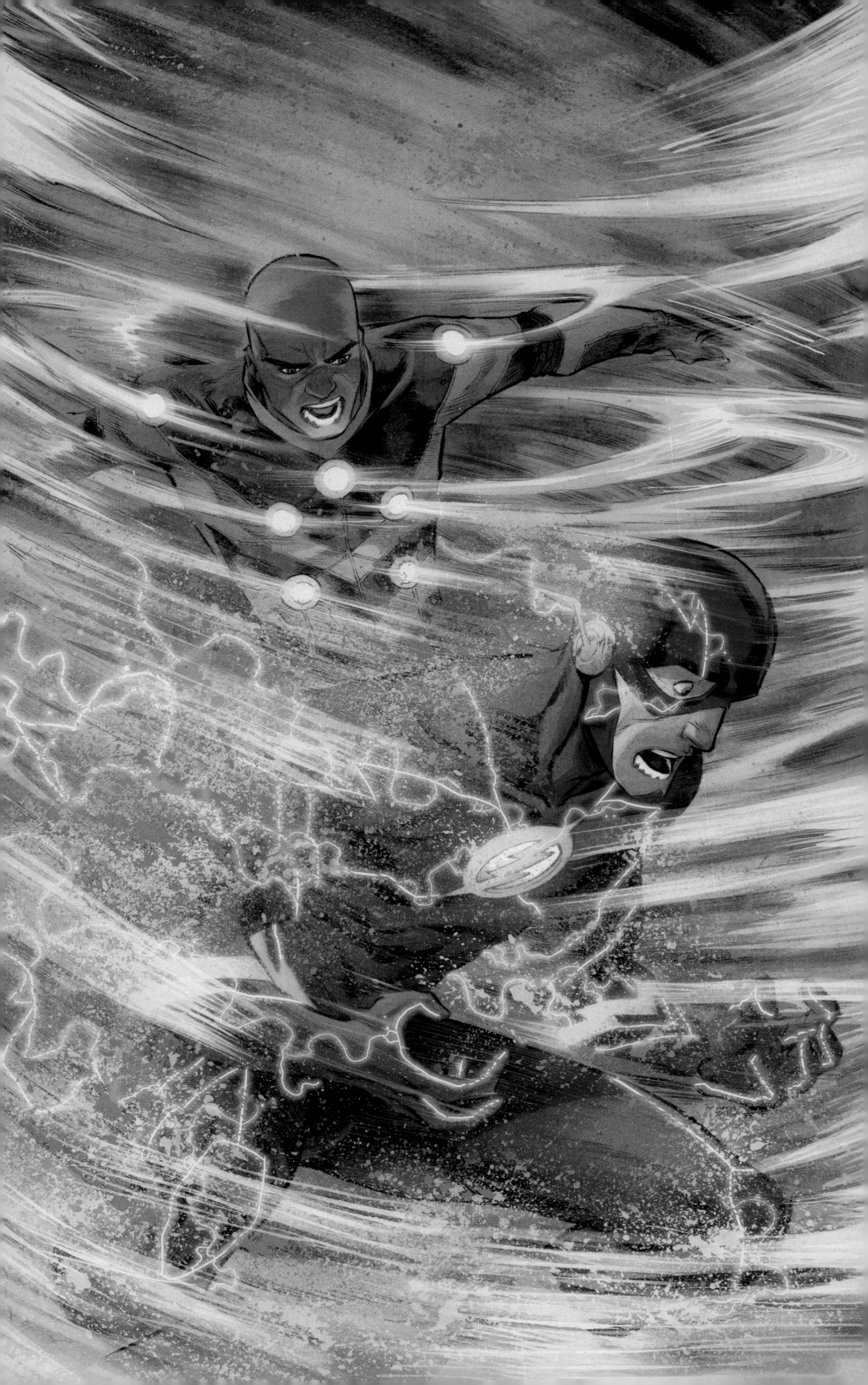

THE FLASH #8

variant cover by BERNARD CHANG

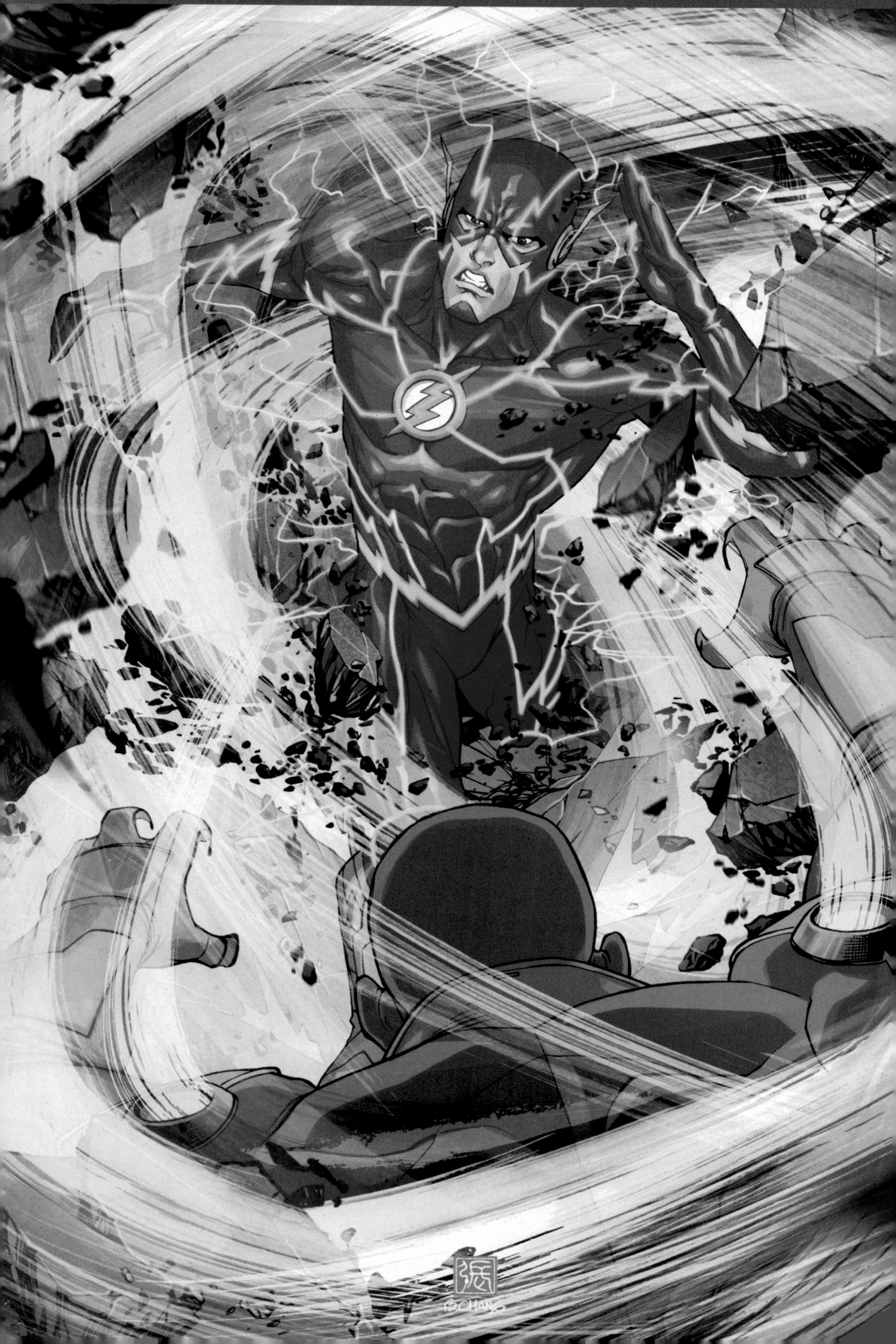
B.CHANG

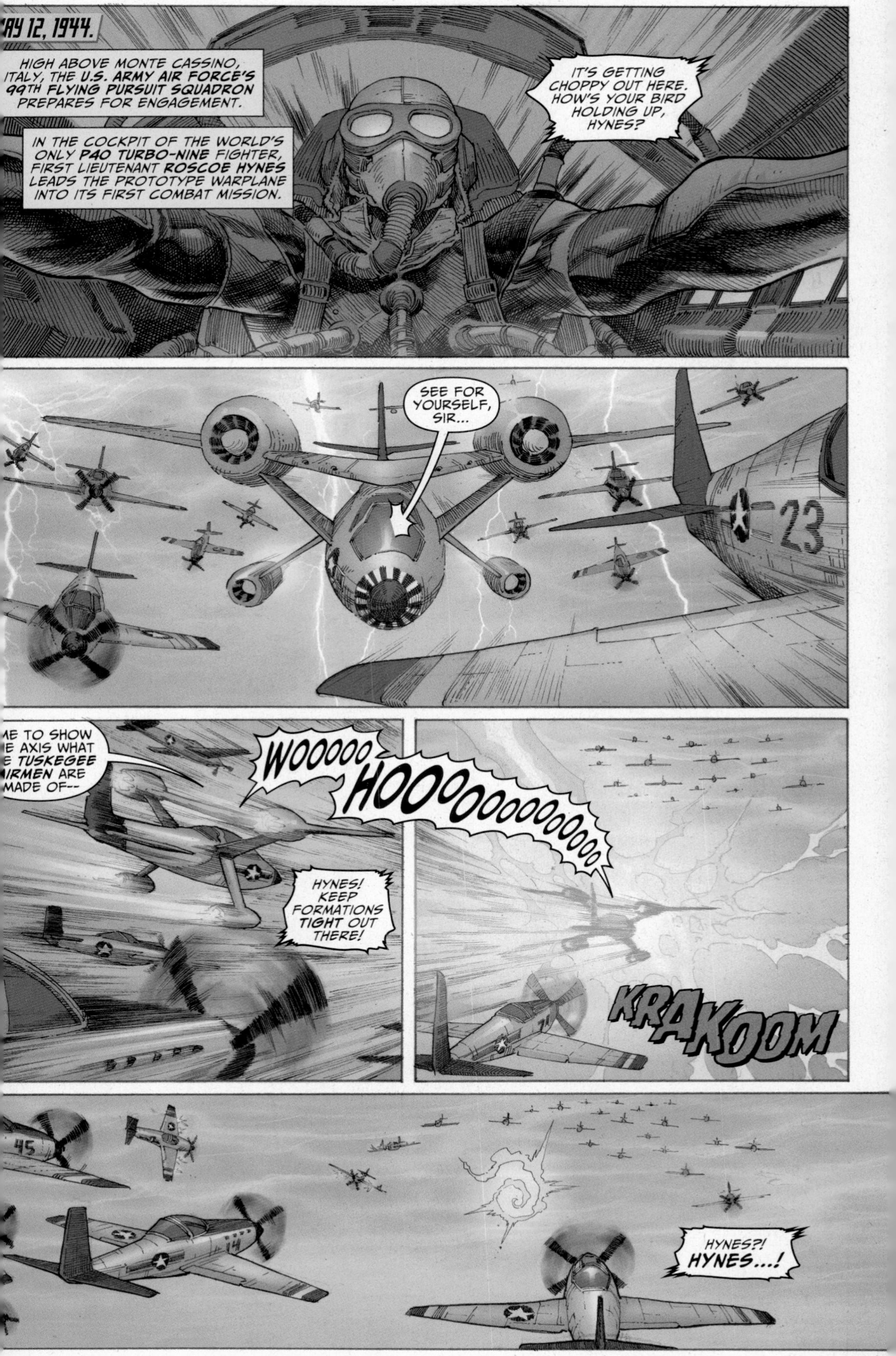

AY 12, 1944.
HIGH ABOVE MONTE CASSINO, ITALY, THE U.S. ARMY AIR FORCE'S 99TH FLYING PURSUIT SQUADRON PREPARES FOR ENGAGEMENT.
IN THE COCKPIT OF THE WORLD'S ONLY P40 TURBO-NINE FIGHTER, FIRST LIEUTENANT ROSCOE HYNES LEADS THE PROTOTYPE WARPLANE INTO ITS FIRST COMBAT MISSION.
IT'S GETTING CHOPPY OUT HERE. HOW'S YOUR BIRD HOLDING UP, HYNES?
SEE FOR YOURSELF, SIR...
23
ME TO SHOW E AXIS WHAT E TUSKEGEE IRMEN ARE MADE OF--
WOOOOO HOOOOOOOOOOOOOO
HYNES! KEEP FORMATIONS TIGHT OUT THERE!
KRAKOOM
45
HYNES?! HYNES...!

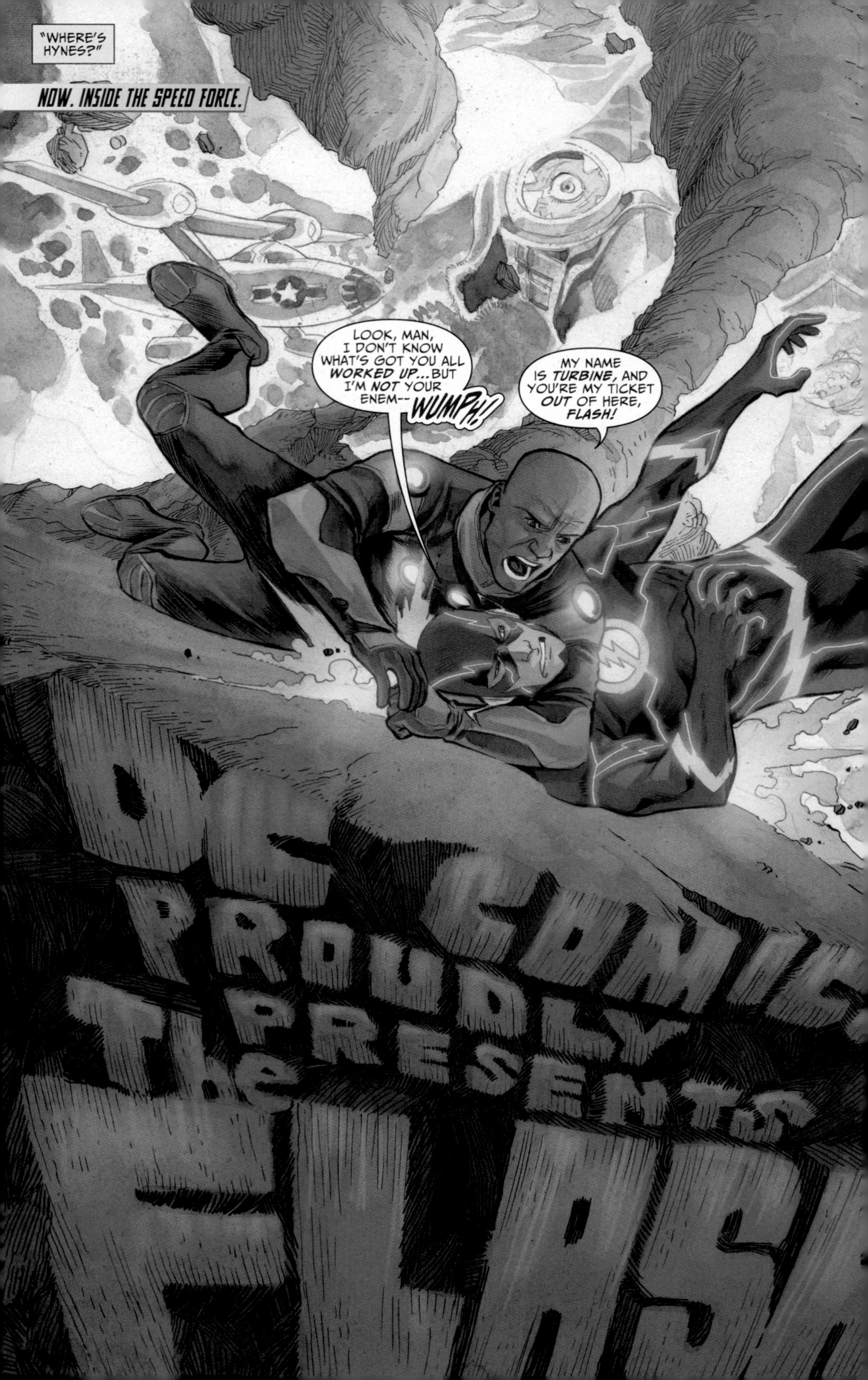
"WHERE'S HYNES?"
NOW. INSIDE THE SPEED FORCE.
LOOK, MAN, I DON'T KNOW WHAT'S GOT YOU ALL WORKED UP...BUT I'M NOT YOUR ENEM--
WUMPH!
MY NAME IS TURBINE, AND YOU'RE MY TICKET OUT OF HERE, FLASH!
PROUDLY
THE

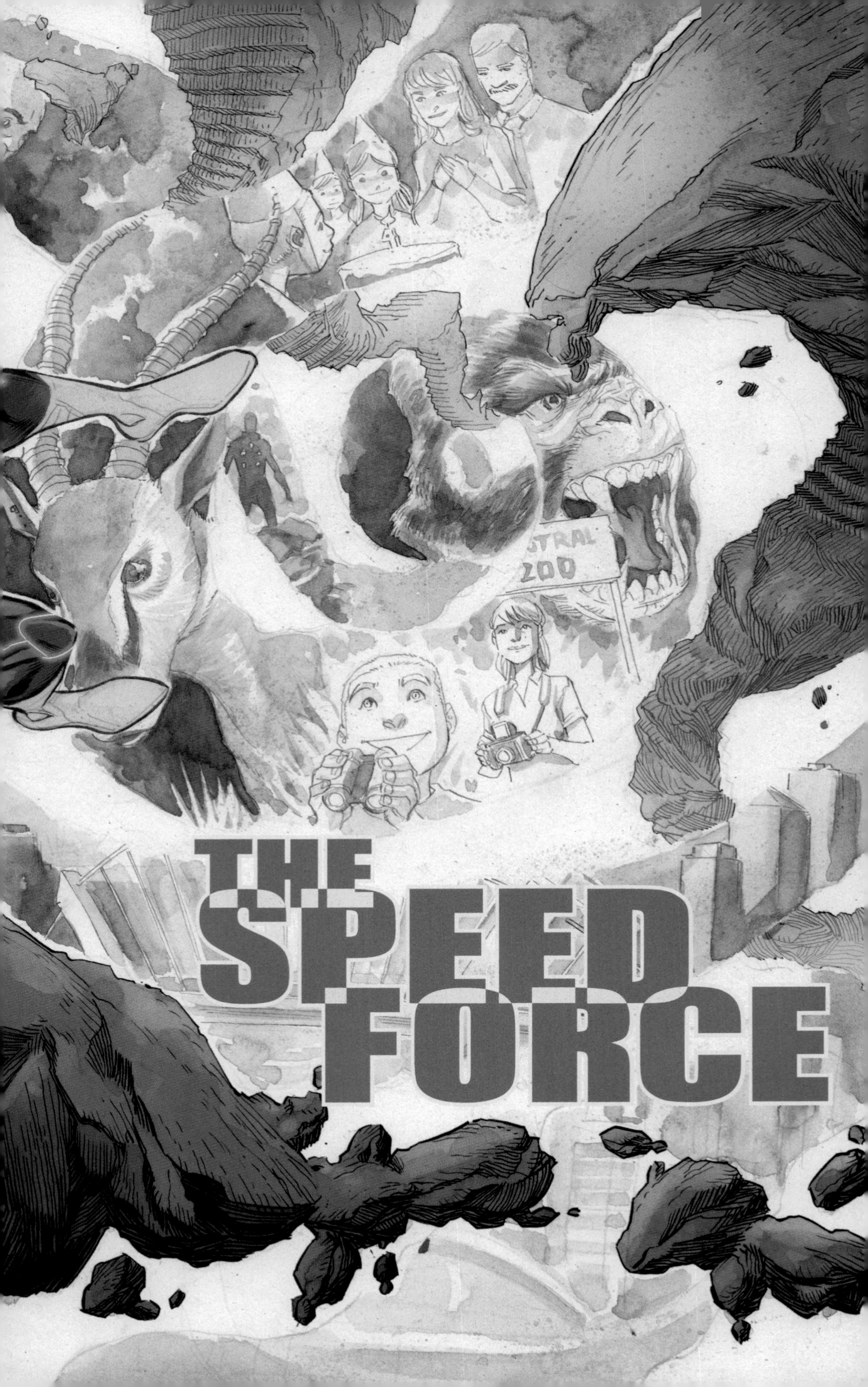
STRAL
ZOO
THE SPEED FORCE

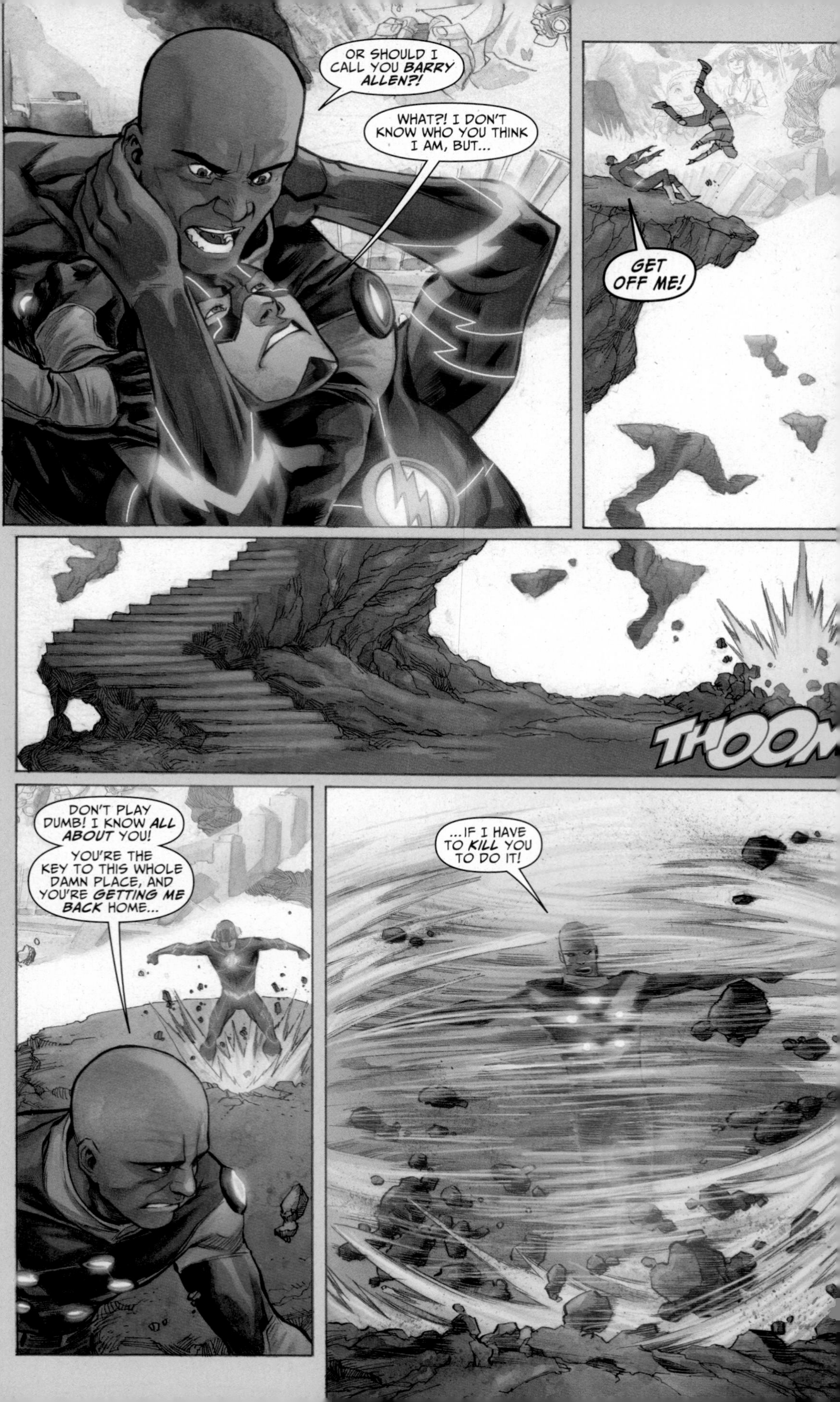
OR SHOULD I CALL YOU BARRY ALLEN?!
WHAT?! I DON'T KNOW WHO YOU THINK I AM, BUT...
GET OFF ME!
THOOM
DON'T PLAY DUMB! I KNOW ALL ABOUT YOU!
YOU'RE THE KEY TO THIS WHOLE DAMN PLACE, AND YOU'RE GETTING ME BACK HOME...
...IF I HAVE TO KILL YOU TO DO IT!

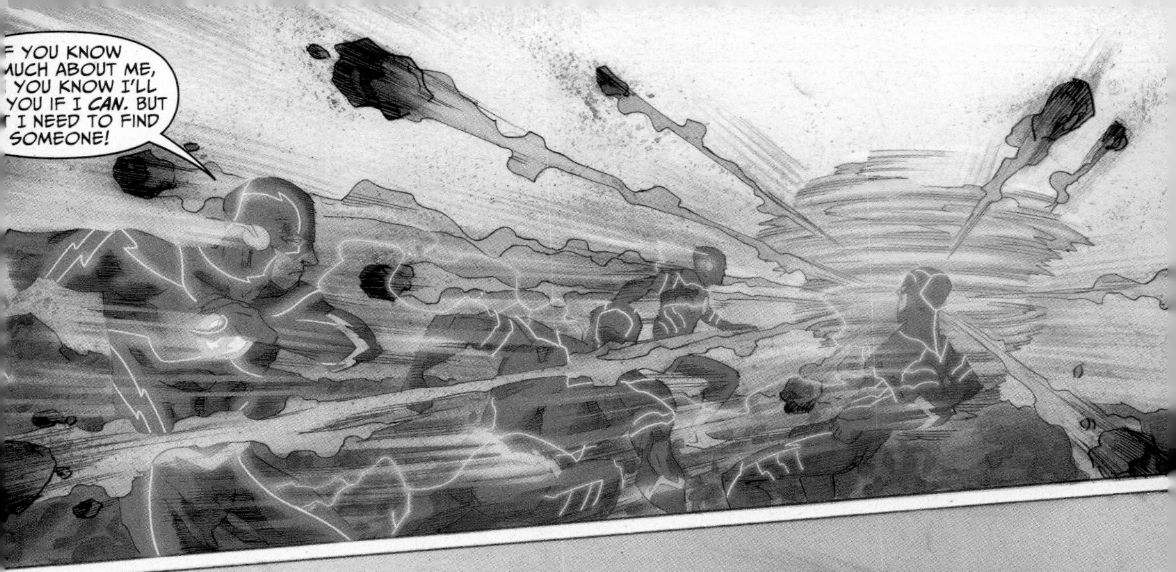
F YOU KNOW MUCH ABOUT ME, YOU KNOW I'LL YOU IF I CAN. BUT I NEED TO FIND SOMEONE!

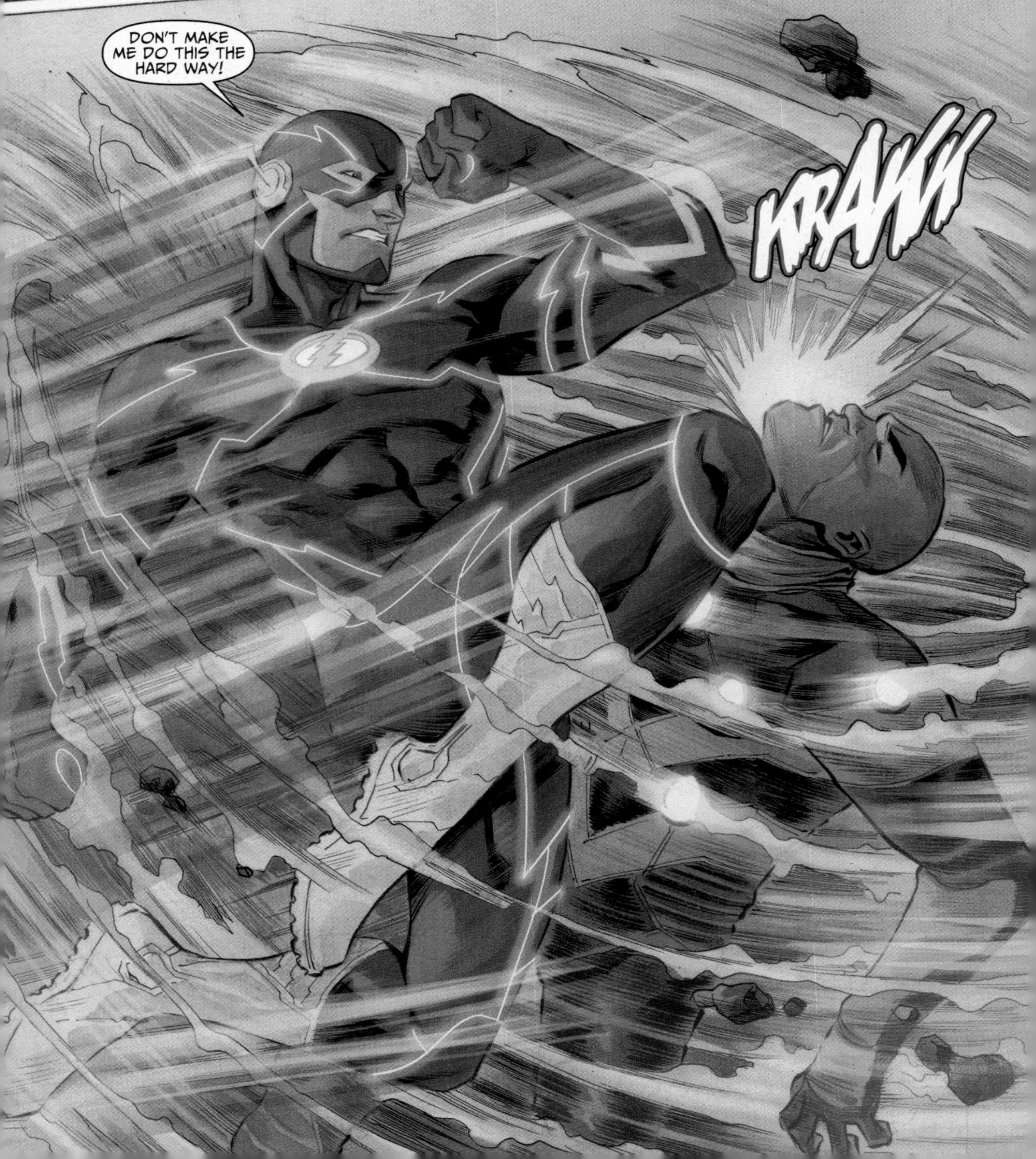
DON'T MAKE ME DO THIS THE HARD WAY!
KRAWW

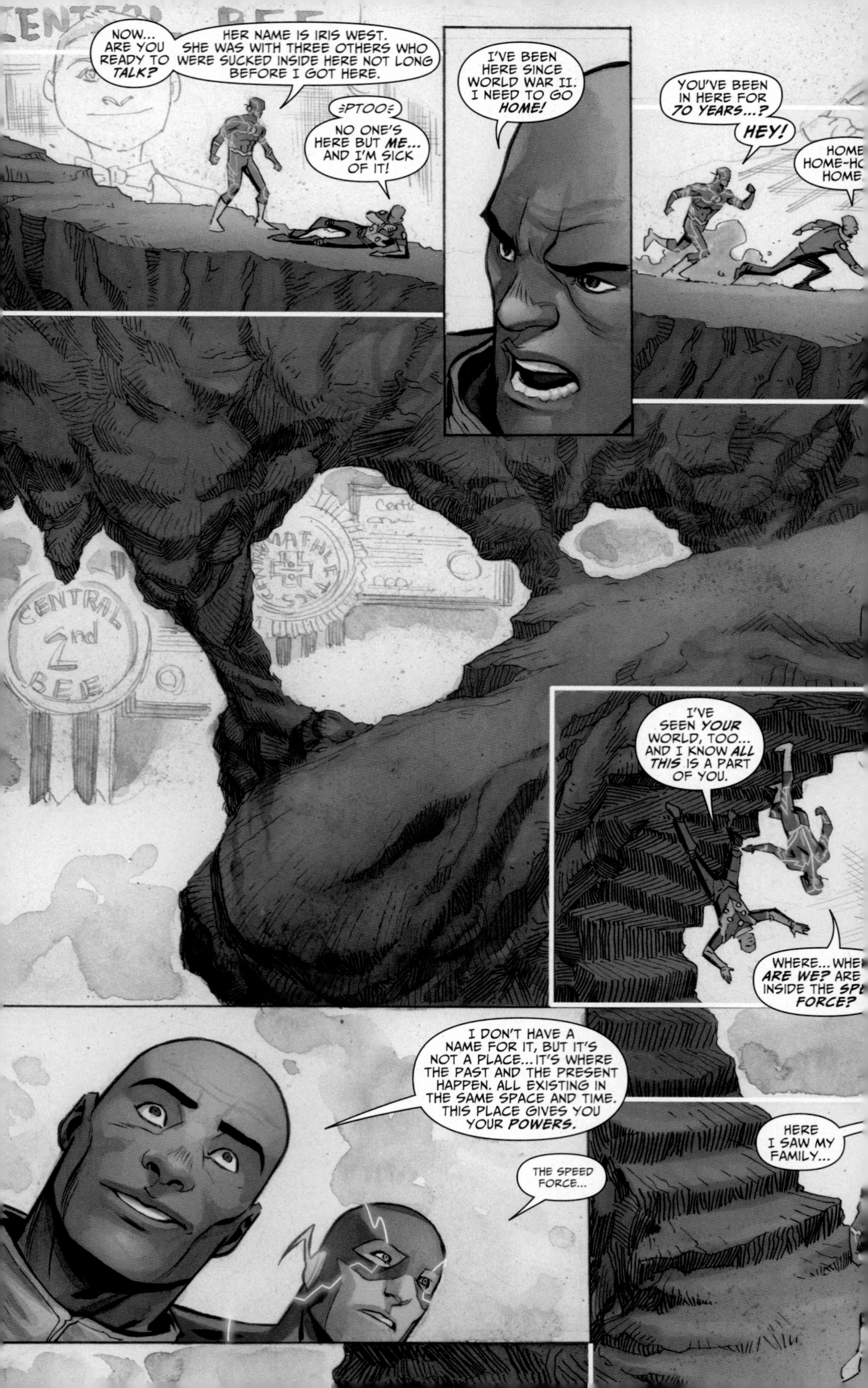
NOW... ARE YOU READY TO TALK?
HER NAME IS IRIS WEST. SHE WAS WITH THREE OTHERS WHO WERE SUCKED INSIDE HERE NOT LONG BEFORE I GOT HERE.
PTOO
NO ONE'S HERE BUT ME... AND I'M SICK OF IT!
I'VE BEEN HERE SINCE WORLD WAR II. I NEED TO GO HOME!
YOU'VE BEEN IN HERE FOR 70 YEARS...?
HEY!
HOME HOME-HO HOME
CENTRAL 2nd BEE
I'VE SEEN YOUR WORLD, TOO... AND I KNOW ALL THIS IS A PART OF YOU.
WHERE... WHE ARE WE? ARE INSIDE THE SP FORCE?
I DON'T HAVE A NAME FOR IT, BUT IT'S NOT A PLACE... IT'S WHERE THE PAST AND THE PRESENT HAPPEN. ALL EXISTING IN THE SAME SPACE AND TIME. THIS PLACE GIVES YOU YOUR POWERS.
THE SPEED FORCE...
HERE I SAW MY FAMILY...

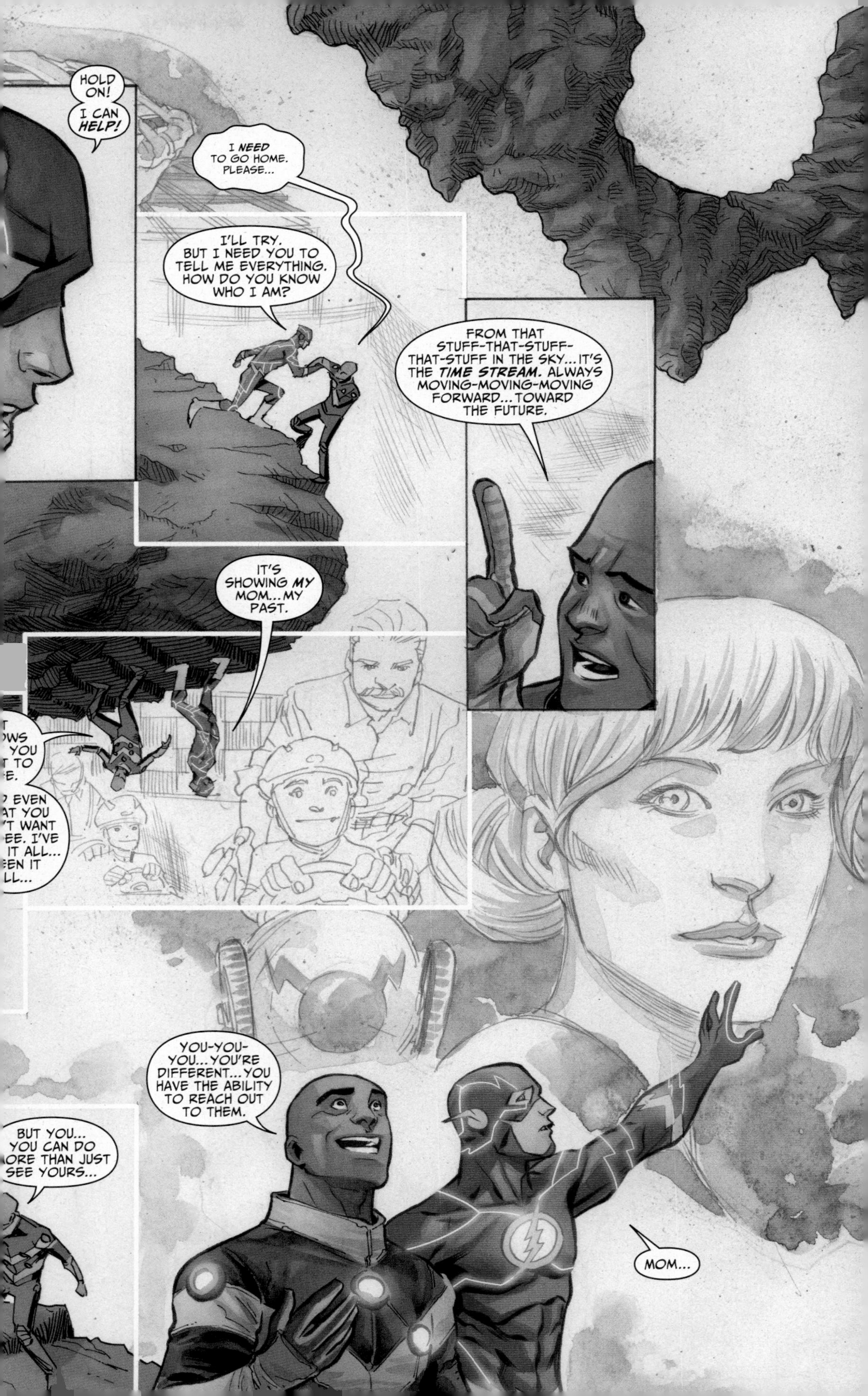

HOLD ON! I CAN *HELP!*
I *NEED* TO GO HOME. PLEASE...
I'LL TRY. BUT I NEED YOU TO TELL ME EVERYTHING. HOW DO YOU KNOW WHO I AM?
FROM THAT STUFF-THAT-STUFF-THAT-STUFF IN THE SKY...IT'S THE *TIME STREAM.* ALWAYS MOVING-MOVING-MOVING FORWARD...TOWARD THE FUTURE.
IT'S SHOWING *MY* MOM...MY PAST.
T OWS YOU T TO E. D EVEN AT YOU 'T WANT EE. I'VE IT ALL... EEN IT LL...
YOU-YOU-YOU...YOU'RE DIFFERENT...YOU HAVE THE ABILITY TO REACH OUT TO THEM.
BUT YOU... YOU CAN DO ORE THAN JUST SEE YOURS...
MOM...

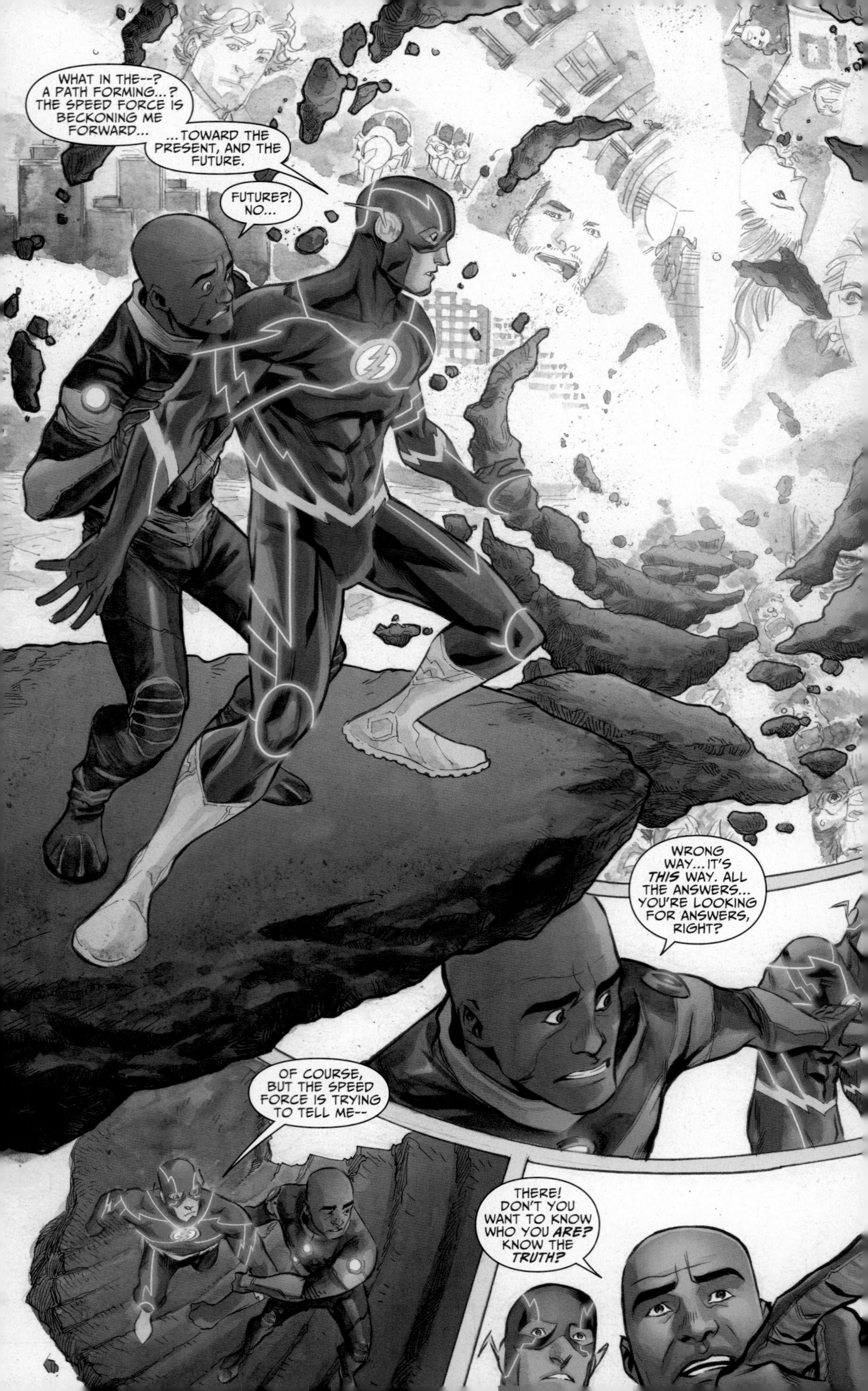
WHAT IN THE--? A PATH FORMING...? THE SPEED FORCE IS BECKONING ME FORWARD...
...TOWARD THE PRESENT, AND THE FUTURE.
FUTURE?! NO...
WRONG WAY... IT'S *THIS* WAY. ALL THE ANSWERS... YOU'RE LOOKING FOR ANSWERS, RIGHT?
OF COURSE, BUT THE SPEED FORCE IS TRYING TO TELL ME--
THERE! DON'T YOU WANT TO KNOW WHO YOU *ARE?* KNOW THE *TRUTH?*

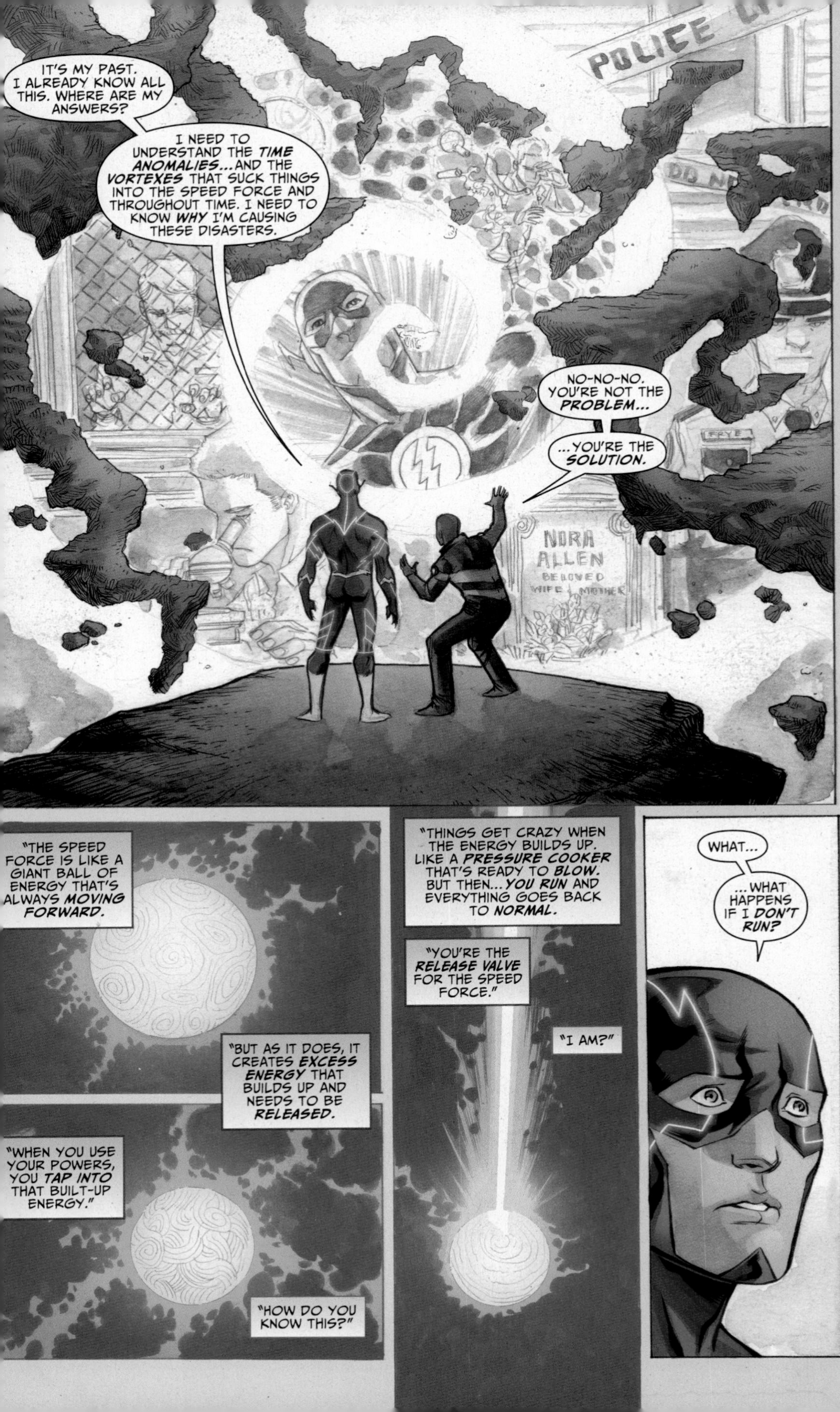
POLICE LI
IT'S MY PAST. I ALREADY KNOW ALL THIS. WHERE ARE MY ANSWERS?
I NEED TO UNDERSTAND THE *TIME ANOMALIES*...AND THE *VORTEXES* THAT SUCK THINGS INTO THE SPEED FORCE AND THROUGHOUT TIME. I NEED TO KNOW *WHY* I'M CAUSING THESE DISASTERS.
NO-NO-NO. YOU'RE NOT THE *PROBLEM*...
...YOU'RE THE *SOLUTION.*
FRYE
NORA ALLEN BELOVED WIFE & MOTHER
"THE SPEED FORCE IS LIKE A GIANT BALL OF ENERGY THAT'S ALWAYS *MOVING FORWARD.*
"BUT AS IT DOES, IT CREATES *EXCESS ENERGY* THAT BUILDS UP AND NEEDS TO BE *RELEASED.*
"WHEN YOU USE YOUR POWERS, YOU *TAP INTO* THAT BUILT-UP ENERGY."
"HOW DO YOU KNOW THIS?"
"THINGS GET CRAZY WHEN THE ENERGY BUILDS UP. LIKE A *PRESSURE COOKER* THAT'S READY TO *BLOW.* BUT THEN...*YOU RUN* AND EVERYTHING GOES BACK TO *NORMAL.*
"YOU'RE THE *RELEASE VALVE* FOR THE SPEED FORCE."
"I AM?"
WHAT...
...WHAT HAPPENS IF I *DON'T RUN?*

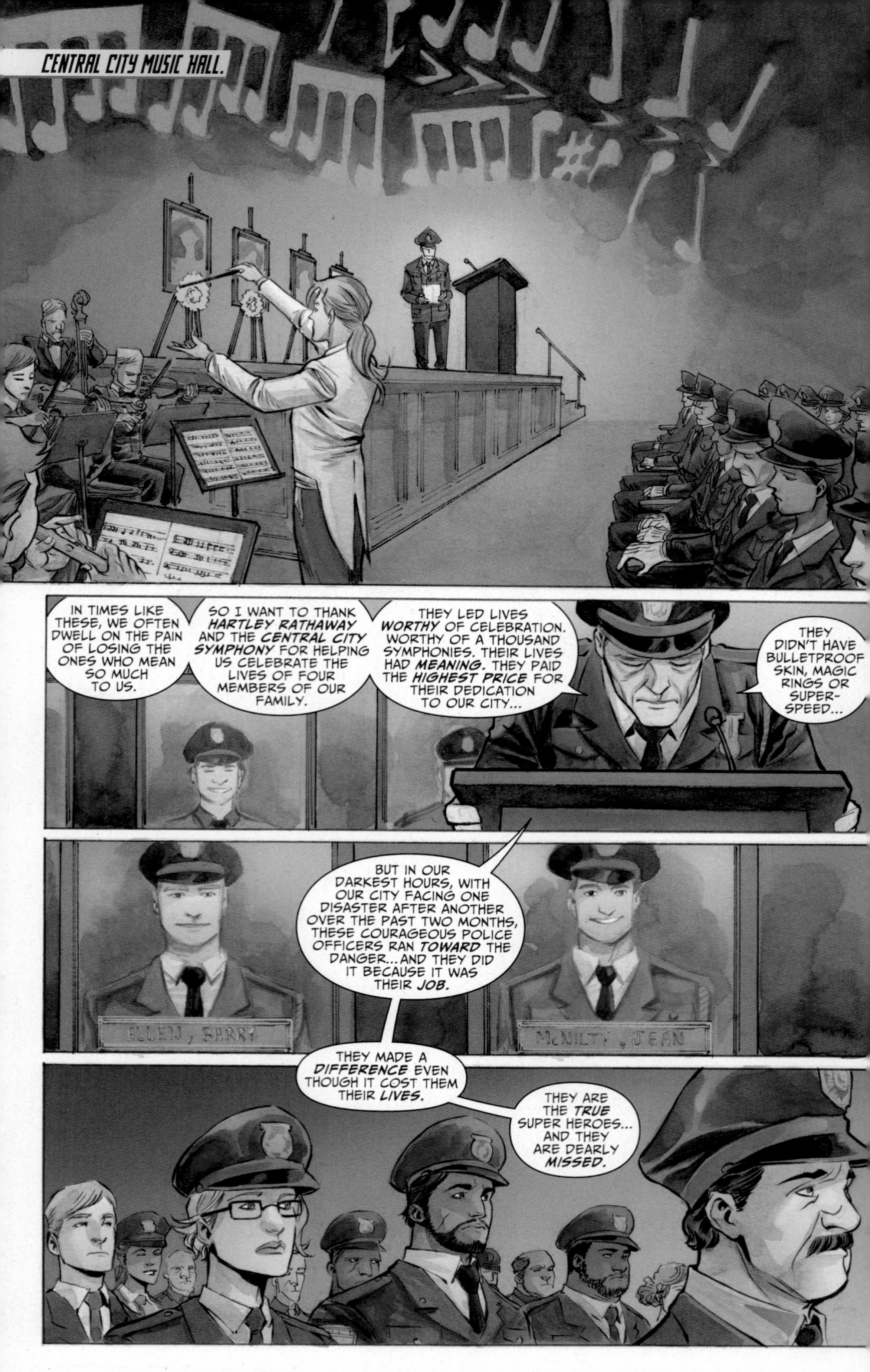
CENTRAL CITY MUSIC HALL.
IN TIMES LIKE THESE, WE OFTEN DWELL ON THE PAIN OF LOSING THE ONES WHO MEAN SO MUCH TO US.
SO I WANT TO THANK HARTLEY RATHAWAY AND THE CENTRAL CITY SYMPHONY FOR HELPING US CELEBRATE THE LIVES OF FOUR MEMBERS OF OUR FAMILY.
THEY LED LIVES WORTHY OF CELEBRATION. WORTHY OF A THOUSAND SYMPHONIES. THEIR LIVES HAD MEANING. THEY PAID THE HIGHEST PRICE FOR THEIR DEDICATION TO OUR CITY...
THEY DIDN'T HAVE BULLETPROOF SKIN, MAGIC RINGS OR SUPER-SPEED...
BUT IN OUR DARKEST HOURS, WITH OUR CITY FACING ONE DISASTER AFTER ANOTHER OVER THE PAST TWO MONTHS, THESE COURAGEOUS POLICE OFFICERS RAN TOWARD THE DANGER...AND THEY DID IT BECAUSE IT WAS THEIR JOB.
ALLEN, BARRY
McNILTY, JEAN
THEY MADE A DIFFERENCE EVEN THOUGH IT COST THEM THEIR LIVES.
THEY ARE THE TRUE SUPER HEROES... AND THEY ARE DEARLY MISSED.

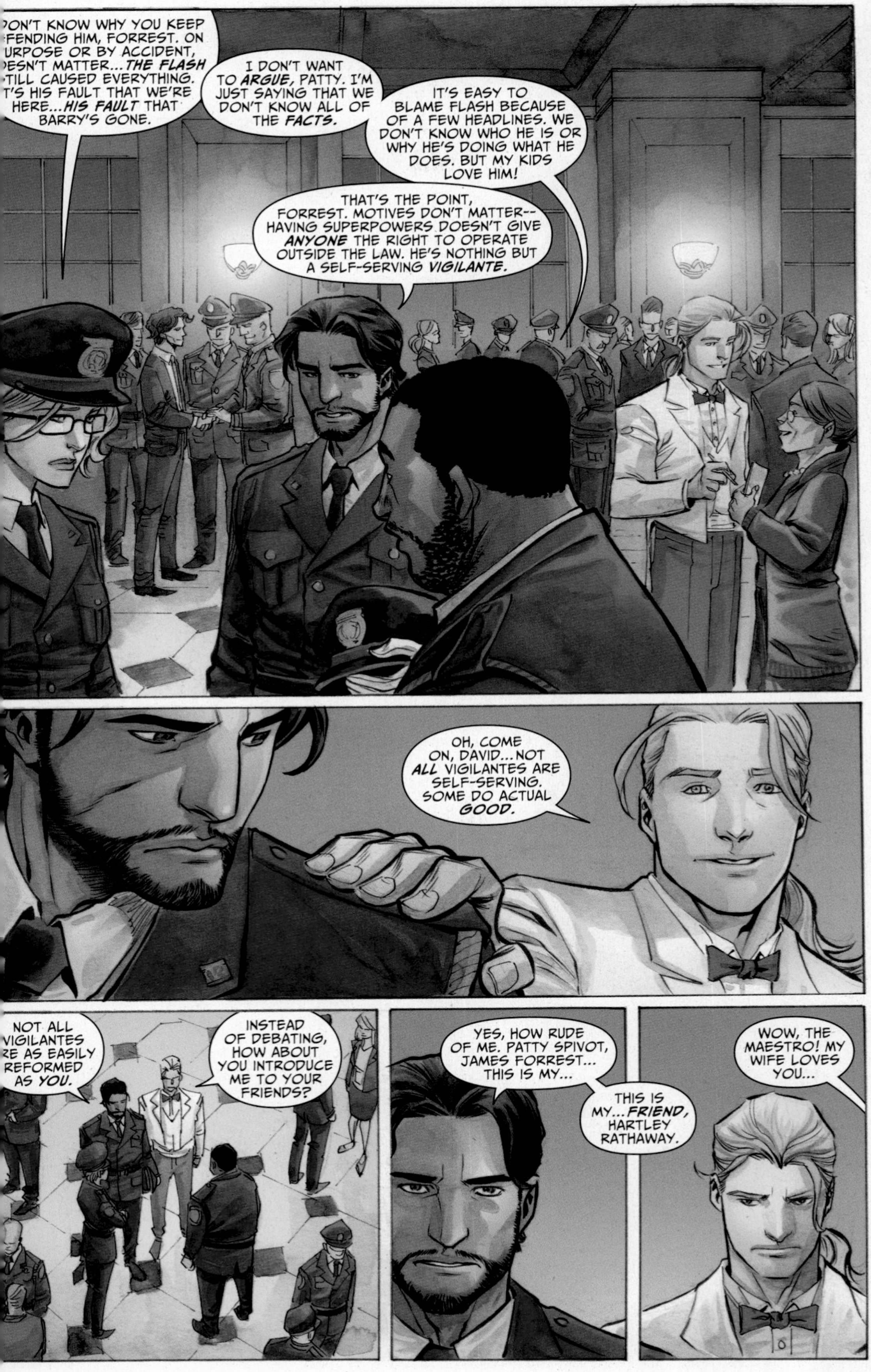
ON'T KNOW WHY YOU KEEP FENDING HIM, FORREST. ON URPOSE OR BY ACCIDENT, ESN'T MATTER... THE FLASH TILL CAUSED EVERYTHING. T'S HIS FAULT THAT WE'RE HERE... HIS FAULT THAT BARRY'S GONE.
I DON'T WANT TO ARGUE, PATTY. I'M JUST SAYING THAT WE DON'T KNOW ALL OF THE FACTS.
IT'S EASY TO BLAME FLASH BECAUSE OF A FEW HEADLINES. WE DON'T KNOW WHO HE IS OR WHY HE'S DOING WHAT HE DOES. BUT MY KIDS LOVE HIM!
THAT'S THE POINT, FORREST. MOTIVES DON'T MATTER-- HAVING SUPERPOWERS DOESN'T GIVE ANYONE THE RIGHT TO OPERATE OUTSIDE THE LAW. HE'S NOTHING BUT A SELF-SERVING VIGILANTE.
OH, COME ON, DAVID... NOT ALL VIGILANTES ARE SELF-SERVING. SOME DO ACTUAL GOOD.
NOT ALL VIGILANTES RE AS EASILY REFORMED AS YOU.
INSTEAD OF DEBATING, HOW ABOUT YOU INTRODUCE ME TO YOUR FRIENDS?
YES, HOW RUDE OF ME. PATTY SPIVOT, JAMES FORREST... THIS IS MY...
THIS IS MY... FRIEND, HARTLEY RATHAWAY.
WOW, THE MAESTRO! MY WIFE LOVES YOU...

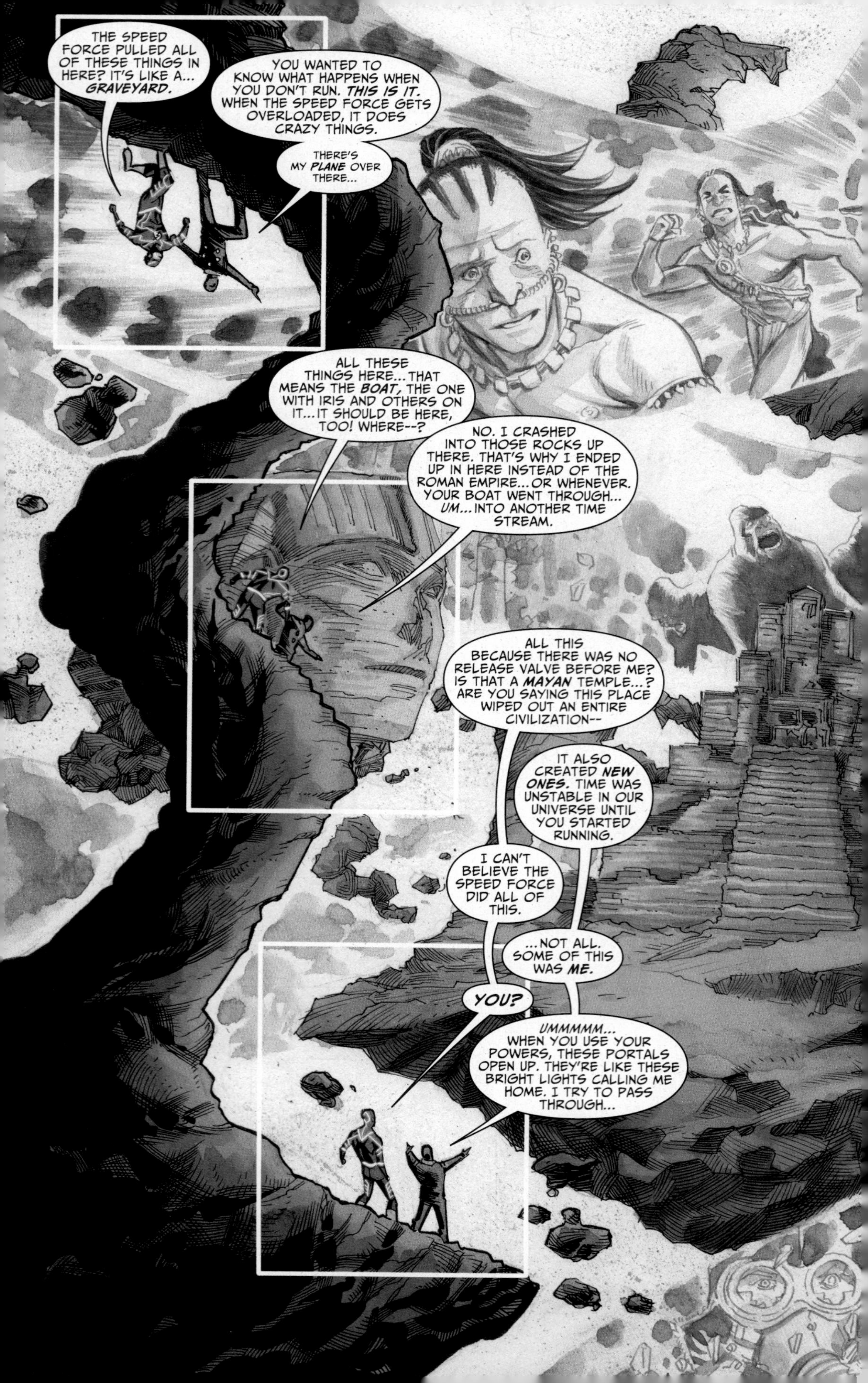
THE SPEED FORCE PULLED ALL OF THESE THINGS IN HERE? IT'S LIKE A... GRAVEYARD.
YOU WANTED TO KNOW WHAT HAPPENS WHEN YOU DON'T RUN. THIS IS IT. WHEN THE SPEED FORCE GETS OVERLOADED, IT DOES CRAZY THINGS.
THERE'S MY PLANE OVER THERE...
ALL THESE THINGS HERE... THAT MEANS THE BOAT, THE ONE WITH IRIS AND OTHERS ON IT... IT SHOULD BE HERE, TOO! WHERE--?
NO. I CRASHED INTO THOSE ROCKS UP THERE. THAT'S WHY I ENDED UP IN HERE INSTEAD OF THE ROMAN EMPIRE... OR WHENEVER. YOUR BOAT WENT THROUGH... UM... INTO ANOTHER TIME STREAM.
ALL THIS BECAUSE THERE WAS NO RELEASE VALVE BEFORE ME? IS THAT A MAYAN TEMPLE...? ARE YOU SAYING THIS PLACE WIPED OUT AN ENTIRE CIVILIZATION--
IT ALSO CREATED NEW ONES. TIME WAS UNSTABLE IN OUR UNIVERSE UNTIL YOU STARTED RUNNING.
I CAN'T BELIEVE THE SPEED FORCE DID ALL OF THIS.
...NOT ALL. SOME OF THIS WAS ME.
YOU?
UMMMMM... WHEN YOU USE YOUR POWERS, THESE PORTALS OPEN UP. THEY'RE LIKE THESE BRIGHT LIGHTS CALLING ME HOME. I TRY TO PASS THROUGH...

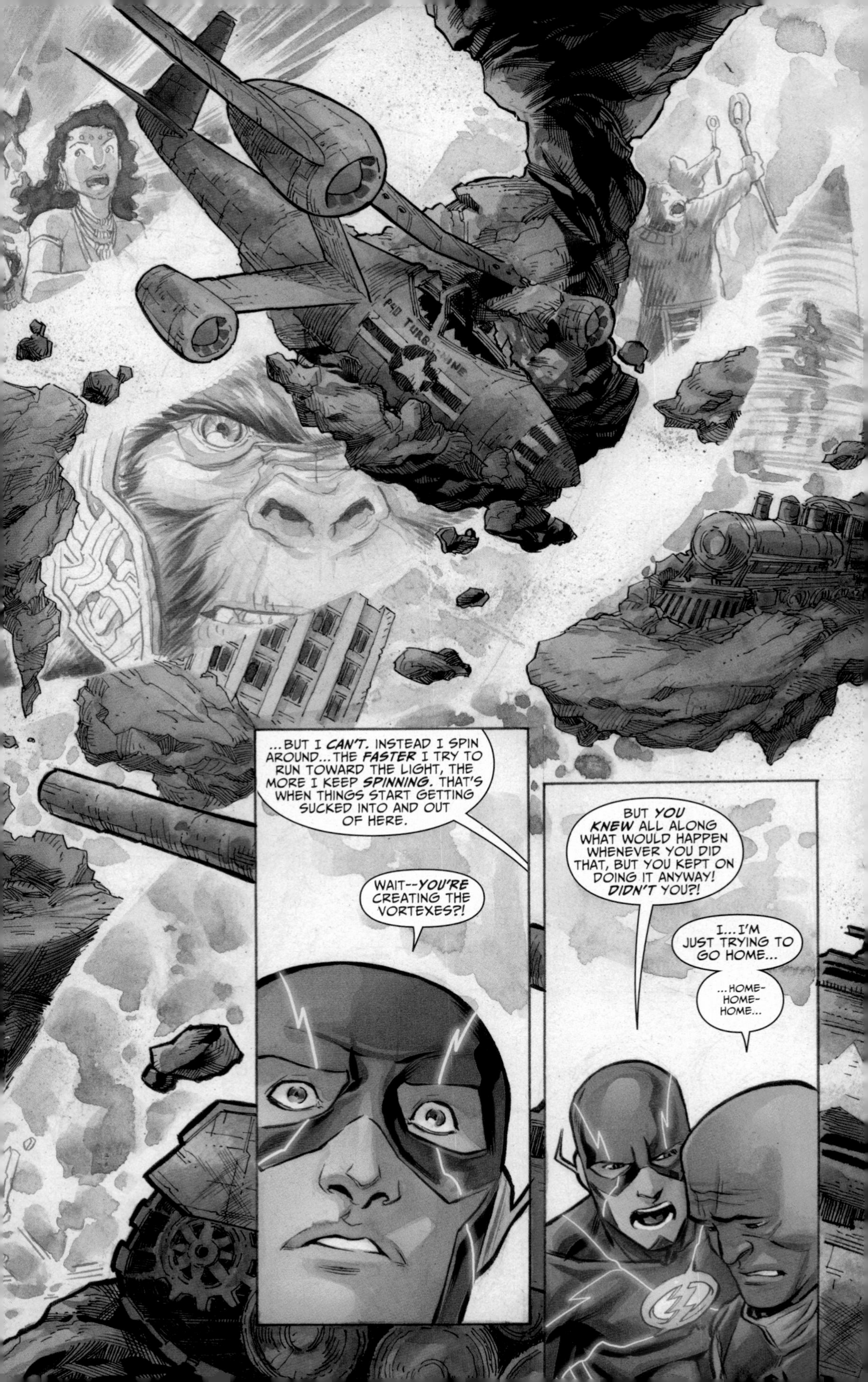

P-40 TURBO-NINE
...BUT I *CAN'T.* INSTEAD I SPIN AROUND... THE *FASTER* I TRY TO RUN TOWARD THE LIGHT, THE MORE I KEEP *SPINNING.* THAT'S WHEN THINGS START GETTING SUCKED INTO AND OUT OF HERE.
WAIT--*YOU'RE* CREATING THE VORTEXES?!
BUT *YOU KNEW* ALL ALONG WHAT WOULD HAPPEN WHENEVER YOU DID THAT, BUT YOU KEPT ON DOING IT ANYWAY! *DIDN'T* YOU?!
I... I'M JUST TRYING TO GO HOME...
...HOME-HOME-HOME...

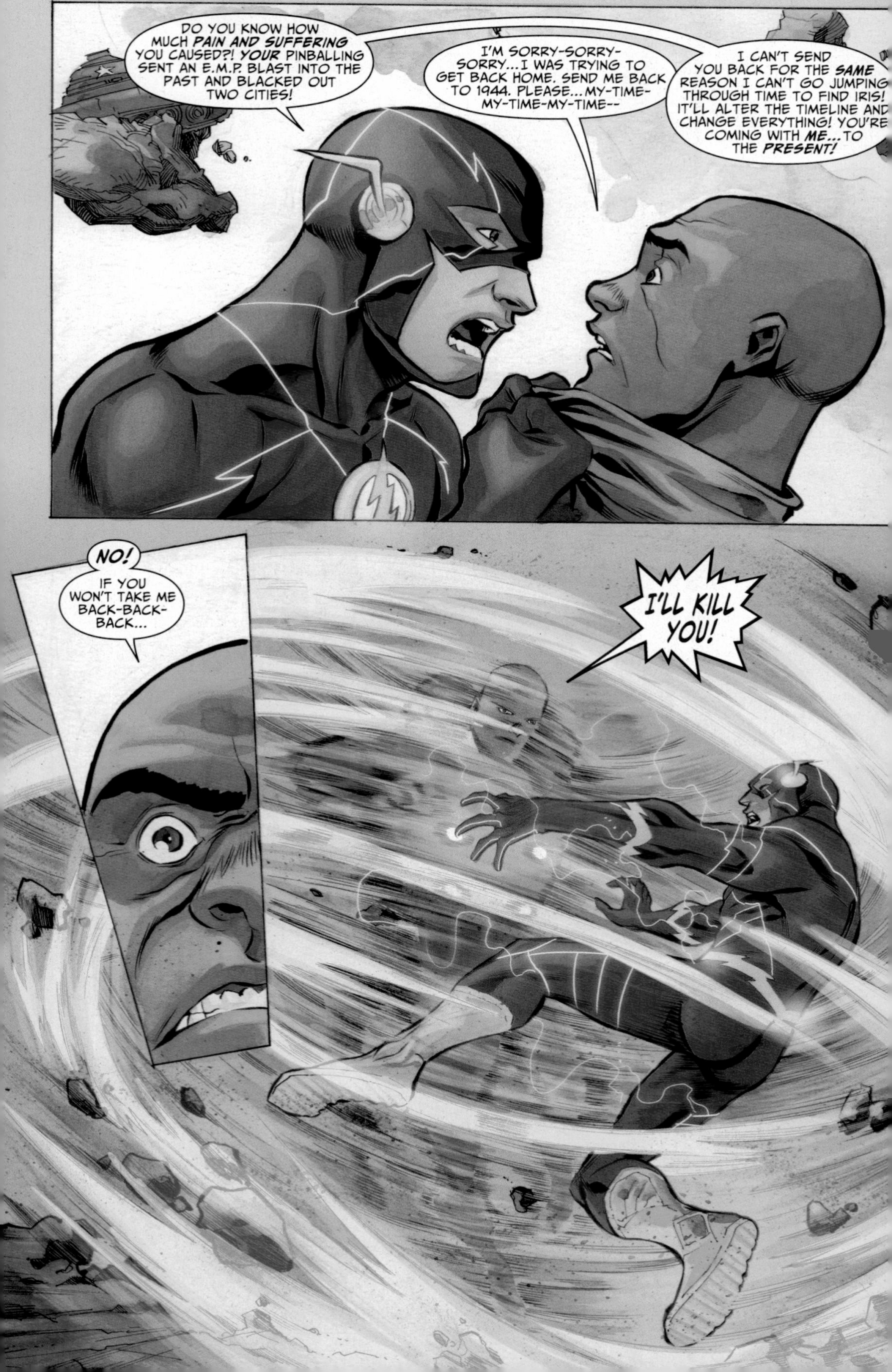
DO YOU KNOW HOW MUCH PAIN AND SUFFERING YOU CAUSED?! YOUR PINBALLING SENT AN E.M.P. BLAST INTO THE PAST AND BLACKED OUT TWO CITIES!
I'M SORRY-SORRY-SORRY... I WAS TRYING TO GET BACK HOME. SEND ME BACK TO 1944. PLEASE... MY-TIME-MY-TIME-MY-TIME--
I CAN'T SEND YOU BACK FOR THE SAME REASON I CAN'T GO JUMPING THROUGH TIME TO FIND IRIS! IT'LL ALTER THE TIMELINE AND CHANGE EVERYTHING! YOU'RE COMING WITH ME... TO THE PRESENT!
NO!
IF YOU WON'T TAKE ME BACK-BACK-BACK...
I'LL KILL YOU!

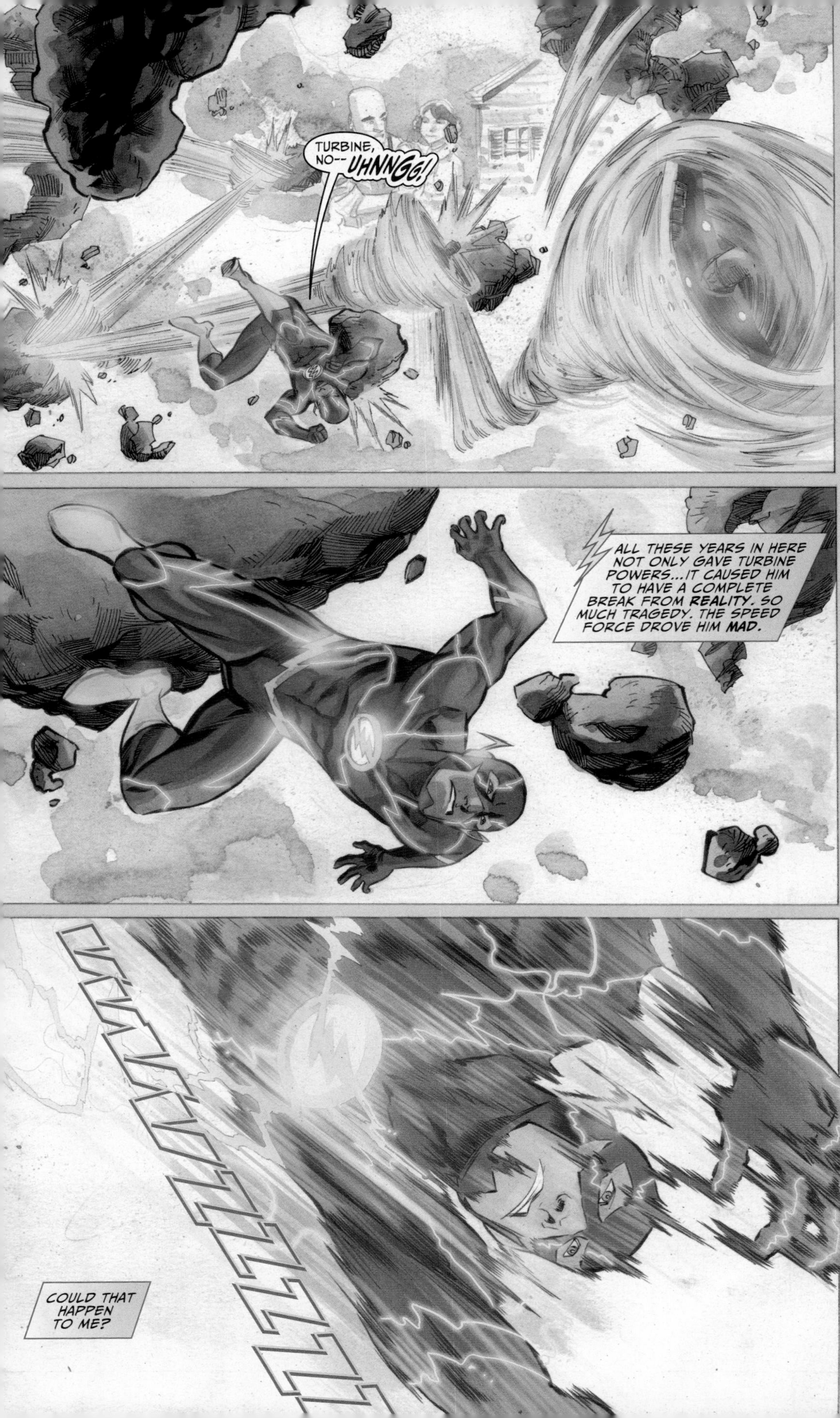
TURBINE, NO-- UHNNGG!
ALL THESE YEARS IN HERE NOT ONLY GAVE TURBINE POWERS...IT CAUSED HIM TO HAVE A COMPLETE BREAK FROM REALITY. SO MUCH TRAGEDY. THE SPEED FORCE DROVE HIM MAD.
COULD THAT HAPPEN TO ME?

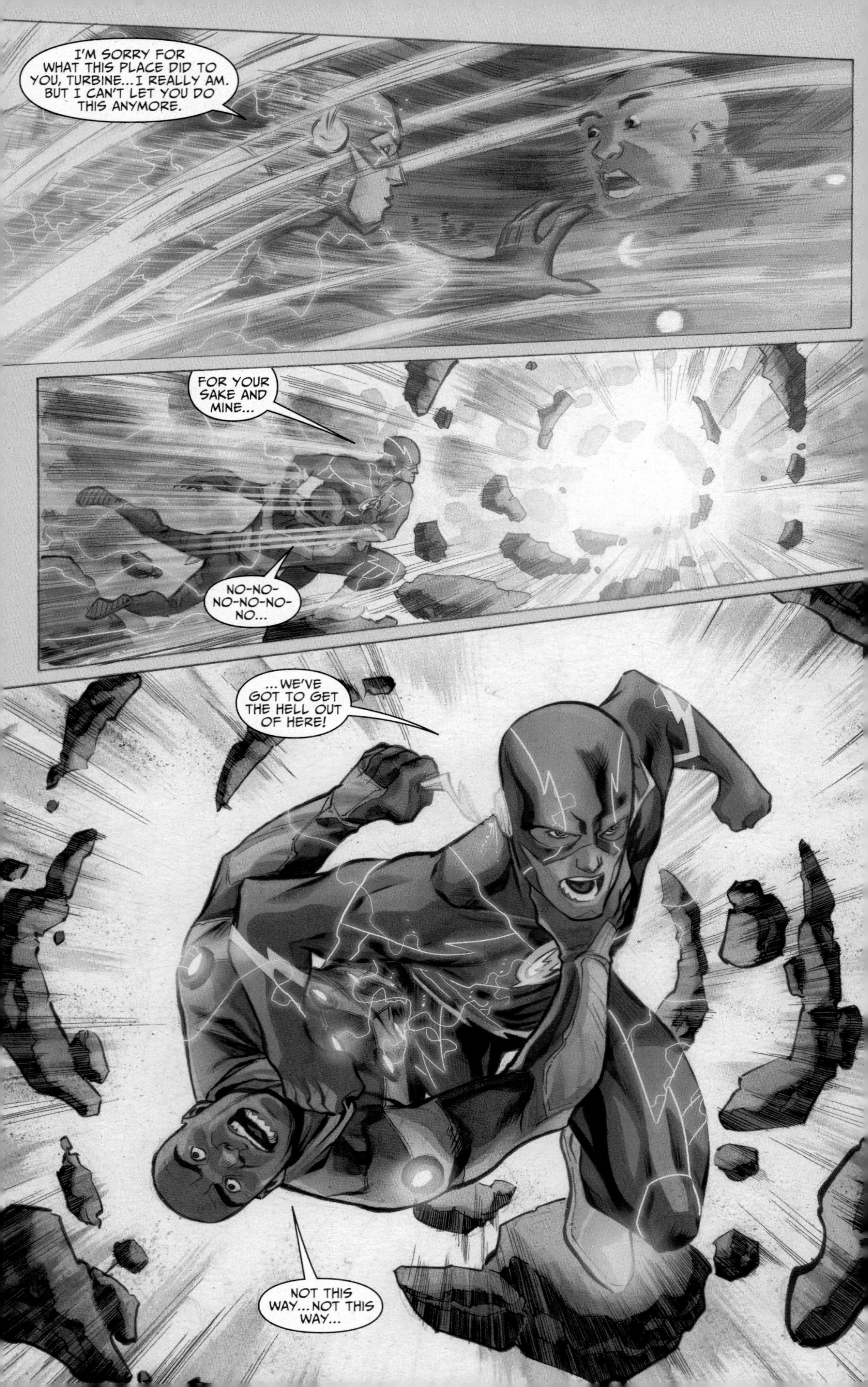
I'M SORRY FOR WHAT THIS PLACE DID TO YOU, TURBINE...I REALLY AM. BUT I CAN'T LET YOU DO THIS ANYMORE.
FOR YOUR SAKE AND MINE...
NO-NO-NO-NO-NO-NO...
...WE'VE GOT TO GET THE HELL OUT OF HERE!
NOT THIS WAY...NOT THIS WAY...

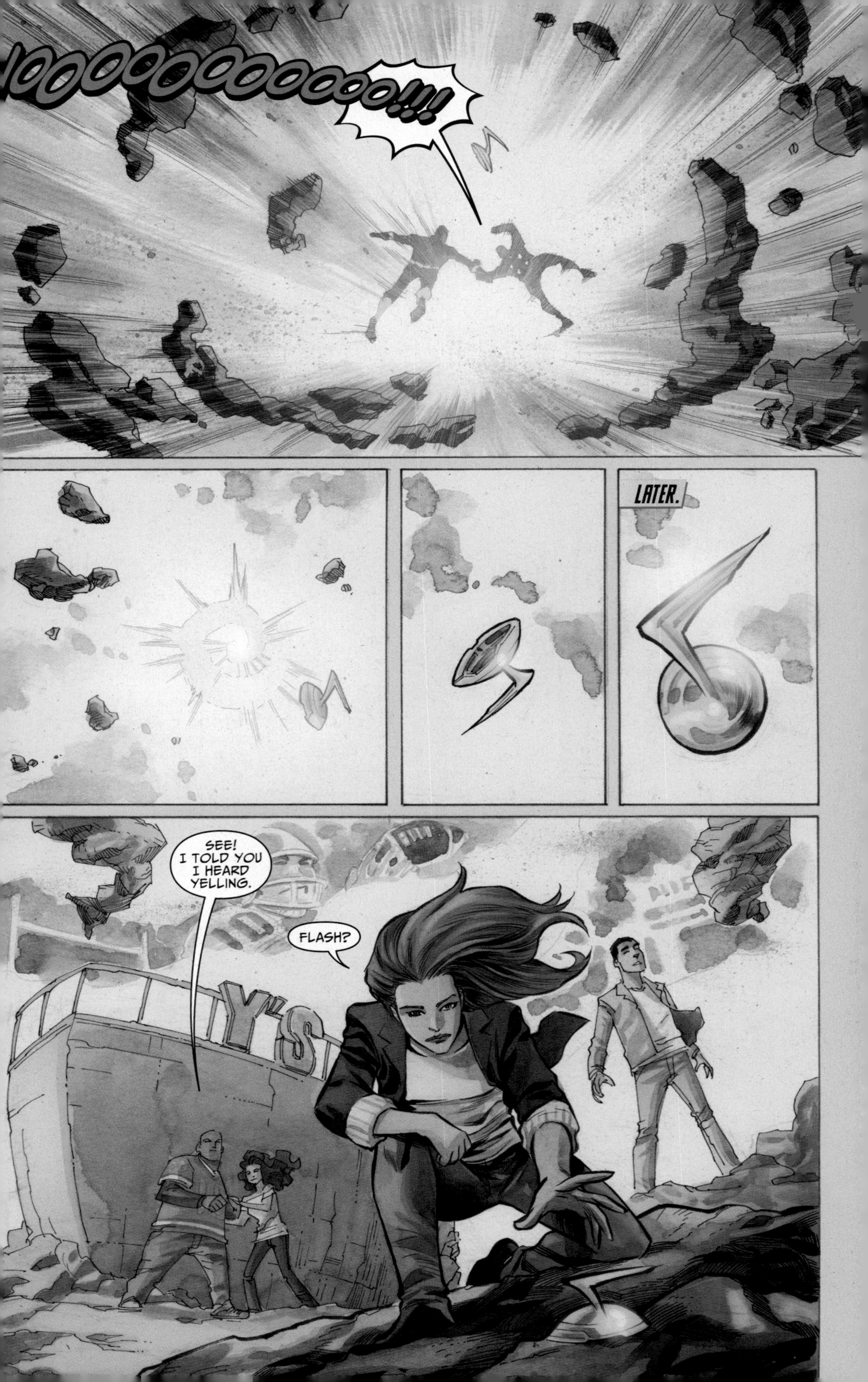
OOOOOOOOOOO!!!
LATER.
SEE! I TOLD YOU I HEARD YELLING.
FLASH?

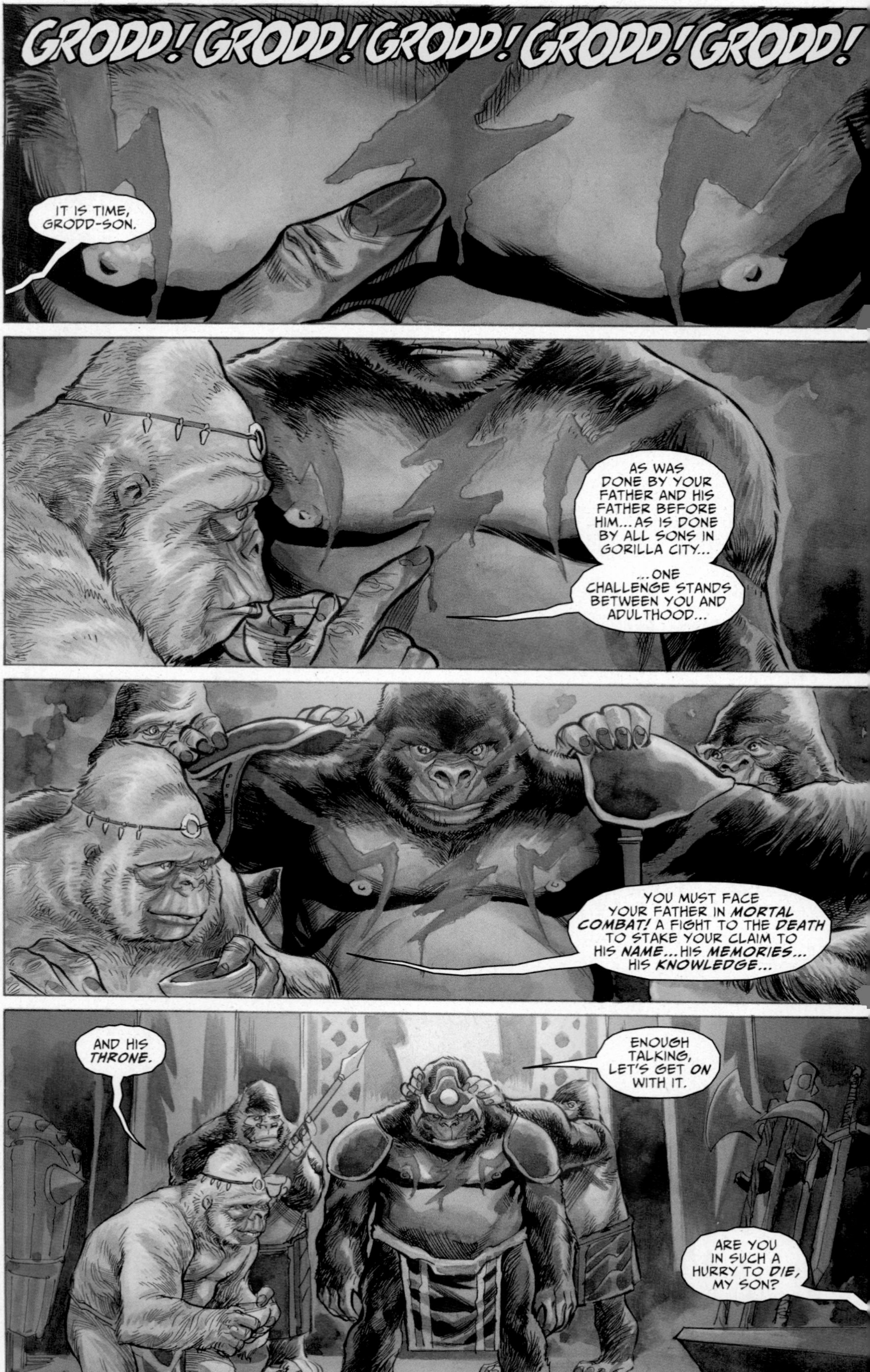
GRODD! GRODD! GRODD! GRODD! GRODD!
IT IS TIME, GRODD-SON.
AS WAS DONE BY YOUR FATHER AND HIS FATHER BEFORE HIM... AS IS DONE BY ALL SONS IN GORILLA CITY...
...ONE CHALLENGE STANDS BETWEEN YOU AND ADULTHOOD...
YOU MUST FACE YOUR FATHER IN MORTAL COMBAT! A FIGHT TO THE DEATH TO STAKE YOUR CLAIM TO HIS NAME... HIS MEMORIES... HIS KNOWLEDGE...
AND HIS THRONE.
ENOUGH TALKING, LET'S GET ON WITH IT.
ARE YOU IN SUCH A HURRY TO DIE, MY SON?

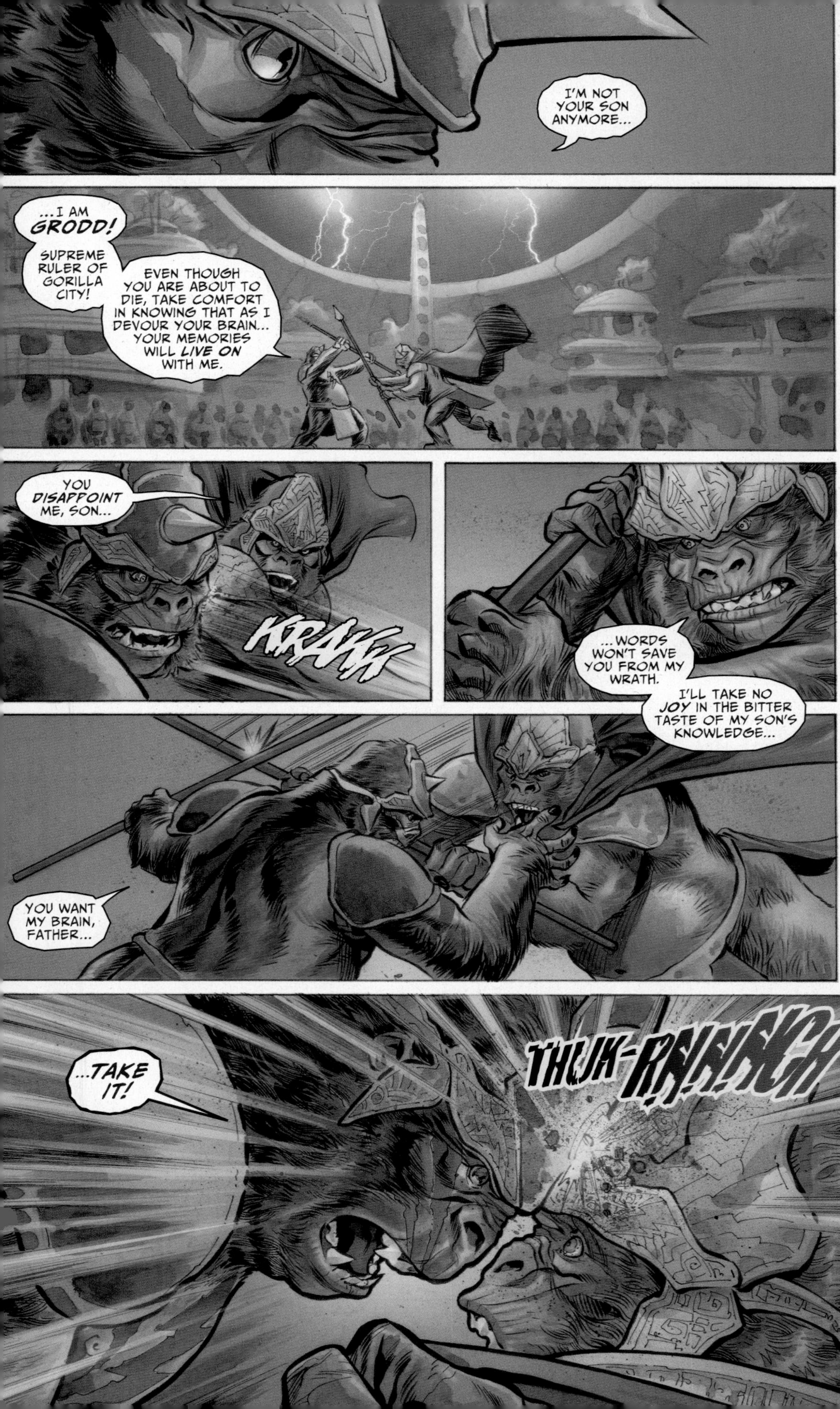
I'M NOT YOUR SON ANYMORE...
...I AM GRODD!
SUPREME RULER OF GORILLA CITY!
EVEN THOUGH YOU ARE ABOUT TO DIE, TAKE COMFORT IN KNOWING THAT AS I DEVOUR YOUR BRAIN... YOUR MEMORIES WILL LIVE ON WITH ME.
YOU DISAPPOINT ME, SON...
KRAKK
...WORDS WON'T SAVE YOU FROM MY WRATH.
I'LL TAKE NO JOY IN THE BITTER TASTE OF MY SON'S KNOWLEDGE...
YOU WANT MY BRAIN, FATHER...
...TAKE IT!
THUK-RRRRSCH

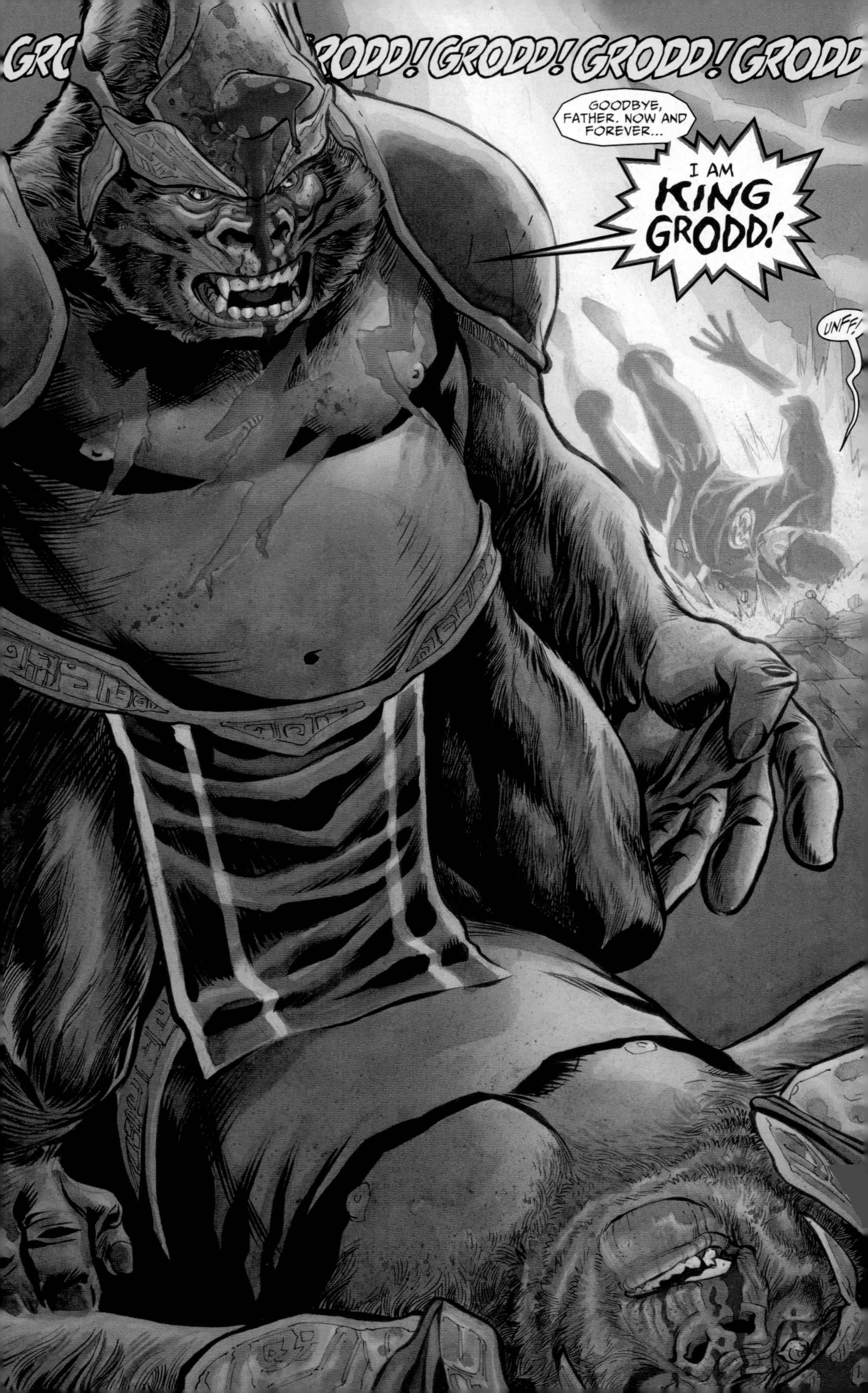
GRODD! GRODD! GRODD! GRODD! GRODD
GOODBYE, FATHER. NOW AND FOREVER...
I AM KING GRODD!
UNFF!

THE FLASH

BEHIND THE SPEED FORCE

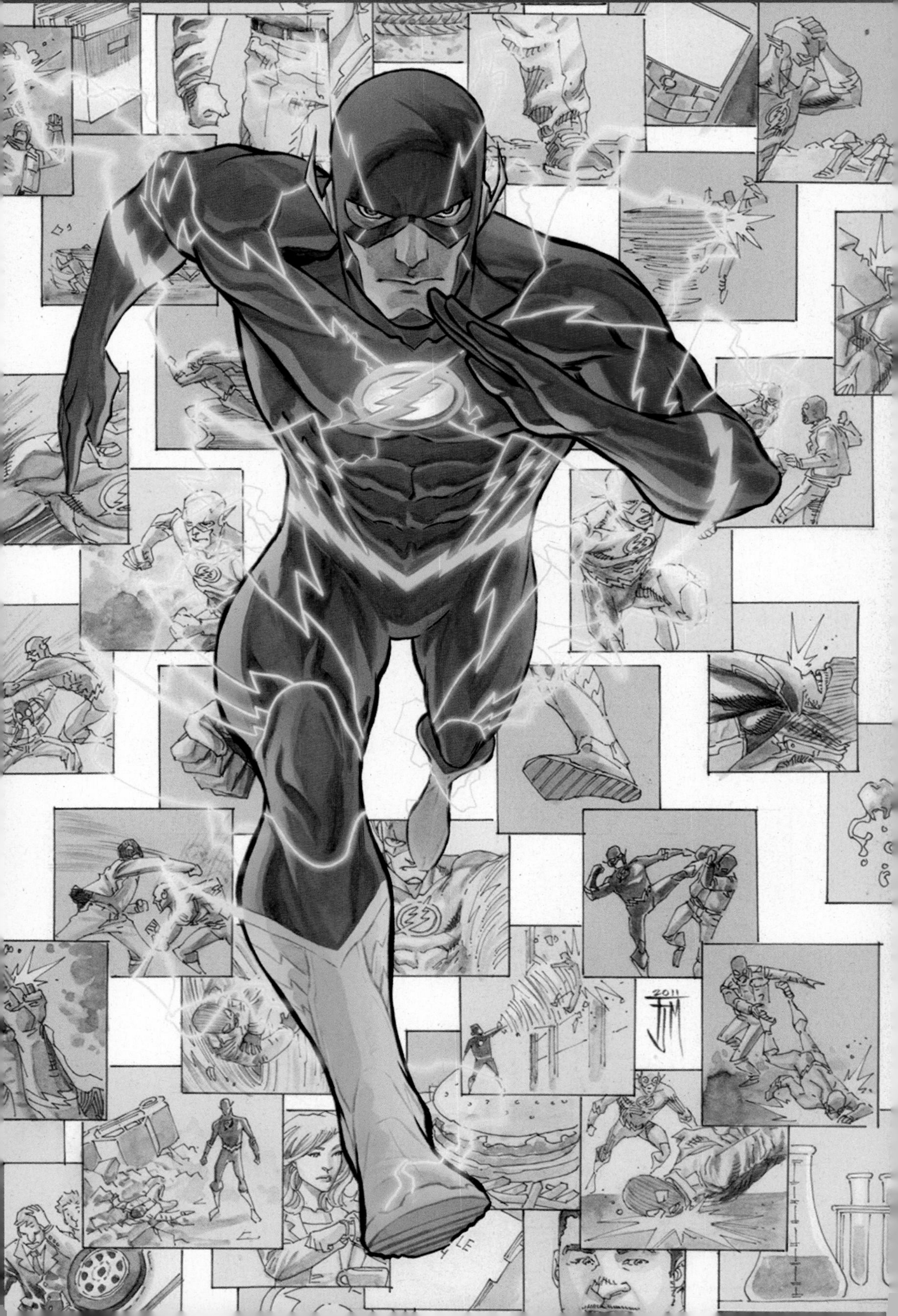

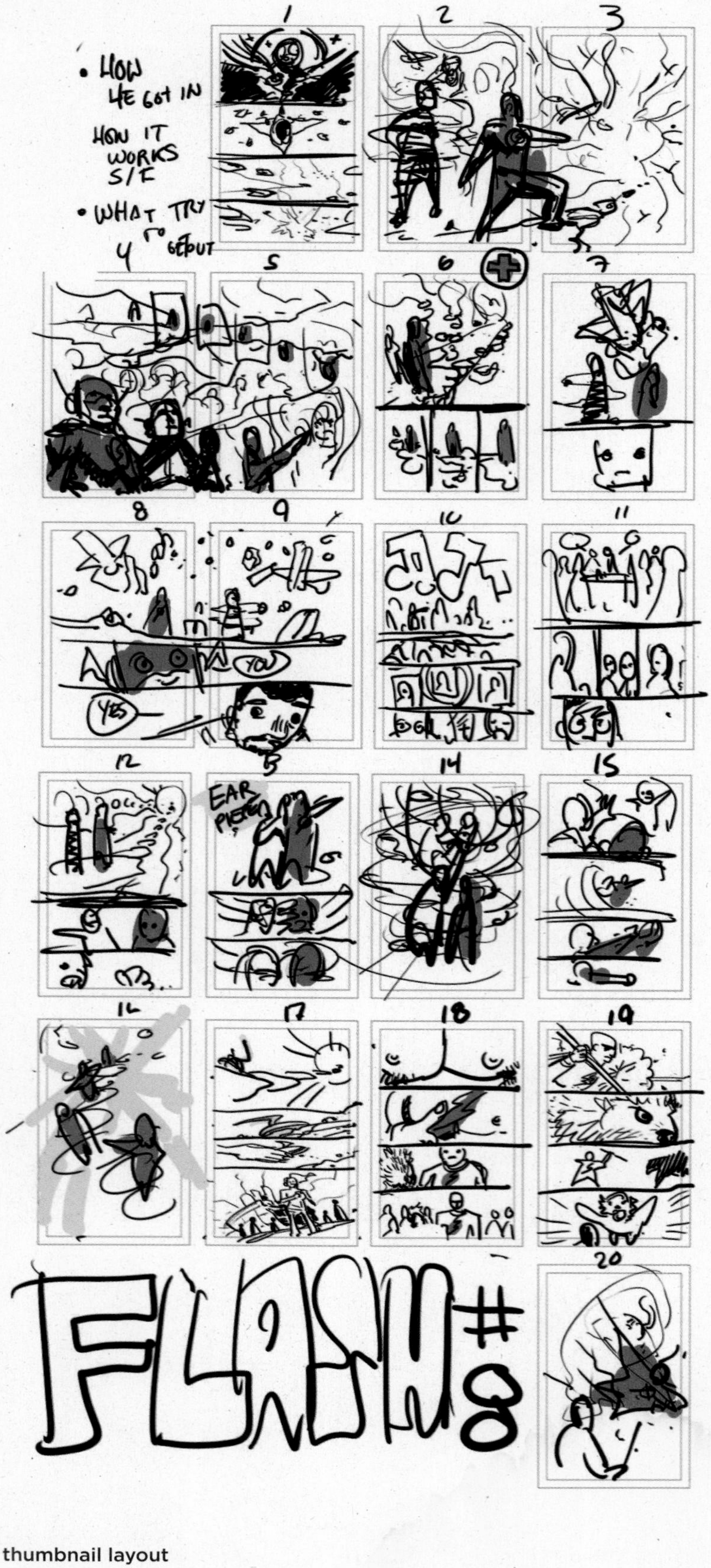
• HOW HE GOT IN
HOW IT WORKS S/F
• WHAT TRY TO GET OUT
EAR PIECE
YOU
YES
FLASH #8

THE FLASH #8 thumbnail layout

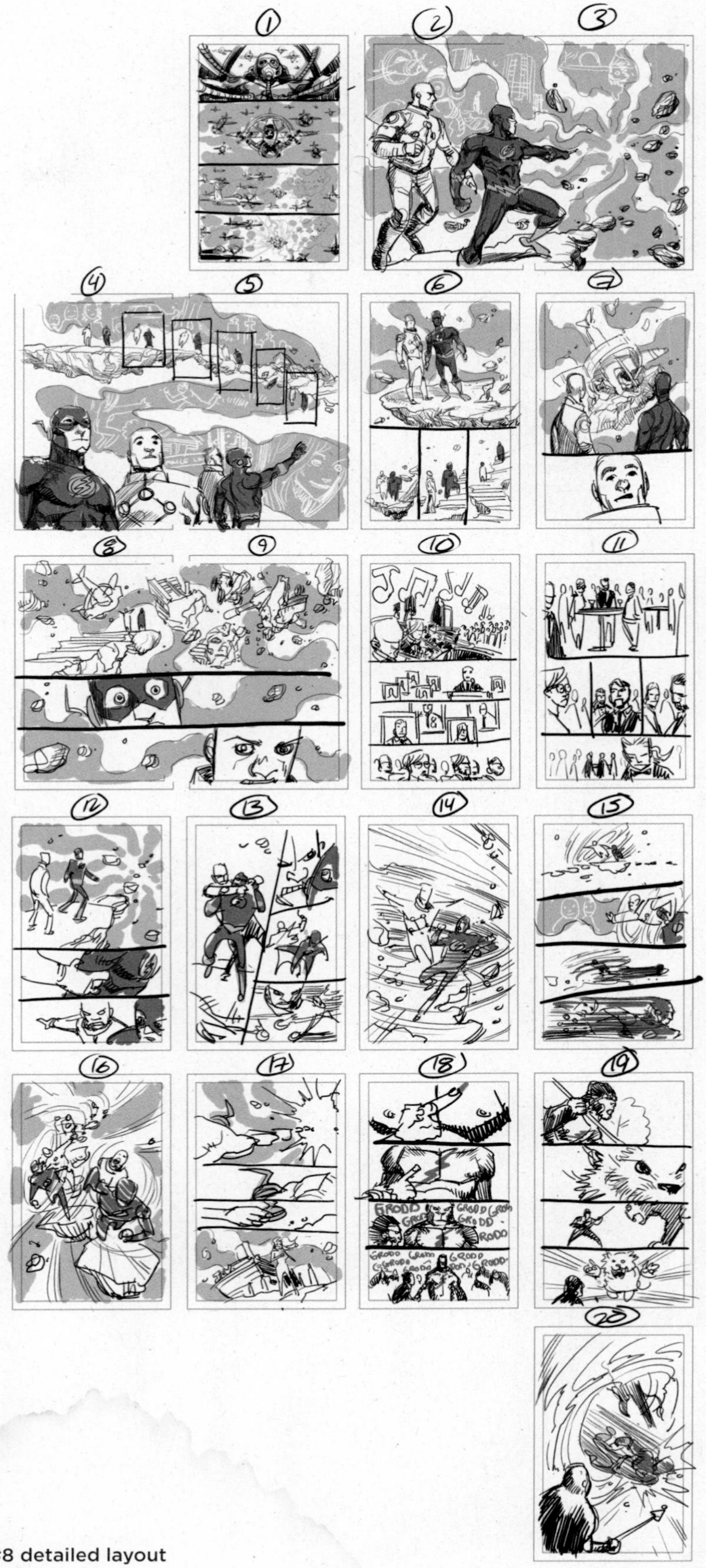
1
2
3
4
5
6
7
8
9
10
11
12
13
14
15
16
17
18
19
20
GRODD

THE FLASH #8 detailed layout

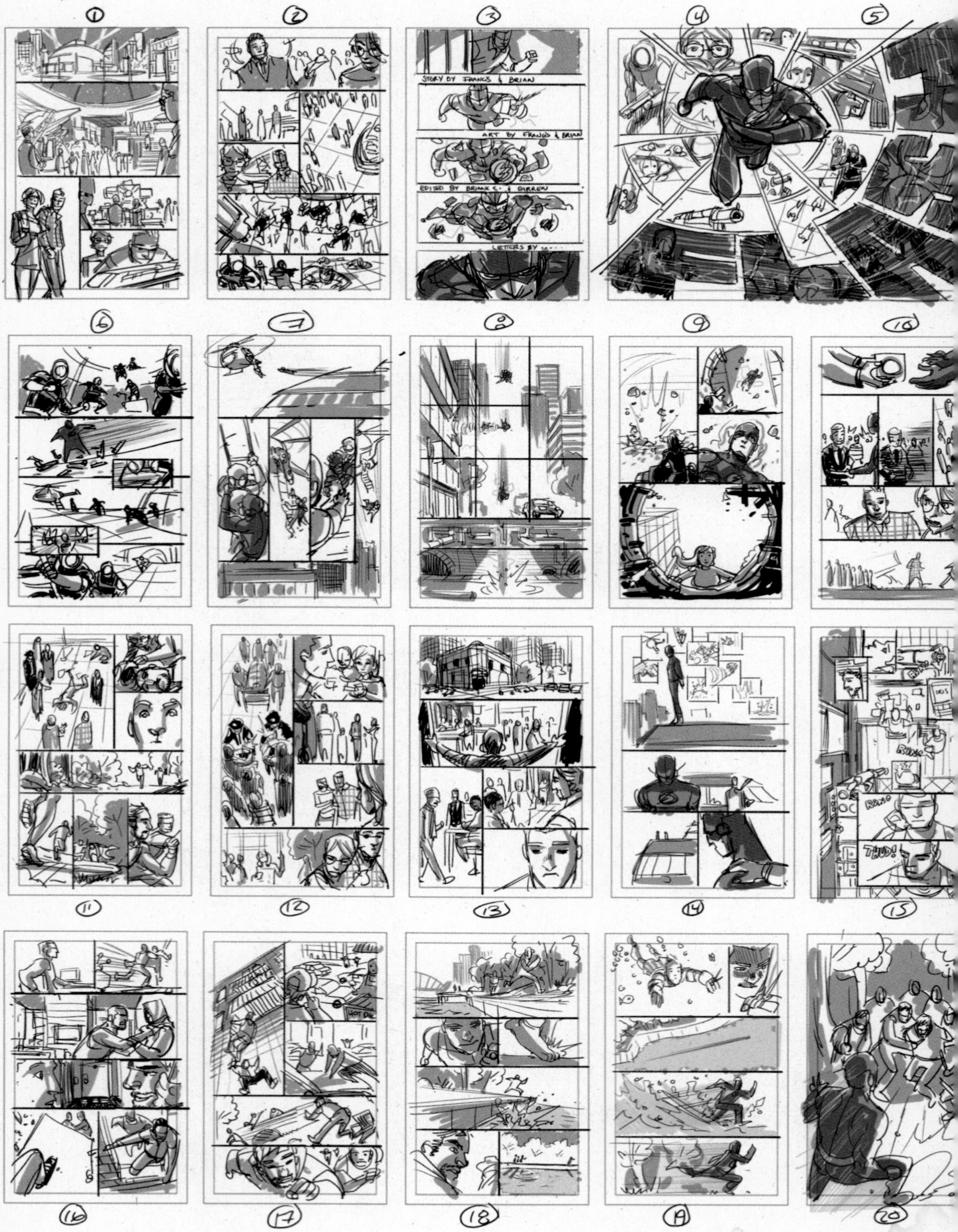
1
2
3
STORY BY FRANCIS & BRIAN
ART BY FRANCIS & BRIAN
EDITED BY BRIAN C. & DARREN
LETTERS BY ....
4
5
6
7
8
9
10
11
12
13
14
15
THUD!
16
17
18
19
20

THE FLASH #1 layout

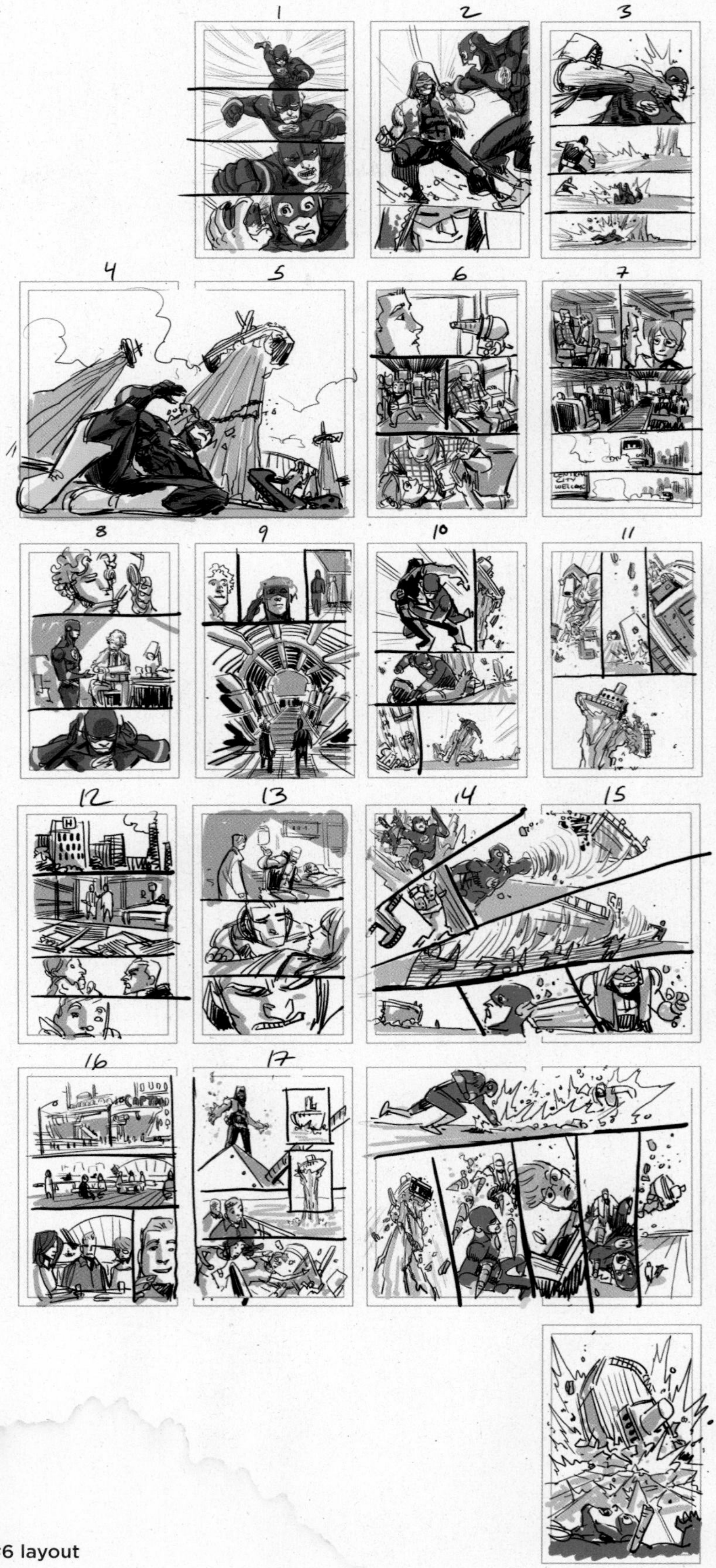
1
2
3
4
5
6
7
8
9
10
11
12
13
14
15
16
17

THE FLASH #6 layout

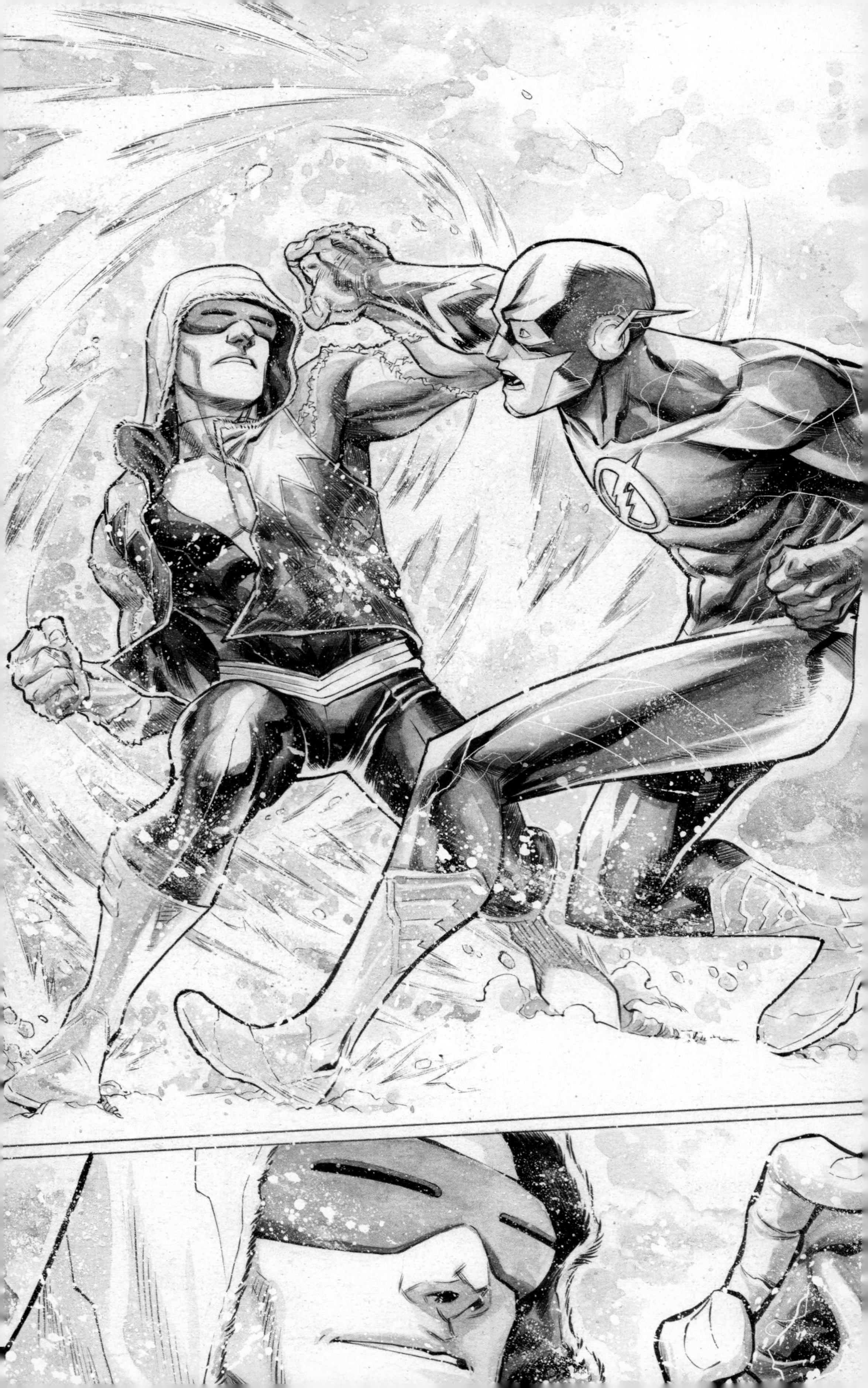

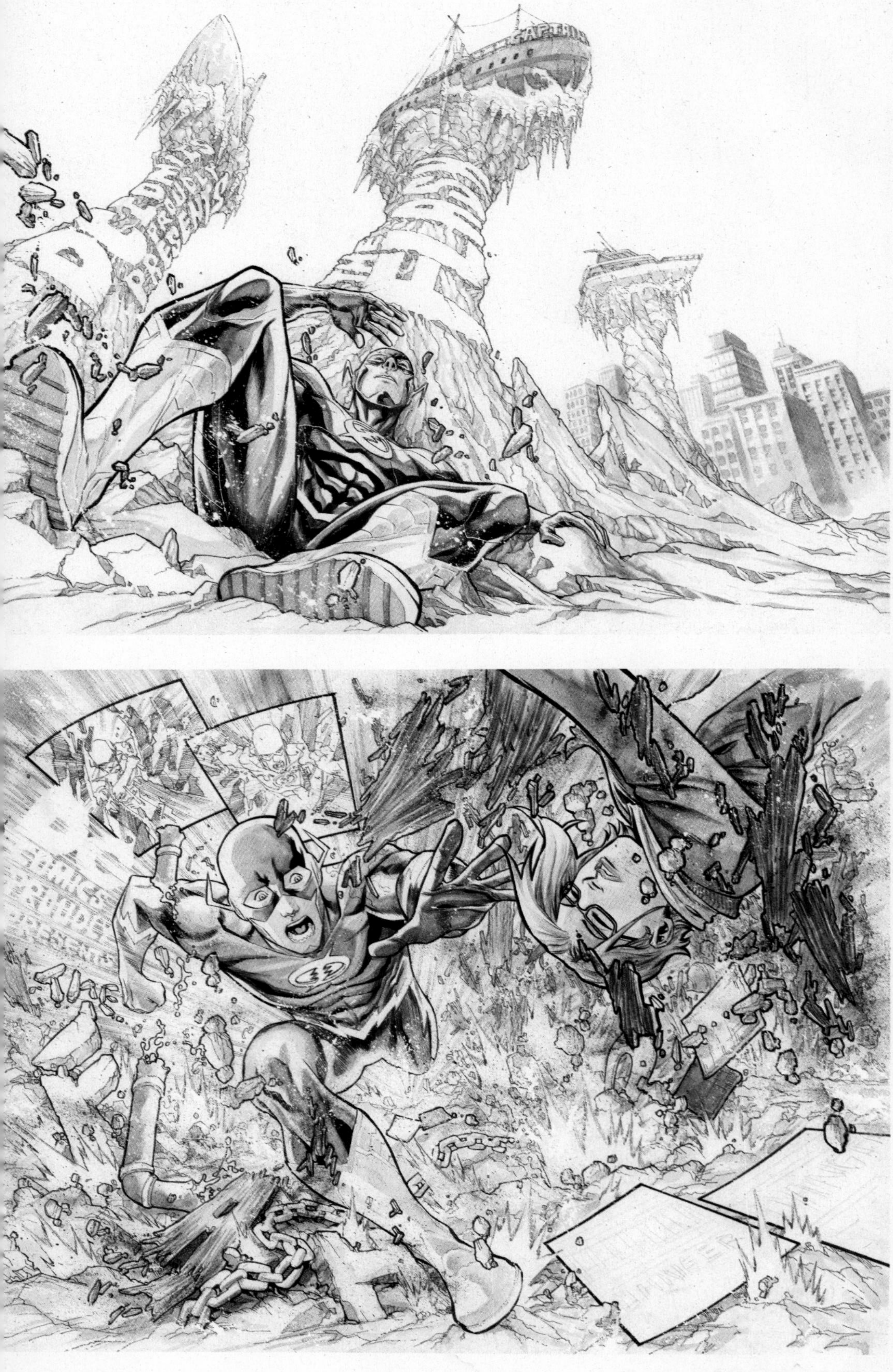

THE FLASH #3 PG 1 FRANCIS MANAPUL

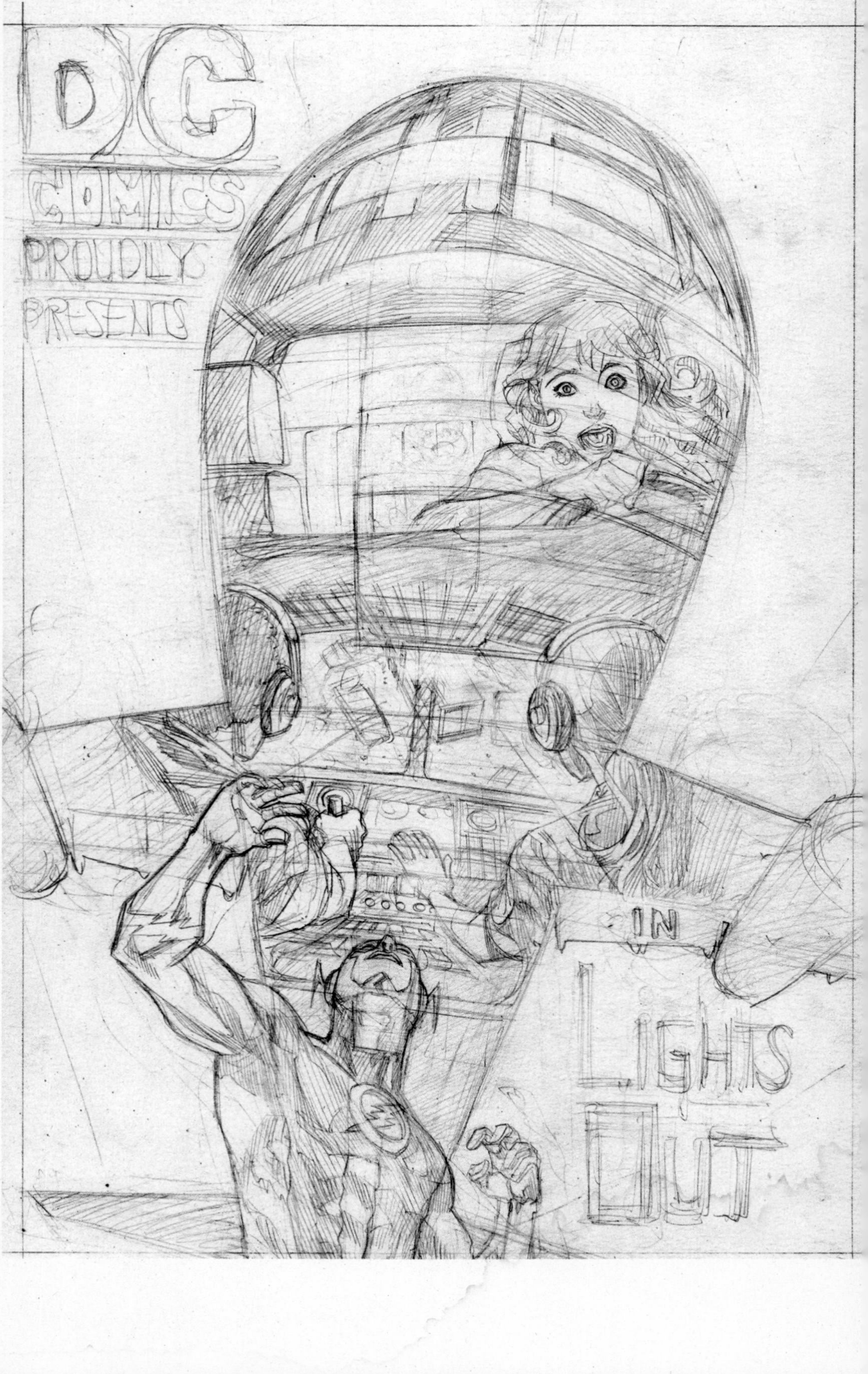
DC
COMICS
PROUDLY
PRESENTS
IN
LIGHTS
OUT

THE FLASH #3 PG 2 & 3 FRANCIS MANAPUL

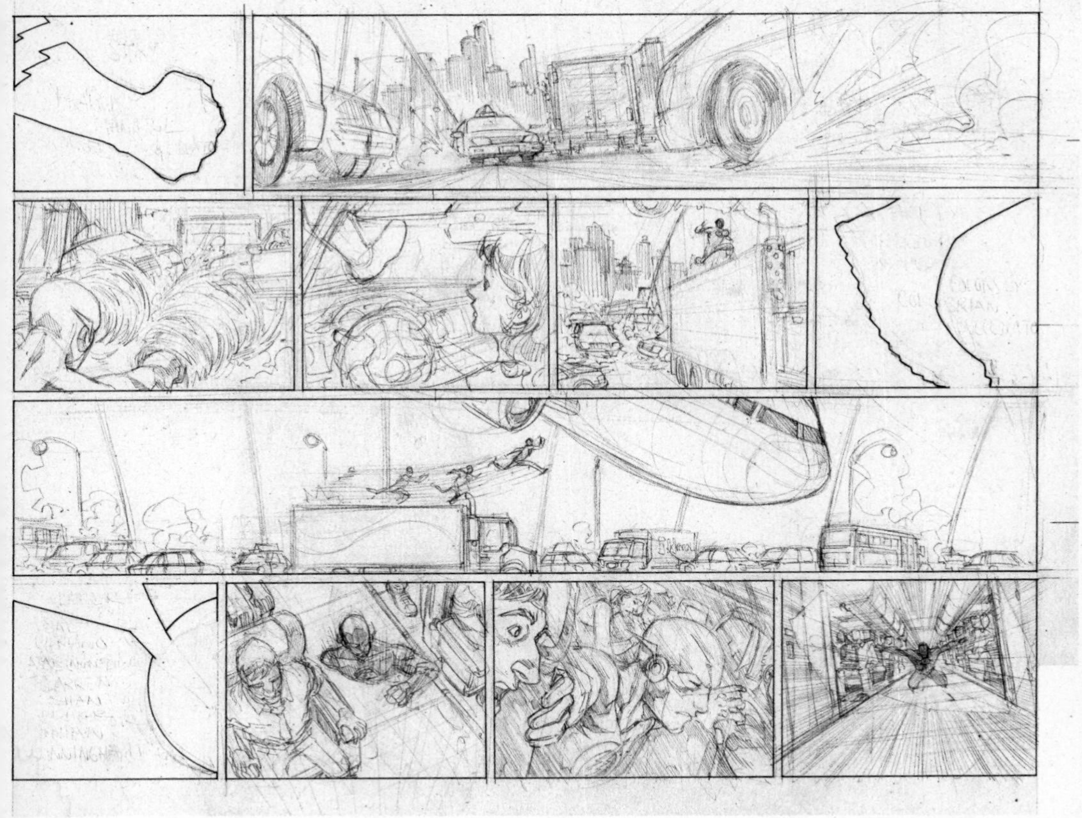

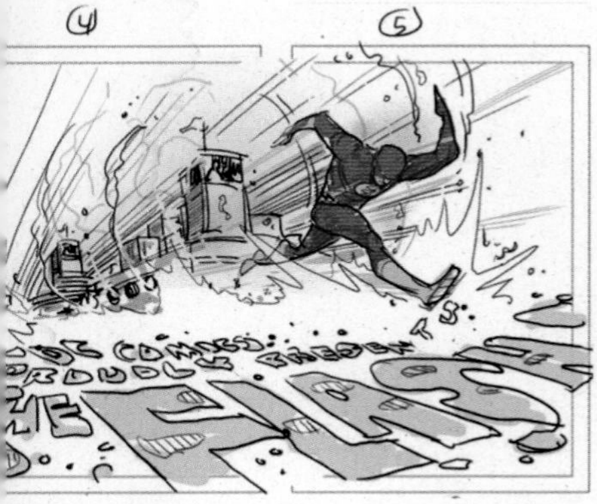

4
5

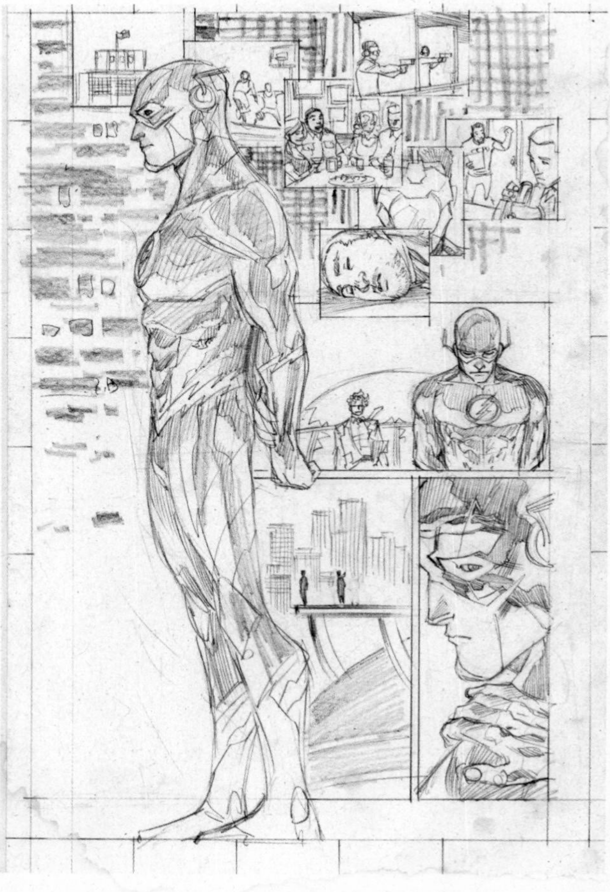

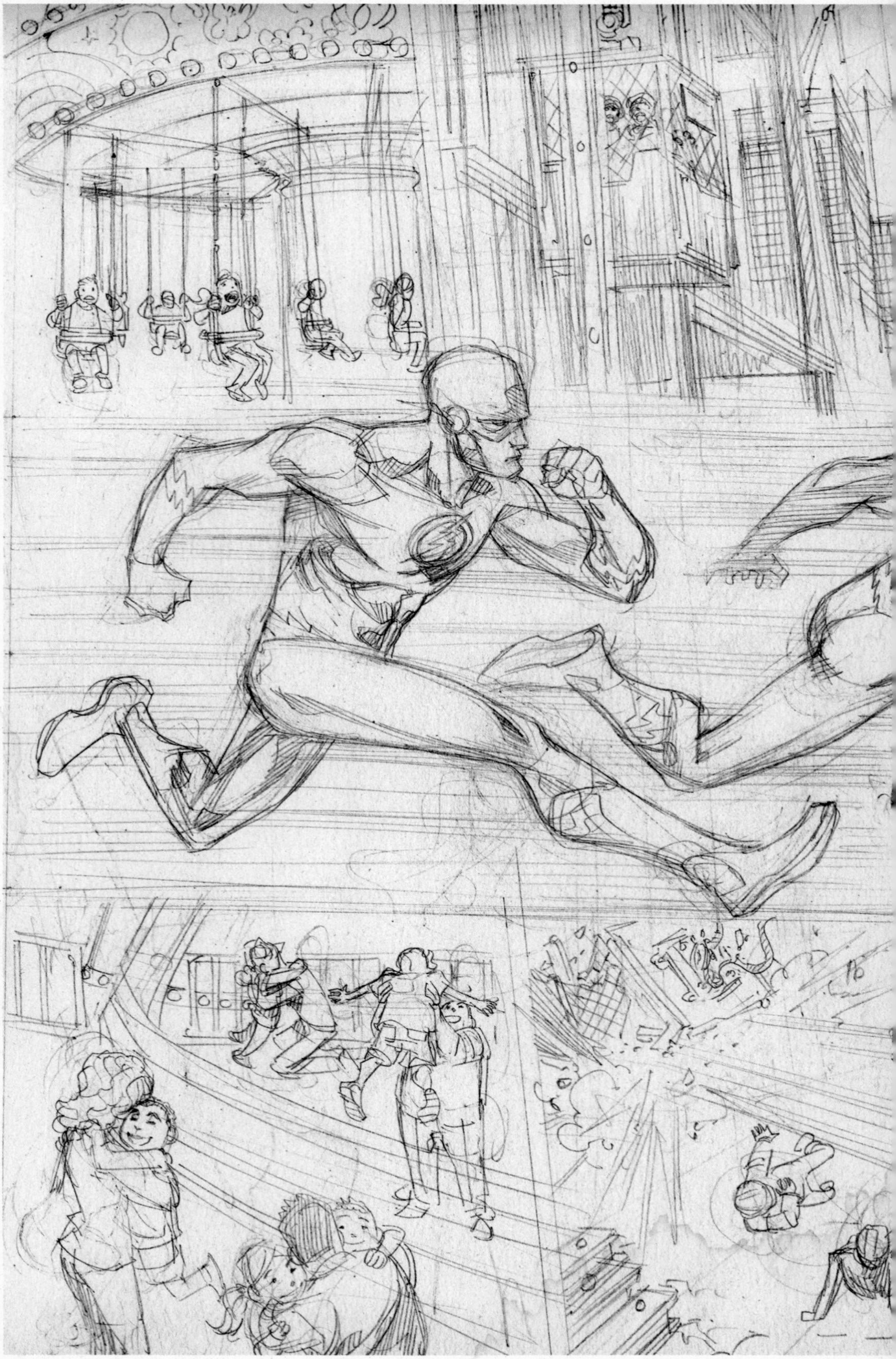

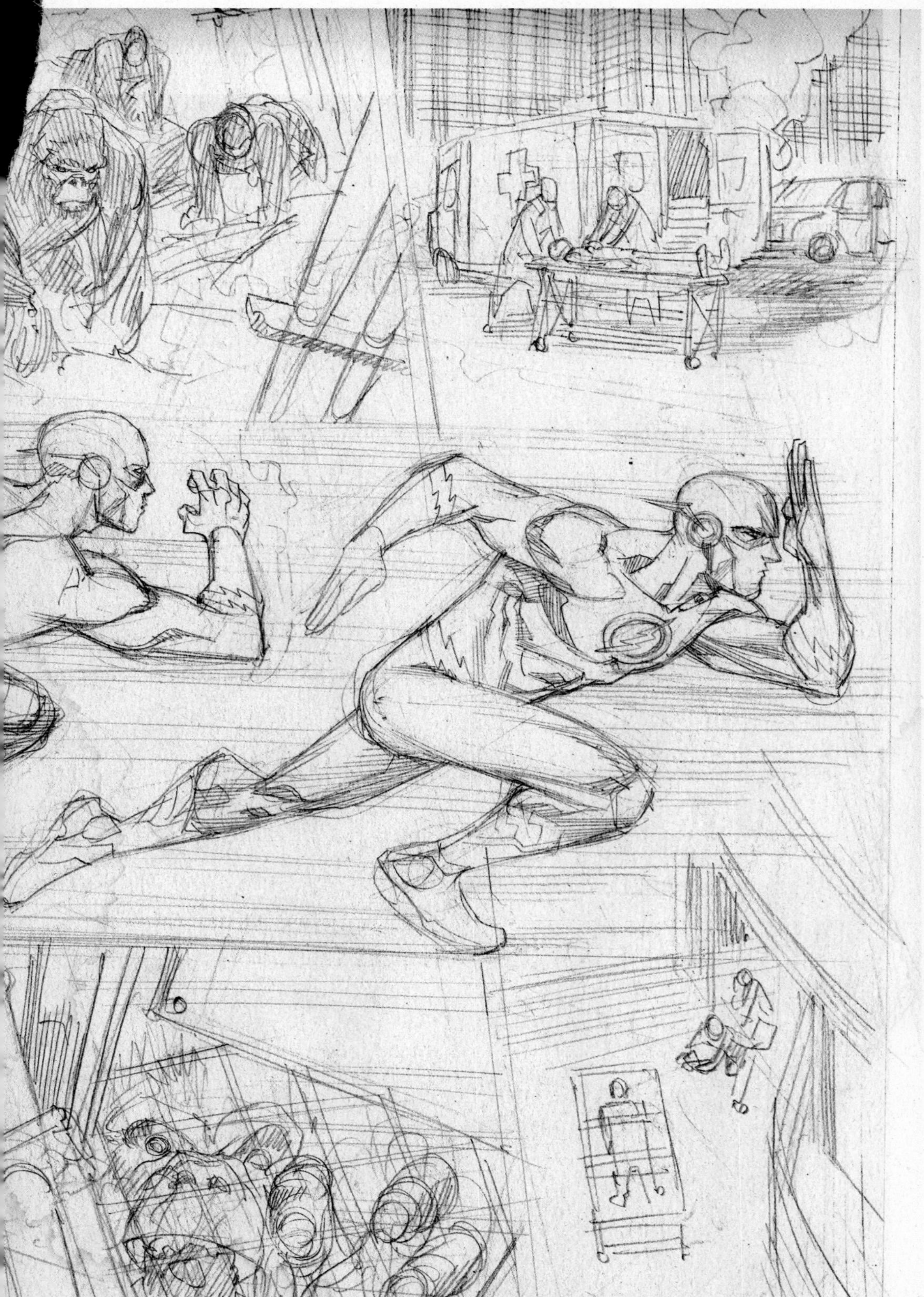

TITLE: ISSUE # PAGE # ARTIST: FRANCIS MANAP

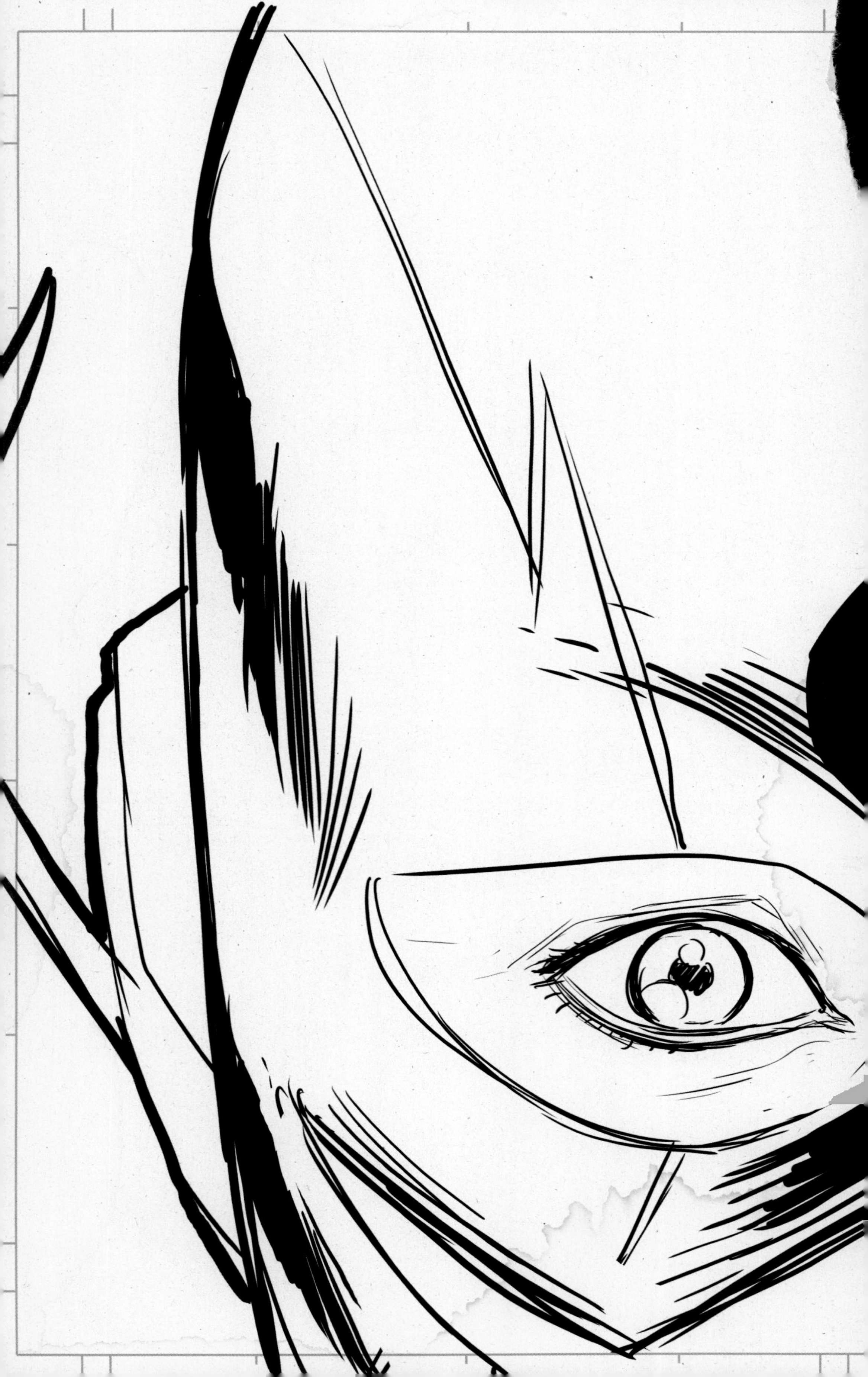